The Lexicon

The Lexicon

An Unauthorized Guide to Harry Potter Fiction
and Related Materials

Steve Vander Ark

with

John Kearns
Lisa Waite Bunker
Belinda Hobbs

RDR Books
Muskegon, Michigan

The Lexicon

RDR Books

1487 Glen Avenue

Muskegon, MI 49441

phone: 510-595-0595

fax: 510-228-0300

www.rdrbooks.com

email read@rdrbooks.com

ISBN 978-1-57143-174-5

Library of Congress Control Number 2008942656

Text design and typography: Richard Harris

Cover design and production: Carl Lemyre, Pegasus Design

Distributed in the United Kingdom by

Roundhouse Publishing Ltd., Atlantic Suite, Maritime House,

Basin Road North, Hove, East Sussex BN41 1WR, United Kingdom

Printed in the United States of America

Dedications

To Katie and Chris, my favorite Harry Potter fans.   –SVA

To Trish . . . my Ginny, who befriended an orphan boy named Harry, just her age, and brought his world into ours.   –BH

To Caroline (who introduced me to Harry), and all the wonderful chapters in our story — especially those still to be written.

–JK

For Carey, you're the best! And for my nieces and nephews Devin, Torin, Isabel, Reed, Ruby, Eli, and Sophia, a new generation discovering the joy and solace of reading. Hey Arrow — Walk time!   –LWB

Introduction &
Acknowledgements

Welcome to the *Lexicon*. As many of you know, in 2007 the original book with this title was the subject of a lawsuit and was ultimately enjoined by the court. After the trial in April 2008, I worked to create a new, different book with a new focus and purpose, mindful of the guidelines of the court. That's the book I am proud to be placing in your hands now.

One of the most important goals of this new book is to avoid giving too much away or using J.K. Rowling's own unique expressions. There will always be new readers discovering the magic of the Harry Potter books, and those new readers deserve to be mystified, surprised, and delighted as they read the series, with the plot unfolding for them the way the author intended. This is how we Potter fans encountered the stories over the past ten years. We read each book voraciously, then waited eagerly for the next installment, all the while wondering and guessing about what was to come. I certainly do not want the *Lexicon* book to spoil that experience for anyone.

This new Lexicon book is a convenient reference that provides chapter citations if you want to explore further in J.K. Rowling's Harry Potter books. If you want to do more research, consult J.K. Rowling's *Fantastic Beasts and Where to Find Them* and *Quidditch Through the Ages* or dig into the Lexicon website at www.hp-lexicon.org.

Throughout this book you'll find some things capitalised and others lower case. This may strike you as a bit haphazard, but it's intentional. We have tried to capitalise words which are capitalised in the books and vice versa. Trouble is, the capitalisation isn't always consistent even within the books. We've done our best, though, because we know that fans like to know that kind of thing, especially fan fiction writers, who are some of our best supporters.

Finally, I want to thank my family, Brenda, Katie, and Chris Vander Ark, who have been a wonderful support over the years. I can't tell you how excited I am to be able to put this book in your hands. My best friend and sounding board, Rodney Te Slaa, deserves a big thank-you for listening to me blather on and on about Harry Potter and the Lexicon for longer than he'd care to remember; maybe I'll finally get him to read the books. Huge thanks to Rachael Livermore for her support of the Lexicon and for everything she's done for this book. Thanks to Roger Rapoport and Richard Harris, along with Megan Trank, Colleen Weesies, Jeremy Nash, Louis Jeannot, Amanda Grycki, Sarah Sheehan, Abby Schmeling, Sarah Ferriby, Kellie Norman, and Zachary Trank, all of RDR Books. I am also grateful to attorneys David Hammer, Lizbeth Hasse, Tony Falzone, Julie Ahrens, and rest of the team from Stanford University Law School's Fair Use Project, as well as Robert Handelsman and Craig Monette. A special thanks also to Peter Tummons and Helen Zaltzman of Methuen Books for their invaluable assistance and encouragement.

The Lexicon website started out as a one-man show, but it definitely isn't that any more. So to my website staff — Belinda Hobbs, John Kearns, Lisa Waite Bunker, Michele L. Worley, Penny Linsenmayer, Clint Hagen, Paula Hall, Kip Carter, and Denise Proctor — thank you from the bottom of my heart. Without you, neither the website nor this book could exist. And of course, a special thank-you has to go to the three people who put in many, many hours making this book a reality. Lisa, John, and Bel, I love you all.

I also want to offer a heartfelt thank-you to all those people who stood by us through the months of working on this project. We have learned the true meaning of the word 'friend' from you. There are no words that can fully express our gratitude.

Steve Vander Ark

Abbreviations Used in This Book

All the information in the Harry Potter Lexicon comes from J.K. Rowling, either in the novels, the 'schoolbooks,' from her interviews, or from material which she developed or wrote herself. The novels are abbreviated as indicated on the list below, with a chapter number following. Page numbers are not used as pagination varied between editions.

The Harry Potter books by J. K. Rowling:
- **SS** *Harry Potter and the Sorcerer's Stone*
- **PS** *Harry Potter and the Philosopher's Stone*
- **CS** *Harry Potter and the Chamber of Secrets*
- **PA** *Harry Potter and the Prisoner of Azkaban*
- **GF** *Harry Potter and the Goblet of Fire*
- **OP** *Harry Potter and the Order of the Phoenix*
- **HBP** *Harry Potter and the Half-Blood Prince*
- **DH** *Harry Potter and the Deathly Hallows* (DH/e indicates the epilogue)
- **FB** *Fantastic Beasts and Where to Find Them*
- **QA** *Quidditch Through the Ages* (QA/i indicates the introductory material)
- **TBB** *The Tales of Beedle the Bard*
- **/f** from the film version of the book (e.g. PA/f)
- **/g** from the video game version of the book

Other Canon sources:
- **AOL** 'America Online chat transcript,' AOL.com, 19 October 2000.
- **AOK1** 'Magic, Mystery, and Mayhem: An Interview with J.K. Rowling,' Amazon.com, Early spring 1999.

BFT 'The Noble and Most Ancient House of BLACK,' a hand-drawn tree that J.K. Rowling donated to Book Aid International in January of 2006 and auctioned 22 February 2006.

BLC 'J.K. Rowing and the Live Chat', Bloomsbury.com, 30 July 2007.

BN 'Barnes and Noble & Yahoo! chat with J.K. Rowling,' barnesandnoble.com, 20 October 2000.

BP Blue Peter (CBBC), 12 March 2001.

BP2 'Harry Potter: A Blue Peter Special.' Blue Peter (CBBC), 20 July 2007.

CBC Rogers, Shelagh. 'INTERVIEW: J.K. Rowling,' Canadian Broadcasting Co., 23 October 2000.

Con J.K. Rowling interview transcript, The Connection (WBUR Radio), 12 October 1999.

CR 'Comic Relief live chat', March 2001.

DP *Daily Prophet* newsletters, written by J.K. Rowling for Bloomsbury's Harry Potter fan club (late 1990s)

EBF 'J K Rowling at the Edinburgh Book Festival', 15 August 2004.

ET de Bertodano, Helena. 'Harry Potter Charms a Nation.' *Electronic Telegraph*, 25 July 1998.

FW Famous Wizard cards, created by J.K. Rowling for the EA video games.

HC Thomas, Sherry. 'J.K. Rowling has the future mapped out for Harry Potter,' *The Houston Chronicle*, 20 March 2001.

HE Fry, Stephen. 'Launch Day interview aboard the Hogwarts Express,' *Bloomsbury Press,* 8 July 2000.

HE2 Mzimba, Lizo. 'JK Rowling talks about Book Four aboard the Hogwarts Express,' BBC *Newsround,* 2 November 2001.

HPM 'Harry Potter and Me' (BBC Christmas Special, British version), BBC, 28 December 2001.

Ind1 Williams, Rhys. 'The spotty schoolboy and single mother taking the mantle from Roald Dahl,' *The Independent* (London), 29 January 1999.

ITV Edinburgh 'cub reporter' press conference, ITV, 16 July 2005

ITV-YIL 'J.K. Rowling, A Year in the Life' ITV1 30 December 2007

JKR J.K. Rowling Official Site

Mac Bethune, Brian. 'The Rowling Connection: How a young Toronto girl's story touched an author's heart,' *Maclean's*, 6 November 2000

NPC National Press Club author's luncheon, NPR Radio, 20 October 1999.

Nr on BBC *Newsround*, 27 April 2001

NR2 Mzimba, Lizo. 'Newsround talks exclusively to J.K. Rowling,' CBBC *Newsround*, 19 September 2002.

OBT/CH 'Open Book Tour: Carnegie Hall' 19 October 2007.

PC-JKR1 J.K. Rowling's first interview on the Pottercast podcast 17 December 2007

PC-JKR2 J.K. Rowling's second interview on the Pottercast podcast 24 December 2007

PA/dvd Interview with David Heyman, Steve Kloves, Mark Radcliffe, Alfonso Cuaron, and J.K. Rowling, *Prisoner of Azkaban* DVD 'Extra,' 23 November 2004.

Pax Paxman, Jeremy, interviewer. 'JK's OOTP interview,' BBC *Newsnight* 19 June 2003.

R4 Fry, Stephen. 'Living with Harry Potter,' on BBC Radio 4, 10 December 2005.

RAH Fry, Stephen. 'J.K. Rowling at the Royal Albert Hall,' 26 June 2003.

RC Raincoast Books interview, Raincoast Books (Canada), March 2001.

Sch1 Online chat transcript, Scholastic.com, 3 February 2000.

Sch2 'About the Books: transcript of J.K. Rowling's live interview on Scholastic.com,' Scholastic.com, 16 October 2000.

Scot2002 Fraser, Lindsay. 'Harry Potter — Harry and me,' *The Scotsman*, November 2002.

SDNY transcript of the trial of *JKR/WB v. RDR Books* 14-16 April 2008 in the Federal District Court, Southern District of New York.

SFC Chonin, Neva. 'Harry Potter's Wizard: Creator of children's book series tours Bay Area,' *The San Francisco Chronicle*, 30 October 1999.

SLG McGarrity, Mark. 'Harry Potter's creator meets her public: Author J.K.Rowling answers questions from students at a school in Montclair,' *The Star-Ledger* (Newark, NJ), 16 October 1999.

SN 'World Exclusive Interview with J K Rowling,' South West News Service, 8 July 2000.

TLC Anelli, Melissa, and Emerson Spartz. 'The Leaky Cauldron and MuggleNet interview Joanne Kathleen Rowling,' The Leaky Cauldron, 16 July 2005.

Today1 Vieira, Meredith. 'JK Rowling One-On-One: Part One.' *Today Show* (NBC), 26 July 2007.

Today2 Vieira, Meredith. 'JK Rowling One-On-One: Part Two.' *Today Show* (NBC), 27 July 2007.

WP1 Weeks, Linton. 'Charmed, I'm Sure,' *The Washington Post*, 20 October 1999.

WBD 'JK Rowling's World Book Day Chat,' 4 March 2004.

Other abbreviations:

JKR (when not used as a reference) J. K. Rowling
FAQ Frequently Asked Questions
NSOED New Shorter Oxford English Dictionary

Many other sources were used for research. A bibliography appears at the end of the book. In no cases have direct quotations been used from these sources without attribution.

Standard indexing abbreviations:

c.f. compare with
ed. editor
e.g. for example
esp. especially
ff. and following
i.e. in other words
L. Latin
Gr. Greek

Eng. English

Brit. British

q.v. see . . .

[**sic**] the preceding, while in error, is used as it is in the books

Information about characters:

Under each name, where applicable, is a list of the basic dates of that character's life. For example, Hannah Abbott's entry shows the following:

(b. circa 1980; Hufflepuff, 1991; Prefect 1995; Dumbledore's Army).

This indicates that she was born in approximately 1980, that she entered Hogwarts and was sorted into Hufflepuff in 1991, that she became a Prefect in 1995, and that she was a member of Dumbledore's Army.

Dates:

The dates of the Harry Potter stories and characters have been established both from clues in the books and from information from J.K. Rowling. According to this information, Harry was born in 1980 and started Hogwarts in 1991. These are the dates seen throughout this book. A number of characters' birth year cannot be determined exactly because all we know is that they were in the same year as other characters. Students begin Hogwarts in the September when they're eleven years old, which means that their birth years fall between two possible years.

The following abbreviations are used for dating events:

c. circa (approximately)

b. born

d. died

B.C. literally means 'Before Christ', used to indicate years before the arbitrary year zero. While other more neutral forms are available, we use B.C. here because that's what J.K. Rowling uses in the books.

About the Famous Wizard cards, *Quidditch Through the Ages,* and *Fantastic Beasts and Where to Find Them*:

While most of the material available about the Harry Potter universe is in the form of stories and narratives, a few sources are already in encyclopedia format. These include the A-to-Z listing of magical creatures in *Fantastic Beasts* and the lists of teams and fouls in *Quidditch Through the Ages.* Rather than reproduce those listings in this book, we direct readers to those books to discover a wealth of information about magical creatures and about the sport of Quidditch. The descriptions on the Famous Wizard cards are typically a single sentence, also similar to what one would find in an encyclopedia. Again, rather than simply reproduce that information, we give only the most basic facts and point readers to the full text of the cards, available in the video games, online in various places including the Harry Potter Lexicon, and in some cases, on J.K. Rowling's website (as Wizard of the Month entries).

A

Abbott

Family name on a headstone in the graveyard in Godric's Hollow, probably ancestors of Hannah, since wizarding families tended to live close together in certain villages after the Statute of Secrecy went into effect in 1692 (DH16).

Abbott, Hannah

(b. circa 1980; Hufflepuff, 1991; Prefect 1995; Dumbledore's Army)

A blonde girl who wears her hair in pigtails (PS7), Hannah is a close friend of Ernie Macmillan (CS11, 15), who shares her hobby of collecting chocolate frog cards (GF19). Both Hannah and Ernie became prefects in August of 1995 (OP10) and joined Dumbledore's Army that October (OP16, DH36). Hannah's mother was killed by Death Eaters (HBP11) during her sixth year at Hogwarts and Hannah left school. (*See also* OBT/CH).

Abbott, Mrs

(d. 1996)

Hannah's mother. She was found dead in the fall of 1996, murdered by Death Eaters (HBP11).

Abercrombie, Euan

(b.1984; Gryffindor, 1995)

A small boy with prominent ears; it's implied that at the beginning of his first year that he believed the *Daily Prophet*'s smear campaign (OP11).

Aberdeen

A city of about 100,000 people on the eastern coast of Scotland. During Harry's first trip on The Knight Bus, the bus moved to Aberdeen abruptly, spilling his hot chocolate (PA3).

Abergavenny

A market town, located in southeastern Wales on the English border, where the Knight Bus dropped off Madam Marsh on 6 August 1993 (PA3).

'abstinence'

After over-indulging during the Christmas holidays, the Fat Lady decided that 'abstinence' would be the

new password to get into the Gryffindor common room (HBP17).

Abyssinia

Another name for Ethiopia, and presumably the home of the Abyssinian
Shrivelfig (PA7).

*The use of the ancient name for this place
is similar to the use of other archaic place
names in the books, indicating that Wizards don't always keep up with the latest
developments in Muggle politics.*

Abyssinian shrivelfig

Second-year Herbology students work
with these plants, learning to prune
them (CS15). When peeled, shrivelf-
igs are used as an ingredient in Shrinking Solution (PA7).

Acanthia Way

A street in Little Norton. Number
eighteen is the home of Doris Purkiss,
a witch with an interesting and improbable theory about the identity of
Sirius Black (OP10).

Accidental Magic Reversal Squad

A team of wizards, including Obliviators, who step in when Muggles have
been exposed to magic or when magic
goes wrong; the team members fix any
damage, undo any magical effects,
and modify the memories of the witnesses so they don't remember seeing
anything unusual (PA3). They also
deal with cases of Splinching (GF6).
The Squad is headquartered on Level
Three of the Ministry of Magic, part
of the Department of Magical Accidents and Catastrophes (OP7).

*In early editions of book three, the Squad
was referred to as the Accidental Magic
Reversal Department (PA3). J.K. Rowling explained the organisation of the
Ministry of Magic for the first time in*
Fantastic Beasts and Where to Find
Them, *which was published several
years later. It seems likely that she hadn't
worked out the details of the Ministry
until that point, which resulted in a few
continuity errors in previous material.*

Accio

(AK-ee-oh, AK-see-oh, or AH-see-oh)
'Summoning Charm'

Causes an object to fly to the caster,
even over quite some distance; the target object is said to have been Summoned. The caster must know at least
the general location of the object Summoned. Harry first learned the Summoning Charm for the First Task of
the Triwizard Tournament (GF20). An
object can be placed under counter-
charms to prevent it being summoned
(DH10, 26).

'accio' = L. *'send for, summon'*

The pronunciation of this spell has been debated by fans. The pronunciation from Scholastic's website is 'A-see-oh'. This is the pronunciation used in the US audio version of the books. In the UK version, the pronunciation is 'AK-see-oh'. However, a correct classical Latin pronunciation would be 'AH-kee-oh', since the letter 'c' was never pronounced as an 's' and double consonants were simply given more emphasis. A possible fourth pronunciation is AH-chee-oh, although there was no 'ch' sound in classical Latin.

accountant

Molly Weasley's second cousin. His mundane profession embarrasses the rest of the family; Ron says that they never talk about him (PS6).

J.K. Rowling discusses the accountant cousin on her website, referring to him as a stockbroker who married a Muggle (implying that he himself was not a Muggle). In early drafts of book four, this second cousin was very rude to the Weasleys and was the father of a girl named Mafalda who was just as rude as her father. When he discovered that his daughter was a witch, he sent her to live at the Burrow for the summer before her first year at Hogwarts to 'introduce her to Wizarding society'. This part of the story was eventually dropped (JKR).

Achievements in Charming

Hogwarts textbook for fifth-years (OP31).

Acid Pops

Magical sweets, sold at Honeydukes, which will burn a hole in your tongue (PA10). One of the passwords for admittance to Dumbledore's office (HBP10).

Ackerley, Stewart

(Ravenclaw, 1994)

Hogwarts student (GF12).

Ackerly Town Hall

This town hall was damaged in a performance of the infamous 'Wizarding Suite' (FW).

aconite

Extremely poisonous plant (hence its other name of wolfsbane). It is also called monkshood because the shape of the flowers somewhat resembles a monk's cowl (PS8).

Acorn, the

A tea leaf fortunetelling symbol, from *Unfogging the Future* pages five and six, which signifies 'windfall, unexpected gold' (PA6).

In tasseography (tea leaf reading), the 'acorn' indicates good fortune, happiness, and contentment.

Acromantula

A gigantic black spider, capable of human speech. While a student at Hogwarts, Hagrid raised an Acromantula named Aragog in the castle which he eventually released into the Forest (CS15). An Acromantula was used in the Third Task of the Triwizard Tournament (GF31, OP16). (*See also* DH32).

'acro' = L. 'highest point, peak' + 'mantula' suggesting 'tarantula', the name for a species of large hairy spider; the name might be loosely interpreted as meaning 'the very largest hairy spider', which certainly fits.

Acromantula (Rune)

A rune for the number 8, according to the book *Ancient Runes Made Easy*. A reference to the eight eyes of the giant spiders (JKR).

Acromantula venom

Highly useful potions ingredient. It is almost impossible to collect from a living Acromantula, for obvious reasons. When the beast dies, its venom dries out very quickly. As a result, the venom is very rare and may fetch as much as one hundred Galleons a pint (HBP22).

action figures

At the Quidditch World Cup, Ron bought a small model of Viktor Krum, the famous Bulgarian Seeker (GF7, 9, 24). Xenophilius Lovegood has moving models of bizarre creatures hanging from his ceiling (DH20).

Advanced Potion-Making
by Libatius Borage

The N.E.W.T.-level textbook for Potions during Harry's sixth year (HBP9), which cost nine Galleons brand new (HBP11). The book was written around the year 1946 (HBP16). The book contains instructions for making the Draught of Living Death starting at page 10 (HBP9).

Advanced Rune Translation

Hermione was reading a copy of this after her pre-sixth-year trip to Diagon Alley; presumably it is one of the N.E.W.T.-level Ancient Runes textbooks (HBP7).

'Adventures of Martin Miggs, the Mad Muggle, The'

A comic book Ron has in his bedroom at the Burrow the first time Harry visits (CS3).

Aeaea

In ancient Greece, the legendary island of Aeaea was the home of the famous sorceress Circe (FW).

A number of possible locations have been

suggested for this legendary island but none are conclusive. The story of Circe and Odysseus is found in Homer's Odyssey.

Aesalon, Falco

An ancient Greek Animagus; for more information, see the Famous Wizard cards (FW).

A subspecies of the European Merlin falcon bears the Latin name Falco aesalon.

Ageing Potion

Causes the person drinking it to grow older. The more Ageing Potion one drinks, the more one ages. Fred Weasley, George Weasley, and Lee Jordan took a few drops of Ageing Potion in an attempt make it seem that they were a few months older. It didn't work (GF16).

Age Line

A thin golden line drawn on the floor which jinxes anyone who crosses it if they are too young. Albus Dumbledore used an Age Line to protect the Goblet of Fire (GF16).

Agnes

Patient in the Janus Thickey ward for permanent spell damage at St. Mungo's Hospital. Agnes' entire head was covered with fur and she barked instead of speaking (OP23).

Agrippa, Cornelius

(1486–1535)

The full name of this wizard was Heinrich Cornelius Agrippa von Nettesheim. Agrippa appears on a Chocolate Frog trading card (FW, PS6). 'Agrippa' is one of the Chocolate Frog cards that Ron is missing from his collection (PS6).

Cornelius Agrippa wrote about magic in his book De Occulta Philosophia *(1531). He believed that the study of magic was the best way to learn more about God. His writings were controversial during his lifetime. After his death, rumours and legends sprang up about him, including tales of him summoning demons and having a large black dog for a familiar.*

Aguamenti

(AH-gwa-MEN-tee)

Charm that conjures a fountain or jet of water from the caster's wand. This spell can be used for putting out fires (HBP11, 17, 26, 28, DH12, 31).

'agua' = Sp. 'water' (from Latin 'aqua') + 'menti' = L. 'mind'

Albania

A small European country along the Adriatic Sea with ties to Helena Ravenclaw, the daughter of one of the Founders of Hogwarts (DH31). Voldemort fled to Albania when he lost his body in 1981 (GF33).

Albania during the 1980s was a closed state. Only small numbers of tourists were allowed into the country and these were followed by secret police. When J.K. Rowling was writing the books in the 1990s, she chose this mysterious, hidden country as a good place for Voldemort to hide away from the outside world.

Alderton

Alleged Muggle-born accused of 'stealing magic' by the Muggle-born Registration Commission. Claimed to be the son of Arkie Alderton, a wizard (DH13).

Alderton, Archibald

(1568–1623)

Accident-prone wizard baker; for more information see Famous Wizard cards (FW).

Alderton, Arkie

Well-known broomstick designer (DH13). Probably the current proprietor (or his namesake) of 'Arkie Alderton's Kwik-Repair Shop' for magical brooms (BLC).

Algie, Great Uncle

Neville Longbottom's relative and a rather odd fellow, from the sound of it.

Algie tried to trick Neville into showing some magical ability as a child, even at the risk of subjecting him to danger. Algie bought Trevor the Toad (PS7) and a *Mimbulus mimbletonia* (OP10) for Neville.

Alguff the Awful

Goblin with a body-odour problem; for more information, see the Famous Wizard cards (FW).

Alihotsy

Magical plant (JKR).

The word 'alihotsy' is used in sikidy, a form of geomancy, for one of the sixteen geometric figures used for divination; it is also known as Aquisitio and means 'gain'. J.K. Rowling said that it also means 'lightness of spirit' (SDNY).

All-England Best-Kept Suburban Lawn Competition

A fictional competition used by the Order of the Phoenix to trick the Dursleys into leaving the house one evening (OP3).

All-England Wizarding Duelling Competition

Won in 1430 by Alberta Toothill; for more information, see the Famous Wizards cards (FW).

alley behind the Leaky Cauldron

Nondescript alley behind the Leaky Cauldron pub, with brick walls and a few trash bins. This unlikely place is one of the primary gateways between the Muggle and the Wizarding worlds. Tapping the right combination of bricks in the wall opens a magical portal into Diagon Alley (PS5).

alley between Wisteria Walk and Magnolia Crescent

Located in Little Whinging a block or two from Privet Drive, this alley has been the scene of two of the biggest incursions into Harry's Muggle existence by elements of the Wizarding world: an errant Knight Bus in 1993 (PA3) and several Dementors in 1995 (OP1).

Alohomora

(AL-o-ho-MOR-ah)

Charm that causes a locked door to open (PS9). Some doors are charmed in a way that makes them impervious to this spell (OP34).

The term 'Alohomora' comes from sikidy, a form of divination from the Malagasy people of Madagascar. It is the name of a magical symbol which means 'favourable to thieves' (SDNY).

Altheda

A character from the story 'The Fountain of Fair Fortune' from *The Tales of Beedle the Bard*. Altheda travels to the fabled fountain for a cure for her feelings of helplessness and finds much more along the way (TBB).

The name is possibly derived from 'Althos', Greek for 'healing', and related to the female names Althea/Althaea.

Amata

A character from the story 'The Fountain of Fair Fortune' from *The Tales of Beedle the Bard*. Amata seeks a cure from the fountain for grief and longing. Along the way she meets two other witches, Asha and Altheda, and rescues a Muggle knight named Sir Luckless (TBB).

'Amata' = Italian 'beloved'

Amortentia

(a-mor-TEN-tee-ah)

The most powerful love potion in the world, recognisable by its shininess and by the patterns in the steam rising over the cauldron. The potion smells differently to different people according to what attracts them (HBP9).

'amor' = L. 'love' + 'tempto' = L. 'to try to influence or tempt'

amulets

Any of a variety of objects which are thought to bring good luck. Lockhart claimed to have dealt with a case of Transmogrifian Torture in Ouagadougou by giving the townsfolk protective amulets (CS9). In 1992, when danger lurked the halls of Hogwarts, a booming trade in magical remedies and defences was carried on in secret, including protective amulets (CS11).

Anapneo

(ah-NAHP-nay-oh)

Spell that clears the target's airway if blocked. Can be used when someone is choking (HBP7).

'anapneo' = Gr. 'breathe'

ancient magic

A form of magic is not cast by wizards with wands but which is part of the 'magical-ness' of the universe. The ancient magic is integrally connected to the concepts of love and of death. This magic cannot be altered or blocked by the actions of wizards. Rather, it must be taken into account and accepted as part of the way the world functions. In some cases, this magic can be invoked, but usually it simply exists when certain conditions are present, particularly as the intentions and attitudes of wizards. (*See also* WANDLORE.)

These two ancient magic concepts of love and death are integral to the plot of the Harry Potter books. Firstly, complete self-sacrificial love gives magical protection, as we see particularly in the protection that Lily gave Harry (esp. GF33). Secondly, saving another person's life creates a life debt. Snape owed James a life debt because James warned him away from a potentially deadly encounter (PS17). The reactions of characters to these two magical realities drive the entire plot (esp. DH33).

Ancient Runes

Magical symbols and hieroglyphs used for writing some old texts (DH7) and for other magical writing. Students at Hogwarts can take an elective class in Ancient Runes which is taught by Bathsheba Babbling (JKR). The textbooks for this class include *Ancient Runes Made Easy* (CS14, JKR), *Magical Hieroglyphs and Logograms, Spellman's Syllabary* (OP26), and various runes dictionaries (PA12). Rune symbols are carved around the edge of Dumbledore's Pensieve (GF30). The known runes are Demiguise (zero), Unicorn (one), Graphorn (two), Runespoor (three), Fwooper (four), Quintaped (five), Salamander (six), Acromantula (eight), Hydra (nine) (JKR), as well as Ehwaz (partnership), and Eihwaz (defence) (OP31).

8

Runes are a carved alphabet used to write the Germanic languages of Northern Europe, beginning in the 2nd century. According to Scandinavian legend, the runes were given by the gods. Because they were carved in wood or stone, runes consisted only of straight lines. In the Harry Potter universe, runes apparently are not connected to actual runic alphabets. The fact that they are named after magical creatures suggest that J.K. Rowling intends her 'runes' to be magical symbols from the Wizarding tradition, not derived from the ancient Muggle alphabets.

Ancient Runes Made Easy

Hermione began reading this during her second year, not long after signing up to take Ancient Runes the following year (CS14). One page of this book shows a collection of magical creature-related runes that stand for the numbers zero through nine. Interestingly, the symbol for the number seven is not identified because it has yet to be discovered (JKR).

Andorra

Located in the mountains between Spain and France, tiny Andorra is one of the smallest countries in the world. However, it has a Ministry of Magic (GF28) and participates in international affairs.

J.K. Rowling seems to enjoy giving prominence to places that in our world are quite small and insignificant on the world stage. She mentioned Lichtenstein, for example, as one of the top Quidditch contenders. In the UK, she places Quidditch teams in small towns like Tutshill and ignores the large cities entirely. This reinforces the idea that Wizarding society is separated from the Muggle world.

Andros the Invincible

A wizard from ancient Greece famous for the size of his Patronus; for more information, see the Famous Wizard cards (FW).
'andro-' = Gr. 'man'

Anglesey

An island off the west coast of Wales, almost due east across the Irish Sea from Dublin. Anglesey is one of the places the Knight Bus visited the first time Harry rode it (PA3).

Animagi / Animagus

(an-i-MAH-jus, an-i-MAY-jus)
plural: Animagi

A wizard who can Transfigure into an animal while retaining the ability to think as a human. Complex and difficult magic is required for this transformation. The magic is performed without a wand (e.g. PA19) or incantation.

An Animagus' appearance as an animal reflects his or her physical condition in human shape. For example, one character's rat Animagus form lacked a toe on one of his front paws because he had lost a finger (PA19). Another character's cat form had square markings around its eyes like her spectacles (PS1). The Improper Use of Magic Office maintains a register of all known Animagi (PA19).

'animal' = L. 'animal' + 'magus' = Persian 'magic user, wise man'

Animagi registry

A record kept in the Improper Use of Magic Office of all known Animagi. It is a matter of public record; Hermione Granger at age thirteen could consult it for the information therein, including the names of registered persons (PA19). For each known Animagus the Ministry records the kind of animal and distinguishing markings (GF26). Penalties for failing to register are rather severe (GF37). There are only six names on the list from the 1900s (PA19).

Annual *Daily Prophet* Grand Prize Galleon Draw

A prize was won in the summer of 1993 by Arthur Weasley. He took the family on a month-long trip to Egypt with most of the winnings. The prize amount was 700 Galleons, which is the equivalent of £3500, or about US$5350 (PA1).

This chance windfall which sent the Weasleys on a holiday in Egypt is one of the key events in the books, believe it or not. If Arthur hadn't won this money, the Weasleys wouldn't have had their picture printed in the Prophet, *and the picture would never have been seen by Sirius, precipitating his escape. This was the catalyst for the rest of the events of the books.*

Annual International Wizarding Gardening Competition

Includes many interesting divisions, including the Contorting Cereals competition (DP1).

antechamber

A small chamber adjacent to a larger room. There is an antechamber connected to the Great Hall, through a door behind the high table, with a fireplace and many portraits (including that of the Fat Lady's friend Violet) (GF17, 31).

Anthology of Eighteenth Century Charms, An

One of the books that Harry, Ron, and Hermione examined while preparing for the Second Task of the Triwizard Tournament (GF26).

Anti-Burglar Buzzer

This magical device or charm buzzes when anyone tries to steal the item it's attached to (GF8).

Anti-Cheating spell

Cast on quills at Hogwarts before exams (PS16).

Anti-Disapparition Jinx

Prevents someone from Apparating. Most wizarding dwellings are magically protected against unwanted Apparators, according to Albus Dumbledore, who confirmed that 'you can't Apparate anywhere inside the buildings or grounds' of Hogwarts (HBP4). However, the Headmaster or Headmistress can temporarily lift the restriction from a specific area of the school for short periods, so that someone already within that area can Apparate to another place within the same area, although they cannot leave the area entirely (HBP18).

antidotes

A substance which counteracts the effects of a poison. There are antidotes for many poisons and for the effects of potions in the Wizarding world. Perhaps the most effective is a bezoar, which will act as an antidote to most poisons (PS8, HBP18, 19).

Mandrakes are an ingredient in most antidotes (CS6).

anti-gravity mist

An innocent-looking magical mist which hovers above the ground. A person stepping into this mist immediately finds that up and down have reversed and they are hanging from the ground over the endless sky (GF31).

anti-jinx

Any of a variety of spells which are cast to reverse or block the effects of a jinx (PA12, OP9, HBP5).

antler jinx

Causes the victim to sprout antlers. Students at Hogwarts have been known to hit each other with this jinx on occasion (OP30).

Aparecium

(a-par-EE-see-um)

Makes invisible ink become visible. Hermione tried this on the mysterious diary, but it had no effect (CS13).

'appareo' = L. 'to appear'

apothecary

A shop selling potion ingredients in Diagon Alley (PS5).

An apothecary is a person or a shop that sells herbs, drugs, and other medical items;

it is the historical version of the modern-day chemist or pharmacy. On the film set, the name of this shop is Slug & Jiggers.

Apparition
(A-pa-RI-shun)
Spell used to disappear from one place and appear almost instantly somewhere else. The sensation is like being squeezed (HBP4). Apparition is difficult magic; some wizards choose to stick with using brooms. Performed incorrectly, Apparition can result in the caster being 'splinched': leaving part of one's body behind (GF5, DH14, 19). Apparition becomes more difficult as distance increases; even Voldemort didn't try intercontinental Apparition (DH23). Apparating directly into someone's house is considered rude (HBP4). It's impossible to track anyone who Apparates. If, however, a person grabs hold of a wizard as they Apparate, that person is taken along by Side-Along Apparition (DH11).
from 'appareo' = L. 'to appear'

Apparition, Side-Along
A form of Apparition in which the Apparator touches someone else, such as a child too young to Apparate, and Apparates with that person as a 'passenger' (HBP3, 4, 25, DH3, 11).

Apparition Test Centre
This test centre itself is located on Level Six of the Ministry of Magic, part of the Department of Magical Transportation (OP7). To legally Apparate, a witch or wizard must be of age and must successfully pass a test to acquire a license. To pass the test, the candidate must successfully Apparate to a specified destination without splinching himself or herself (GF6, HBP22). The Ministry of Magic offers a twelve-week series of lessons from a Ministry of Magic Apparition instructor, given at Hogwarts. The cost for these lessons in Harry's sixth year was twelve Galleons (HBP17).

Appeal Against House-Elf Slavery
This campaign was unfortunately defeated in 1973 (JKR).

Appleby Arrows
Quidditch team from the small town of Appleby in northeast England, southeast of York (DP1-4).

Appraisal of Magical Education in Europe, An
This book discusses, among other things, Beauxbatons Academy of Magic (GF9, 11).

Aquavirius Maggot

A creature, probably fanciful, which Luna Lovegood thought she spotted in the Department of Mysteries (OP34). *'aqua' = L. 'water' + possibly 'virus' = L. 'slime, poison'; a maggot is a fly larva which eats decomposing flesh*

Aragog

(c. 1942–1997)

A male Acromantula, acquired as an egg c. 1942 by Hagrid from a traveller. Hagrid hid Aragog in a cupboard in the castle and reared him on table scraps until circumstances forced him to release the creature into the Forest (CS15). Aragog died of old age in the spring of 1997 (HBP22). *'ara' from 'aranea' = L. 'spider' + 'gog' from 'Gog' = a legendary giant who appears along with Magog, his fellow giant, in the Bible and in folklore from many cultures.*

Archie

Old wizard who, when forced to dress as a Muggle, favoured flowered nightgowns. Archie refused to wear trousers at the World Cup campground, saying that he liked 'a healthy breeze around his privates' (GF7).

Arcus

One of two wizards in historical accounts thought to have taken the Elder Wand from Loxias (DH21).

Argyllshire

A county in western Scotland. A map of Argyllshire hangs on the second floor of Hogwarts. This map is where the Fat Lady hid after being attacked by an intruder (PA9).

Arithmancy

A branch of magic that is concerned with the magical properties of numbers; someone who practices Arithmancy is called an Arithmancer. There have been famous Arithmancers in history who have added to magical knowledge. For example, in the 1200s, Bridget Wenlock, a famous Arithmancer, discovered the magical properties of the number seven (FW). An O.W.L. in Arithmancy is required to apply for a curse-breaker's job at Gringotts' (OP29). Arithmancy at Hogwarts is taught by Professor Vector. In her class, students are expected to write essays and to be able to understand complicated number charts, which are part of their homework (PA12). Arithmancy is Hermione's favourite subject (PA12,16). *J.K. Rowling described Arithmancy as 'predicting the future using numbers', and added, 'I've decided there's a bit of numerology in there as well . . .'*

(RAH). It's surprising, then, that Hermione would be so keen on this subject. She is typically disdainful of Divination techniques. Despite what J.K. Rowling said in that interview, it seems unlikely that Arithmancy as taught at Hogwarts is as much about telling the future as it is about understanding the inherent magical nature of things. After all, numbers do have magical effects and symbolism, as we see for example in Voldemort's obsession with splitting his soul into seven parts.

Arkie Alderton's Kwik-Repair Shop

This shop is the place to go for a wizard whose racing broom 'has a terrible knack of veering left' (BLC).

Armando Dippet: Master or Moron?
by Rita Skeeter

A bestselling biography written about one of the headmasters of Hogwarts (DH13).

armour

Hogwarts contains many enchanted suits of armour, some of which stand on plinths around the castle (PA12) while others are in an armour gallery (PS9). They move on their own, muttering and creaking and watching as people pass by (e.g. CS5, GF15). At Christmas time, lights (everlast-ing candles, evidently) shine from inside every suit of armour in the castle (PA11, HBP15). During some years they are bewitched to sing Christmas carols as well (GF22). The armour in the castle was summoned to fight against the Death Eaters in the Battle of Hogwarts (DH30).

armour-bewitching charm

Bewitches a suit of armour to sing Christmas carols. This charm was used as part of the Christmas decorations in 1994 (GF22).

armour gallery

Room filled with armour adjacent to the trophy room on the third floor of Hogwarts (PS9).

armour, goblin-made

Some armour in the Wizarding world is made by goblins, and is quite valuable (e.g., HBP20). According to Phineas, the swords can absorb powerful substances such as Basilisk venom to become stronger (DH15).

Arnold

A purple Pigmy Puff which Ginny Weasley purchased from her brothers' shop in Diagon Alley. She named him Arnold and took him along with her to Hogwarts in a cage (HBP6, 7, 11, 14).

ash

A magical wood used for both brooms and wands (JKR).

Ash wood, in tree lore, signifies 'strength of purpose'. The great tree at the centre of world in Norse mythology was vast ash tree called Yggdrasil.

Asha

A character from the story 'The Fountain of Fair Fortune' from *The Tales of Beedle the Bard*. Asha is a witch with a painful, incurable malady who seeks wellness at the fountain (TBB).

Asha means 'wish, desire, hope' in Hindi, and 'life' in Swahili.

Asiatic Anti-Venoms

Harry consulted this book while doing some fifth-year Potions homework (OP16).

asphodel

Powdered root of asphodel is used in the Draught of Living Death (PS8).

In Greek mythology, the asphodel plant was thought to be the favourite food of the dead. Ancient Greeks often planted asphodel around graveyards.

Assyria

Assyria was where his great uncle Algie got Neville's *Mimbulus mimbletonia* (OP10).

Assyria is an ancient name for an empire which no longer exists, mainly including modern-day Iraq, Syria, and Lebanon, another example of the Wizarding world being a bit out of touch with current Muggle events.

astrology

The study of the movements of the stars and planets and their influence on people's lives. Astrology requires a careful study of star charts relating to the date of a person's birth. The students in Trelawney's Divination classes have to create complicated charts and determine which planets were where and how that all affects their lives. Trelawney, it transpired, was not particularly adept at interpreting this form of divination (GF13).

astronomical models

Miniature versions of stars and planets, useful for studying astronomy. A model of the galaxy in a glass ball and globes of the moon were for sale in Diagon Alley (PA4). Trelawney used a miniature model of the solar system to teach Divination (GF29). Hepzibah Smith had celestial globes in her collection (HBP20). A huge room-sized model of the solar system is to be found in the Department of Mysteries (OP35).

Astronomy

A class, taught by Professor Sinistra, which meets at midnight at the top of the Astronomy Tower (esp. PS8, OP14, 31).

In the Harry Potter universe, the moon, stars, and planets directly influence the effects and strength of magic spells and potions. The class in Astronomy is not primarily a class of memorising facts about the heavens, but of learning about one of the underlying foundations of magical theory. Therefore, it's curious that they would have to learn about things like the surface features of the moons of Jupiter (OP14).

Astronomy Tower

The tallest tower of Hogwarts. It is here that the students study Astronomy at midnight and where they took their Astronomy O.W.L. (OP31). The top of this tower is more or less directly above the front entrance of the castle (OP31). A steep spiral staircase leads to the top of the tower (PS14, OP31). The Battle of the Tower was fought in, atop, and at the base of this tower (HBP27).

Atmospheric Charm

A spell which creates the weather effects seen in the magical windows of Ministry of Magic headquarters in London, and probably the spell which had gone wrong making it rain in people's offices (OP7).

Atrium

A large entrance hall on Level Eight of Ministry of Magic headquarters, lined with Floo Network fireplaces. At one point, the Fountain of Magical Brethren stood in the Atrium. Later, that fountain was replaced by a vast black sculpture of a witch and wizard sitting on thrones made of hundreds of naked Muggles, with the words MAGIC IS MIGHT on the base. At the end of the Atrium are golden gates beyond which are the lifts (OP7, DH12).

Aubrey, Bertram

(Hogwarts, 1970s)

Hogwarts student, a contemporary of the Marauders. James Potter and Sirius Black once received detention for hexing Aubrey (HBP24).

Augurey

A small magical bird (JKR).

'augury' = Eng. 'generally, the art of divination, but specifically, the art of the augur (one who interprets omens based on the behaviour of birds)'

Auror Headquarters

Auror Headquarters is located on Level Two of the Ministry of Magic. It consists of a series of open cubicles, each Auror being assigned a space to work. The cubicles are decorated with pictures of known Dark wizards, maps, clippings from the *Daily Prophet*, and other odds and ends (OP7).

Aurors

An elite group of witches and wizards who battle the Dark Arts, in some ways as soldiers but more often as intelligence agents. Aurors hunt down Dark wizards and defeat them, often in fierce wizard duels. The Aurors were responsible for bringing to justice many of the Dark wizards who supported Voldemort during the 1970s. They also battled the giants, killing many and driving the rest from Britain. (*See also* BLC).

'aurora' = L. 'dawn'

The name suggests the coming of light to defeat the darkness of evil. However, the Aurors are under the direct control of the Ministry and as such carry out the will of the government. In some cases, this has led the Aurors to behave almost as badly as the Dark Wizards they fight. For example, under the leadership of Bartemius Crouch senior in the 1970s, the Aurors were given sweeping powers, allowing them to bypass the normal channels of justice. Sirius Black was imprisoned during this time without a trial because of these policies (GF27). Under Fudge and then under the Death Eaters, the Aurors became enforcers of a corrupt regime. However, after the Second Wizarding War, reforms of the Aurors were undertaken by the new Minister for Magic, so there is hope (JKR).

Auror training

Training to be an Auror takes three years after leaving Hogwarts; the Aurors ask for a minimum of five N.E.W.T.s, with nothing less than an 'Exceeds Expectations' grade. Apart from Defence Against the Dark Arts, the recommended N.E.W.T.s include Charms, Potions (particularly the study of poisons and antidotes), and Transfiguration (OP29). Candidates with the required academic qualifications must then pass a criminal background check and must pass 'a stringent series of character and aptitude tests' to assess skill in practical defence, perseverance, dedication, and the ability to react well to stress (OP29).

Australia

Australia is both the smallest continent and its own country, located on a large island entirely in the southern hemisphere. One character sent her parents to Australia to protect them from Death Eaters (DH6).

Auto-Answer Quill

These magical quills are banned during O.W.L.s (OP31).

Avada Kedavra

(uh-VAH-duh kuh-DAH-vruh)

'Killing Curse'

Causes instant death in a flash of green light. One of the Unforgivable Curses (GF14), said to be unblockable and with no counter-curse. This spell produces a jet (OP36) or flash (GF14) of green light, and a sound as though some huge invisible thing is rushing at the target (GF1, 14). Harry is the only known person to survive the Killing Curse (esp. PS1, GF14, also GF34, DH17, 34).

'adhadda kedhabhra' = Aramaic 'let the thing be destroyed'

A number of alternate etymologies have been discussed for this spell. Abracadabra is a cabbalistic charm in Judaic mythology that is supposed to bring healing powers. One of its sources is believed to be from Aramaic avada kedavra, *another is the Phoenician alphabet which begins with the sequence of letters* a-bra-ca-dabra.

The Avada Kedavra spell, or Killing Curse, was used indiscriminately by Voldemort. However, his use of the spell repeatedly against Harry always failed. Harry proved that he was capable of using these terrible weapons as well, casting both the Imperius and Cruciatus Curses at various times. However, he chose not to use this spell of ultimate evil against Voldemort.

Avalon

An island in the British Isles ruled by Morgan le Fey, a famous witch and contemporary of King Arthur and Merlin (FW).

Avalon is a legendary island somewhere off the coast of England which figures in Arthurian legend. It is the place where the sword Excalibur was forged and, by some accounts, where King Arthur was buried.

Avery

(b. late 1920s)

A friend and follower of Tom Riddle while at Hogwarts (HBP17), Avery became one of the first group of Death Eaters in the mid-1950s (HBP20). He is possibly the father of the Avery who attended Hogwarts with Severus Snape in the 1970s.

Avery

(b. circa 1960; Slytherin c. 1971)

Attended Hogwarts with Severus Snape (GF27, DH33). A Death Eater who protested his innocence after Voldemort disappeared in 1990 by saying he acted under the Imperius Curse (GF27); he was later punished by Voldemort with the Cruciatus Curse (GF33). Possibly the son of the Avery that attended Hogwarts with Tom Riddle.

Avis

(AH-vis)

A spell which conjures a flock of small, twittering birds (GF18).

'avis' = L. 'bird'

Award for Special Services to the School

Gold shield once awarded to Tom Riddle for his actions when the school was in danger. His award is kept in the trophy room at Hogwarts (CS13). Harry and Ron also received Special Awards for Service to the School in their second year (CS18).

Axminster

A type of carpet. The Crouch family used to have a flying Axminster that seated twelve — before flying carpets were banned, of course (GF6).

Azkaban Fortress

Wizarding prison, located on a small island far out in the icy waters of the North Sea (PA3, Sch1). Azkaban is a terrible place. For years, prisoners were guarded by Dementors, horrible creatures who have been described as 'sightless soul-sucking fiends' (GF2, 27). (*See also* OP25, HBP1, DH5, BLC).

The name 'Azkaban' evokes the name of Alcatraz, an infamous prison on an island in the middle of San Francisco Bay in California. Alcatraz had the reputation for being one of the toughest prisons in the United States, and the worst criminals served their time there. Its location on an island surrounded by icy, treacherous currents gave it the reputation for being escape-proof. For a period of a few years, Alcatraz even had a strict policy of silence. There are stories of prisoners driven mad by this terrible enforced silence.

B

Babayaga

Russian hag; for more information, see the Famous Wizard cards (FW).

Baba Yaga is a well-known character in Slavic folk tales, typically depicted as vicious and bloodthirsty. Baba Yaga lives in a house which stands on chicken legs. She flies through the air in a gigantic mortar, using the pestle to steer and a broom to sweep away her tracks. 'Baba' means 'grandmother' in Russian and other Slavic languages; 'Yaga' is shortened from the name 'Jadwiga'.

Babbitty Rabbitty

A witch in the Wizarding fairy tale 'Babbitty Rabbitty and the Cackling Stump' from *The Tales of Beedle the Bard*. In this fable, Babbitty Rabbitty outwits a greedy king and his 'charlatan' sorcerer who try to get rid of wizards and witches so they can have all the magic to themselves (TBB).

This name (and story title) may be a tongue-in-cheek reference to the books J.K. Rowling wrote when she was five or six years old:

'The first finished book I did was a book called 'Rabbit,' um, about a Rabbit called Rabbit, thereby revealing the imaginative approach to names that has stood me in such good stead ever since' (HPM).

'Babbity Rabbitty and her Cackling Stump'

A Wizarding fairy tale from the book *Tales of Beedle the Bard*. The story tells of a witch who uses magic to get the better of a foolish Muggle king (DH7, TBB).

Babbling, Bathsheda

Hogwarts Professor for the Study of Ancient Runes (JKR).

'babble' = Eng. 'gibber, talk nonsense'
The name of this teacher comes from an early planning draft for Prisoner of Azkaban, *included on J.K. Rowling's website. The first name is unclear on the handwritten manuscript and may be 'Bathsheba'.*

Babbling Beverage

Potion which causes the target person to talk nonsense (OP32).

Babbling Curse

Exact effect not mentioned, but one can assume it causes the victim to babble (CS4).

Backfiring Jinx

The Office for the Detection and Confiscation of Counterfeit Defensive Spells and Protective Objects investigated the use of this illegal spell (HBP5).

Baddock, Malcolm

(Slytherin, 1994)

Hogwarts student (GF12).

badger

The badger is the animal symbol for Hufflepuff house at Hogwarts (PS3, GF15).

Bagman, Ludovic 'Ludo'

Famous Beater for the Wimbourne Wasps c. 1980 who was accused of passing information to the Death Eaters (GF30). Ludo joined the Department of Magical Games and Sports (c. 1993), serving as its head until resigning in late June 1995 due to his own irresponsibility and foolishness (GF37). Ludo was always more interested in the fun of sport than in taking his position with the Ministry seriously.

'ludo' = L. 'play'

'bagman' = Eng. slang: while in the U.S. this carries the sense of someone who collects money for a scam, in the U.K. it carries the meaning 'travelling salesman'.

Bagman, Otto

Got into trouble with the Muggle Artefacts Office because of an 'unusual' lawnmower, but Arthur Weasley straightened things out for him. Out of gratitude, Otto's brother Ludo arranged the Weasleys' tickets to the Quidditch World Cup (GF5).

Bagman (Sr.)

Father of Ludo and Otto, friend of the Death Eater Augustus Rookwood (GF30).

Bagnold, Millicent

Minister of Magic before Fudge, from 1980 to 1990 (OP5, JKR).

Bagshot, Bathilda

(b. mid-1800s–d. 1997)

Author of the famous book *A History of Magic*. Bagshot lived in Godric's Hollow and was a neighbour of the Dumbledore family. Her great-nephew was Gellert Gindelwald, who became friends with Albus Dumbledore on a visit to Bathilda's home in the summer of 1899 (DH 18, 32, 35).

'Bagshot' is the name of a town in Surrey,

to the west of London and in the general area where Little Whinging would be located.

Bagshot House

Now filled with the 'odour of old age, of dust, of unwashed clothes and stale food', this house was home to Bathilda Bagshot for many years. The house is located in Godric's Hollow, in between the town square and the Potter cottage (DH17). It was here that Grindelwald stayed when he came to Godric's Hollow as a teen, when he befriended Albus Dumbledore (DH18, 35). Harry and Hermione visited this house, too, in December 1997.

'balderdash'

Password to get into the Gryffindor common room (GF12, 14).
'balderdash' = Eng. 'nonsense'

balloons

Balloons can be enchanted to produce magical effects when they burst (DH8) — or not to burst at all (PS12).

Ballycastle Bats

Quidditch team from Ballycastle, a town on the north coast of Northern Ireland. The captain of the team is Finbar Quigley (DP1).

'banana fritters'

Password to get into Gryffindor Tower (GF25).

Ban on Experimental Breeding

An important law which prevents wizards from creating new and dangerous creatures (GF24).

Ban on Importing Flying Carpets

Because the carpet is classified as a Muggle artefact, the Ministry has in place a Ban on Importing Flying Carpets (GF7).

Bandon Banshee, the

A Dark creature supposedly defeated by Gilderoy Lockhart (CS6), but which actually was defeated by a witch with a hairy chin (CS16). Bandon is a small market town located in southern Ireland, roughly ten miles from the Celtic Sea.

The original text read 'witch with a harelip', but this was changed to 'hairy chin' in later editions.

Bane

A black-haired, unfriendly centaur who dislikes and mistrusts humans (OP33). In spite of his attitude, and although he preferred not to get involved, Bane eventually took sides and fought against the Death Eaters (DH36).

'bane' = Eng. 'something which causes misery or death'
Centaurs in mythology were always male and had a reputation for carrying of human women for mating. J.K. Rowling doesn't specify what happens to Umbridge when she's carried off by Bane, which is probably a good thing; the implications aren't pleasant to contemplate.

Banishing Charm

reverse of Summoning Charm
Depulso (PA/g)
Sends an object away from the caster; the target object is said to have been Banished (GF26).

banshee

A Dark creature with the appearance of a woman with a frightening face and black hair so long it touches the floor. Its screams will kill (PA7, CS6, DP4).
Banshees are female spirits from Irish mythology — and not surprisingly, Seamus Finnigan, who is Irish, is particularly afraid of them (PA7). Their wailing cries are said to foretell death. The Irish banshee is not particularly hideous, but because it is described as combing its long hair, superstition suggests that it's bad luck to pick up a comb found lying on the ground because it could be a left there by a banshee as a lure to trap the unwary.

Barbary, Heathcote

(b. 1974)
One of The Weird Sisters; for more information, see the Famous Wizard cards (FW).

Barkwith, Musidora

(1520–1666)
Wizard composer; for more information, see the Famous Wizard cards (FW).
'Musidora' from 'music'; 'Barkwith' = might be connected to the idea that dogs bark when they hear music being played or sung poorly, so the name suggests that this composer's music is 'bark-worthy'.

Barnabas the Barmy

A tapestry of this wizard, depicting his ill-advised attempt to train trolls how to dance, hangs on the seventh floor of Hogwarts Castle, opposite the entrance to the Room of Requirement (OP18, HBP20).
'barmy' = Brit. slang 'crazy'

Barnabus Finkley Prize for Exceptional Spell-Casting

Albus Dumbledore won this prize during his years at Hogwarts (DH18).

Barnsley

Barnsley is a town in South Yorkshire. The Five Feathers in Barnsley is home to Bungy the waterskiing budgerigar, about whom Harry heard a news story while listening to the Muggle news (OP1).

Baruffio

Wizard who mispronounced a charm and suffered for it (PS10).

Baruffio's Brain Elixir

During the weeks before O.W.L.s, older students tried to make money selling aids to concentration and memory to gullible fifth-years, such as Baruffio's Brain Elixir (OP31).

We don't know much about the enigmatic figure of the wizard Baruffio, but it's humorous that someone who couldn't pronounce a charm properly would lend his name to a brain stimulant.

Bashir, Ali

A flying carpet merchant who was very interested in importing his wares into Britain, even if he had to resort to smuggling (GF7, 23).

Basic Blaze Box

One of the range of fireworks products offered by Weasley's Wizard Wheezes (OP28).

Basic Hexes for the Busy and Vexed

Harry and Hermione looked in this book while searching for a simple spell for dealing with a dragon (GF20).

Basil

Ministry wizard, wearing a kilt and a poncho in an attempt to dress like a Muggle, who worked at the Portkey terminus at the Quidditch World Cup (GF7).

Basilisk

A wizard-bred Dark creature of enormous power, a huge serpent with extremely poisonous fangs. Only a Parselmouth can control a Basilisk (CS17). Its stare can kill. Spiders flee from the Basilisk, but it fears the crowing of a rooster (CS16).

J.K. Rowling's basilisk doesn't exactly match that in the various legends and bestiaries in which it appears. Those descriptions range from a small poisonous snake to a grotesque chicken. The basilisk was said to have been hatched from a serpent's egg placed under a rooster. Besides the deadly stare, many other terrible powers have been assigned to the basilisk, including breathing fire and withering plants with a glance.

Basilisk venom

One of the most potent magical substances known, Basilisk venom remains poisonous long after the creature has died. It is one of the few substances able to destroy a Horcrux (CS17). The only antidote to Basilisk venom is the tears of a phoenix (CS17, DH6).

bat, Beater's

In Quidditch, the Beaters use enchanted wooden bats to hit the Bludgers in an effort to affect their flight (away from fellow team members and/or toward opposing team members) (PS10).

Bat-Bogey Hex

Enlarges an opponent's 'bogies' to bat-size, gives them wings, and sets them to attacking his or her face (OP6, 33, HBP7).

'bogey' = Brit. slang 'booger' (nasal mucous)

Bath

Located in southwestern England near Bristol, Bath was so named because it was once home to an elaborate Roman public bath, the ruins of which still stand in the town. Ron told Harry a story he had heard of a witch in Bath who owned a book that had been bewitched so you could never stop reading it (CS13).

Many fans suspect that the Harry Potter books are bewitched in the same way...

bathrooms (UK: toilets)

There are a number of bathrooms located around Hogwarts castle (PS10). One girls' toilet is out of order because it is haunted place and frequently flooded (CS9, 16). There are also bathrooms on the fourth floor (OP28) and sixth floor (HBP24), and an elaborate Prefects' Bathroom on the fifth floor (GF23). The Room of Requirement created a bathroom for the students hiding from the Carrows during the 1997–1998 school year. However, that bathroom only appeared 'once girls started turning up' (DH29).

battle

During the Second Wizarding War, battles were fought between Death Eaters and allies of the Ministry, including Aurors and members of the Order of the Phoenix. Some of these battles were single combats, but others were pitched battles between larger groups of combatants.

The first three of the main battles in the Second War, while not identified by name in the books, have been given various names by fans for reference. In the Lexicon, we refer to them as the Battle of the Department of Mysteries, the Battle of the Tower, and the Battle of the Seven Potters. The final battle is called the Battle of Hogwarts in the book.

Battle of the Department of Mysteries

June, 1996

Fought in the lower levels of the Ministry of Magic between Death Eaters, Dumbledore's Army, and the Order of the Phoenix. The battle ended in a spectacular duel in the Atrium of the Ministry (OP35, 36).

Battle of Hogwarts

2 May, 1998

The climactic final showdown between the side of good and the side of evil. The Death Eaters enlisted giants, Dementors, and Acromantulas to fight for them, while the defenders of Hogwarts included centaurs, house-elves, students and their parents, shopkeepers from Hogsmeade, enchanted armour and statues and desks, and many others. Hogwarts castle was damaged in this battle and many people died defending it (DH31–36).

Battle of the Seven Potters

27 July, 1997

Fought in the skies over southern England between the Order of the Phoenix and over thirty Death Eaters on brooms (DH4).

Battle of the Tower

June, 1997

Members of the Order of the Phoenix and of Dumbledore's Army battled a party of Death Eaters atop and in the corridors around the Astronomy Tower of Hogwarts (HBP27, 28).

'baubles'

Password to get into Gryffindor Tower (HBP15).

'bauble' = Eng. 'cheap jewellery; shiny ball-shaped decoration; a jester's baton'

Bayliss, Hetty

Muggle living in Norfolk; on 1 September 1992 she was sure she spotted a flying car while hanging out her wash (CS5).

Hetty would have seen the car fly over sometime around noon, when Harry and Ron were following the Hogwarts Express north from London. Norfolk is quite some distance to the east of any reasonable route north to Scotland, however. Perhaps the Hogwarts Express took a magical detour to avoid a Muggle train at some point, and Ron followed it. At any rate, Hetty's report ended up in the evening edition of the Daily Prophet, *unfortunately for Ron and Harry (CS5).*

Beamish, Oswald

(1850–1932)

Proponent of goblin rights; for more information, see the Famous Wizard cards (FW).

Beaters

Quidditch players who use an enchanted bat to hit Bludgers, protecting their own team and attacking the opposing players (esp. PS10).

Beautifying Potion / Beautification Potion

Potions to improve the physical beauty of the drinker (FW).

Beautifying Robes

Sold at Madam Malkin's Robes for All Occasions (DP1).

Beauxbatons Academy of Magic

One of at least three magical schools in Europe, Beauxbatons is a French school whose students participated alongside those of Hogwarts and Durmstrang in the Triwizard Tournament. Both male and female students wear sky-blue robes. The headmistress is Madame Maxime (GF15 ff.).

'beaux' = Fr. 'handsome, beautiful' + 'batons' = Fr. 'sticks, wands'

The film version of GF shows Beauxbatons as an all-girl school, but it is not so in the book.

Bedazzling Hex

A cloak with this hex cast upon it can function as an Invisibility Cloak (DH21).

Beedle the Bard

Author of Wizarding children's fairy tales including 'The Fountain of Fair Fortune,' 'The Wizard and the Hopping Pot,' 'Babbitty Rabbitty and her Cackling Stump,' 'The Warlock's Hairy Heart,' and 'The Tale of the Three Brothers' (DH7, DH21, TBB).

Befuddlement Draught

ingredients: sneezewort, scurvy-grass, and lovage

A potion studied by fifth-year students at Hogwarts (OP18). Also known as a Confusing and Befuddlement Draught, similar in effect to a Confusing Concoction.

Beginner's Guide to Transfiguration, A

by Emeric Switch

The required textbook for Transfiguration for first and second year students at Hogwarts (PS5).

The surname of the author is an obvious one, considering the subject matter of the book; 'switch' means 'to change one thing for another'.

Belby, Flavius

(1715–1791)

Wizard who survived a Lethifold attack while in Papua New Guinea in 1782. He wrote about the experience, revealing for the first time the exist-ence of this terrible creature and also the fact that a Patronus Charm will drive a Lethifold away. Belby had at one time been voted the president of the local Gobstones Club (FW).

Belby, Marcus
(Ravenclaw, mid-1990s)
A 'thin and nervous-looking' boy whose Uncle Damocles invented Wolfsbane potion (HBP7).

Belch Powder
Yet another delightful product to buy at Zonko's to antagonise Filch (PA8).

Belcher, Humphrey
A wizard who mistakenly thought a cheese cauldron would be a good idea (HBP10).

Bell, Katie
(b. 1978; Gryffindor, 1990; Chaser 1991–1997; Dumbledore's Army)
One of the three Chasers on the Gryffin-dor team during most of Harry's years at Hogwarts. Oliver Wood considered her to be a superb Chaser (PA8). Katie has had her share of injuries during her years at Hogwarts, on and off the Quidditch pitch (PS11, HBP12). She was a member of the D.A. (OP17) and fought bravely against the Death Eaters (DH30, PS11).

Benson, Amy
A Muggle child from the orphan-age where Tom Riddle grew up who was terrorised while on an outing, al-though no one could work out what actually happened to her (HBP13).

Bermuda Triangle
An area of the Atlantic Ocean where many ships and aircraft have sup-posedly been lost under mysterious circumstances. The Wizarding travel agency Terrortours arranges excursions for witches and wizards to visit the wrecks there (DP3).
The Bermuda Triangle is an imaginary triangle formed by drawing lines be-tween Miami, Bermuda, and San Juan which is famous for unexplained disap-pearances of ships and planes. There is actually little evidence of there being any unusual happenings in that region, but the legends surrounding mysterious disappearances persist. J.K. Rowling enjoys making references to various leg-ends and folklore in the books, suggest-ing that they are actually examples of creatures and events in the Wizarding world.

Bertie Bott's Every Flavour Beans
One of the most famous sweets in the Wizarding world. These beans are essentially the same as Muggle jelly

beans but with flavours that Muggles would never expect, such as ear wax and vomit (PS6, 17). Bertie Bott's Every Flavour Beans were created by inventor Bertie Bott quite by mistake when he dropped a pair of dirty socks into the mix when he was making sweets (FW). Hogwarts students buy them from the lunch trolley on the Hogwarts Express (PS6) and from Honeydukes in Hogsmeade (PA10).

Bethnal Green

A district of London's East End, historically known as a poor area. In 1995, a series of magical pranks on Muggles in that area were investigated by the Ministry of Magic (OP7).

Bewitched Sleep

Puts the target person into a deep sleep; the subject is in a state almost like suspended animation and does not breathe for the duration of the spell (GF27).

bezoar

A shrivelled kidney-like 'stone' (HBP18) that comes from the stomach of a goat; it protects from most poisons (PS8, HBP18, 19).

Bezoars are actually fairly common in animals; even humans can get them. They're very similar to a hair-ball, a hard lump of indigestible material which stays in the stomach. In folklore, bezoars were thought to have magical powers, including being a universal antidote for poison.

bicorn

Horn of this creature is used as a potion ingredient. For example, powdered bicorn horn is used in Polyjuice Potion (CS10).

'bi-' = L. 'two' + 'cornus' = L. 'horn'

The Bicorn is a demonic creature which eats human flesh found in British and French folklore. It eats only husbands who have been bullied by their wives, and therefore, according to the tales, it is well fed and fat.

Bighead Boy

Fred and George Transfigured Percy's Head Boy badge to read this (PA4).

Bilius

Ron Weasley's Uncle Bilius saw a Grimm and died twenty-four hours later, or so the family story goes (PA6); Fred said Uncle Bilius was always good for a laugh (DH8). Bilius is Ron's middle name (DH7).

Bill of Goblin Rights

Subject of a meeting between the Ministry of Magic and B.O.G. in the early 1990s. It didn't go well (DP3).

binding/fastening magic

Spells which fasten chains or ropes to restrain someone or something. Examples include magical chains which bind prisoners to the chair of the accused in the Ministry's courtroom (GF30, OP8, DH13) and the spell *Incarcerous* (OP33), which sends magical ropes to bind up a target (c.f. PS17, 19). (*See also* ROPES, MAGICAL and CHAINS, MAGICAL.)

Binky

Lavender Brown's pet rabbit which was killed by a fox in the fall of 1993 (PA8).

Binns, Cuthbert

History of Magic teacher, the only professor at Hogwarts who is a ghost: ancient and shrivelled in appearance and semi-transparent (PS8). Binns' classes are remarkable only for their utter dreariness. He reads through endless details of goblin uprisings and other events 'in a flat drone like an old vacuum cleaner' which puts everyone to sleep (CS9, GF22, OP12). Binns prides himself on sticking to the facts and not going on about myths and legends (CS9).

Professor Binns' first name, 'Cuthbert', appears on a list J.K. Rowling created while planning Prisoner of Azkaban *(JKR). St. Cuthbert is a well-known Anglo-Saxon holy man who died in 687.*

Like Binns, St. Cuthbert didn't stay put even in death. For the next four hundred years, his bones were moved from one place to another until they were finally given a proper resting place in a shrine built in Durham Cathedral.

Birch, Brevis

Captain of the Tutshill Tornados who tried to make excuses for his team losing to the Ballycastle Bats (DP2).

Birmingham

Birmingham is located in west-central England and, after London, is the country's second most populated city. On one of its journeys, the Knight Bus jumped from Grimmauld Place to 'just outside Birmingham,' according to Stan Shunpike (PA3).

Bishop, Dennis

A Muggle child from the orphanage where Tom Riddle lived. Dennis, along with Amy Benson, was terrorised while on an outing, although no one could work out what actually happened to him (HBP13).

Black (Family)

The Black family is one of the most prominent pure-blood wizarding families. They call themselves 'The Noble and Most Ancient House of

Black'. The family motto is *'Toujours pur'* (French for 'always pure') (OP6, BFT), so it is not surprising that many of its members were supporters of pure-blood supremacy.

Black, Alphard

(died c.1976–77)

Uncle to Sirius and Regulus. Alphard was their mother's brother; however he has been removed from the tapestry because he 'gave gold to his runaway nephew' (Sirius), and is therefore represented by a burn hole in the Black Family Tree (OP6, BFT).

Alphard = the brightest star in the constellation Hydra

Black, Annis

A hag , living in a cave in a place called Deadmarsh, who protested what she saw as unfair criticism of hags as 'monsters' (DP1).

'Black Annis' is the name of a legendary hag who lived in a cave in the Dane Hills in Leicestershire which she dug herself with claws as hard as iron. Black Annis is reputed to have eaten children and hung their skins on the walls of her cave.

Black, Arcturus

(1901–1991)

Sirius Black's grandfather (BFT), possibly the one who was awarded Order of Merlin, First Class for 'Services to the Ministry'. Sirius says it was probably just because he gave them gold (OP6).

Arcturus = the brightest star in the constellation Boötes, the third brightest star in the sky

Black, Cygnus

(1929–1979)

Father of Bellatrix, Andromeda, and Narcissa; Sirius Black's uncle (BFT).

Cygnus = the constellation of The Swan

Black, Elladora

(1850–1931)

This is likely the Aunt Elladora mentioned by Sirius who started the family tradition of beheading house-elves when they got 'too old to carry tea trays' (OP6, BFT).

Black, Marius

(1900s)

Member of the Black family who was disowned for being 'a squib' (BFT).

Black, Orion

(1929–1979)

Father of Sirius and Regulus; he heavily fortified the family home at number twelve Grimmauld Place, London. Married his second cousin, Walburga Black (BFT).

Orion = constellation of The Hunter, one of the most prominent and well-known constellations in the sky

Black, Phineas

Disowned because he 'supported Muggle rights' (BFT).

Phineas = poss. ancient Egyptian 'Nubian, dark skinned'

Black, Phineas Nigellus

(1847–1925; Slytherin, c. 1858; later Headmaster)

Great-great-grandfather of Sirius Black, sometimes referred to as the least popular Headmaster Hogwarts has ever had (OP6). Phineas' portrait hangs in the Headmaster's office and he grudgingly helped Dumbledore when pressed. His portrait also hangs in number twelve Grimmauld Place (OP37). Phineas was a snide, sarcastic fellow with little patience for the feelings and the problems of others, particularly young people, whom he found tedious and self-absorbed (OP23, DH12, 15).

Phineas = poss. ancient Egyptian 'Nubian, dark skinned'

'Nigellus' = a Latinised version of the word 'black'

Black, Pollux

(1912–1990)

Sirius Black's grandfather (BFT). *See* BLACK, ARCTURUS.

Pollux = the brightest star in the constellation Gemini (The Twins); one of the brightest stars in the night sky

Black Family Tree tapestry

A tapestry which hangs on the wall of number twelve Grimmauld Place that has been in the family for seven centuries, according to Kreacher (OP6). On it the family's births, marriages, and deaths are embroidered with gold thread; family members who have been disowned have had their names 'blasted' from the fabric (a small burn like a cigarette burn appears where their name should have been).

When the producer of the Harry Potter films, David Heyman, realised that they would need to reproduce this tapestry on the set, he asked J.K. Rowling for help. As he tells it, she faxed him the entire family tree a short time later. J.K. Rowling also created a hand-drawn version of the family tree to be auctioned off for charity, which included the lovely note 'there are many stories between the lines'. There are indeed. Names from all through the series turn up on the Black family tree, suggesting relationships and connections between characters. Such delightful background information is typical of J.K. Rowling's commitment to creating a richly detailed world for her stories. We have included many of the more interesting names from that document in this book.

Black, Regulus Arcturus
(1961–1979; Slytherin, 1972; Quidditch Seeker; Death Eater)
Regulus was the younger brother of Sirius Black. Unlike his brother, Regulus was favoured by his parents because he shared their pureblood prejudices. Soon after leaving Hogwarts, he became a Death Eater (OP6, DH10). The family house-elf, Kreacher, was particularly fond of Regulus, as the boy was the only one who treated him well (DH10).
Regulus = L. 'the little king' and the brightest star in the constellation Leo. Regulus was also the family name of Marcus Atilius Regulus, a Roman naval commander who was legendary for his heroic self-sacrifice. Arcturus = the brightest star in the constellation Boötes, the third brightest star in the sky

Black, Sirius
(1960–1996; Gryffindor, 1971; Order of the Phoenix)
James Potter's closest friend, Harry Potter's godfather, and an Animagus. Sirius rejected his family's pure-blood philosophy (OP6). At Hogwarts he was a Gryffindor and one of The Ma-

rauders, a group which included James Potter and Remus Lupin. After Hogwarts, Sirius worked for the Order of the Phoenix. After the death of his closest friends (PA18), he was falsely accused of their murder and imprisoned in Azkaban (PA10). After years in Azkaban, he escaped and supported Harry and the Order of the Phoenix in any way he could (OP6, esp. OP35).
Sirius = the 'Dog Star', the brightest star in the Canis Major ('Great Dog') constellation

Black, Walburga
(1925–1985)
Mother of Sirius and Regulus, married to Orion Black. She was fanatical about purity of blood. Now that she is dead, her portrait hangs in Number 12 Grimmauld Place from which she shrieks and screams about 'bloodtraitors and Mudbloods' being in her house (BFT, OP4 etc.).

blackboard, magical
The Quidditch World Cup stadium had a huge blackboard upon which gold writing appeared as if written by a huge invisible hand. The space displayed advertising before the match, and then became a scoreboard once play commenced (GF8).

Blackpool Pier

Famous holiday destination on the northwestern coast of England on the Irish Sea. The Longbottoms have visited Blackpool, for this was where Neville as a young boy was pushed off the end of the pier by his Great Uncle Algie to try to 'force magic out of him'; Neville nearly drowned (PS7).

There are actually three separate piers at Blackpool, all built in the mid- to late 1800s and featuring theatres, restaurants, rides, and other entertainment facilities. In 1990, a Ferris wheel was added to the central pier.

blackthorn

A wand wood (DH20).

Blackthorn wood is traditionally associated with strong outside influences that are difficult to resist, so it's not surprising that Harry didn't find that a blackthorn wand worked well for him.

'bladvak'

Word meaning 'pickaxe' in Gobbledegook, the language of Goblins (GF24).

Blane, Balfour

(1566–1629)

Famous Ministry wizard; for more information, see the Famous Wizard cards (FW).

Blast-Ended Skrewt

A strange hybrid creature bred by Hagrid in the fall of 1994 by crossing manticores and firecrabs. Skrewts can belch fire and, when fully grown, sport magic-resistant armour (GF13, 18, 21, 31).

What happened to that one remaining Skrewt? We might guess that the final remaining specimen, once it recovered from the curse, was released into the Forbidden Forest, where all wild things are released in the end (BP).

Blasting Curse

See CONFRINGO.

Blenkinsop, Barnabus

His obituary in the *Daily Prophet* offering a reward for information about how he died, which was under very mysterious circumstances involving a tin of anchovies and an empty bed (DP2).

Blenkinsop, Timothy

Puddlemere United supporter who attended a recent match against the Holyhead Harpies and was caught in the ensuing riot. He still has a tail because of it (DP4).

Bletchley

A Ministry of Magic employee whose office was 'raining' (DH13).

Bletchley, Miles

(Slytherin, c. 1989; Quidditch Keeper c. 1991–1996)

Slytherin Quidditch player who hit Alicia Spinnet from behind with a jinx prior to the autumn 1995 Gryffindor–Slytherin match (OP19).

Blibbering Humdinger

One of the odd creatures Luna Lovegood believes to exist (OP12, 36).

Blocking Jinx

See IMPEDIMENTA.

Blood Blisterpod

A small purple sweet, invented by Fred and George. Half of it causes a nosebleed. The other half of the sweet stops the bleeding (OP14).

Blood Brothers: My Life Amongst the Vampires

by Eldred Worple

Worple, the author of this autobiographical book, showed up at Slughorn's Christmas party with a vampire friend of his (HBP15).

blood-flavoured lollipops

Sweets for sale at Honeydukes under a sign saying 'Unusual Tastes' (PA10).

Blood-Replenishing Potion

Medical magic: this potion makes up for lost blood (OP22).

blood-sucking bugbear

The suspected culprit when roosters were being killed at Hogwarts. Hagrid was understandably concerned (CS11).

The bugbear in English folklore is a huge bear which lurks in the woods and attacks children who don't mind their parents.

blood traitors

A pure-blood who doesn't hold the usual prejudiced views of other pure-blood families who tend to be exclusive and to look down on those who are half-blood or Muggleborn. The Weasley family has been branded 'blood traitors', although it doesn't seem to bother them much (OP6).

Bloody Baron, The

(Slytherin c. 1000; now Slytherin ghost)

The Bloody Baron is a grim, silent, terrifying ghost covered with bloodstains. He is never heard to speak (PS16). The Baron is the ghost of a man who a millennium ago murdered the woman he loved when she spurned him, then committed suicide with the same knife (DH31). Peeves, who respects the

Baron for some unknown reason, calls him 'Your Bloodiness' and 'Mr Baron' (PS16).

In the film version of the first book, the Bloody Baron is inexplicably depicted as rather frilly and goofy, not at all like the character in the books.

Bloxam, Beatrix

(1794–1910)

Author of the much-maligned series of books; for more information, see the Famous Wizard cards (FW).

Possibly this is a reference to Beatrix Potter, who wrote whimsical books for children. There appeared to be a discrepancy between the image of Bloxam on the card (as an elderly lady) and her birth and death dates, which were given as 1794–1810, indicating that she died at the age of 16. In Tales of Beedle the Bard, *the corrected date of 1910 solved this problem.*

Bludd, Blodwyn

(b. 1923)

Known as the 'Vampire from the Valleys.' For more information, see the Famous Wizard cards (FW).

Tom Jones is one example of a famous Welsh singer 'from the Valleys', a term referring to the valleys of South Wales.

Bludger

A round black iron ball, ten inches in diameter (slightly smaller than a Quaffle). Two Bludgers are used in a game of Quidditch. Bludgers are enchanted to attack and attempt to unseat the nearest player, which is why Beaters attempt to knock Bludgers toward opposing players (PS10).

bluebell flames

Creates a quantity of blue flame which can be directed to a specific place or carried around in a jar (PS11, 16, CS11, DH19).

Bluebottle

A type of broom, designed for family use, advertised at the Quidditch World Cup (GF8).

boa constrictor

Large snake living in a Surrey zoo who escaped under unusual circumstances in June 1991 when Harry Potter visited the zoo with his cousin Dudley (PS2).

Boardman, Stubby

The lead singer of the Hobgoblins, who retired c. 1980 after being hit in the ear by a turnip at a concert in Little Norton Church Hall (OP10).

boarhound

A large breed of dog used in hunting wild boars, another name for the Great Dane. Hagrid's pet Fang is a black boarhound. Like Hagrid, Fang looks much fiercer than he is (PS8).

In the films, Fang is depicted as a Neapolitan mastiff, but in the books he's a Great Dane.

boar statues

On either side of the wrought iron gates into the Hogwarts grounds stands a pillar topped by a statue of a winged boar (PA5, DH31). These symbols of Hogwarts are probably derived from the legend that Rowena Ravenclaw chose the location for the castle after dreaming of being led to the cliff by the lake by a warty hog (JKR).

Bob

Works at the Ministry, probably in the Department for the Regulation and Control of Magical Creatures, since he was riding the lift carrying a chicken that breathed fire (OP7).

Bobbin, Melinda

(Hogwarts 1990s)

Hogwarts student who in 1996 was recommended as a member of the Slug Club because 'her family owns a large chain of apothecaries' (HBP7).

Bode, Broderick

(c.1946–1996)

A wizard with a greyish complexion and sad expression who worked for the Department of Mysteries (GF7, OP8). Bode was seriously injured under mysterious circumstances in late 1995 and was sent to St. Mungo's (OP19, 23, OP25).

According to a (non-canon) planning chart for Order of the Phoenix, *Death Eater Walden Macnair was the wheezing old man with the ear trumpet visiting Bode at St. Mungo's on Christmas Eve. It is very likely that Macnair was the 'friend' who brought Bode the Devil's Snare (JKR).*

Bodrig the Boss-Eyed

Bodrig is the spokesgoblin of the Brotherhood of Goblins. He somewhat disingenuously told the *Daily Prophet* that the B.O.G. does not condone violence (DP3).

'boss-eyed' = 'cross-eyed or squinty'

Bodrod the Bearded

Possibly the name of a Goblin rebel leader, but since he's only mentioned by Ron trying to remember a list of names for an exam, one never knows (GF31).

Body-Bind Curse

An alternate name for the Full Body-Bind, *Petrificus Totalus* (PS17).

Boggart

A magical creature without a natural form. When a boggart encounters a human it changes its shape into whatever is most feared by that person (OP9). A boggart appears to feed on the emotion of fear, hence its classification as a Dark creature (PA7).

The boggart is a malevolent household spirit from British folklore, described as small, dark, and hairy. It attaches itself to a family and will stay with them for years, tormenting them, even if they move to a new house. Some boggarts are said to live under bridges.

Bogrod

Gringotts goblin who in the spring of 1998 had a most unusual day involving the high security vaults (DH26).

boil cure potion

ingredients: dried nettles, crushed snake fangs, stewed horned slugs, porcupine quills (added after taking the cauldron off the fire)

A very simple potion to cure boils is taught to first-years in their first Potions class with Snape (PS8).

When incorrectly mixed, however, this potion is extremely dangerous. How typical of Snape to start his first year class out with a potion that, if they make a single mistake, will make them break out in painful boils, melt their cauldrons, and burn through their shoes. In contrast, Flitwick waited several weeks before letting the first-years do any real magic in Charms, and then it was simply levitating a feather.

Bole

(b. 1977; Slytherin, 1988; Quidditch Beater c.1993–1995)

Member of the Slytherin Quidditch team who is not above cheating during a match (PA15).

'bole' = Eng. 'tree trunk', which might indicate either that he's rather large or that he's as dumb as a piece of wood.

Bonaccord, Pierre

First Supreme Mugwump of the International Confederation of Wizards. Bonaccord wanted to improve wizards' relationship with trolls but found that some wizards were not very keen on the idea (OP31).

'bon' = Fr. 'good' + 'accord' = Eng. 'harmony or reconciliation'

bond of blood

The bond of blood is an extremely powerful ancient magic which is formed when a person sacrifices himself or herself for a family member, out of love. The sacrifice creates a lingering protection in the blood of the person who was saved. It is not activated, however, until the charm is actually cast, and it is not sealed and functioning until another member of the family accepts the saved person as his or her own. As with most ancient magic, the bond of blood is mysterious and very strong and is not completely understood by most wizards (esp. OP37, DH3).

Bones, Amelia Susan
(d. 1996)
Head of the Department of Magical Law Enforcement until her death and a very powerful witch (HBP1). Bones was a short-haired witch who wore a monocle. She was known to be very fair (OP7, 8).

Bones, Edgar
According to Moody, he was a great wizard. He was the brother of Amelia Susan Bones, uncle of Susan Bones, and member of the Order of the Phoenix in the 1970s (OP9).

Bones, Susan
(b. circa 1980; Hufflepuff, 1991; Dumbledore's Army)

A Hufflepuff student in Harry's year. Susan wears her hair in a long plait down her back. In October 1995, Susan became a member of Dumbledore's Army (OP16, esp. 38). A number of Susan's family members have been killed in the battle against the Death Eaters over the years (BN, OP9, 25, HBP1).

Bonham, Mungo
(1560–1659)
A famous healer and the founder of St. Mungo's Hospital for Magical Ailments and Injuries (FW).
St. Mungo is the founder and patron saint of the city of Glasgow in Scotland.

Boomerang, Ever-Bashing
One of an extensive list of magical items banned at Hogwarts by Filch (GF12).

boomslang
African snake, the skin of which is an ingredient in Polyjuice Potion. Snape keeps boomslang skin in his private stores (CS10, 11, GF27).
The boomslang, Dispholidus typus, is native to sub-Saharan Aftica, where it lives in trees. The skin, which is mostly green in males and mostly brown in females, serves the snake well as camouflage. Boomslangs are highly venomous,

but since they are timid and don't attack unless threatened, they are not a serious threat to people. The name 'boomslang' is Afrikaans and Dutch for 'tree snake'.

Boot, Terry
(b. circa 1980; Ravenclaw, 1991; Dumbledore's Army)
Student in Harry's year who joined Dumbledore's Army in October 1995 (OP16, DH31).

Borage, Libatius
(c. 1940s)
The author of *Advanced Potion-Making*. *'libatio' = L. ' to pour wine, as part of a religious ceremony'; 'borage' = a prickly herb with blue or purplish star-shaped flowers'*

Borgin
Proprietor of Borgin and Burkes of Knockturn Alley; an oily, smooth-talking fellow who fawned on Lucius and Draco Malfoy but then grumbled about them after they left the shop (CS4, HBP6).

Borgin and Burkes
A shop located in Knockturn Alley which engages in the buying and selling of Dark Magic items (CS4, HBP6). The shop has had some very unusual employees over the years (HBP20).

Boris the Bewildered
Statue on the fifth floor of Hogwarts near the Prefects' bathroom (GF23).

Bott, Bertie
(b. 1935)
Inventor of Bertie Bott's Every Flavour Beans (FW).

Bottom Bridge
A bridge near the Lovegood house in Devon, a good spot for fishing (DH20, 21).

Bouncing Bulbs
Fourth-years re-pot these in Herbology class (GF18).

Bowtruckle
A small insect-eating tree creature with long sharp fingers, small eyes, and a general appearance of a flat-faced little stickman made of bark and twigs, Although ordinarily peaceful, a Bowtruckle will attack a human if provoked. A witch or wizard seeking to take leaves or wood from a Bowtruckle-inhabited tree should offer woodlice or fairy eggs to the Bowtruckle to placate and distract it (OP13).

'Boy Who Lived'
Harry's famous title, because he is the only wizard to ever survive a Killing

Curse. And he's done it three times now, actually (PS1, DH34).

Bozo
A paunchy man working as a photographer for the *Daily Prophet* who worked with Rita Skeeter (GF18, 19, 24).

Bradley
(Ravenclaw, 1990s; Quidditch Chaser c.1995–1996)
Hogwarts student (OP30, 31).

Bragge, Barberus
Chief of the Wizards' Council in 1262 who began the practice of catching a live Golden Snidget as part of the game of Quidditch (FW).
'Barberus' is similar to 'barbaric'; 'brag' means to boast about oneself. Each of these words suggests his character, which is bullying and crude.

Brain Room
A long, rectangular room in the Department of Mysteries dominated by a large tank of green liquid in which float a number of brains. Apparently the room is used to study thought or memory (OP34, 35).
When Ron is attacked by the brains in this room during the Battle of the Department of Mysteries, he is injured quite se-

verely. Later, Madam Pomfrey treats his injuries and notes that thoughts can 'leave deeper scarring than almost anything else' (OP38). J.K. Rowling has commented in various interviews about her own struggle with depression and is speaking here from the heart; she knows just how deep those kinds of scars can be.

Braithwaite, Betty
Daily Prophet reporter who landed an exclusive interview with Rita Skeeter to talk about Skeeter's then upcoming book, *The Life and Lies of Albus Dumbledore* (DH2).

Braking Charm
Charm used on a broomstick to allow it to stop effectively. The Firebolt had an 'unbreakable braking charm' (PA4).

Bran the Bloodthirsty
A giant from medieval times who lived in a castle on top of an enchanted beanstalk; for more information, see the Famous Wizard cards (FW).
The reference on the Famous Wizard card is obviously a nod to the fairy tale of 'Jack and the Beanstalk'. However, Bran is a famously violent giant in Celtic folklore. According to legend, he led the giants of Wales in their invasion of Ireland, but was killed by a poisoned arrow.

Branstone, Eleanor
(b. circa 1983; Hufflepuff, 1994)
Hogwarts student (GF12).

Brazil
The largest country in South America (and also the only one with a primary language of Portuguese, rather than Spanish). The boa constrictor which Harry freed from the zoo was native to Brazil, though it was bred in captivity (PS2). Bill Weasley once had a pen friend here (GF7).

Break With a Banshee
by Gilderoy Lockhart
One of the many required textbooks for Defence Against the Dark Arts in Harry's second year (CS4).

British and Irish Quidditch League
The association of professional Quidditch teams in Great Britain. There are thirteen teams in the League (DP1–4). The headquarters of the League is located on Level Seven of the Ministry of Magic in London (OP7).

Brockdale Bridge
The Brockdale Bridge was less than ten years old when, thanks to Death Eaters, it collapsed in the summer of 1996 (HBP1).

Brocklehurst, Mandy
(b. circa 1980; Ravenclaw, 1991)
Sorted at the same time as Harry (PS7).

Broken Balls: When Fortunes Turn Foul
Harry saw a copy of this at Flourish and Blotts while buying his Divination textbook (PA4).

Brookstanton, Rupert 'Axebanger'
Hermione came across this name when she was searching for someone with the initials 'R.A.B.' (HBP30).

Broom Regulatory Control
Broom Regulatory Control is part of the Department of Magical Transport (OP7).

brooms
The most common form of personal flying transportation in the Wizarding world. Most witches and wizards own at least one broom. A flying broomstick is not simply a 'normal' broomstick pressed into service as a mode of transportation. Rather, it is a magical item with built-in charms (esp. PS9,10, PA4).
There's probably no image more closely associated with witches than the flying broomstick. The first record of an accused

witch claiming to ride a broomstick was in 1453.

brooms, school

Older brooms kept in the school broomshed. They don't fly especially well (PS9, PA10, HBP11). These brooms are used primarily for flying lessons, which first-years take with Madam Hooch (PS9).

broomshed

A small outbuilding used to store brooms. The Hogwarts broomshed is located near the Quidditch pitch (PS11). The Weasleys have a broomshed near their house, described as an old stone outhouse. It is full of spiders (HBP4).

broomstick servicing kit

Present given by Hermione to Harry for his thirteenth birthday. It includes a *Handbook of Do-It-Yourself Broom Care*, a tin of Fleetwood's High-Finish handle polish, and Tail-Twig Clippers (PA1).

Brotherhood of Goblins, The (B.O.G.)

A group pressing for goblin rights, including the right to carry and use wands, which caused a bit of a ruckus in Chipping Sodbury recently. The leader of the organisation is Bodrig the Boss-Eyed (DP3).

Brown, Lavender

(b. circa 1980; Gryffindor, 1991; Dumbledore's Army)

A Gryffindor in Harry's year and best friend of Parvati Patil. Lavender tends to squeal and giggle a lot and generally gives the impression of being silly. She's keen on Divination (PA8). Lavender was Ron's girlfriend for few months in their sixth year, a relationship which consisted mostly of snogging (HBP21, DH7). Lavender was a member of Dumbledore's Army (esp. OP16, DH31).

bruise-healing paste

Medical magic: this is a thick yellow paste used to heal bruises, most likely invented by the Weasley twins (HBP6).

Bryce, Frank

(1917–August 1994)

Elderly Muggle caretaker of the Riddle house in Little Hangleton. Resident of Little Hangleton for most of his life, except for his military service during World War II (in which he was wounded, leaving him with a certain amount of permanent disability). After the war he worked for the Riddle family as a gardener. He continued to look after the house for fifty years after the Riddle family died (GF1).

Bubble-Head Charm

Encloses the head of the caster with a bubble of breathable air, which is useful when swimming to the bottom of the Lake (GF26) or avoiding the stench of Stink Pellets and Dungbombs (OP29).

bubbles, magical

Bubbles can be enchanted in many ways. Magical bubbles filled with light float near the ceiling in St. Mungo's (OP22). A *Scourgify* spell cast on a person washes their mouth out with soap so that pink soap bubbles come out of their mouth (OP28). Magical bubbles can also serve as decorations (PS11). A faulty wand has been known to give off purple bubbles (CS13).

Bubotuber

A rather unpleasant plant, black and wriggling, which is covered with large fluid-filled lumps (GF13). As Professor Sprout taught her fourth-year students, this fluid reacts with human skin. Undiluted, it will raise horribly painful boils on contact (GF28), but properly diluted and processed can be used to cure acne (GF13). The pimple-curing properties of bubotuber pus were discovered by Sacharissa Tugwood (FW).

Buckbeak

A grey hippogriff brought to Hagrid's first Care of Magical Creatures lesson in the fall of 1993. Buckbeak was at one time condemned as a dangerous beast (PA15), but was rescued (PA22) and eventually renamed Witherwings (HBP3).

Budleigh Babberton

A small Muggle town with a war memorial in the square and a church. Horace Slughorn took up residence in a Muggle house there for a week while its owners were on holiday in the Canary Islands, and this is where Harry and Dumbledore visited him (HBP4). *There is no Budleigh Babberton in the Muggle world. Its namesake, however, is most likely Budleigh Salterton, a coastal town southwest of Exeter. Also nearby are Chudleigh and Ottery St. Mary, two towns whose names J.K. Rowling similarly tweaked to create Chudley and Ottery St. Catchpole.*

Bulbadox Powder

Substance which causes the skin of a person who touches it to break out in boils (OP12).
'bulbous' = Eng. 'bulging, swollen' + 'dox', pehaps to sound like 'toxic'

Bulgaria

A country in Eastern Europe. The Bulgarian National Quidditch team played Ireland for the World Cup in 1994. Bulgaria's Minister for Magic is Mr Oblansk (GF8).

Bulstrode, Millicent

(b. circa 1980; Slytherin, 1991; Inquisitorial Squad)

Slytherin girl in Harry's year. With a square build and heavy jaw, Millicent was 'no pixie' in her second year; by their fifth year she was still able to physically overpower Hermione. Both Ron and Harry consider Millicent ugly; she reminds Harry of a hag (CS11, OP32).

Bulstrode, Violetta

Her husband was the son of Phineas Nigellus Black and Ursula Flint (BFT). Probably an ancestor of Millicent, a Slytherin girl in Harry's year (PS7).

Bundimun

A magical pest (JKR).

Bungs, Rosalind Antigone

Hermione came across this name when she was searching for someone with the initials 'R.A.B.' (HBP30).

Bungy the Budgie

In the summer of 1996, Harry knew that Voldemort must not be attacking in the open yet because the Muggle television news was reporting on something as mundane as Bungy the budgie, a bird which could water-ski (OP1).

Burbage, Charity

(d. 1997; Muggle Studies professor, c. 1990-1997)

Hogwarts Professor of Muggle Studies. She wrote a defence of Muggleborns in the *Daily Prophet* during the summer of 1997 and subsequently disappeared under mysterious circumstances (DH1, 2).

The scene at the beginning of the seventh book is horrifying, but it's also a bit of a let-down. How much more effective would it have been if the victim had been someone we knew, like Sprout, perhaps? Or at least someone we'd heard of? On the other hand, this is a book for all ages. The scene is intense, especially when Burbage pleads with Snape for help, to say nothing of the gruesome ending. Perhaps Rowling's choice to keep the reader somewhat emotionally detached makes sense. The name, 'charity', means 'love', which fits for a woman who writes impassioned statements defending others.

Burke, Caractacus

One of the founders of Borgin and Burkes, a shop in Knockturn Alley, described as a small old man with 'a thatch of hair that completely covered his eyes'. Burke was an underhanded fellow who didn't mind cheating people who came to him to sell their treasures (HBP13) or sending his employees to wheedle rich wizards out of their precious magic heirlooms (HBP20).

The name has two possible sources. William Burke was a famous murderer and grave robber in Scotland in the early 1800s, and from that the phrase 'to burke' has come to mean 'to smother someone to death'. Alternately, the British slang term 'berk' means an idiot or objectionable person. Sirius Black refers to himself and James as 'arrogant little berks' when they were at Hogwarts together (OP29).

Burke, Herbert

Husband of Belvina Black, the daughter of Hogwarts Headmaster Phineas Nigellus Black. They had two sons and one daughter (unnamed) (BFT). Possibly related to Caractacus Burke of Borgin and Burke's.

Burkina Faso

A tiny country in western Africa. It has a Ministry of Magic. One of Gilderoy Lockhart's supposed adventures that took place in Burkina Faso, specifically in its capital, Ouagadougou (CS9).

burn-healing paste

Medical magic: an orange ointment used by Madam Pomfrey to treat burns (GF20).

Burrow

A wizard house, owned by the Weasley family. It's at least four stories tall, built so crazily that it must certainly be held up by magic (CS3). It's located outside of the village of Ottery St. Catchpole, but so well hidden that the postman may not even know where it is (GF3). The ground floor consists of the living room and kitchen. The next several floors are bedrooms, with Ron's at the very top. A ghoul lives in the attic (CS3, GF10, DH6). Harry Potter loves this house and it has often served as a refuge for him. The garden outside the Burrow has gnarled trees lining the walls, plenty of weeds and overgrown grass, a large pond, and lots of gnomes (CS3). The property includes a small field hidden by trees where the kids play Quidditch (GF10) and a stone outbuilding which is used as a broom-shed (HBP4). When the entire family is home during summer holidays and Hermione and Harry are staying as well, there are simply too many people for the small kitchen so they eat dinner in the garden (GF5, DH7)

Weasels are solitary animals which live in burrows which they've taken over from other animals. J.K. Rowling places the solitary Weasley family in a house — taken from a farm outbuilding ('[i]t looked as though it had once been a large stone pigpen') — which they call The Burrow. Interestingly, just outside of the real town of Ottery St. Mary is a farm called Burrow Hill Farm.

Butterbeer

Very popular drink served cold in bottles (PA12 etc.), or hot by the mug at the Three Broomsticks (PA8 etc.). House-elves can get drunk on butterbeer, but it doesn't have that effect on humans (GF28).

Cadogan, Sir

A little knight in a painting that hangs in a seventh-floor corridor near the South Tower, a silly fellow whose bravura outshines his common sense and who glories in quests and challenges. In a pinch, Sir Cadogan was once called upon to guard the Gryffindor Common Room (he was the only painting brave enough to take the job). He thought up ridiculous passwords and changed them on a daily basis. Sir Cadogan has a huge sword and a little fat pony (PA6, 9, OP12). (*See also* DH31).

A cadogan, pronounced kuh-DUH-guhn, is an odd type of teapot with no opening on top.

Cadwallader

(Hufflepuff, 1990s; Quidditch Chaser c. 1996–1997)

A burly Quidditch player on the Hufflepuff team (HBP19).

Caerphilly Catapults

A professional Quidditch team from the Welsh town of Caerphilly (DP1-4).

café on Tottenham Court Road

An grubby late-night Muggle cafe on Tottenham Court Road which was damaged in a wizard battle on the evening of 1 August 1997 (DH9, c.f. DH20).

Cairo

Cairo is the capital of Egypt, as well as its largest city. In the late 1800s, while still a student at Hogwarts, Albus Dumbledore won a gold medal for 'Ground-Breaking Contribution to the International Alchemical Conference in Cairo' (DH18).

Callisto

A moon of Jupiter studied in Astronomy class at Hogwarts. Ron spent some time writing an essay for Professor Sinistra about Jupiter's moons. He incorrectly listed the largest moon as Callisto instead of Ganymede (OP14).

Calming Draught

Madam Pomfrey gave this to Hannah Abbott to deal with the stress of the O.W.L. exams (OP27).

Campaign for Greater Freedom for Wizards

Glinda Crook spoke for this group in the *Daily Prophet*, decrying the actions of the Ministry of Magic designed to reign in the actions of wizard-kind on Hallowe'en (DP4).

Campbell, Angus

Caerphilly Catapults Chaser who replaced Alasdair Maddock (DP3).

Campbell, Lennox

Seeker for the Montrose Magpies (DP2).

campground

Located next to a wood and a twenty minute walk away from a nice deserted moor and the Quidditch World Cup Stadium. It was looked after by a Muggle, Mr Roberts, who had to receive regular Memory Charms so he wouldn't notice all the magic around him. There were other similar campgrounds in the vicinity as well (GF7, DH14).

Canary Creams

Magical treats created by Fred and George. They have the appearance and taste of ordinary custard creams, but they will Transfigure the eater into a huge canary. The effect is short-lived, however, since the person moults a few moments later and becomes his or her normal self (GF21).

Custard creams are popular biscuits (cookies) in Britain. They consist of two cookie wafers with a vanilla cream centre, rather like a vanilla Oreo (and often eaten the same way, by twisting the cookies apart and eating the centre first).

Canary Transfiguration hex

A temporary hex to change someone into a giant canary (GF21).

candle magic

Candles are used for lighting in Hogwarts, and they are often used in magical ways. The Great Hall is lit with thousands of floating candles (PS7). Rita Skeeter uses magic to light and suspend a candle overhead when she's trying to conduct an interview in a broom cupboard (GF18). Poisonous candles are sold in Knockturn Alley (CS4). Strings of enchanted candles hang in the trees of Hogsmeade at Christmastime (PA10). Nearly Headless Nick's Deathday party was lit by black candles with thin blue flames (CS8). An everlasting candle is placed inside each suit of armour in the castle at Christmastime (PA11, HBP16).

candy and sweets

You never know what you might get when you buy sweets in the Wizarding world. Unusual tastes, magical effects, and strange ingredients are common. Bertie Bott's Every Flavour Beans will surprise you with flavours like pepper and sprouts (PS17). Acid pops will burn a hole through your tongue. Cockroach Clusters contain real cockroaches. And Drooble's Best Blowing Gum will fill the room with coloured bubbles that last for days. The best place to buy magical candy is Honeydukes Sweet Shop in Hogsmeade (PA10).

'caput draconis'

Password to get into the Gryffindor common room (PS7).

'caput draconis' = L. 'dragon's head'; this term is used for one of the sixteen figures of sikidy, a form of geomancy used in Madagascar. J.K. Rowling borrowed a number of other terms from this source, including 'fortuna major', another Gryffindor password.

car, enchanted

Although a car is defined as a Muggle artefact, and is therefore illegal to enchant under wizarding law (CS3), nevertheless there are a few enchanted cars in Britain. The Ministry of Magic has cars that navigate traffic with mag-

ical ease (PA5, OP23, HBP6). Arthur Weasley, who actually wrote the law banning such things, owned a Ford Anglia which he had enchanted to fly (esp. CS3).

cards, Exploding Snap

Cards specially made for the game of Exploding Snap, which means that the cards may blow up noisily at any time (e.g. CS12). These cards are occasionally used to build a house of cards, which can get interesting (GF22).

cards, fortune telling

Tarot cards for fortune telling, used by Professor Trelawney (HBP10, 25).

This method of fortune telling is called 'cartomancy'. Trelawney's interpretations of the meanings of the cards are fairly accurate, although naturally she's reading them as darkly as possible. Her reference to 'The Lightning-Struck Tower' card is spot on, however, not only because of its meaning in cartomancy — 'impending disaster' — but also because it predicts the Battle of the Tower (HBP27).

cards, Self-Shuffling playing

Ron had a deck of these in his room at the Burrow (CS3).

Care of Magical Creatures

A class offered at Hogwarts. Students

start Care of Magical Creatures in their third year (PA6). They study the life cycles of various magical creatures, some of which can be rather dangerous. They learn to care for, feed, and manage the creatures, along with lore about them and how to use them (or parts of them) for magical purposes (GF24, PA6, OP13, etc.). The class was taught by Professor Kettleburn until June 1993, then by Hagrid. Occasionally, Professor Grubbly-Plank substituted for Hagrid (GF24, OP11). The textbooks used are *Fantastic Beasts and Where to Find Them* (OP27) and *The Monster Book of Monsters* (PA4).

Carmichael, Eddie

(Ravenclaw, 1990)

An enterprising student a year ahead of Harry who tried to profit from the fact that he earned nine 'Outstanding' O.W.L.s (OP31).

carriage, flying

A huge powder-blue flying carriage as big as a house, used by the Beauxbatons students to attend the Triwizard Tournament at Hogwarts. The carriage was drawn by twelve gigantic Abraxans, flying horses bred by Madame Maxime, the headmistress of Beauxbatons (GF15, OP20, HBP30).

carriages, horseless

About a hundred carriages wait for arriving Hogwarts students along a rough, mud road near the railway station on September first each year, and take them back to the station at the beginning of the summer holidays. Most students consider them 'horseless carriages' because they do not appear to be pulled by anything (PA5, GF11, 12, 37). They are actually pulled by Thestrals, which are visible only to those who have seen death. The coaches smell of mould and straw (PA5).

A 'horseless carriage' was a term used for early automobiles in the U.S.

Carrow, Alecto

The sister of Amycus Carrow; a Death Eater who fought in the Battle of the Tower (HBP27) and a year later served as Hogwarts Muggle Studies teacher (DH12).

Alecto was one of the three Furies in Greek mythology, female embodiments of vengeance. Her name means 'unceasing in anger'. Alecto is found in Virgil's Aeneid.

Carrow, Amycus

Alecto Carrow's brother, a squat, 'lumpy'-looking wizard with a lopsided leer and a wheezy giggle. Although he fought in the Battle of the Tower

(HBP27), Amycus was made the Defence Against the Dark Arts teacher in the following school year (DH30).

Amycus is the name of two characters in Greek mythology. One is the son of Poseidon who figures in the tale of the Argonauts, the other a centaur.

cart, Gringotts

Magical transportation into the deep underground vaults of Gringotts Wizarding Bank. The cart is self-propelled and apparently guides itself along the underground passages, because the goblin doesn't steer as it winds its way along railway tracks in the floor. The cart has only one speed, according to Griphook: breakneck (PS5, DH26).

Catalonian Fireball Dragon

A species of dragon found in Catalonia, a region in the northeastern tip of Spain (JKR).

Though not mentioned in Fantastic Beasts and Where to Find Them, *a sketch of the Catalonian Fireball can be found in the pages of* Dragon Breeding for Pleasure and Profit, *shown on J.K. Rowling's website. Appearing along with the Portuguese Long- Snout, the Fireball brings the total number of known dragon species to twelve.*

catapult, winged

U.S.: slingshot

One of the many items not allowed for students at Hogwarts (HBP24).

Catchlove, Greta

(b. 1960)

Author of *Charm Your Own Cheese* (CS3, FW).

On J.K. Rowling's website, in an advertisement on the Rumours page, the author of the book is listed as Gerda Curd. Apparently this author uses a penname which is more 'cheesy' (JKR).

caterpillars

Potion ingredient. Sliced caterpillars are used in Shrinking Solution (PA7).

Caterwauling Charm

A spell which sets off an alarm. When an unauthorised person enters the target area while the effect is running, a caterwauling noise will be set off like a siren. Hogsmeade was under a Caterwauling Charm that would go off if anyone moved around outside while curfew was in effect (DH28).

'caterwaul' = Eng. 'to make a screaming noise like that of a cat during mating season'

'cat's among the pixies, the'

Mrs Figg uses this expression. It's synonymous with the Muggle cliché 'the cat's among the pigeons', meaning that something has stirred up trouble (OP2).

Cattermole: Alfred, Ellie, and Maisie
Children of Reg and Mary Cattermole who were scared for their mother's safety (DH13).

Cattermole, Mary Elizabeth
Wife of Reg Cattermole of Magical Maintenance at the Ministry of Magic. Her parents were Muggle greengrocers. Mary, a small woman with dark hair pulled back into a bun, was brought before the Muggle-Born Registration Commission to explain from whom she 'stole' her wand (DH13).

Cattermole, Reginald
Wizard who worked for Magical Maintenance at Ministry of Magic headquarters in London. He is the husband of Mary Elizabeth Cattermole. Reg figured unwittingly into a plan devised by Harry, Ron and Hermione to enter the Ministry (DH12, 13).

cauldron
A basic part of every witch and wizard's kit, a metal pot with a handle. These versatile items are used to brew potions, but can also be used to carry supplies, and, in a pinch, to clobber an attacker. Many cauldrons are at least partially magical. Self-stirring and collapsible cauldrons are for sale in a shop on Diagon Alley, for example (PS5). Gaspard Shingleton invented Self-Stirring Cauldrons (FW), a fact which the first years had to remember for their History of Magic exam (PS16). Cauldrons can carry a lot of books, which suggests that they might have enchantments on them to make them bigger on the inside than on the outside (CS4).

Cauldron Cakes
Something delicious sold on the Hogwarts Express (PS6, PA5, GF11) and baked by Bathilda Bagshot as a housewarming present for the Dumbledores (DH11).

'Cauldron Full of Hot, Strong Love, A'
A song performed by Celestina Warbeck. It is a 'particularly jazzy number' with sentimental associations for Mrs Weasley, as she and her husband danced to it when they were eighteen. It features not only Celestina Warbeck, but also her chorus (HBP16).

cauldron shop
This shop on Diagon Alley, the closest shop to the entrance from the alley be-

hind the Leaky Cauldron, sells all sorts of cauldrons (PS5).

Cauldwell, Owen
(b. 1983; Hufflepuff, 1994)
Hogwarts student (GF12).

cave by the sea
An extensive series of sea caves, nearly inaccessible except by magic, where Tom Riddle terrorised two children while on a day trip from the orphanage where he grew up (HBP13). Years later, Voldemort used dark enchantments and Inferi in the deep chambers of the cave to secure and protect a Horcrux (HBP28, DH10).

cave above Hogsmeade
A cave, located in the mountains above Hogsmeade which has served as a hideout and a refuge over the years (GF27, HBP8, DH31).

Cave Inimicum
(CAH-vay i-NIM-eekum)
One of the protective spells Hermione used (DH14, 22).
'cave' = L. *'beware'* + *'inimicum'* = L. *'of enemies'*

Cecilia
The pretty, snobbish Muggle girl on a grey horse that Tom Riddle was with when he rode past the Gaunt family shack. She was heard to say 'My God, what an eyesore!' (HBP10).

ceiling, enchanted
Some wizarding institutions have enchanted ceilings in their largest and most important rooms. The ceiling of Hogwarts' Great Hall is enchanted so that it mimics the sky outside (e.g. PS7, PA9, GF12, 13). At times the enchantment has been modified for a special occasion. Warm, dry enchanted snow fell from it for a Christmas celebration (CS12) and colourful confetti rained down during Lockhart's Valentine's Day festivities (CS13). The ceiling of the Atrium of the Ministry of Magic also seems to be enchanted to resemble the sky. It glows peacock blue early in the morning (OP7) and dark blue in the evening (OP34).

Centaur
Reclusive magical being, a horse with human body and head. Centaurs are only male, not female (JKR). Centaurs watch and read the signs in the stars and planets and they do not take sides in the events unfolding around them, preferring simply to observe (PS15). A herd of centaurs live in the Forbidden Forest, including Ronan (PS15), Bane (PS15), Magorian (OP30) and up un-

til Harry's fifth year, Firenze (PS15, OP27). The centaurs fought in the Battle of Hogwarts against the Death Eaters (DH36).

Centaurs figure in Greek mythology. In many cases, centaurs represent animalistic behaviour — carrying off human women, for example — but they also appear as wise teachers. The centaurs in the Harry Potter books demonstrate both traits. Bane carries off Umbridge when she insults and attacks the herd. Firenze, on the other hand, becomes a teacher at Hogwarts, even though he is banished from the herd because of associating with wizards.

Centre for Alchemical Studies

The foremost such institute is in Egypt (JKR).

chains, magical

A spell which causes magical chains to snake out of a chair and bind a person to it. The chair in the Court of Magical Law has these magical chains on it (GF30, OP8, DH13).

See BINDING/FASTENING MAGIC.

Challenges in Charming

One of the scholarly journals of the Wizarding world; Albus Dumbledore had at least one paper published in it when he was still quite young (DH2).

Chamber of Secrets

A legendary secret room deep underneath Hogwarts castle, constructed by Salazar Slytherin to house a monster which would finish his 'noble work' by ridding the school of non-pureblood students. Over the centuries, many have searched for the Chamber without success. Eventually, the whole thing was assumed to be purely fiction (CS9). It was not, however. The chamber is large and temple-like, with a huge statue of Slytherin dominating (CS16, 17, cf. DH31).

chamber pot room, magical

A mysterious room in Hogwarts discovered accidentally by Dumbledore; the room happened to be very conveniently filled with chamber pots. Although he did not realise it, this room was the Room of Requirement (GF23).

Chambers

(Ravenclaw, 1990s; Quidditch Chaser c.1995–1996)

Ravenclaw Chaser in the final Quidditch match with Gryffindor of the 1995–1996 school year (OP31).

chambers of the Philosopher's Stone

A series of chambers located deep underneath Hogwarts, used to conceal the Philosopher's Stone and protect it from would-be thieves. Dumbledore placed the Stone there sometime in 1991 or 1992. The stone was protected by several magical traps and devices such that stealing the Stone would be quite a feat (PS16, 17).

Where was the Stone all year, though? When was it placed in the Mirror and when was the Mirror placed in the underground chamber? After all, the mirror was in a disused third floor classroom at Christmas. Quite honestly, hiding the Stone in a mirror tucked away in some dusty corner of the castle seems a bit more secure than placing it behind a series of obvious magical barriers, calling attention to it and almost daring someone to try to get through. And let's face it, any magical defences which can be penetrated by three first-years, no matter how clever, aren't all that impressive. The most logical explanation is that the whole forbidden chamber thing was a ruse to cover for the fact that the Stone was actually somewhere else, and that Dumbledore intended for Harry to go down into the Chamber after Quirrell. What Dumbledore hadn't counted on, it would seem, was the fact that Voldemort was involved.

chameleon cloaks

There were rumours that the Puddlemere United team was investigating chameleon cloaks for new robes (DP1).

Chameleon Ghouls

These ghouls are known to pretend to be suits of armour (CS10).

Chang, Cho

(Ravenclaw, 1990; Quidditch Seeker, 1993–7?; Dumbledore's Army)

A popular, pretty Ravenclaw student who was Harry's girlfriend for awhile (esp. OP21, 26). She loves Quidditch — she has been a fan of the Tutshill Tornados since she was six — and was the Seeker for the Ravenclaw Quidditch team (PA13 etc.). In her sixth year, Cho joined Dumbledore's Army along with her friend Marietta Edgecombe (OP16).

Charing Cross Road

A busy shopping street located in central London, Charing Cross Road is the site of the Leaky Cauldron (PS5, PA3, HBP6).

True, Charing Cross Road is a very mundane, Muggle-filled street, but on the other hand, there is some magic to be found. Bookshops and music stores abound. Denmark Street, which connects to Charing Cross Road near the intersection with Oxford Street, is known as the 'British Tin Pan Alley'. Here Elton John wrote his first hit, 'Your Song', and legendary acts such as the Beatles and Jimi Hendrix recorded. Farther down the street is the London Hippodrome, which a hundred years ago was home to elaborate circus performances which included acts in a huge water tank that filled the stage. Muggles who want a taste of the magic of Diagon Alley can wander Cecil Court, just off Charing Cross Road, and buy anything from antique maps to crystal balls and stuffed owls.

Charms Club

A student organisation at Hogwarts (OP13).

Charms

A spell which adds to or changes the properties of an object. Charms are somewhat less scientific and more artistic and creative than Transfiguration spells (JKR), doing things such as such as making objects flash different colours or levitate. Some charms make a person laugh or dance or even create a bubble of breathable air around a person's head. Other Charms can be extremely powerful. Memory Charms, for example, can be so strong that they completely remove a person's memory

or even damage his or her mind permanently. Flitwick teaches the Charms classes at Hogwarts (PS8, etc.).

Charms Classroom

Classroom where Flitwick teaches Charms (PS10, etc.). Because the effects of the students' magic attempts can be somewhat random and haphazard, Flitwick is resigned to being pummelled, smacked on the head, and Summoned across the room. It is located down the Charms corridor on the third floor (PS9) and has a window overlooking the front drive (OP30).

Charm to Cure Reluctant Reversers

This spell comes from page twelve in Harry's *Handbook of Do-It-Yourself Broomcare* (PA2).

Charm Your Own Cheese

by Greta Catchlove (FW), also known as Gerda Curd (JKR)

The Weasleys keep a copy of this cookbook in their kitchen (CS3).

Chaser

Quidditch players who pass the Quaffle between them, trying to throw it through the goal to score; there are three on a Quidditch team (PS10, etc.).

Cheering Charm

A charm that cheers a person up. Cheering Charms were part of the Charms curriculum for the third-years (PA15). They were also part of the written Charms O.W.L. exam (OP31). Cheering Charms were invented by Felix Summerbee during the 1400s (FW).

cheese cauldron

Not a good idea, despite what Humphrey Belcher thinks (HBP10).

cherry

Neville's new wand is made from this wood (HBP7).

In Danish folklore, forest demons were said to live in cherry trees. Vila (which J.K. Rowling calls Veela in her stories) were believed to live near cherry trees according to Serbian folklore. Culpeper's Complete Herbal, a book J.K. Rowling mentions as one of her sources, lists a number of remedies using cherry fruit and sap.

chess, wizard

See WIZARD CHESS.

chestnut

Chestnut is a wand wood. Peter Pettigrew's wand was made of chestnut (DH24).

The lore of the chestnut tree doesn't fit Pettigrew particularly well. It signifies honesty and a well-developed sense of justice.

Chimaera

A vicious, bloodthirsty creature with a lion's head, a goat's body, and a dragon's tail. Fiendfyre sometimes takes the form of a Chimaera (DH31).

Chimera is a monstrous creature found in Greek mythology. Homer describes it as 'a thing of immortal make, not human, lion-fronted and snake behind, a goat in the middle, and snorting out the breath of the terrible flame of bright fire'. In Turkey there is a volcanic mountain called Mount Chimaera which, according to ancient writers, had lions on the peak, pastures with goats in the middle, and nests of snakes at the base, corresponding to the appearance of the Chimera monster.

China

The most populated country in the world, with over one billion people. Two Chinese wizards of note were the magical creatures specialist Quong Po and the alchemist Dzou Yen (FW). China is also the home of the Chinese Chomping Cabbage (OP16).

Chinese Chomping Cabbage

Hermione studied a diagram of this for a homework assignment (OP16).

Chinese Fireball

A species of dragon native to China. The Fireball is a bright red dragon with golden spikes on its head (GF19, 20).

Chipping Clodbury

This town was the location of a late-night meeting between Ministry representatives and the Brotherhood of Goblins intended to discuss the creation of a goblin bill of rights. Things got a little out of hand (DP3).

Chipping Clodbury does not actually exist in the Muggle world. The name is a play on words for the town J.K. Rowling grew up in, which is called Chipping Sodbury.

Chittock, Glenda

(b. 1964)

Radio personality; for more information see the Famous Wizard Cards (FW).

Chizpurfle

A magical pest (JKR).

Chocoballs

Sweet sold at Honeydukes (PA5).

chocolate

Chocolate has special properties. Not only does it make a wonderful treat but it also serves as a particularly pow-

erful antidote for the chilling effect produced by contact with Dementors and other particularly nasty forms of Dark Magic (PA5, 21).

Chocolate's magical effect isn't limited to witches and wizards. Chocolate actually makes us Muggles feel good because it contains small amounts of stimulants which increase endorphins in the brain. Part of chocolate's appeal comes from the fact that it melts at almost exactly body temperature, so popping a bit of chocolate into your mouth results in that melting goodness everyone loves.

Chocolate Cauldrons

Chocolates which typically have fire-whiskey in them, although unscrupulous witches have been known to substitute a love potion for the whiskey (HBP18).

Chocolate Frog cards

These cards, each bearing the face of a famous witch or wizard, come in Chocolate Frogs candy (along with a real chocolate frog) (PS6). Hogwarts students collect and trade them (e.g. PS13, GF19, OP10). The faces on some of the cards are famous even to Muggles, although their magical abilities were not always recognised.

Chorley, Herbert

A Muggle and a Junior Minister to the British (Muggle) Prime Minister. Chorley had to take some time off recently when he started acting very strangely (HBP1).

Christmas

The first of the two-week breaks between terms at Hogwarts, encompassing the Christmas and New Years holidays. Most students go home over this holiday break, but a few stay at Hogwarts. Traditionally, twelve Christmas trees are set up in the Great Hall by Hagrid and decorated by Flitwick. Sometimes the armour in the castle is enchanted to sing carols. Wizards use real, live fairies in place of decorative light strings (PA10, GF23). A feast is held on Christmas day, culminating in a round of Cribbage's Wizarding Crackers (e.g. PS12).

Christmas seems to be celebrated more as a cultural than religious holiday at Hogwarts, which is a 'multi-faith school', according to J.K. Rowling (MTV). British schools traditionally have breaks between terms at Christmas and Easter, just like Hogwarts.

Chudley Cannons

Quidditch team from the town of Chudley. The Cannons are Ron's favourite Quidditch team even though they do tend to lose rather often (CS3, etc.). The Cannons wear orange robes with a speeding black cannon ball and a double letter C on them (CS4). Some famous (and not so famous) players for the Cannons include Seeker Galvin Gudgeon (DP1), Beater Joey Jenkins (GF22), and Chaser Dragomir Gorgovitch, who transferred in 1995 and since holds the record for the most dropped Quaffles (DH7). The manager is Ragmar Dorkins (DP1).

Though there is no Chudley in Britain, there is a Chudleigh. It is located in Devon not far from the likely location of Ottery St. Catchpole and the Burrow.

Circe

A famous enchantress of ancient Greece; for more information see the Famous Wizard Cards (PS6, FW).

Circe, in Greek mythology, lived on the island of Aeaea. In the Odyssey, *she captured Odysseus' crew and turned them into pigs. He used an antidote revealed to him by the god Hermes to avoid being poisoned himself and rescued his men.*

Clagg, Elfrida

(1612–1687)

Chieftainess of Warlock's Council, Clagg made the Golden Snidget a protected species (JKR, FW).

The dates given on Clagg's Chocolate Frog card conflict with information from QA4 which says she was the 'Chief of the Wizard's Council' in the mid-1300s.

Clankers
Small metal objects which when shaken produce a loud metallic clanking sound; used to control dragons in Gringotts (DH26).

Clapham
Clapham is an area of southwest London that, at number two, Laburnum Gardens, is home to Sturgis Podmore (OP14).

Class B Tradeable Materials
The Ministry restricts trade in these materials because they are so dangerous (DH20, 21).

Class C Non-Tradeable Substances
Prohibited by Ministry regulations, but not as dangerous as Class A or B materials. Venomous Tentacula Seeds fall into this category (DH9).

classes at Hogwarts
Classes at Hogwarts are designed to train a young witch or wizard to be a competent, capable, and wise member of Wizarding society. They learn the basic theory and practice of the standard domains of magic: Transfiguration,

Charms, Potions, and Herbology. They also learn to discern between good and evil uses of magic, and to deal with the forms evil takes, such as Dark creatures and curses.

The following classes are offered at Hogwarts:
  Ancient Runes
  Arithmancy
  Astronomy
  Care of Magical Creatures
  Charms
  Defence Against the Dark Arts
  Divination
  Herbology
  History of Magic
  Muggle Studies
  Potions
  Transfiguration
  Extra-curricular:
    Flying (first year),
    Apparition (sixth year)
    Duelling

Classroom eleven
Located along the ground floor corridor, opposite the Great Hall, this classroom was used by Firenze to teach Divination beginning in 1995. When students entered the classroom, they discovered that it had been magically transformed into a forest, complete with starry sky (OP27).

Cleaning Charms

Various spells which are useful around the house (JKR). An example is *Scourgify* (OP3).

cleaning solutions, magical

Cleaning and polishing is usually accomplished with magical means, including various potions. 'Mrs Scower's Magical Mess Remover' is used regularly (CS9, GF18). Use number twelve of dragons' blood is oven cleaner (SFC).

Cleansweep series

A series of sport broomsticks produced by the Cleansweep Broom Company beginning in 1926 (PS9, CS7, PA12, HBP11, DP2). The current model is the Cleansweep 11, which came out in the summer of 1995 (OP9). Ron, Fred, and George Weasley all rode on Cleansweeps.

Clearwater, Penelope

(b. 1976; Ravenclaw, 1987; prefect 1992)

Girlfriend of Percy Weasley, who calls her Penny; she has long curly hair (CS12). She appreciates the Firebolt as a first-class broomstick, and is serious about Quidditch (PA13).

The text of CS14 has been corrected in current editions to put Penelope in the same year as Percy; Madam Pomfrey is now said to be 'bending over a sixth-year girl with long, curly hair'.

Cliodna

Famous Irish Druidess; for more information, see the Famous Wizard cards (PS6, FW).

Cliodna in Irish mythology was a goddess of love and beauty. She was accompanied by three birds whose songs had healing properties.

Cloak of Invisibility

One of the Deathly Hallows, according to legend a Cloak originally owned by Death himself. In fact, the Cloak was created many, many years ago by the Peverell brothers and belonged originally to Ignotus Peverell (DH21). Unlike any other Invisibility Cloak, this Cloak was perfect, never fading, and most importantly, could be used to protect others as well as the person who wore it. The Cloak was passed along the Peverell line for generations until it was given finally to the last living descendent of Ignotus: Harry Potter (DH35).

clocks, magical

In the kitchen of the Burrow was a clock with only one hand and no numbers. It was marked 'Time to make tea,' 'Time to feed the chickens,' and 'You're late!'

(CS3). Also in the Burrow is a grandfather clock with nine hands, one for each Weasley family member. These hands point to inscriptions around the face which indicate where that person is at the moment, such as 'home', 'school', or 'mortal peril' (GF10). In number twelve, Grimmauld Place was a somewhat more sinister grandfather clock. This rather nasty clock would shoot heavy bolts at passers-by (OP6, DH10).

There is a minor continuity error with the clock showing the location of the Weasley family members. In book two, it's a grandfather clock (CS3), but during the Second War, it was the size of a carriage clock and Molly was in the habit of carrying it around with her, even though it constantly said 'Mortal peril' for her entire family (HBP5). Considering that the clock is magical, however this is easily explained. There's nothing to say that it has to stay the same size all the time.

Clogg, Edgar
Ghost who has been hanging around the Hogwarts Quidditch pitch as long as anyone can remember ('Quidditch World Cup' video game).

clothing, Wizard
For the most part, wizards wear robes, without Muggle clothing underneath (GF7). There are varying types of robes, including dress robes for fancy occasions (GF10) and Quidditch robes designed for athletes (PS11). Depending on weather, travelling cloaks and hats can be added as well (DH11). At Hogwarts, school robes are plain and black (PS5) and seem to have something that identifies the house, although what this might be is never stated. Students wear pointed black hats as a regular rule (PS5, CS5).

The robes seen in the films do not match those described in the books at all; instead they look like school uniforms and use school ties to show house colours. The 'robes' are more like cloaks over Muggle-style clothing. The pointed black hats mentioned in the books were shown in the earlier films but were abandoned after that.

Club, The
A tea leaf fortunetelling symbol, from *Unfogging the Future* pages five and six, which means 'an attack' (PA6).

cobbing
Quidditch foul. During the World Cup final in 1994, this foul is described as the 'excessive use of elbows' (GF8).

cockatrice
A magical creature which is a combination of a rooster and a dragon or

snake. A cockatrice went on a rampage in the Triwizard Tournament of 1792 (GF15).

The legendary creature called the cockatrice is actually almost a twin of the basilisk. Some of the characteristics of the basilisk in the Potter books are actually those of the cockatrice, such as the ability to turn people into stone with a glance. Some medieval bestiaries say that the weasel is the only animal which is immune to its petrifying stare.

Cockroach Cluster

Sweets for sale at Honeydukes, most likely with real cockroaches inside (PA10).

J.K. Rowling has mentioned that she is a Monty Python fan (Sch2). Cockroach clusters come directly from a sketch from 'Monty Python's Flying Circus'.

Code of Wand Use

Clause 3 of this Code says that no non-human creature is permitted a wand (GF9). The passage of this Ministry of Magic Decree, called the Wand Ban, in 1631 led to goblin riots (JKR). This is still a serious point of contention with the goblins (DH24).

Cokeworth

The home of the Railview Hotel, where Vernon Dursley drove the fam-ily in a desperate attempt to escape Harry's letters from Hogwarts (PS3).

The name of the town of Cokeworth may be borrowed from the grim industrial city of Coketown in Charles Dickens' novel Hard Times. *'Coke' in this context refers to a fuel derived from coal, used in iron-making blast furnaces.*

Cole, Mrs

The matron of Tom Riddle's orphanage. Mrs Cole appeared to be harried and overworked, but her manner and appearance was not unkind (HBP13).

Collapsible Cauldron

A cauldron which can be made smaller, perhaps to make it easier to carry (PS5).

Colloportus

(ko-lo-POR-tus)

Seals a door, making an odd squelching noise (OP35).

'colligo' = L. 'to bind together' + 'portus' = L. 'doorway, opening, portal'

Colour Change Charm

A Charm that is required during the practical portion of the Charms O.W.L. Possibly the same as the flashing paint charm (OP31).

CoMC

Commonly used abbreviation in fandom for Care of Magical Creatures.

Come and Go Room

The House-elves' name for the Room of Requirement (OP18).

Comet series

A series of racing brooms built by the Comet Trading Company. Malfoy rode a Comet 260 (PS10), as did Cho Change (PA13) and Tonks (OP3).

Committee for the Disposal of Dangerous Creatures

A Ministry committee that considers cases of brutality of magical creatures. They hold a hearing and consider evidence, then pronounce judgment (PA11, 16, 21).

Committee on Experimental Charms

This Ministry committee deals with unusual and potentially dangerous new spells (CS3). The committee was founded by Balfour Blane c. 1600 (FW). One of its current personnel, Gilbert Whimple, presently has horns, presumably from handling some dangerous magic (GF7).

Common Magical Ailments and Afflictions

A standard book of medical information for wizards (GF2).

common rooms

Each Hogwarts house has a common room, adjacent to its dormitories, where many students spend their free time. Each room is unique, reflecting the founder of the House and the characteristics of its students. Gryffindor and Ravenclaw each have a tower with a circular common room at the base (PS7, DH30); Hufflepuff has a 'cosy and welcoming' common room near the kitchens (BLC); and Slytherin has a dungeon underneath the lake (DH23).

Common Welsh Green

Dragon species native to the higher mountains of Wales (PS14, JKR).

Compendium of Common Curses and Their Counter-Actions, A

The Room of Requirement contained a copy of this book during the D.A.'s first meeting there (OP18).

'complimentary medicine'

Treating patients using Muggle techniques along with the magical approaches. The practice is considered very dodgy by wizards (OP23).

Comstock, Magenta
(1895–1991)

Comstock was a magical artist. She was famous for painting portraits with strangely enchanted eyes (JKR).

Magenta is a purplish-red colour, a fitting name for an artist. The last name may be a nod to Anna Botsford Comstock, an American artist and educator in the early 20th century.

Confringo
(kon-FRIN-go)
'Blasting Curse'

Causes the target to explode (FW, DH4, 17).

'confringo' = L. 'to smash, crush; to ruin, undo'

Confronting the Faceless

The N.E.W.T.-level textbook for Defence Against the Dark Arts during Harry's sixth year (HBP9).

Confundo
(kon-FUN-do)
'Confundus Charm'

Causes confusion. A person who is affected by this Charm is said to be Confunded (PA21, HBP11, 14, DH1, 15, 16, 26, 33, /e). The Confundus Charm can be cast on a magical object as well as a person (GF17).

'confundo' = L. 'to mix up, jumble together, confuse, bewilder, perplex'

Confundus Charm
See CONFUNDO.

Confusing and Befuddlement Draught
ingredients: sneezewort, scurvygrass, and lovage

Harry had to study the ingredients and their effects during his fifth year (OP18).

Confusing Concoction

A potion that third-years were asked to brew for their exams (PA16).

Conjunctivitis Curse

A spell that affects the eyes and vision of the target (GF19, 20).

'conjunctiva' = L. 'connecting (as in membrane of the eye)' + '-itis' = L. 'inflammation'

conjured items

A spell that creates objects out of thin air (e.g. CS11, PA9). Most things conjured out of thin air will disappear after a couple of hours (SN). Some things simply can't be conjured; Gamp's Law of Elemental Transfiguration states that there are five of these exceptions, one of which is food (DH15, 29). Wizards occasionally will 'draw up a chair' (conjure a chair out of thin air) (e.g. OP8, 22). Conjuring spells are advanced magic — considered N.E.W.T. level at Hogwarts (OP13).

Connolly

Beater for the Irish National Side Quidditch team (GF8).

Contorting Cereals

A category in the Annual International Wizard Gardening Competition which causes some confusion in Muggles, who call them 'crop circles' (DP1).

contract, magical

This spell or spells makes a contract magically unbreakable. Placing a name in the Goblet of Fire constituted a binding magical contract. The people whose names were chosen were obliged to participate in the contest (GF16). *See* UNBREAKABLE VOW.

Cooper, Buckley

Wrote a letter to the *Daily Prophet* asking for legal advice in the running feud he's been having with his brother, wondering if he could get away with turning his nephews and nieces into animals (DP3).

Coopey, Howland

Wrote a letter to the *Daily Prophet's* Problem Page asking for medical advice about his alarming and rather colourful symptoms (DP3).

Coote, Ritchie

(Gryffindor 1990s; Quidditch Beater 1996–?)

Coote is a 'weedy-looking' fellow, but he 'aims well'. He is put on the Gryffindor Quidditch team playing Beater along with Peakes (HBP11).

Corner, Michael

(b. circa 1980; Ravenclaw 1991; Dumbledore's Army)

Michael is a dark-haired boy who met Ginny Weasley at the Yule Ball. Through Ginny, Michael and his friends joined the D.A. (OP16, DH29).

Michael Corner was listed as a Hufflepuff on J.K. Rowling's list of students in Harry's year (HPM) but became a Ravenclaw in the books.

Cornfoot, Stephen

(b. circa 1980; Ravenclaw 1991)

Student in Harry's year (HPM).

Stephen's name appears in the draft of the class list of Harry's year that J.K. Rowling displayed during the 'Harry Potter and Me' TV interview (HPM). According to the list he is a pure-blood. Stephen has never appeared in canon, but his name is listed here because he apparently existed in early plans for the books.

Cornwall

County which comprises the south-western tip of England. Cornwall is the location of Tinworth, a Muggle coastal town which includes a significant magical population (including Bill and Fleur Weasley's home, Shell Cottage) (DH16). Cornwall is also the location of Falmouth, home of the Falcons Quidditch team, and Bodmin Moor, where a Quidditch pitch is located (DP2, 3, 4). Cornish Pixies, the type let loose in the classroom by Gilderoy Lockhart (CS6), are native to here, and in fact in the 17th century Dymphna Furmage experienced an 'unfortunate incident' with pixies while on holiday in Cornwall (FW).

Cotswolds

The Cotswolds is a small area in England famous for beautiful rolling hills. The town of Bath is located in the Cotswolds. Trolls have historically lived in the hills here; troll specialist Gondoline Oliphant was clubbed to death by trolls in the Cotswolds while she was sketching in 1799 (FW).

Cotton, Gregory

Appleby Arrows Seeker (DP3).

cough potion

The Wizarding world's equivalent to Muggle cough elixir (cough syrup in the U.S.) (HBP15).
See PEPPERUP POTION.

Council of Magical Law

Likely another name for what was in later books called the Wizengamot, this Council was responsible for conducting several key Death Eater trials following the initial fall of Voldemort in 1981. The Council was overseen by Barty Crouch, Sr., the Head of the Department of Magical Law Enforcement at that time (GF27, 30).
Beginning in book five, the primary court of law in the Wizarding world is called the Wizengamot; quite possibly this is the same court but that J.K. Rowling hadn't invented the name yet. On the other hand, the Council of Magical Law may be a special court set up for the purpose of dealing with captured Death Eaters.

Courtrooms, Ministry

The Ministry courtrooms are located in the lower levels of Ministry headquarters in London. They are intimidating places. In some cases the accused persons are brought in by Dementors and find themselves sitting on a chair which chains their arms in place magically.

The various judges and other members of the court sit far above the accused in rows of seats around the perimeter of the high-ceilinged chamber. Among other things, they have been used for hearings conducted by the Council of Magical Law (GF30), the Wizengamot (OP8), and the Muggle-Born Registration Commission (DH13).

Crabbe, Irma
(1912–1990)
The wife of Pollux Black, and grandmother to Sirius and Regulus Black, as well as to Bellatrix Lestrange, Andromeda Tonks, and Narcissa Malfoy (BFT).

Crabbe, Mr
A Death Eater, the father of Vincent Crabbe. Like his son, Mr Crabbe is a large fellow and a bit dim (GF33, OP26).

Crabbe, Vincent
(c. 1980–1998; Slytherin 1991; Inquisitorial Squad; Quidditch Beater 1995–?)
A thickset Slytherin in Harry's year (PS6), and the son of a Death Eater (GF33). He was quite dense, although he seemed a little brighter than Goyle (PS9). He spent much of his career at Hogwarts trailing Draco Malfoy as something of a bodyguard for him (e.g. PS6, PA5, HBP18, DH31). Be-ginning his fifth year he also played Beater on the Slytherin Quidditch team (OP19) and joined the Inquisitorial Squad (OP32).
'crab' = Eng. slang. 'gripe, complain'

Cragg, Elfrida
Someone whose portrait hangs in St. Mungo's (OP22).
This is probably a misprint for Elfrida Clagg, the famous Chieftess of the Wizard's Council in the 1600s.

Creevey, Mr
A Muggle milkman (CS6) who has two sons who are wizards, Colin (CS6) and Dennis (GF12).

Creevey, Colin
(1981–1998; Gryffindor, 1992; Dumbledore's Army)
A very excitable, short boy with mousy brown hair who was just tickled to death to discover that he was a wizard and to find out about Hogwarts (CS5, 6). Colin's heart is in the right place, certainly, but he does tend to get run over once in a while in the rush of events. Colin joined Dumbledore's Army in October 1995 (OP16). What Colin lacks in size he makes up for in bravery (esp. DH34).

Creevey, Dennis

(b. 1983; Gryffindor, 1994; Dumble-dore's Army)

The younger brother of Colin, and like Colin has 'mousy' brown hair (GF12). Dennis was the smallest kid in his year when he arrived, and thus almost certainly the smallest kid in Hogwarts; he needed to stand on his seat in the Great Hall to be able to see the Goblet of Fire properly, and still only just came up to everyone else's eye-level (GF12, 16). Dennis joined Dumbledore's Army in October 1995 (OP16).

Dennis managed to get into Hogsmeade for the initial meeting of the D.A. at the Hog's Head, even though at the time he was a second year student and technically not allowed off school grounds. This may be a continuity error on J.K. Rowling's part, but could also just indicate that Dennis is a bit cleverer than meets the eye.

Cresswell, Dirk

(d. 1998)

A gifted student while at Hogwarts, Cresswell went on to become the Head of the Goblin Liaison Office (HBP4, DH15, 22).

A man named Derek Cresswell serves on the Nottingham City Council and was the Sheriff of Nottingham some years

back. *Sure, it's probably just a coincidence, but it is interesting nevertheless to discover such a similar name while researching.*

Cribbage's Wizarding Crackers

Part of the Christmas feast celebration, similar to Muggle crackers, but these are magical and contain very interesting and unusual things. When pulled, a wizard cracker goes off with a very loud blast (PS12, PA11, GF23). Some items found in Wizarding Crackers include a wizard chess set, grow-your-own-warts kit, and a pack of nonexplodable luminous balloons (PS12).

Christmas crackers are a tradition in Britain but little known in the United States. They consist of a cardboard tube decorated with ribbons and lace with a small gift inside. When pulled apart by two people, they give off a bang and reveal the gift.

Croaker

Arthur Weasley identified this wizard as being an Unspeakable, someone who works for the Department of Mysteries (GF7).

Crockford, Doris

A witch in the Leaky Cauldron on July 31, 1991, who was just so delighted to meet Harry Potter that she came back more than once to shake his hand (PS5).

Cromer

Cromer is a small seaside town on the east coast of England, almost straight east of London, in Norfolk. In the early eighteenth century, this was the home of the feared Sea Serpent of Cromer (FW).

Cronk, Crispin

(1795–1872)

Wizard who was inordinately fond of sphinxes; for more information, see the Famous Wizard cards (FW).

'cronk' = Australian slang 'fraudulent'

Crook, Glinda

Works for the Campaign for Greater Freedom for Wizards. Quoted in the *Daily Prophet* decrying the actions of the Ministry of Magic designed to reign in the actions of wizard-kind on Hallowe'en (DP4).

Glinda is the name of the Good Witch of the North in the Wizard of Oz stories.

Crookshanks

Crookshanks is a half-Kneazle (JKR) that Hermione purchased from Magical Menagerie in Diagon Alley before her third year at Hogwarts (PA4). He appears to be a large ginger cat with a squashed flat face, a bottle-brush tail and bandy legs. Crookshanks' Kneazle ancestry accounts for his unusual intelligence and his ability to identify suspicious characters and activities (esp. PA4, 19, GF14).

J.K. Rowling based Crookshanks on a fluffy ginger cat she enjoyed watching on her lunch hours (although she is allergic to cats) (JKR). Crookshanks' name refers to his bandy legs ('shank' is Old English for leg, or shinbone). George Cruikshank (1792–1878) was a caricaturist who illustrated Charles Dickens' book Oliver Twist.

Crop-related charms

The Ministry of Magic report 'A Study into Muggle Suspicions about Magic' recommended that the International Confederation of Wizards address problems created by crop-related charms (DP1).

Cross, the

A tea leaf fortunetelling symbol, from *Unfogging the Future* pages five and six, which means 'trials and suffering' (PA6).

Trelawney got this one right. The meaning of the cross in tasseography is 'trouble, delay, or death'.

Cross-Species Switches

Classification of Transfiguration magic in which one type of creature is Transfigured into another (GF22).

Apparently it's easier to do the spell when the creatures have similar names (e.g. guinea fowl into guinea pigs), similar appearance (e.g. hedgehogs into pincushions), or both (e.g. beetles into buttons).

Crouch, Bartemius 'Barty', Sr.

(d. June 1995)

Ministry official, famous for aggressively prosecuting Dark Wizards in the 1970s. His fervour led him to authorise methods almost as bad as those of the Death Eaters they were hunting. Crouch was much admired at the time, but fell from grace around 1982 due to personal failures and mistakes and was moved to the Department of International Magical Cooperation (GF27).

'crouch' from Old Fr. 'crochir' = 'to become bent'

Crouch, Bartemius 'Barty', Jr.

(b. circa 1963, d.? 24 June 1995)

Barty Crouch Jr. was the only child of Ministry official Barty Crouch, Sr. He was a gifted and promising young wizard, but became a Death Eater, much to his father's shame (GF30, 36, 37).

Crouch, Caspar

Wizard who appears on the Black family tree tapestry in the drawing room of Number 12 Grimmauld Place (BFT).

Crouch, Mrs

A frail witch, married to Barty Crouch Sr. (GF27, 30, 35).

Cruciatus Curse

See CRUCIO.

Crucio

(KROO-see-oh)

Cruciatus Curse

This Unforgivable Curse is the most extreme method of torture in the Wizarding world, causing almost intolerable pain (esp. GF14, 34, DH23, 29). If used for extended periods of time, it is also capable of driving its subject insane (GF30).

'crucio' = L. 'torture, torment'

Crumb, Gideon

(b. 1975)

A member of The Weird Sisters; for more information, see the Famous Wizard cards (FW).

Crumple-Horned Snorkack

An elusive, non-flying creature which seems to be popular among readers of *The Quibbler* (OP13). The Snorkack has a very distinctive horn (DH20). (*See also* BLC).

Crup
Magical creature which looks like a small dog, except that a Crup has a forked tail (OP25).

'crying over spilt potions'
Mrs Figg uses this expression. It's synonymous with the Muggle cliché 'no use crying over spilt milk' (OP2).

crystal balls
Tools for Divination (PA15) which came in handy as weapons in a pinch (DH32).

crystal bell jar
A huge jar standing in a room in the Department of Mysteries, filled with some sort of moving liquid. Floating with the current inside is a small bird. As the bird moves though its path, it changes from egg to baby bird to adult bird and back to egg. The jar is used to study time (OP34).

Cuffe, Barnabas
Editor of the *Daily Prophet* (HBP4).

cupboard under the stairs
Harry's 'bedroom' at the Dursleys for ten years. The cupboard had spiders in

it and when he awoke each morning he would be looking up at the underside of the stairs (PS3, DH4).
'cupboard' = 'closet' (US)

Cup of Hufflepuff
See HUFFLEPUFF'S CUP.

Curd, Gerda
Author of *Charm Your Own Cheese* (possibly a penname, since the author's name on the famous wizard card is Greta Catchlove) (JKR).

curse-breaker, Gringotts
A very adventurous job involving breaking into ancient tombs and recovering gold (PA1, OP29, HBP5).

Curse of the Bogies
A curse that Ron threatened to learn and use on his friends at one point, although this was probably just talk (PS9).
'bogey' could be derived from:
  'Old Bogey' = The Devil (c. 1836), or
  'bogle' = Scottish phantom or goblin (c. 1505), or even
  'bogge' = terror, possibly from 'bwg' = Welsh 'ghost' and 'bwgwl' = Welsh 'fear'
Yeah, maybe. But more likely:
  'bogey' = Brit. slang 'booger, nasal mucous'

curses

Spells cast for evil purposes (JKR).

Curses and Counter-curses: (Bewitch Your Friends and Befuddle Your Enemies with the Latest Revenges: Hair Loss, Jelly-Legs, Tongue-Tying, and Much, Much More)

By Vindictus Veridian

A book with a tempting (and very lengthy) title which Harry spotted in Flourish and Blotts on his first visit to Diagon Alley (PS5).

Cushioning Charm

The Cushioning Charm creates an invisible 'pillow' in the air (DH26).

Cyclops

A one-eyed ancient Greek giant; for more information, see the Famous Wizard cards (FW).

This Cyclops from The Odyssey *is Polythemus, the son of Posiedon. He is one of a race of one-eyed giants who live on the island of Cyclops. When Odysseus accidentally enters Polyphemus' cave, the giant kills several of his men. He in turn gets the giant drunk and puts out his one eye. In order to escape the giant's clutches, the men strap themselves to the underside of Polyphemus' sheep. When the now-blind giant lets the sheep out to graze, he is suspicious and feels the back of each animal to make sure that Odysseus' men aren't riding them. Feeling nothing but wool, he lets the sheep go.*

D.A., the

The name for the group of students who banded together to learn defensive spells during the time that Umbridge was at Hogwarts. The name D.A. stands for Dumbledore's Army (OP18 ff).

DADA

Commonly used abbreviation in fandom and even by J.K. Rowling herself for Defence Against the Dark Arts.

Dagworth-Granger, Hector

Founder of the Most Extraordinary Society of Potioneers (HBP9).

Daily Prophet

The primary newspaper of the Wizarding world. The current editor is Barnabas Cuffe (HBP4). It has offices in Diagon Alley (DP) and publishes an edition every morning. Typically, the *Prophet* is delivered each morning by owl post (PS5, GF28, OP12, HBP11). An evening edition, called *The Evening Prophet*, is also printed (CS5).

J.K. Rowling does not show much sympathy for the press in her stories. The Prophet is not the only publication in the Wizarding World, but it is almost certainly the most widely read. J.K. Rowling shows the Prophet allowing itself to become a tool of the Ministry's propaganda, shifting from one position to another at the drop of a hat. For a year, the Prophet reported the Ministry line that Harry Potter was crazy and dangerous. Within two weeks of Voldemort's appearance at Ministry headquarters, however, they were calling Harry 'The Chosen One'. But J.K. Rowling's indictment of those reading and believing what the Prophet prints is even more scathing. Perhaps the most disturbing example of this is when Molly Weasley acts coolly toward Hermione based on the gossip Rita Skeeter wrote. You'd think Molly of all people would know better. But J.K. Rowling makes the point that even good, well-intentioned people can be subverted by things they read in the press . . . or on the Internet.

daisy roots

An ingredient, chopped, used in Shrinking Solution (PA7).

According to Culpeper's Complete Herbal, crushed daisy leaves can reduce swelling (as well as act as a remedy for a lot of other things).

Damocles, Uncle

Uncle of Marcus Belby and the inventor of the Wolfsbane Potion. Marcus's father and his Uncle Damocles have had a bit of a falling out of late (HBP4).

dandelion juice

Beverage Hagrid served when Harry dropped by (OP38).

Dark Arts

Magic that is intentionally evil.

What makes magic 'Dark'? This has been the subject of a lot of discussion among fans. Is Harry using the Dark Arts when he uses the Imperius Curse to control Bogrod and Travers during their break-in of Gringotts? True, he doesn't intend to harm anyone when he does it. But what about when he casts Crucio? What about when Ginny casts her infamous Bat Bogey Hex on people? Certainly she intends to hurt the person she's cursing. Is she using Dark magic? This is a very difficult distinction to make, but one which is of key importance for witches and wizards in training. This is why Defence Against the Dark Arts is such an important class for students at Hogwarts — and why Voldemort cursed the position, attempting to subvert that training.

Dark Arts Outsmarted, The

A book found in the Room of Requirement when it was being used for the D.A. to practice (OP18).

Dark Creatures

Magical creatures which harm or kill, but not as part of their natural life cycle (as a predator, for example, which kills to eat) but as a form of evil intention. For example, a hinkypunk lures travellers into bogs not to eat them but simply to cause mischief (PA9).

Dark creatures are not simply animals with magical abilities. Fantastic Beasts refers to many of them as 'demons,' not in a religious sense, but because it describes a key aspect of them all: they exist to actively do harm and damage. Dark creatures aren't simply predators, although some do feed on fear and other negative emotions. They attack for the sake of hurting someone, not simply to eat. One way of thinking about it is to say that they are a physical embodiment of an evil, harmful intent, a physical embodiment of Dark Magic. For this reason,

Dark Creatures are studied in Defence Against the Dark Arts classes, not Care of Magical Creatures.

Dark Detectors

Magical devices, such as Sneakoscopes and Foe Glasses, which warn of the presence of enemies or of Dark Magic (GF20). While useful, Harry is quick to point out that they can be fooled (OP18).

Dark Force Defence League

An organisation which fights against the Dark Arts (CS6, GF31).

Dark Forces: A Guide to Self-Protection, The

By Quentin Trimble

First year textbook for Defence Against the Dark Arts classes at Hogwarts (PS5).

Dark Items

Magical items which are filled with Dark Magic. These include cursed items like the opal necklace (HBP12) and objects used for Dark rituals, such as Voldemort's Horcruxes (esp. HBP23). Dark Items can affect the people around them in negative ways (e.g. DH15).

Dark Lord, The

A title used for Voldemort by his followers (esp. OP26).

Dark Mark *(spell)*

See MORSMORDRE.

Dark Mark

A symbol used by Voldemort and his Death Eaters. As a spell, it creates a huge glowing green skull and snake which they cast over a house where they'd murdered (GF9, HBP27). Voldemort branded a Dark Mark on his inner circle of Death Eaters (esp. GF33, DH23, 28, 30).

Dark Side, The

A name for Voldemort's supporters.

The term 'Dark Side' is used in books one through four, but never in books five, six and seven. Once Voldemort returned and the battle became centred on the Order of the Phoenix and the Death Eaters, the terminology became more personal.

Dark Wizard Catchers

Another name for Aurors (GF11).

Davies, Roger

(b. circa 1978; Ravenclaw, c.1989; Quidditch Chaser and Captain c.1993-1996)

A popular, athletic Ravenclaw student a year or two older than Harry (GF22, 23, OP25, 30).

Davis, Tracey

(b. circa 1980; Slytherin, 1991)

Hogwarts student in the same year as Harry (HPM).

Tracey Davis' name appears in the draft of the class list of Harry's year that J.K. Rowling displayed during the 'Harry Potter and Me' TV interview (HPM). The chart appears to indicate that Tracey is a Half-blood witch (HPM). She has never appeared in canon.

Dawlish, John

Auror, very capable and self-assured. He left Hogwarts with Outstandings in all his N.E.W.T.s. Dawlish is described as a tough-looking wizard with very short, gray, wiry hair (OP27, 31, 36, HBP8, 17, DH1, 15, 29).

The name 'Dawlish' comes from the name of a seacoast town in Devon. It is located near Exeter, where J.K. Rowling attended university. His first name was given to him by J.K. Rowling in a conversation with fans at the book release readings for book seven. Dawlish is named after John Noe of The Leaky Cauldron website.

Deadmarsh

The hag Annis Black lived in a cave in Deadmarsh (DP1).

Dearborn, Caradoc

Member of the Order of the Phoenix in the 1970s (OP9).

Death (character)

In the children's story 'The Tale of the Three Brothers', the character of Death accosted three brothers who tricked him into giving them amazingly power magical items: an invincible wand, a stone which could raise the dead, and a cloak of invisibility (DH21).

d'Eath, Lorcan

(b. 1964)

A popular singer who is part vampire (JKR).

Death Chamber

A strange chamber deep in the Department of Mysteries where an ancient archway stands on a dais. The archway holds a curtain or veil which moves as if touched by a gentle breeze. Some people can hear voices coming from the archway, although there is apparently nothing behind it. The voices are those of the dead, and the chamber and archway are used to study death (OP34, 35).

Deathday Party

Party held in the dungeons on 31 October 1992 to celebrate Nearly Headless Nick's 500th Death Day. Harry, Ron, and Hermione attended but didn't stay long (CS8).

Death Eaters

Voldemort's followers. The original group consisted of Hogwarts students (HBP17). After leaving school, Voldemort gave his followers the name Death Eaters (HBP20) and branded a Dark Mark on their left forearm (GF23, etc.). After Voldemort disappeared, many of the Death Eaters were imprisoned (GF30). Others claimed to have been Imperiused (GF27). (*See also* GF33, OP25, DH1, 30, 31, 36).

Deathly Hallows, The

Three legendary magical items of great power: the Elder Wand, the Resurrection Stone, and the Cloak of Invisibility. Their origin is told in 'The Tale of the Three Brothers' from *The Tales of Beedle the Bard* (DH21). Harry found his destiny wrapped up in the incredible tale of these legendary objects, in ways he could never have imagined (esp. DH 18).

Death Omens: What To Do When You Know The Worst Is Coming

A book for sale in the Divination section of Flourish and Blotts (PA4).

Deathstick

Legends tell of a powerful wand called the Deathstick, which some believe to be the same as the Elder Wand, one of the Deathly Hallows (DH21).

Decoy Detonators

Small horn-like devices on short legs which, when dropped, run off some distance away and then emit an explosive sound and black smoke (HBP6, DH13)
Reminds me of an old greenish-gold AMC Gremlin I owned back in the 1970s . . .

Decree for the Restriction of Underage Wizardry

Law which states that, because of a lack of full training and sometimes a lack of common sense (HBP19), underage wizards are not allowed to use magic out of school (CS5, PA3, etc). The Decree making this a law, passed in 1875 (OP8), is designed to protect the students and their families and also to avoid breaches of the most important wizarding law, the Statute of Secrecy. There are exceptions to this law in a case where the young witch or wizard is in a life-threatening situation (OP7). The Ministry keeps track of any underage magic by placing a Trace on each student (DH4).

Defence Against the Dark Arts

This class, one of the most important at Hogwarts, teaches students to identify and deal with Dark magic. Students learn about Dark spells and creatures and to use offensive and defensive spells. Since the mid-1950s, Hogwarts has had a new Defence Against the Dark Arts teacher every year (HBP20). As a result, the curriculum and quality of instruction varied widely from year to year, although the basic subject matter was prescribed by the Ministry (GF14).

Defence Against the Dark Arts classroom

A classroom located on the first floor. The Defence Against the Dark Arts classroom has windows looking out onto the grounds and an iron chandelier (CS6).

Defence Against the Dark Arts professor's office

Office and quarters of the Defence Against the Dark Arts teacher. Since each year there is a new teacher in that post, the office has undergone a makeover every September (CS6, PA8, GF20, OP13).

While the classroom is on the first floor, the Defence Against the Dark Arts professor's office is on the second (CS6). This

was nicely portrayed in the second film by having Lockhart enter the classroom by means of a staircase from his office.

defensive charge

An unnamed and apparently involuntary magical effect which produces something like an electrical charge to protect a wizard (OP1).

Defensive Charm

Type of magic which is used for self defence (FW). Training for the Magical Law Enforcement Squad includes learning the latest Defensive Charms (DP2).

Defensive Magical Theory
By Wilbert Slinkhard

The textbook Umbridge assigned to her Defence Against the Dark Arts students which more than anything taught how to avoid using magic. In other words, it was totally worthless, especially when the Wizarding world was facing the re-emergence of Voldemort. Fudge, however, was worried that Dumbledore might use the Defence Against the Darks Arts classes to train students as a personal army (OP15).

Deflagration Deluxe

One of the range of fireworks packages available from Weasley's Wizard Wheezes. It cost twenty Galleons (OP28).

Deflating Draught

An antidote to Swelling Solution (CS11).

Defodio

(deh-FO-dee-oh)

'gouging spell'

A spell which digs through dirt or rock (DH26).

'defodio' = L. 'dig down, hollow out'

de-gnoming

Getting rid of the gnomes from a garden. This involves grasping the gnomes by the ankles, swinging them around a few times to disorient them, and then tossing them out of the garden. Gnomes are rather dim, so when they realise a de-gnoming is going on, they all come rushing up out of their holes to see what's going on, making them a lot easier to catch (CS3).

Delacour, Apolline

Married to Monsieur Delacour and mother of Fleur and Gabrielle Delacour (GF31, DH8). Madame Delacour, who is at least part Veela, is described as being a beautiful blonde woman and accomplished at household spells (DH6).

'Apolline' = derived from the male name Apollo who in Greek mythology was, among other things, the god of beauty.

Delacour, Fleur

(b. circa 1977; Beauxbatons, 1988)

Talented, self-assured girl and Triwizard champion from Beauxbatons. She is part Veela, stunningly beautiful with long blond hair (GF16). After leaving school, Fleur took a job at Gringotts in London to improve her English (OP4). (*See also* HBP29, DH8). *'Fleur Delacour' means 'flower of the court' in French, according to J.K. Rowling (AOL).*

Delacour, Gabrielle

(b. 1986)

Fleur's younger sister (GF26). According to Fleur, Gabrielle talks about Harry all the time (HBP5, c.f. DH6, 8).

Delacour, Monsieur

Married to Apolline Delacour and father of Fleur and Gabrielle Delacour. Attended the Third Task of the Triwizard Tournament (GF31). Monsieur Delacour is described as short, plump, and as having a little, pointed black beard (DH6).

Delaney-Podmore, Sir Patrick

A bearded ghost who is the leader of the Headless Hunt. Nick bitterly refers to him as 'Sir Properly Decapitated-Podmore' (CS8, DH31).

Deletrius

(deh-LEE-tree-us)

Erases the ghost images of spells revealed by *Priori Incantato*. Possibly can be used to remove other spell effects as well (GF9).

'deleterius' = L. 'destroy, eradicate'

Deluminator

Small magical object that looks like a cigarette lighter. When clicked, the Deluminator pulls into itself all light from a place. When reversed with another click, balls of light fly back out of the Deluminator, restoring the light or lights that were extinguished (PS1, OP3). According to Rufus Scrimgeour, the Deluminator was designed by Albus Dumbledore and is both valuable and rare (DH7). It has a hidden ability to transport a person to the location of someone who says their name (DH19).

In the earlier editions of the books, this device was called a Put-Outer. The new name, which fits the style of names in the books much better, was first used when book seven was released. Many fans have noted the similarities between the Deluminator and the multi-function tool called the Sonic Screwdriver shown on the television programme Doctor Who.

Dementors

Horrible, spectral creatures, hooded and robed, which feed on human emotions. Dementors drain 'peace, hope, and happiness out of the air around them,' according to Lupin (PA10). Even before a Dementor is seen, its presence is obvious; they are surrounded by an unnatural darkness and terrible icy cold (PA5). Dementors affect even Muggles, although the Muggles can't see the foul, black creatures. They were the guards at Azkaban and made that place horrible indeed. The Ministry used Dementors as guards in its courtrooms as well (GF30, DH13). When they breed, they create chill mist which permeates everything (HBP1).

J.K. Rowling created Dementors as a personification of depression. She described it this way:

> *'It was entirely conscious. And entirely from my own experience. Depression is the most unpleasant thing I have ever experienced . . . It is that absence of being able to envisage that you will ever be cheerful again. The absence of hope. That very deadened feeling, which is so very different from feeling sad. Sad hurts but it's a healthy feeling. It's a necessary thing to feel. Depression is very different.' Treneman, Ann. 'J.K. Rowling, the interview', The Times (UK), 30 June 2000.*

Dementor's Kiss

A Dementor's 'last and worst weapon' (PA12). The Dementor puts back its hood and places its jaws on the mouth of the victim and removes his soul, leaving him an empty shell, alive but completely, irretrievably 'gone' (PA12, 20).

Demiguise

A peaceful, herbivorous primate that can make itself invisible. Its hair can be woven into Invisibility Cloaks (DH21). *'demi' = Fr. 'half' + '-guise' = from Eng. 'disguise', to hide or conceal identity*

Demiguise (Rune)

A rune for the number zero, according to the book *Ancient Runes Made Easy*. A reference to the fact that a Demiguise can make itself invisible (JKR).

Demiguise Derby

An event organised by the underhanded goblin Urg the Unreliable (FW).

Dennis

A Muggle boy living in Little Whinging, part of Dudley's gang (PS3).

Densaugeo

(den-sah-OO-gi-oh)

Causes the victim's teeth to enlarge grotesquely (GF18).

'dens' = L. 'tooth' + 'augeo' = L. 'grow'

Deprimo

(de-PREE-mo)

A spell which pushes something down forcefully (DH21).

'deprimo' = Spanish 'depress or push down'

Derek

(b. 1982; Hogwarts student, 1993)

Hogwarts student a couple of years younger than Harry who, like Harry, was stuck at Hogwarts over the holidays in 1993 (PA11).

Derrick

(b. 1977; Slytherin, 1988; Quidditch Beater c. 1993-1995)

A Beater on the Slythyerin Quidditch team (PA15, OP19).

Dervish and Banges

A magical equipment shop on the High Street in Hogsmeade (PA5, GF27).

'Dervish' = a Sufi Muslim ascetic; one group of dervishes are famous for a whirling ritual dance which they perform, which may be the connection here, since a magical equipment shop is likely to contain items that spin or otherwise move around by magic.

'Bang' is obvious for a shop specialising in magical odds and ends; consider, for example, that at the Burrow, 'small explosions from Fred and George's bedroom were considered perfectly normal' (CS4).

Derwent, Dilys

(1722–1741; St. Mungo's Healer; Head-mistress of Hogwarts 1741–1768)
Previous Hogwarts Headmistress; she has long silver ringlets. Copies of her portrait hang not only in the Head's office but also in the main admitting area for St. Mungo's (OP22).

Descendo

(deh-SEN-doe)
Causes something to descend or lower itself (DH6, 31).
'descendo' = L. 'descend, come down'

Despard, Dragomir

A pseudonym used by Ron on one of their adventures (DH26).

Detachable Cribbing Cuffs

Banned items during O.W.L. exams, not surprisingly (OP31).

detentions

Punishments given at Hogwarts for rule-breaking. Teachers are given the freedom to choose the type of punishment. Some teachers assign writing lines or doing unpleasant tasks like cleaning without using magic (e.g., CS7). Some teachers overstepped their powers, however (GF13, OP12 ff, DH29).

Deverill, Barnabas

One-time possessor of the Elder Wand (DH21).

Deverill, Philbert

Manager of Puddlemere United (DP1, 2).

Devil's Snare

A dangerous plant which uses its creepers and tendrils to ensnare anyone who touches it, binding their arms and legs and eventually choking them. Devil's Snare prefers a dark, damp environment and shrinks away from fire, so a well-placed flame spell such as 'bluebell flames' will drive it away from its victims (PS16, OP22, 25). Devil's Snare is mentioned in the Rumours advertisement for the Toots, Shoots 'n' Roots radio program (JKR).

Devon

A county located in England's West Country. Nicolas and Perenelle Flamel made their home there (PS13). Chudley, home of the Cannons, and the Burrow are located in Devon. Ilfracombe, the site of the famous Ilfracombe Incident of 1932, is found along the northern coast of Devon (FW).
The books place Ottery St. Catchpole, and therefore the Burrow, on the south coast of the West Country. Looking at a

map of that area, we are given some clues which help us to narrow down the location specifically to Devon. The town of Ottery St. Mary is quite near the coast in Devon. The 'Ottery' part of the name comes from the fact that the town is on the River Otter. Even if Ottery St. Catchpole is not the same town as Ottery St. Mary, it must also be located along the River Otter to have that name. Another suggestive fact is that the town of Chudleigh is located near Ottery St. Mary, and of course the Chudley Cannons are Ron's favourite Quidditch team. To top it all off, there is actually a farm called The Burrow Hill Farm just a mile or so south of Ottery St. Mary.

Diadem of Ravenclaw

A magical Diadem worn by Rowena Ravenclaw which according to legend was able to give wisdom to its wearer. The Diadem was a thin tiara engraved with the words 'Wit beyond measure is man's greatest treasure'. The Diadem was lost for many centuries and some doubted that it even existed (DH29, 31).

Diagon Alley

A long, cobbled Wizarding high street in London lined with a strange and exciting assortment of shops and restaurants. Diagon Alley is accessed through the Leaky Cauldron pub on Charing Cross

Road. Shops there include Flourish and Blotts bookstore, Madam Malkin's Robes for All Occasions, Quality Quidditch Supplies, Eeylops Owl Emporium, Ollivander's Wand shop, and Gringotts Wizarding Bank. Witches and wizards travel to Diagon Alley from all over Britain to spend the day shopping (PS5, CS4, PA4, HBP6, etc.). Near Gringotts is a side street called Knockturn Alley where are to be found shops dealing with the Dark Arts (CS4).

Diary of Tom Riddle

A simple diary, purchased by Tom Riddle in a Muggle shop on Vauxhall Road in London. The diary turned up many years later and was discovered to have many unusual magical powers (esp. CS13, 17).

Didsbury

Didsbury is a suburb of Manchester, in northwest England. It was the home of warlock D.J. Prod, a satisfied Kwikspell customer quoted on their advertisements (CS8).

Diffindo

(dih-FIN-doe)

'Severing Charm'

A useful spell which cuts something open or apart (GF20, 23 35, DH9).

'diffindo' = L. 'cleave, open'

Diggle, Dedalus

A member of the Order of the Phoenix both in the 1970s and again in the 1990s (OP3, 9); he was in the Leaky Cauldron when Hagrid brought Harry in on July 31, 1991 (PS5). Diggle once bowed to Harry in a shop (PS5), much to Petunia Dursley's horror. He lives in Kent and, according to Minerva McGonagall, has never had any sense (PS1). Diggle once served as an escort for the Dursleys, who didn't trust him very much, not surprisingly (DH11).

Diggory, Amos

Ministry Official working for the Department for the Regulation and Control of Magical Creatures. Amos took a great deal of pride in his son, Cedric. Amos was a genial man who was on friendly terms with the Weasleys. The Diggorys live near Ottery St. Catchpole (GF6, 37).

Diggory, Cedric

(1977–1995; Hufflepuff, 1989; Prefect 1992; Quidditch Captain and Seeker, 1993–5)

A handsome boy with grey eyes. In 1993, when he was a fifth-year, he took over as Captain and Seeker of the Hufflepuff House Quidditch team. He was a very good student and a prefect (PA9). Cedric was selected by the Goblet of Fire to represent Hogwarts in the Triwizard Tournament (GF16). *Cedric's name is possibly a nod to one of the main characters in C. S. Lewis' Narnia tales, Digory Kirke.*

Diggory, Mrs

Cedric Diggory's mother, wife of Amos, a very level-headed witch (GF31, 37).

'dilligrout'

One of the Fat Lady's passwords to get into Gryffindor Tower (HBP14). *Dilligrout is a thin porridge with plums in it.*

Dillonsby, Ivor

Wizard interviewed by Rita Skeeter for her book *The Life and Lies of Albus Dumbledore*. Claimed he 'had already discovered eight uses of dragon's blood when Dumbledore 'borrowed' his papers' (DH2). Ivor is of the opinion that Bathilda Bagshot is senile (DH18).

Dimitrov

Bulgarian National Team Chaser (GF8).

Dingle, Harold

(Hogwarts student, 1990s)

Tried to sell what he claimed was powdered dragon claw to other students as a study aid (OP31).

Dippet, Armando

Former headmaster of Hogwarts (until the mid-1950s), Dippet was nearly bald and somewhat feeble (CS13). His portrait hangs in Dumbledore's office (OP37, FW).

Dirigible Plums

A fruit growing near the Lovegood house. The plum looks like an orange radish and supposedly helps a person wearing one to accept the unusual (DH20), which is undoubtedly why Luna wears them as earrings (OP13).

Disapparate

(dis-AP-a-rate)

Apparition, from the point of view of the place a wizard is leaving.

'dis-' = L. 'apart, opposite of' + 'appareo' = L. 'to appear'

Disarming Charm

See EXPELLIARMUS.

Disillusionment Charm

A charm which hides the true, magical nature of something. The spell can be used to make a witch or wizard nearly invisible (OP3, HBP3, DH4, 22, 24, JKR).

An 'illusion' is a false image, often with the suggestion of being fantastic or even magical. The word comes from 'illu-

sionem' = L. 'irony, jest', which itself comes from 'illudere' = L. 'to play with'; (Ludo Bagman's first name comes from the same source word.) The prefix 'dis' suggests the removal of a fantasy image, in this case meaning that the magical appearance of a creature will be concealed by the spell. Interestingly, the definition in Wikipedia seems to be particularly appropriate for the effects of this spell on Muggles:

> *'A feeling that arises from the discovery that something is not what it was anticipated to be, commonly held to be stronger than disappointment especially when a belief central to one's identity is shown to be false; The act of freeing from an illusion, or the state of being freed therefrom.'*

Dissendium

(dis-EN-dee-um)

Opens the secret door in the statue of the hump-backed witch. Harry learnt this word from the Marauder's Map. It is said aloud while the statue is tapped with the caster's wand (PA10).

'dissocio' = L. 'to part or separate'

dittany

One of the plants found in *One Thousand Magical Herbs and Fungi* (PS14). Essence of Dittany is used to heal wounds (e.g. HBP24, JKR, DH14, 17, 27).

Two varieties of dittany are used by herbalists, both having reputed medicinal properties. White dittany, found in southern Europe, Asia, and Africa, gives off an anti-inflammatory oil.

Divination

A branch of magic which attempts to foresee future events. There are several types of Divination. A common form is what is known as 'fortunetelling': predicting events based on things like crystal balls and tea leaves. The second kind of Divination is that which is practiced by the centaurs. They analyse the stars and other portents to determine large scale and long term events (OP27). Many in the Wizarding world consider this type of magic to be imprecise at best (PA6).

Divination (class)

Elective classes taught at Hogwarts starting in third year (CS14), taught by Professor Trelawney and, for a few years, the centaur Firenze. Trelawney's classes consist of learning to read palms, peering into crystal balls, and looking for meaning in dreams and tea leaves (PA6). They spend quite a bit of time on Astrology as well (GF29). Firenze's classes burn mallowsweet and observe the movement of stars and planets as indicators of large scale events on Earth (OP27).

Divination classrooms

Two classrooms were used for Divination classes. Trelawney taught in a round classroom atop the North Tower, overheated by a perfumed fire and filled with stuffed furniture and little tables. Shelves line the walls holding teacups and crystal balls, among other things (PA6). Firenze taught in classroom eleven, on the ground floor, which had been transformed by magic into a forest clearing (OP27).

Dobbs, Emma
(b. 1983)
A new Hogwarts student Harry watched being Sorted (GF12).

Dobby
'A Free Elf'
(b. June 28, year unknown; d. March 1998)
House-elf indentured to the Malfoy family who aspired to change his lot in life. (CS2). After escaping servitude under the Malfoys (CS18), Dobby began working at Hogwarts (GF21). He took every opportunity to help Harry (esp. GF26, OP18). Dobby was fond of socks and used his earnings as a free elf to buy yarn and knit them for himself (GF23). (*See also* DH23, 24).
A 'dobby' is a brownie — a house elf — from Yorkshire and Lancashire folk-

lore. Dobbies were described as thin and shaggy and were very helpful little spirits.

Dr Filibuster's Fabulous Wet-Start, No-Heat Fireworks

Magical fireworks which can be purchased in Gambol and Japes Wizarding Joke Shop (CS4). Fred and George Weasley were particularly fond of these; it is likely that they provided the inspiration for their own range of fireworks, called Weasleys' Wild-Fire Whiz-Bangs (OP28).

Dodderidge, Daisy

(1467–1555)

Builder and first landlady of the Leaky Cauldron. For more information, see the Famous Wizard cards (FW).

Doge, Elphias

(b. circa 1881; Order of the Phoenix)

Elderly wizard with a wheezy voice and silver hair (DH8), a Special Advisor to the Wizengamot and lifelong friend of Albus Dumbledore (DH2). Doge was part of the original Order of the Phoenix and volunteered again in the 1990s. He was part of the Advance Guard in 1995 (OP3). Rita Skeeter called him 'Dodgy' (DH2) and 'Dog-breath' (DH18).

Dolohov, Antonin

(d. 1998?)

One of Tom Riddle's friends after leaving school, an original Death Eater (HBP20, DH9, 36). Dolohov's 'specialty attack' was a jet of purple light cast in a zigzag pattern which causes severe internal injury (OP31).

Donkey, The

Contrary to Trelawney's interpretation, Seamus said he thought Harry's tea leaf looked more like a donkey than a Grim (PA6)

In tasseography, fortune-telling by reading tea leaves, the 'donkey' signifies stubbornness, which is a sly joke in this context. Seamus is, after all, being a bit obstinate when he contradicts Trelawney.

door-opening spell

Sends a jet of sparks out of the wand, opening the target door (PA7).

Dorkins, Mary

Muggle news reporter who filed a report on a waterskiing budgie (OP1).

Dorkins, Ragmar

Manager of the hapless Chudley Cannons (DP1, 2, 3, 4).

Dorset

Dorset is a county in the West Country, located on the southern coast of England, which includes Wimbourne, home of the Wasps Quidditch team. It is where Newt Scamander, author of *Fantastic Beasts and Where to Find Them*, lives with his wife Porpentina and their pet Kneazles (FB).

Dot

Resident of Little Hangleton, who remembered Frank Bryce as a child and wasn't afraid to voice her opinions about him in the pub (GF1).

double-ended newt

When Hermione goes in to buy Crookshanks at the Magical Menagerie, a wizard is at the counter being advised on double-ended newts (PA4).

Doxy

A small fairy-like creature covered with black hair. Doxies have a poisonous bite. They are pests which can infest houses, taking up residence in the draperies. Removing them requires a good supply of Doxycide. It's a good idea to have an antidote for Doxy venom on hand as well (OP6). Their eggs and droppings may be used as potion ingredients and other magical inventions (e.g. OP6) Doxie

eggs are a favourite food of bowtruckles (DH28).

Doxycide

Black liquid, usually delivered by spray bottle, used to knock out Doxies so that they can be safely disposed of. The effects last quite a long time (OP6).

'Draco Dormiens Nunquam Titillandus'

The Hogwarts school motto, which appears on the crest; it means 'Never tickle a sleeping dragon.'

J.K. Rowling wanted the motto for Hogwarts to be practical advice, not some high-sounding platitude like, as she suggests, "reach for the stars' or 'persevere and endure" (CR). Not surprisingly, this 'practical advice' is also an example of her tongue-in-cheek humour.

dragon

Dragons are great winged, fire-breathing lizards, among the most amazing magical creatures in the world. Muggles remember them only as beasts from mythology, which is a credit to the ongoing efforts of the Ministries of Magic in many countries who work tirelessly to keep these huge beasts hidden. Wizards who work with them are called dragon keepers

(GF19). Gringotts uses dragons to guard the high security vaults (PS5, DH26). For more information about the various breeds of dragons, see the book *Fantastic Beasts and Where to Find Them.*

Dragon Breeding for Pleasure and Profit

Hogwarts library book consulted by Hagrid, who always wanted a dragon (PS14). Pages of this book include 'Essential Equipment,' 'Recognising Dragon Eggs,' a map showing 'Dragons of the World,' and 'A-Z Of Ailments' (JKR).

dragon dealer

A profession which must be somewhat shady, since dealing in dragons is against the law (PS14, 16).

dragon dung / dragon manure

Dragon dung is sold by the barrel in Knockturn Alley (CS4) to be used as compost in Herbology. Dragon dung is also great for sending anonymously to Percy Weasley at the Ministry of Magic just to annoy him (GF5). Dragon manure is used as fertilizer in Herbology classes (OP25).

dragon eggs

Highly prized as potion ingredients (particularly Chinese Fireball egg-shells). However, trading in dragon's eggs is illegal so they're a bit tricky to obtain (PS16).

dragon feeder

A position which one might guess is hard to fill. Perhaps that's why Gringotts bank needed to advertise for dragon feeders in the *Daily Prophet* (DP2).

We don't actually meet one of the Gringotts dragons until DH26, but Hagrid mentions to Harry already in the first book that Gringotts uses dragons to guard the high security vaults (PS5).

dragon heartstring

This part of a dragon is used as a wand core (PS5).

Before the age of modern medicine, common belief was that the heart was held in place in the chest by 'heartstrings', which were thought to be nerves or tendons. Apparently dragons (also something which people believed in before the modern era of science) have this anatomical feature.

dragon hide gloves

These gloves are recommended for use by wizards because they offer protection from magical and non-magical dangers (PS5, GF13, 18, OP19, HBP14, 18).

dragon keeper

A rather dangerous job, but one which appeals to people like Charlie Weasley, who works as a dragon keeper at a reservation in Romania (PS8, GF19).

dragon milk cheese

This interesting product is advertised as being included in the book *Charm Your Own Cheese* (JKR).

The concept of dragons giving milk is extremely odd, given that dragons aren't mammals. The term 'dragon's milk', however, is actually a 17th-century term used to describe the strong beer usually reserved for royalty. J.K. Rowling is probably making an allusion to beer, not commenting on the nursing proclivities of dragons.

Dragon Pox

A disease which afflicts witches and wizards. The symptoms of this disease are quite bizarre, including a green and purple rash between the toes and sneezing sparks (DP3). Elphias Doge gives an account of his own bout with dragon pox as a boy, saying that the disease is highly contagious in its early stages, and that even after it has run its course, his skin remained green and pocked for some time (DH2). The famous Gunhilda of Gorsemoor developed a cure for Dragon Pox around 1600 (FW).

Dragon pox is treated on the second floor of St. Mungo's (OP22).

There is a minor continuity error in the dates associated with Dragon Pox. According to the Famous Wizard cards, the first known victim of Dragon Pox was Chauncery Oldridge in the 1300s (FW). However, in Quidditch Through the Ages, *a letter written in the 1100s by a wizard named Goodwin Kneen mentions that his wife, Gunhilda, missed a Quidditch match because she had contracted Dragon Pox (QA3).*

dragon reservations

To protect their native dragons, as well as to keep them out of sight of Muggles, many countries have established reservations for the creatures to live in. These are frequently located in high mountain areas. Charlie Weasley works at a dragon reservation in Romania (e.g. PS6, GF19).

dragon's blood

A very magical substance. Albus Dumbledore discovered that there are twelve uses for dragon's blood (PS6, DH2), one of which is oven cleaner (SFC).

Dragon's Fire

A magical effect which Arthur Weasley added to the flying motorcycle, rather like a jet engine, to push the bike to great speed in a hurry (DH4).

Dragon Species of Great Britain and Ireland
Hogwarts library book consulted by Hagrid, who always wanted a dragon (PS14).

Drakul, Count Vlad
(b. 1390)
Notorious vampire who inspired the fictional Count Dracula created by Bram Stoker. For more information, see the Famous Wizard cards (FW).

Draught of Living Death
ingredients: asphodel in an infusion of wormwood, valerian roots, sopophorous bean
A very powerful sleeping potion (PS8, HBP9, FW).

Draught of Peace
ingredients: includes powdered moonstone and syrup of hellebore
A tricky O.W.L.-standard potion taught to fifth-year students. It calms anxiety and soothes agitation (OP12).
J.K. Rowling intentionally creates humour by contrasting the intended effect of this potion—peace—with the ingredient hellebore, which sounds rather

evil (and is very poisonous as a matter of fact), and also with the difficulty the students have making it. The potion is so tricky to make that it probably generates more anxiety in the preparation than it cures.

Dreadful Denizens of the Deep
One of the books that Harry, Ron, and Hermione examined while preparing for the Second Task of the Triwizard Tournament (GF26).

dream interpretation
Divination method taught by Professor Trelawney at Hogwarts; uses the text book *The Dream Oracle*, by Inigo Imago (OP12, 13).
Dreams were considered by ancient people to be a form of supernatural or divine communication. Certain people were thought to have a gift of interpreting dreams. Today, some modern psychologists still look at a person's dreams as a way of understanding their subconscious mind. Harry might have done himself a favour by paying a little more attention in this part of Divination classes; his dreams quite frequently have hidden meanings.

Dream Oracle, The
by Inigo Imago
Trelawney set out copies of this book

in Divination class during Harry's fifth year; the book appears to have been used only in class. It covers dream interpretation (OP12, 15, 17).

dress robes

Dress robes are worn by wizards for formal occasions (DH8). Students fourth-year and above were required to bring dress robes to Hogwarts for the Yule Ball (GF10, 23).

Droobles Best Blowing Gum

This wizarding sweet will fill the room with bubbles that don't pop for days (PS6, PA5, 10, GF23, OP23).

The name was changed with revisions to the text in 2004 to remove the apostrophe. Earlier editions refer to this as Drooble's Best Blowing Gum.

Drought Charm

Spell to dry up water (GF26).

Dudley, Vernon

Name Harry used as an alias in a pinch to hide his identity from Death Eaters (DH23).

Duelling Club

Extracurricular activity at Hogwarts where students learn the sport of Wizard duelling Dumbledore allowed Lockhart to start a Duelling Club at Hogwarts

during the 1992–1993 school year (CS11).

Duel, Wizard's

Duelling exists as a sport in the same way that fencing is a sport in the Muggle world (PS9, CS11). While it is a friendly sporting competition, it is essentially a form of combat. Wizard duelling as a sport has rules and competitions, but in battle, the same skills come into play in life or death struggles (OP18, ff).

Duelling as a method of settling disputes between people has been common practice all through history, although now it is banned almost everywhere. Duels were always a matter of honour and only fought between men of the upper classes. By the 18th century, a code of rules was created called the code duello, *which laid out the exact procedures for a duel to be fought, including the selection of weapons, the naming of seconds, and so on. The rules for issuing the challenge, for example, are reminiscent of the rules Lockhart taught during the Duelling Club. In an actual battle, however, these niceties aren't particularly helpful; when Voldemort insisted on the formalities in an encounter with Harry, the boy instead used the moment to duck for cover (GF34).*

Duke, Kirley

(b. 1971)

A member of the band The Weird Sisters (FW).

Dukelow, Matilda

A fan of the Holyhead Harpies who wondered what had really happened when Wilda Griffiths, the Puddlemere United Chaser, disappeared during a match (DP4).

Dumbledore, Aberforth

(b. 1883 or 1884; Hogwarts 1895; Order of the Phoenix)

A tall, thin, bad-tempered old man with a lot of long grey hair and a beard (OP16). He was the brother of Albus Dumbledore and the barkeep at the Hog's Head in Hogsmeade (OP16). As a boy, he was very close to his sister and when tragedy struck the family, he blamed Albus (DH2, 18, 28). Aberforth was a member of the original Order of the Phoenix (OP9). He is a morally ambiguous character, hobnobbing with the dodgy clientele and indulging in illegal activities (HBP12), but can be a powerful ally as well (DH31 ff.). He has a strange affinity for goats (GF24, DH2).

Dumbledore, Albus Percival Wulfric Brian

(July or August of 1881–1997; Gryffindor, 1892; Prefect, 1896; Head Boy, 1898; Transfiguration teacher, 1920s–1940s; Headmaster, 1950s–1997; Order of the Phoenix)

Considered by many to be the greatest wizard of the modern age, Dumbledore turned down offers to become Minster for Magic (PS5), preferring to head the Wizengamot and to serve as the Headmaster of Hogwarts, a post he held for almost forty years. In these roles, he spoke with quiet strength and wisdom. As a youth, he fell in love with Gellert Grindewald (OBT/CH) and was for a time taken in by Gellert's dangerous philosophy of wizard superiority and the quest for the legendary Deathly Hallows (DH18). He realised after a time that Grindelwald's path was one of evil and realised his own error in allowing his heart to blind him to reality (DH35). This failure led to tragedy in Dumbledore's family for which he blamed himself for the rest of his life (DH28, 35). Dumbledore devoted the last half of his life to fighting against Voldemort, founding the Order of the Phoenix for that purpose in the 1970s (OP4). Dumbledore had not forgotten the Deathly Hallows, however, and he discovered all three at one time or another (DH33, 35).

'albus' = L. 'white'

Percival after his father

'dumbledore' = 18th C Eng. word for 'bumblebee'

Wulfric = Anglo/Saxon. 'wolf power' or 'wolf ruler.' Also, a 12thC British hermit saint known for his miracles and prophecies

The character of Albus Dumbledore is far more complex than it appears. In the very first chapter of book one, J.K. Rowling introduces us to his eccentricity, gentle humour and belief in giving people second chances. This image of a kindly guardian and guide is maintained throughout the series. However, the character has a darker side, one which doesn't become clear until the seventh book. He was deeply ashamed of some of the things he did — and thought — in his youth. He learned the hard way about the seductiveness of power, and its costs, and spent the rest of his life trying to understand and contain the darker impulses in Wizarding society. Even toward the end of his long life, Dumbledore was so tempted by the potential of the Resurrection Stone that he slipped the ring on his finger and was struck with a deadly curse. Once we realise this darker side of his personality and his past, we can see his actions throughout the series as being as much manipulative as magnanimous.

Dumbledore, Ariana

(1884 or 5–1899)

Younger sister of Albus and Aberforth Dumbledore, daughter of Kendra and Percival Dumbledore. At the age of six, she was attacked by three young Muggles who had seen her performing magic and had panicked; she was so traumatised by the incident that she never recovered, requiring constant care and supervision for the rest of her life. Aberforth was very close to her and years later kept a portrait of her on his mantle (DH2, 28).

Dumbledore, Kendra

(d. summer 1899)

Mother of Albus, Aberforth, and Ariana Dumbledore; wife of Percival. In Rita Skeeter's gossipy book *The Life and Lies of Albus Dumbledore*, she is described as being 'proud and haughty' (DH11, 16).

Dumbledore, Percival

Father of Albus, Aberforth, and Ariana Dumbledore; husband of Kendra. He got the reputation of being a Muggle-hater when he attacked the three Muggle boys who severely traumatised his daughter Ariana c. 1850 (DH2, 28).

Dumbledore's Army

A group of students who banded together to learn Defence Against the Dark Arts during the 1995-6 school year. The students called themselves the D.A., which stood for Dumbledore's Army (OP18). Members of the D.A. fought in the major battles of the Second Wizarding War, suffering some casualties (HBP27, DH4, 31, 36).

Dungbomb

Smelly joke item invented by Alberic Grunnion (FW). When thrown, these magical stink bombs give off a putrid odour, very handy for creating a diversion or just annoying Filch (e.g. PA10, 11, OP30).

dungeons

The lower levels of Hogwarts castle are mostly dungeons. One large dungeon room is used as a potions classroom (PS8). The dungeons connect to the Slytherin common room, which is under the lake (DH23), and to Snape's office and quarters (CS5).

Durmstrang Institute

A magical school located in a castle in the north of Europe. Until recently, the Headmaster was Igor Karkaroff. Durmstrang students wear uniforms consisting of furs and blood-red robes. The Durmstrang castle is not as big as Hogwarts, having only four floors. Its

fires, according to Viktor Krum, 'are only lit for magical purposes' (GF23). Durmstrang has the reputation of teaching Dark Arts, and it does not admit Muggle-born students (GF11). Gellert Grindelwald was a student here once, and he carved 'his' symbol into one of the walls, where it remains today (DH8).

The name Durmstrang comes from the German phrase 'Sturm und Drang' which translates to 'Storm and Stress.' The phrase refers to a movement in German literature in the late 1700s which emphasized the expression of raw, sometimes negative emotions over the rationalism of the Enlightenment. Examples of 'Sturm und Drang' artwork and literature include elements intentionally designed to frighten or disturb their audience.

Durmstrang ship

The students from Durmstrang arrived at Hogwarts aboard a magical sailing ship which rose from the depths of the Hogwarts lake, obviously having travelled from one body of water to another by magic (GF15).

Duro

(DUR-oh)

Turns the target object to stone (DH32).

'duro' = L. 'to harden, solidify'

Dursley, Dudley

(b. June 23, 1980)

Harry Potter's Muggle cousin and the only son of Vernon and Petunia Dursley. Dudley, in contrast to Harry, has been grossly overindulged by both his mother and father (HBP3). Petunia pets him and coddles him and turns a blind eye to his bullying. Vernon, on the other hand, encourages his son's manipulations, greed and violent behaviour (e.g., PS2, OP1). Dudley attends a private school named Smeltings and spends his school holidays terrorising Harry and the younger children of the neighbourhood with his gang (OP1).

The name 'Dursley' comes from a town in Gloucestershire, England. J.K. Rowling chose the name because it sounded 'dull and forbidding.'

Dursley, Aunt Marjorie 'Marge'

Vernon Dursley's loathsome sister. She lives in the country in a house where she raises bulldogs (PA3). Marge looked a lot like her brother Vernon: 'large, beefy, and purple-faced'; she even had a moustache (PA2).

Dursley, Petunia (Evans)

(b. late 1950s)

Lily Potter's older sister and the wife of Vernon Dursley. As children, Petunia and Lily were very close; however, when Lily began to show signs of being a witch, Petunia was horribly jealous and hurt. As an adult, Petunia was a nosey gossip who doted on her son Dudley, kept an obsessively immaculate house, and deferred to her smug, blustering husband. In 1991, she agreed to Dumbledore's request to take Harry in when he was orphaned, knowing it would seal the powerful protective charm. While she overindulged Dudley, she treated Harry very poorly, like an unwanted servant (CS2).

Dursley, Vernon

The husband of Harry's aunt Petunia. He is about as much a Muggle as a person can get. He has no use for imagination at all. He is the director of Grunnings, a firm that makes drills (PS1, 2). Vernon considered magic to be 'dangerous nonsense' (PS3) and Harry something to be ignored, controlled, or locked away (e.g. CS2). Vernon encouraged his son Dudley to be boorish and greedy, just like he was (e.g., PS2).

dwarfs

Short, surly-looking fellows who were hired by Lockhart to play the role of 'card carrying cupids' and deliver Valentines to the students. They were quite aggressive about their well-wishing, at times tackling students and sitting on them to force them to listen to some affectionate message (CS13).

The status of 'dwarf' in the Harry Potter universe is unclear. This is the only place where they are mentioned. The text indicates that they're a separate type of magical being, not simply short wizards.

Dzou Yen

(4th Century B.C.)

Chinese Alchemist (FW).

Some scholars consider China to be the origin of alchemical teaching and traditions, connected with the practice of medicine more than transmuting metals. The 'elixir of life', sometimes called 'drinkable gold' was a compound made from various substances, including arsenic and mercury. Elixirs made from those substances, far from giving immortality, were dangerous poisons. A number of Chinese emperors apparently died from elixirs given them by their alchemists.

eagle

The symbol, in bronze on a blue background, representing Ravenclaw house (GF15).

eagle owl

Draco Malfoy received letters and packages from home from a large eagle owl (PS9).

It's not surprising that the Malfoys used an eagle owl, the largest variety of owl found in Britain.

Eargit the Ugly

(14th century)

Goblin representative at a Wizard's Council; for more information see the Famous Wizard cards (FW).

earmuffs

These have to be worn when working with Mandrakes, as their cry is fatal (CS6).

Normal earmuffs wouldn't work very well for this, since they don't block out all sound. These must be magical earmuffs.

Edgecombe, Madam

Witch who works in the Floo Network Office. Marietta Edgecombe is her daughter (OP27).

Edgecombe, Marietta

(Ravenclaw, c. 1990; Dumbledore's Army)

A friend of Cho Chang's with curly, reddish-blonde hair, Marietta was dragged to D.A. meetings but wasn't really all that keen to be there (OP16, 27). (*See also* BLC).

Edible Dark Marks

A product sold at Weasleys' Wizard Wheezes. According to the promo, 'they'll make anyone sick!' (HBP6).

Educational Decrees

During Umbridge's memorable year at Hogwarts, the Ministry of Magic passed seven Educational Decrees to help her take more and more control over the school. Among other things, these gave the Ministry the power to appoint teachers (OP15), banned student organisations (OP17), prevented teachers from giving students information unrelated to their subjects (OP25), banned *The Quibbler* (OP26), and promoted Umbridge from teacher to High Inquisitor (OP15) and to Headmistress (OP28). *The series of Decrees instituted by the Ministry are an echo of the type of Laws passed in Germany immediately after Hitler was appointed to be Chancellor in 1933 and the Nazi party worked to silence all its rivals. One of the first of these Laws was the 'Law for the Protection of the German People' which restricted demonstrations, freedom of speech, freedom of press, and ordered the confiscation of literature considered to be dangerous to the state.*

Eeylops Owl Emporium
A dimly lit shop in Diagon Alley which, according to the sign, sells 'tawny, screech, barn, brown, and snowy' owls (PS5). The shop sells treats for owls called 'owl nuts' (HBP6).

Egbert the Egregious
One-time possessor of the Elder Wand (DH21).

egg, golden
A heavy magical object in the shape of a dragon's egg used as a prize in the First Task of the Triwizard Tournament (GF20, 25).

Egypt
A country steeped in magical history, where Bill Weasley worked as a curse breaker for Gringotts. The Weasleys visited him there and toured the pyramids, seeing unbelievable curses the old Egyptian wizards had put on tombs (PA1). Egypt is home to the Centre for Alchemical Studies, the world's largest such research institute (JKR).

Ehwaz
An Ancient Rune, meaning 'partnership' (OP31).

Eihwaz
An Ancient Rune that translates to mean 'defence' (OP31).

Elder Wand
The most powerful and deadly of the Deathly Hallows, a wand which can defeat all others. The Elder Wand, by different names, has left its mark on Wizarding history in tales of violence and murder (DH21). *Elder wood is associated with death and resurrection in folklore, in particular because elder can re-grow a damaged limb easily. Witches were thought to live in elder trees in medieval times and it is a traditional wood for making broomsticks and wands. According to folklore, furniture made from elder was bad luck, which is interesting be-*

cause Ron tells Harry and Hermione that a Wizarding superstition states 'Wand of elder, never prosper' (DH21).

Elephant and Castle

One of the many places that Willy Widdershins pranked Muggles with an exploding toilet (OP7).

Elephant and Castle is an area of South London which several hundred years ago was called Newington. That was a rather common place name at that time, so beginning in the 1700s the area was referred to by the more distinctive name of 'Elephant and Castle' after a pub which stood on the spot.

Elfric the Eager

Was responsible for an uprising that first-years learned about, so he was probably a goblin (PS16).

Elixir to Induce Euphoria, An

A bright yellow potion that Harry brewed during a Potions class. It has occasional side effects of 'excessive singing and nose-tweaking', according to Slughorn, though these can be reduced with the addition of a little bit of peppermint (HBP22).

Elixir of Life

Potion made using the Philosopher's Stone. It extends life, though it requires that the drinker consume it regularly to maintain immortality (HBP23). Nicholas Flamel lived over 650 years by drinking it (PS13).

An elixir of life was one of the main goals of alchemy the world over. This powerful potion was thought to give long or eternal life to the person who drank it. The elixir was envisioned by alchemists from many traditions as a liquid form of various long-lasting precious metals, particularly gold, which does not tarnish and therefore represents eternal life. The Philosopher's Stone, a legendary substance which could turn lesser metals into gold, was therefore considered to be an essential part of creating an elixir of life. There is no evidence that alchemists actually found either the Philosopher's Stone or the Elixir of Life, though many spent their entire lives searching for them.

Elkins, Elveira

Witch who wrote to the *Daily Prophet* Problem Page because she was having trouble with her Fixing Charm (DP3).

Ellis Moor

A moor with a Quidditch stadium (DP4).

While there doesn't appear to be any place called Ellis Moor in Britain, there is a Porkellis Moor in Cornwall which may be where J.K. Rowling got the name. In the 1800s, a number of tin mines were in operation in the Porkellis area, but all that remains now are the ruins of the pump buildings.

elm

A wand wood that was used to make Lucius Malfoy's wand (DH1).

In Celtic lore, elm wood is associated with, among other things, the dark side of a person's psyche, which makes it an interesting choice for the wand of a Death Eater.

Elphick, Wilfred

(1112–1199)

Wizard killed by an Erumpent; for more information, see the Famous Wizard cards (FW).

Emeric the Evil

One of many wizards to possess the Elder Wand (DH21). He was discussed in Harry's first-ever History of Magic class (PS8).

Enchanted Encounters

by Fifi LaFolle

A series of Wizarding romance novels (JKR).

Enchantment in Baking

The Weasleys keep a copy of this in their kitchen (CS3).

Encyclopedia of Toadstools

A book stocked by Flourish and Blotts that hit Lucius Malfoy in the eye during an altercation in the store (CS4).

England National Quidditch Team

Ludo Bagman played for The English National Quidditch Team many years ago (GF30, also GF5).

Engorgement Charm

See ENGORGIO.

Engorgio

(en-GOR-gee-oh)

'Engorgement Charm'

A fairly commonplace charm that is used to enlarge objects (GF4).

'engorger' = Fr. 'swallow greedily'

Enid, Great Aunt

A relative of Neville Longbottom, possibly married to Uncle Algie (PS7).

Enlarging Spell

A spell that makes something bigger (OP26).

Ennervate

(EN-er-vayt)

Spell which can be cast on a person who has been Stunned to bring them back to a normal state of consciousness and control (GF9).

The name of this spell was changed with the 2004 corrections of the books to 'Rennervate' which makes the etymology less confusing. 'Ennervate' means to embolden, to give 'nerve' ('courage', as in the phrase 'that takes a lot of nerve'). Some editions of the book had given the spell as 'Enervate' which would mean exactly the opposite: to remove *courage or nerve.*

Entrail-Expelling Curse

Apparently this curse, invented by Urquhart Rackharrow in the 1600s, causes the victim's insides to come out of them. Yes, you read that correctly. Ew. (OP22).

One wonders why a spell like this would even be necessary, but disembowelling was part of 'drawing and quartering', an extreme form of punishment for the crime of treason in that era. Considering that this person's name includes the word 'rack', also a form of medieval torture punishment, this might have been where J.K. Rowling got the idea. Believe it or not, 'drawing and quartering' was only abolished in Britain in 1870.

entrance hall

The oak front doors of Hogwarts lead directly into an absolutely enormous entrance hall (CS15), 'so big you could have fit the whole of the Dursleys' house in it' and with a ceiling that, at night, can't be made out for its height (PS7). All the Hogwarts students can fit in it at once, which they memorably did the night Fred and George left dramatically, flying off into the sunset (OP29).

Entrancing Enchantments

A type of love spell (CS13).

Entwhistle, Kevin

(Ravenclaw, 1991)

Kevin's name appeared in an early draft of the class list of Harry's year. He is Muggle-born. Despite his presence on the list, Kevin has never appeared in canon (HPM).

Episkey

(eh-PIS-key)

A type of healing spell that repairs damage, such as a broken nose (HBP8) or a bleeding mouth (HBP14).

'episkeyazo' = Gr. 'to repair'

Erecto

(e-REK-toh)

A useful spell that Hermione uses to set up a tent (DH14).

'erecto' = L. 'erect, set up'

Errol

An old, decrepit gray owl belonging to the Weasley family. He often collapses unconscious after deliveries, making it easy to confuse him with a feather duster (CS4).

Errol's name is likely related to the words 'error' and 'errant'.

Erumpent

A huge magical beastwith an exploding horn. Apparently the horn of a Crumple-Horned Snorkack is similar to that of the Erumpent, except for the blowing up part (DH20).

The name of this creature comes from the idea of 'erupt', meaning 'to explode suddenly', and 'pent', which means 'confined', giving the idea of something pent up and waiting to explode.

Ethelred the Ever-Ready

Medieval wizard known for having a short temper (FW).

The name comes from Aethelred II, 'the Unready,' a king of England, who far from being too aggressive was noted for trying to buy his way out of trouble.

Eton

Eton College is a famous private boys' boarding school in England. Justin Finch-Fletchley once told Harry that his name was down for Eton before he found out he was a wizard and elected to attend Hogwarts instead (CS6).

Eton is one of the most prestigious schools in Britain. Famous students include eighteen former Prime Ministers and members of the Royal family. If Justin was set to attend, he probably comes from an upper-class, well-connected family.

Europa

One of Jupiter's moons, studied in Astronomy class (OP14).

Evanesco

(ev-an-ES-ko)

'Vanishing Spell'

A spell which makes something go away completely 'into non-being' (DH30). It seems to be a handy everyday spell for many wizards, though it isn't taught until the fifth year (OP13).

'evanesco' = L. 'to disappear'

Evans family

A family living in the same town as the Snape family of Spinner's End in the 1960s. Mr and Mrs Evans had two daughters, Petunia and Lily. They were proud to discover that Lily was a witch (PS4) and enjoyed finding out about the Wizarding world (DH33).

See POTTER, LILY *and* DURSLEY, PETUNIA.

Evans, Mark

A Muggle boy living near Privet Drive, who, at age ten, was beaten up by a fifteen-year-old Dudley (OP1). Despite his last name, he is unrelated to Lily's family (JKR).

Evening Prophet

The late edition of the *Daily Prophet* (CS5).

The evening edition of the Prophet *reported a Muggle in Peebles seeing a flying car within an hour or two of it occurring, and Snape had a copy shortly thereafter. This suggests that the paper was magically delivered, since even a fast owl couldn't travel from London, where the* Prophet's *offices are located, to Scotland in less than an hour. Perhaps the evening edition is not a separate newspaper but simply the standard morning edition with the text magically updated through the day to show breaking news.*

Everard

A celebrated former headmaster of Hogwarts. His portraits now hang in the headmaster's office and the Ministry of Magic (OP22).

Ever-Bashing Boomerangs

Became the four hundred thirty-seventh item to be banned at Hogwarts, at the start of Harry's fourth year (GF12).

Everlasting Elixirs

Studied in sixth-year Potions; information on these can be found in *Advanced Potion-Making* (HBP15).

Everlasting Icicles

A Christmas decoration often hung from trees and banisters at Hogwarts (PS12, GF22).

Everlasting Ink

Over the years, a number of visitors to Godric's Hollow have used this ink to sign messages on the sign commemorating the fall of Voldemort in 1981 (DH17).

Exmoor

Large area of moorland in northern Devon, most of which is a national park, where a professional Quidditch stadium is located (DP2). Also the site of a 'Singing Sorceress' concert by Celestina Warbeck (JKR).

Expecto Patronum

(ex-PEK-toh pa-TROH-num)
'Patronus Charm'

Spell that conjures a Patronus, a silvery phantom which in its strongest ('corporeal') form takes the shape of an animal (OP27). The Patronus is the embodiment of the positive thoughts of the caster, and is the only known defence against Dementors (PA12). In order to cast it, one has to focus on a 'single, very happy memory' (PA12). See PATRONUS.

'expecto' = L. 'expect or look for' + 'patronus' = L. 'a protector, defender'

Expelliarmus

(ex-pel-ee-AR-mus)

'Disarming Spell'

Causes an opponent's wand to fly out of his or her hand (PA19, OP18). Harry learned this spell from Snape (CS11, 16, OP18). The spell can have some unforeseen consequences (GF34). An Expelliarmus spell can 'defeat' a witch or wizard, changing their wand's allegiance (DH35).

'expelo' L. 'to drive out' + 'arma' L. 'weapon' While Voldemort uses the Killing Curse indiscriminately, Harry relies on this non-aggressive spell. J.K. Rowling defines Harry's character in this way, using Expelliarmus even when the Death Eaters have pegged it as his signature move (DH4). In the end, J.K. Rowling writes Harry as a person not of violence and murder, but of compassion and mercy — of love. And it is love which defeats evil in the end: the love of family seen in the actions of Narcissa Malfoy, the love of friends demonstrated between the members of the D.A., the love shown to the weak and downtrodden as seen in Harry's attitude toward house-

elves and goblins, and the love shown even to enemies when Harry will not commit murder even at the potential cost of his own life.

Exploding Bonbons

A delicious and dangerous sweet sold at Honeydukes (PA10).

Exploding Snap

A wizarding card game made more interesting by the fact that the cards occasionally blow up (e.g. GF22).

Expulso

(ex-PUL-soh)

A spell which creates an explosion (DH9).

'expulsum' = L. 'drive out, expel, force out, banish'

Extendable Ears

An invention of Fred and George's that allows listening in on conversations from long distances and through closed doors, (though the Ears are foiled by Imperturbable Charms). Extendable Ears look like long flesh-coloured strings. To use them, one end of the string is inserted into the ear, then the word 'Go!' is spoken. The other end then wriggles off toward whatever needs listening to (OP4, 22, 23, HBP6, DH12, 15).

Extinguishing Spell

A spell used by dragon keepers to put out inadvertent fires (GF19).

eye, magical

Mad-Eye Moody has a magical eye that allows him to see in all directions, as well as see through walls, ceilings, and Invisibility Cloaks (GF25, OP9, DH14).

Fainting Fancies

Magical sweets, invented by Fred and George, which cause the person eating them to pass out (OP6, 13).

fairy

A tiny creature that looks like a very small human with insect wings. Fairies are extremely vain, liking nothing better than to serve as decoration (e.g. PA10, GF23).

Fairies are common in folklore the world over, usually depicted as small ethereal beings which live out of sight of humans, often in woodlands. Fairies have magical powers to fly, cast spells, and predict the future. They can be friendly but are sometimes depicted as mischievous or even malevolent. J.K. Rowling's version of fairies is quite different from the traditional type, more like insects than intelligent nature spirits.

fairy eggs

A favourite food of Bowtruckles (OP13).

fairy lights

Christmas light strings (OP23). Also a password used by the Fat Lady (GF23).

This is a play on words. In the Wizarding world, real live fairies are used to decorate; the British term for Christmas light strings is 'fairy lights'.

fake wands

A Weasley invention which look just like normal wands but transform into something funny when used, such as rubber chickens or pairs of underpants (US: a tin parrot or a rubber haddock). The most expensive variety beat the unwary user about the head and neck (GF22).

Falcon, the

A tea leaf fortune-telling symbol, from *Unfogging the Future* pp.5-6, which signifies 'a deadly enemy' (PA6).

Falmouth Falcons

Quidditch team hailing from Falmouth at the south-western tip of Britain (DP1-4).

Fancourt, Perpetua

(1900–1991)

Witch inventor (FW). For more information, see the Famous Wizard cards.

Fang

Hagrid's pet and companion. Fang is an enormous black boarhound (PS8, GF13) with a booming bark (CS15). Fang appears a rather scary beast but is at heart a coward. He seems to like Ron particularly (PS8). Fang lives in Hagrid's cabin; his basket sits in the corner of the cabin's single room.

The boarhound is another name for the Great Dane. Boarhounds have a reputation for being gentle, even with small children, though they earned their name because they were used to hunt fierce wild animals such as boars and stags.

Fanged Frisbees

Similar to a Muggle Frisbee, but with a nasty personality. Forbidden inside Hogwarts castle by Filch (GF12, HBP9).

Fanged Geranium

Magical plant which bites, studied in Herbology class (OP31).

Fantastic Beasts and Where to Find Them

By Newt Scamander

Standard reference book about magi-

cal creatures in the Wizarding world (PS5, OP27, DH20, FW).

The book Fantastic Beasts and Where to Find Them *is available in Muggle shops. Many of the creatures listed here, as well as many more, can be found in the second part of that book, which is an encyclopaedia of magical creatures filled with fascinating information. We do not reproduce that information in here; instead, we encourage you to buy a copy of* Fantastic Beasts *for yourself and find out more.*

Fat Friar, the

(Hufflepuff, medieval)

A wizard who was once a Hufflepuff and is now is their resident ghost. He is a jolly, friendly ghost who cheerfully wishes the first-years good day and hopes they'll be placed in Hufflepuff (PS7).

The image of a fat, jovial friar who cares a bit too much about the pleasures of food and drink is a familiar one in literature, particularly to anyone who remembers the character of Friar Tuck in the legends of Robin Hood. The religious orders which take the name 'friar' date back to the 1200s so the Fat Friar couldn't have been the Hufflepuff ghost until that era. Of the four main Orders of the Catholic Church, the Augustinian ideals seem to most closely match those of Hufflepuff, and it is likely that the Fat Friar was a follower of Augustine. Augustinians do not seek out the exceptional or exclude those who are marginalized in society. They seek to build community founded on love and respect for all.

Fat Lady

Portrait of a heavy-set lady wearing a pink silk dress who hangs over the round doorway into the Gryffindor Common Room. To gain admittance, a person must give the correct password to the Fat Lady, whereupon she swings her frame out from the wall (PS8). She has been known to get a bit testy with people who wake her up for no good reason and is prone to wandering out of her frame late at night to go visiting, making it impossible to enter Gryffindor Tower (PS9). She is friends with Violet, a portrait in the antechamber off the Great Hall (GF17, 23, HBP17).

Fawcett family

Wizarding family living near Ottery St. Catchpole (GF6).

Fawcett, Miss S

(b. 1980; Ravenclaw, 1991)

Hogwarts student, possibly part of the Fawcett family of Ottery St. Catchpole. Attended the Duelling Club in 1992 (CS11) and the Yule Ball in 1994 (GF23). For a short time she had a long white beard, but she got better (GF16).

There is a discrepancy between the British and American first editions of Goblet of Fire. *In the first British edition, we read:*

> *'Ten points from Hufflepuff, Fawcett!' Snape snarled as a girl ran past him (GF23).*

In the most recent American edition, Snape deducts her points from Ravenclaw.

Fawkes

Dumbledore's pet phoenix (CS12, GF36, HBP29, 30). Fawkes is a very intelligent magical bird who serves as a messenger and a lookout for his owner (e.g. OP22). Like all phoenixes, Fawkes periodically burst into flames and was reborn from the ashes as a chick (CS12).

Fawkes borrows the name of the infamous Guy Fawkes, who in 1606 was involved with the Gunpowder Plot to blow up Parliament. Fawkes wasn't actually the leader of the Plot, but his name has gone down in history as the man responsible. The fifth of November is now called Guy Fawkes Day and celebrations involve bonfires and fireworks in memory of the explosion that never happened back in 1606. Since the phoenix bird burns up entirely every so often and is reborn as a tiny chick, a name associated with fire makes sense.

feather-light

An unnamed spell that makes the target object weigh practically nothing (PA3).

This spell isn't named in the book, but Harry does think that he might make his trunk 'feather-light' using magic so that he can carry it with his broom.

Felix Felicis

Gold-coloured potion which gives luck (HBP9, 22).

'felix' = L. lucky + 'felicis' = L. lucky (same word, different declensions)

'fell off the back of a broom'

An expression synonymous with the Muggle cliché 'fell off the back of a truck' to indicate goods which come from a questionable source (OP2).

fen

An alkaline wetland, in Britain mostly found near the eastern coast of England in and around Norfolk. According to one of the Sorting Hat's songs (GF12), Salazar Slytherin came from 'fen', suggesting that he was very possibly from that area.

Fenwick, Benjy

Member of the Order of the Phoenix in the 1970s, killed by Death Eaters; according to Moody. they only found 'bits of him' (OP9).

Fergus

Seamus Finnegan's annoying cousin (HBP17).

Ferula

(feh-ROO-lah)

Spell that conjures a wooden rod, used to create a splint for an injured leg. (PA19).

'ferula' = L. 'stick or rod (as used for punishment)'

Fever Fudge

A Weasley invention, part of the Skiving Snackbox, which gives a person a high fever. The ingredients include murtlap essence (OP26).

Fidelius Charm

(fih-DAY-lee-us)

A very powerful spell, extremely complex and difficult to cast, which hides a place and people inside it so that they cannot be detected by any means. One person is designated the Secret Keeper for the spell, and that person alone can reveal the location (PA10) by giving that knowledge either verbally or in writing (OP4). After the death of a Secret Keeper, each of the people to whom he or she had confided the secret will become a Secret Keeper. The power of the Fidelius Charm will be diluted more and more as the number of Secret Keepers grows (DH6, JKR). *'fidelis' = L. 'trustworthy, faithful'*

Fiendfyre

Highly dangerous cursed magical fire, made up of flames of abnormal size and heat that can crumble fairly substantial objects, even magical artefacts, to soot at a mere touch. Left burning long enough, the fire will take the shapes of gigantic fiery beasts (including serpents, chimaeras, dragons, and birds of prey) which will pursue any target humans (DH31). *'fiend' = Eng. 'an inhuman, cruel person' + 'fyre' from Old Eng. 'fyr' = 'fire'*

Figg, Arabella Doreen (Mrs)

A member of the Order of the Phoenix, a squib living near the Dursleys in Little Whinging. She is an eccentric old woman who wears carpet slippers and a housecoat everywhere. She watched over Harry as he grew up (PS2, GF36, OP1, 2) and seemed unusually interested in how he was getting on (PS3). She raises Kneazles (OP1, 2, JKR).

Filch, Argus

The Hogwarts caretaker, a cantankerous, vindictive man who detests the students. Filch's horrible attitude in part arises from his frustration at being a Squib. Filch has a cat called Mrs Norris with whom he has an almost psychic connection. She wanders the corridors of the castle just as he does, and if she spots anyone breaking a rule, Filch is there within minutes. He knows the secret passageways and hidden doors of Hogwarts better than almost anyone (except possibly the Weasley twins) (PA9). Filch may be romantically involved with Madam Pince (HBP15, 30). *Argus was a giant in Greek mythology, a watchman with a hundred eyes; 'filch' = Eng. slang 'to steal'*

Filch's office

Located on the ground floor, this office contains a messy desk with an oil lamp hanging over it. The room smells of fried fish. Here Filch stores filing cabinets full of the details of the infractions of generations of students (c.f.HBP24). From the ceiling hang chains and manacles, just in case he gets the chance to use them on students (CS8, PA10).

Finch-Fletchley, Justin
(b. 1980; Hufflepuff, 1991; Dumbledore's Army)
A curly-haired Muggle-born wizard who was down for the exclusive Muggle school Eton until he got the letter from Hogwarts (so it is quite likely that his parents are very wealthy) (CS11). He was a member of the D.A. (OP16).

Finite
(fi-NEE-tay)
Stops the effects of a currently operating spell (OP36, DH31).
'finio' = L. 'settle, end, die, cease'
This spell is probably just a shortened form of Finite Incantatem.

Finite Incantatem
(fi-NEE-tay in-kan-TAH-tem)
Stops the effects of a currently operating spell (CS11).
'finio' = L. 'settle, end, die' + 'incantationem' = L. 'the art of enchanting'

Finnigan, Mrs
Seamus's mother (GF7, OP11). She is a witch, which Seamus's father, a Muggle, didn't find out until after they married (PS7).

Finnigan, Seamus
(b. 1980; Gryffindor, 1991; Dumbledore's Army)
Irish boy with sandy hair in Harry's year. He is a Half-blood, with a Muggle father and a witch mother (PS7). He is good friends with Dean Thomas (GF7). Seamus is a Kenmare Kestrals fan (OP11).

Firebolt
Released in the summer of 1993, the Firebolt was at that time the fastest racing broom in the world (PA4). Harry resisted the temptation to buy one, but to his surprise he received a Firebolt for Christmas from an anonymous person (PA11). The Irish International Side flew Firebolts in the 1994 Quidditch World Cup (GF8).

Fire-Crab
A magical creature from which Hagrid created Blast-Ended Skrewts by crossing them with manticores (GF24).

Firenze
(fee-REN-zeh)
(Divination professor, 1996-?)
A centaur with white hair, a golden-yellow body, and blue eyes (PS15). He trusts humans more than the rest of the centaurs do and believes that the centaurs must be willing to take a stand against the rising evil. At Dumbledore's request, he joined the Hogwarts staff as a Divination teacher at Hogwarts,

an act that caused the other centaurs to consider him a traitor and banish him from their herd (OP27, 30, 38, HBP9, DH36). (*see also* BLC).

Firenze is the Italian form of the name for the city of Florence, the capital city of Tuscany in Italy.

Firewhisky

Wizard liquor. While many types of drinks are available in the Wizarding world, nothing has as much kick as Ogden's Old Firewhisky (CS6, GF10, DH5, 25).

The spelling is almost always given without an 'e' before the final 'y', indicating that Firewhisky is Scottish, not Irish. However, the Irish spelling is used on one occasion in HBP15, referring to the alcohol in Romilda Vane's Chocolate Cauldrons.

First Wizarding War

(c. 1970 through 1981)

By the early 1970s, Voldemort become so fearsome that few dared speak his name. In addition to his Death Eaters, Voldemort formed alliances with werewolves and Dementors and controlled armies of Inferi (HBP3). During this time, Voldemort and his minions attacked anyone who resisted or who defended the rights of Muggles and Muggle-born wizards, and marked the scenes of murder with the Dark Mark (GF9). Whole families

were wiped out and many others went into hiding. The Ministry could not cope with the situation, so Albus Dumbledore began organising the resistance, creating the Order of the Phoenix (OP6, 9). The War only ended with the mysterious disappearance of Voldemort in Godric's Hollow (PS1).

Fixing Charm

Spell that magically fastens one thing to another (DP3).

Fizzing Whizzbees

Magical sherbet balls that make you float off the ground when you eat them (PA5, 10, GF23). A password to get into Dumbledore's office (OP22).

Flagrante Curse

Causes the target object to burn anyone who touches it (DH26).

Flagrate

(fla-GRAH-tay)

Spell creating a burning, fiery line in the air which can be 'drawn' with the wand into specific shapes. The shape lingers for some time (OP34).

'flagro' = L. 'blaze, burn'

Flame-Freezing Charm

Spell changing the properties of fire so that its heat feels like a warm breeze.

Used in medieval times by witches and the wizards being burned at the stake; they would cast this spell, then scream and pretend to be burning up (PA1).

Flamel, Nicolas
(b. circa 1326–d. mid-1990s)
Celebrated alchemist (DH2), famous for creating the only known Philosopher's Stone in existence. As a result, Flamel and his wife Perenelle (b. circa 1333) lived for over 600 years (PS17, JKR). Dumbledore did some alchemical work with him in the 1900s (PS17).

flashing paint charm
This 'tricky little charm' makes paint flash different colours (PS11).

Fleet, Angus
Muggle living in Peebles who thought he saw a flying car (CS5).

Fleetwood's High-Finish Handle Polish
A component of Harry's Broom Servicing Kit (PA1).

Flesh-Eating Slug
Apparently a frightening creature, since someone was scared enough of them to turn a Boggart into one (PA7, CS4).

Flesh-Eating Trees of the World
Book used for sixth-year Herbology. Among other things, the book discusses methods of getting the juice out of Snargaluff pods (HBP14).

flesh memory
A form of magic cast on some items which allows them to 'remember' and identify the first human to touch them. A Snitch has flesh memory so it can identify the first Seeker to touch it in the event of a disputed catch (DH7).

Fletcher, Mundungus
(Order of the Phoenix)
A crook whose shady business dealings are always getting him into trouble (e.g., HBP12). However, Albus Dumbledore believes that despite his dodginess he can be mighty handy to have around since he hears things others don't (OP5, 16). Harry and the Weasley boys think he is a lot of fun to spend time with, as his stories keep his listeners in stitches. Mundungus, or 'Dung' as he's called, is a keen drinker, smokes a smelly pipe, and swears magnificently (OP5). Mundungus is a completely untrustworthy scoundrel (CS4, GF10, DH4).
'mundungus' = Eng. from Spanish 'a foul-smelling tobacco'

Fletwock, Laurentia

(b. 1947)

Witch who breeds winged horses; she has spoken out against widespread use of broomsticks, mostly to encourage people to use flying horses instead. For more information, see the Famous Wizard cards (FW, JKR). *'Fletwock' is a sound-alike (not quite a homonym) for the word 'fetlock', the ankle joint of a horse's leg.*

'flibbertigibbet'

A password to get into Gryffindor Tower (PA15)

The most common modern meaning of this word is 'an irresponsible, silly person', but a somewhat rarer meaning implies that the person is a mischief-maker if not actually a fiend. In other words, someone like Peeves.

'flint'

An honest-to-goodness error in the books has come to be called a 'flint' after Marcus Flint, the Slytherin Quidditch captain whom J.K. Rowling inadvertently included in one book too many, making him an 'eighth-year' student. The term was coined by one of the members of the Harry Potter for Grown Ups online group. Remarkably few genuine flints exist, considering the vast scope of the story. Incidentally, the original error of

Flint's year has been corrected in later editions.

Flint, Marcus

(Slytherin, 1987; Quidditch Chaser, Captain c.1991–1993)

The Captain of the Slytherin Quidditch team for the first three years Harry played. Harry thought he looked like he might be part troll. Flint wasn't beyond a bit of cheating to win a match (PS11, CS7, 10, PA13).

Flint, Ursula

The wife of Hogwarts Headmaster Phineas Nigellus Black (BFT).

Flitterbloom

An innocuous potted plant which is similar to Devil's Snare in appearance, though not in temperament (OP25).

Flitwick, Filius

(b. October 17, year unknown; Ravenclaw, Head of House)

Charms professor at Hogwarts, Head of Ravenclaw House. He is very short, needing to stand on a pile of books to see over his desk (PS8), with white hair and a squeaky voice. He is an accomplished wizard and, according to rumour, was a duelling champion when he was younger (CS11). Flitwick has taught students how to 'swish and flick' at Hogwarts since at least the 1970s (PA11) and is well-respected by everyone, even Dolores Umbridge (OP15).

'filius' = L. 'son'

'Flitwick' is the name of a town in Bedfordshire, England. The town name is pronounced 'FLIT-ick'. J.K. Rowling may have chosen the name because it fits the character's personality to some extent: 'flit' = 'flutter'; Br. slang for an effeminate man (OED).

Flitwick's Office

Located on the seventh floor, Flitwick's office is the thirteenth window from the right of the West Tower (PA21).

Flobberworm

A magical worm which prefers to be left alone and to do nothing (PA6).

Floo Network

Network connecting wizarding fireplaces all over Britain. When Floo Powder is thrown into a fireplace that is connected to the network, the fire burns a brilliant green colour. To travel, a witch or wizard steps into the fire and states her or his destination (another fireplace on the Floo Network) (esp. CS4). To talk to someone through a fireplace, the witch or wizard throws Floo powder into the flames and inserts only her or his head, again stating the fireplace to which a connection is desired (GF11, 19, OP29).

'flue'= Eng. 'vent or chimney for a fireplace or other heating device', but also a reference to magical travelling ('flew'). In fact, fans have theorised that Hagrid used the Floo Network to travel to the Hut on the Rock, based on this exchange between Harry and Hagrid:

'How did you get here?' Harry asked, looking around for another boat.

'Flew,' said Hagrid.

'Flew?'

'Yeah — but we'll go back in this. Not s'pposed ter use magic now I've got yeh.' (PS5)

Floo Network Authority

Ministry office which maintains and regulates the Floo Network. Employees of the Floo Network Authority have the ability to monitor Floo connections in a manner analogous to wiretapping a Muggle telephone (OP3, 17, 22, 27, 28, DH1, 4, 30). Witches and wizards working for the Floo Network Authority are referred to as Floo Network Regulators (OP28), while the Floo Regulation Panel makes decisions about connections to the Network. It is against regulations for a Muggle fireplace to be connected to the Floo Network, but the Panel makes exceptions in rare cases (GF4).

Floo Powder

Silvery powder, invented in the 1200s by Ignatia Wildsmith (FW), which allows magical travel and magical communication between fireplaces connected to the Floo Network (CS4).

Florean Fortescue's Ice-Cream Parlour

A shop Harry frequented while staying in Diagon Alley. (PA4).

Florence

Probably a student at Hogwarts, a contemporary of Harry's father (GF30).

Flourish and Blotts

A bookshop in Diagon Alley that serves as the primary supplier of schoolbooks for Hogwarts students (PS5, CS4, PA4).

Both of the words in this shop's name relate to writing. A 'flourish' is an embellishment or an ornamental stroke added to handwriting or calligraphy. To 'blot' ink is to use absorbent 'blotting paper' to dry the ink on a page. This was necessary before the introduction of ball point pens and would certainly be required of anyone using a quill and ink, as they do at Hogwarts.

Fluffy

Very dangerous, very large three-headed dog, owned by Rubeus Hagrid.

Fluffy will only sleep if he hears music (PS11, 16). Hagrid released Fluffy into the Forbidden Forest (BP).

The three-headed dog in Greek mythology is named Cerberus and guards the gates of Hades. J.K. Rowling borrowed a number of Cerberus' qualities for Fluffy, particularly the fact that he could be lulled to sleep by music.

Flume, Ambrosius

Owner, along with his wife, of Honeydukes Sweetshop in Hogsmeade (HBP4). The Flumes not only sell a wide variety of sweets, but also make their own fudge and enormous blocks of chocolate.

'Ambrosia' was the food of the gods on Mount Olympus in Greek mythology. It was said to confer immortality on a mortal who would eat (or drink) it.

Flutterby Bush

A species of magical plant which quivers and shakes (DH6). Students pruned these in their fourth-year Herbology class (GF20).

Flying (class)

Teaches the basic fundamentals of broomstick flying to first years early in the school year. Madam Hooch teaches the class, an assignment which sometimes requires her to escort the resulting casualties to the hospital wing (PS9).

flying carpets

Flying carpets rather than brooms are the standard magical means of transportation in Asia and the Middle East. In Britain flying carpets have been banned for many years since they are now on the Registry of Proscribed Charmable Objects, being defined as a Muggle artefact that it is illegal to enchant; therefore it is not lawful to import them (GF7).

flying magic

Generally speaking, wizards are unable to fly without the aid of magical devices, such as broomsticks or flying carpets. Spells can create flying effects, however. For example, *Wingardium Leviosa* levitates objects (PS10, c.f. CS2). (*See also* DH4, 5, 30).

Flying With The Cannons

A book of interesting facts devoted to the Chudley Cannons Quidditch team (CS12). The book is illustrated with moving photographs (GF2, 22).

Foe-Glass

A Dark Detector which resembles a mirror but does not reflect the scene in front of it; instead it shows the enemies — the foes — of its owner. It shows shadowy, out-of-focus figures which become more distinct as the foes get closer (GF20).

The name of this device is a nice play on words. While a 'foe' is an enemy, it is also a homonym for the French word 'faux', meaning 'false' — a fitting term for a looking-glass that isn't a true mirror.

'For the Greater Good'

Albus Dumbledore and Gellert Grindelwald, in their enthusiasm for bringing wizards out of hiding and into their 'rightful place' in larger human society, talked about wizards ruling over Muggles 'for the greater good' (DH18, 35). This became the slogan for Grindelwald as he grew in power in Europe in the early 1940s, and his excuse for committing atrocities (DH18). Grindelwald had even carved the words over the entrance to Nurmengard, the prison he built to hold his enemies (DH18).

Forbidden Forest

A large, dark forest to the east of Hogwarts which is strictly off limits to students except in the course of occasional Care of Magical Creatures lessons (OP21) or detentions (PS15). Often referred to as just 'the forest', the Forbidden Forest is thick with trees; off the paths the way is almost impassable

(CS15). The forest is home to many creatures, including unicorns, Thestrals, Acromantulas, centaurs and the Weasleys' turquoise Ford Anglia (CS15); anything wild and dangerous that needs a place to live is put there (BP).

Ford Anglia, flying

Battered old turquoise automobile bought by Arthur Weasley for the alleged purpose of taking it apart in his shed to see how it worked. In fact, in the process of dismantling and reassembling the car, he also bewitched it to be able to fly and installed an Invisibility Booster. He also magically expanded the inner spaces so that an enormous amount of luggage could fit in the boot and numerous people could sit comfortably in its wide seats (CS3, 15).

Forest of Dean

One of England's last remaining ancient forests (DH19). Hagrid hails from the Forest of Dean (RAH).
J.K. Rowling grew up on the edge of the Forest of Dean, in Tutshill.

Forgetfulness Charm

Perhaps the same as *Obliviate*. It is possible to injure a Muggle if you miscast this spell on them (JKR).

Forgetfulness Potion

Potion taught to first-year students (PS16).
J.K. Rowling uses a subtle bit of word-play when she describes the first-years who 'tried to remember' how to make a Forgetfulness Potion for their exams.

Fortescue, Dexter

Red-nosed, corpulent wizard, a former Headmaster of Hogwarts. His portrait hangs in the Headmaster's office (OP27).

Fortescue, Florean

Wizard who once owned an ice cream parlour in Diagon Alley where Harry Potter worked on his homework while staying at the Leaky Cauldron (PA4).
According to J.K. Rowling, there was a subplot with Florean Fortescue involving the Elder wand which didn't make it into the final book (PC-JKR2).

'fortuna major'

Password to get into the Gryffindor common room (PA5).
'furtuna major' = L. 'good fortune'; this term is used for one of the sixteen figures of sikidy, a form of geomancy used in Madagascar. J.K. Rowling borrowed a number of other terms from this source as well, including 'alihotsy'.

'Fountain of Fair Fortune, The'
One of the fairy tales attributed to Beedle the Bard (DH7). The story tells of four people who are on a quest to find happiness from a fabled magical fountain, only to discover that they didn't need magic at all (TBB).

Fountain of Magical Brethren
The Fountain of Magical Brethren was a grouping of golden figures on a plinth in the centre of a pool halfway down the vast atrium of the Ministry of Magic in London. Water spouted into the pool from figures of a witch and wizard, surrounded by a house-elf, a centaur, and a goblin looking at them in adoration. The ironically-named statue gave testimony to the warped sense of superiority assumed by wizards over other magical races (OP36).

fountain of wine
A spell which produces a fountain of wine from the end of the caster's wand (GF18).

Four-Point Spell
See POINT ME.

Fowl or Foul? A Study of Hippogriff Brutality
Ron used this book while doing research to help Hagrid (PA15).

France
Hagrid and Madame Maxime travelled to France en route to Eastern Europe while on a secret mission (OP20). Hermione also took a trip to France with her parents during one summer holiday, which included a stop in Dijon (OP20). The first meeting of the International Confederation of Wizards was held in France (OP31).

Freezing Charm
According to Slughorn, one simple Freezing Charm will disable a Muggle burglar alarm (HBP4).

Freshwater Plimpies
Fish living in the stream near the Lovegood house (DH20).

Fridwulfa
Giantess and mother of Hagrid who abandoned her human family in c.1931 (GF24). Having deserted Hagrid's wizard father, she later had a second child, a son named Grawp, by another giant. She died 'years and years ago', according to Hagrid in November 1995 (OP20, 30).

Frobisher, Vicky
(Gryffindor, early 1990s)
Hogwarts student involved in many school activities, particularly Charms

Club. Tried out for Gryffindor Keeper in autumn 1995 and flew better than Ron Weasley; however she was rejected because she said that Charms Club would rank higher in her priorities than Quidditch in the event of a schedule conflict (OP13).

Frog Spawn Soap
Something for sale at Zonko's. Sounds dead useful, like so many of Zonko's products (PA14).

From Egg to Inferno: A Dragon Keeper's Guide
Hogwarts library book consulted by Hagrid, who always wanted to own a dragon (PS14).

Fubster, Colonel
A retired Muggle neighbour of Marjorie Dursley who looks after her bulldogs when she's away from home (PA2).

Fudge, Cornelius Oswald
Minister of Magic from 1990 (OP10) until June 1996 (HBP1). Fudge became Minister of Magic upon Millicent Bagnold's retirement. At the beginning of his tenure, he sent Dumbledore owls frequently, seeking advice about what to do (PS5). Fudge is somewhat weak, swayed by money, addicted to his own position and privilege, and impressed by wizarding families with pure bloodlines (OP9). He ignored Voldemort's return for a year. When his folly became apparent, he was sacked (HBP1). Fudge usually wore a green pinstriped suit, long black or pinstriped cloak, and a lime green bowler hat (CS14, PA3).

J.K. Rowling said that she based Fudge on the British Prime Minister Neville Chamberlain who, prior to World War Two, tried to convince himself and the British nation that giving in to some of Hitler's demands would avoid a large scale war. Even more to the point, Chamberlain was accused of lying to Parliament about the strength of Hitler's armed forces and getting rid of people in government who disagreed with his policy toward Germany.

Fudge, Rufus
Cornelius Fudge's nephew who worked for the Improper Use of Magic office but got caught in a scandal involving a vanishing Muggle tube train (subway train) (DP2).

Fudge Flies
A delicious treat from Honeydukes that Scabbers used to like, according to Ron (PA13).

Fulbert the Fearful

(1014–1097)

A very nervous and cowardly wizard; for more information, see the Famous Wizard cards (FW).

Full Body-Bind

See PETRIFICUS TOTALUS.

furballs

Creatures on sale in the Magical Menagerie (PA4); these are probably puffskeins (OP6, HBP6).

Furmage, Dymphna

(1612-1698)

Witch attacked by Pixies; for more information, see the Famous Wizard cards (FW).

Furnunculus

(fur-NUN-kyoo-lus)

Causes the target to break out in boils (GF18, 37).

'furuncle' = Eng. 'painful skin boil'

fur spell

An unnamed spell that causes a person to grow fur (CS11).

Fwooper

African magical bird with brightly-coloured feathers (JKR).

Fwooper (Rune)

The rune for the number four. The four possible colours of the Fwooper are the reason this bird is the symbol for that number (JKR).

Gadding With Ghouls
by Gilderoy Lockhart
One of the many required textbooks for Defence Against the Dark Arts in Harry's second year (CS4).

Gaddley
Town where a Muggle family was found murdered in 1998, during the Second War. The Muggle authorities blamed a gas leak, but it was actually the work of Death Eaters (DH22).
There is no town called Gaddley in Britain, although there is a village called Gaddesby in Leicestershire.

Galleon
The largest of the coins used by wizards, sometimes referred to as a 'gold Galleon'. Along the edge are imprinted a row of numbers, which are the serial number of the goblin who made the coin (OP19). The Galleon is worth about five British pounds (CR). There are seventeen silver Sickles to the Galleon (PS5).
Galleons were large, sturdy wooden warships of the 16th through 18th centuries which were often associated with treas-

ure. For example, the Spanish treasure fleet of that era which brought gold and other precious commodities back from the Caribbean included a large number of galleons.

Galleons, enchanted
Ingenious magical items used for communication in the D.A. In order to get word to members of the D.A. about meetings, a Protean Charm was used on some fake Galleons. When Harry decided on the day and time for a meeting, he changed the numbers on his Galleon. The other fake coins would become warm to alert their owners, then show the new time and date (OP19, DH29).

Gambol and Japes Wizarding Joke Shop
A shop in Diagon Alley, a favourite of Fred and George, which sells a wide variety of tricks and practical joke items (CS4).

Gamekeeper
Hagrid's title, along with Keeper of the Keys (PS4).

Gamp, Hesper

Wife of Sirius Black (1877-1952), who was the oldest son of Phineas Nigellus Black (BFT).

Gamp's Law of Elemental Transfiguration

One of the 'rules' of magic. There are Five Principle Exceptions to Gamp's Law, which are certain types of items which can't be conjured from nothing or Transfigured from completely different materials. Food is one of the exceptions (DH15).

gargoyles

Grotesque winged creatures, usually made of stone. A gargoyle statue guards the moving stairway up to the Head's office (CS11 etc., OP28). Two stone gargoyles flank the staff room and make snide comments at students who dare to try to enter (OP17, DH31). There are stone gargoyles on the castle roof as well (DH31).

Technically, the term gargoyle refers to a stone water spout regardless of the type of creature it's made to resemble. In fact, there is a gargoyle on the National Cathedral in Washington D.C. that looks like Darth Vader (although because that sculpture deflects rainwater rather than channel it through its mouth, it's not a gargoyle but a 'chimera'). Gargoyles weren't placed on building only as fancy gutter spouts, however. They also served as guardians of the building, warding off evil spirits and protecting those inside. The gargoyles outside the staffroom function this way, warding off not evil spirits but students with their wisecracks and snide remarks. Gargoyles as a type of magical creature are usually described as looking like a demon with horns and a tail, after the famous gargoyles of the Notre Dame Cathedral in Paris.

Garrotting Gas

Invisible gas which incapacitates people (OP32).

A garrotte is a simple but very deadly weapon. Typically, it consists of a cord or wire which is wrapped around the victim's throat, killing them by suffocation. Since it is highly unlikely that Fred and George would have released something which was actually deadly, we assume that Garrotting Gas is non-lethal, simply rendering its victims unconscious.

Gaunt house

Miserable hovel located in the woods just outside Little Hangleton, home to Marvolo Gaunt and his two children, Morfin and Merope (HBP10, 23).

'gaunt' = Eng. 'very thin especially from disease or hunger or cold'

Gaunt, Marvolo

Maternal grandfather of Tom Riddle. Marvolo was short and squat, with odd proportions which made him look something like a monkey. Marvolo wore a gold ring with the Peverell symbol carved into a black stone, a symbol he didn't understand, thinking it was a coat of arms (HBP10).

Gaunt, Merope

(b. circa 1908–d. 31 Dec 1926)

Daughter of Marvolo Gaunt and mother of Tom Riddle. Eighteen-year-old Merope was beaten down and abused by her father. Merope's tragic life and death set the stage for the dramatic events of the next fifty years of Wizarding history (HBP10, 13).

The star named Merope is one of the Pleiades, a striking cluster of seven stars in the constellation Taurus. Merope was a character in Greek mythology, a nymph who was the daughter of Atlas, a Titan. Merope married a mortal, Sisyphus, the king of Corinth. She was so ashamed of this that she hid her face among the stars in the sky, which is why the dimmest star of the Pleiades bears her name.

Gaunt, Morfin

Son of Marvolo Gaunt, brother of Merope, a Parselmouth and a sociopath. Morfin was sentenced to Azkaban for his anti-Muggle behaviour (HBP10, 17).

Geminio

(jeh-MIN-ee-o)

Charm which duplicates the target object (DH13).

'geminare' = L. 'to double'

Gemino Curse

Spell which creates multiple worthless copies of an object. Gringotts goblins placed Gemino Curses on the objects in the Lestranges' high security vault. When those objects are touched, the spell created a lot of identical copies of them, making the genuine ones impossible to find. According to Griphook, a would-be thief who continued to handle treasure under such a curse would eventually be crushed by the weight of expanding 'gold' (DH26).

See GEMINIO.

from 'geminare' L. 'to double'

Gernumblies

Alternate name for garden gnomes, according to Xenophilius Lovegood, derived from the Latin name for the species, *Gernumbli gardensi*. Their magic is allegedly very strong; being bitten by a gnome may, according to Lovegood, have all sorts of whimsical and creative consequences, from 'singing opera' to 'declaiming in Mermish' (DH8).

Ghosts

Semi-transparent, non-corporeal beings. Although dead, in many ways they enjoy a full life. There are differences, however: their sensibilities are dulled after their deaths, judging by the music and refreshments at the Deathday Party (CS8). They do not eat (PS7). The Ministry of Magic has some authority over ghostly behaviour (GF25). Only wizards can become ghosts, and then only if they choose that path before they die. They enter a state somewhere between living and dead because they are afraid of death (OP38, EBF). There are at least twenty ghosts at Hogwarts, including the four House Ghosts (PS7).

ghouls

Slimy, buck-toothed, ugly creatures which live in attics or barns of wizards. A ghoul lives in the attic of the Burrow, just above Ron's room (CS4, GF10, DH6).

Ghouls are graveyard-dwelling monsters from Arabian folklore. They are shape-shifting demons who take animal form to lure unwary travellers to their death in the desert. They are also thought to rob graves and eat the dead.

Giants

Full-blooded giants are about twenty feet tall (GF24). They now live in remote mountain areas in tribes, with a leader called a Gurg. They are violent by nature and very mistrustful of wizards and magic (OP20). In the 1970s, the giants allied themselves with Voldemort. Many giants were killed by Aurors and the rest fled (JKR). (*See also* DH31, 34, 36). *See* GRAWP.

Giant Squid

Huge creature living in the Hogwarts lake. Normally giant squids live deep in the ocean, so this one is undoubtedly magical; this is borne out by the fact that the Hogwarts giant squid allows students to tickle its tentacles (PS16) and feed it toast (GF18).

The giant squid and its even larger cousin, the colossal squid, are some of the largest organisms on Earth. The giant squid can grow to over forty feet in length. It lives in the deep oceans the world over (specimens have been found off Scotland, in fact). These elusive creatures are difficult to study and therefore are not completely understood. Similar beasts appear in legends as terrifying monsters, attacking surface vessels or fighting with sperm whales. In Norse folklore the monster was known as the Kraken and was blamed for the disappearances of ships and for creating huge dangerous whirlpools when they submerged.

Gibbon

Death Eater who set off the Dark Mark during the Battle of the Tower (HBP29).

Gilderoy Lockhart's Guide to Household Pests

by Gilderoy Lockhart

Mrs Weasley keeps a copy of this at the Burrow. It discusses gnomes (CS3) and doxies (OP6).

gillywater

A favourite drink of McGonagall at the Three Broomsticks (PA10).

The name for this drink comes from the gillyflower, which is typically identified as the carnation, although other fragrant flowers have been called this as well. Gilliflowers were used to make gilliflower wine, according to a recipe from Cornwall dated 1753.

gillyweed

Native to the Mediterranean, this magical water plant looks like a bundle of slimy, greyish-green rat tails. When eaten, it gives a person gills to breathe underwater and webbed hands and feet for swimming, which last for approximately one hour. Its properties were discovered by Elladora Ketteridge

(FW). Snape keeps gillyweed in his private stores; it is not available to the students (GF26).

Gladrags Wizardwear

A wizarding clothing shop in Hogsmeade that also has additional locations in London and Paris (GF8, 27).

glen

A Scottish term for 'valley'. According to the Sorting Hat's song, Rowena Ravenclaw hails from the 'glen', which suggests that she is most likely from Scotland — and thus perhaps the one of the four founders who lived closest to Hogwarts' present location (GF12). She was, after all, the one who chose the location for the school (JKR).

Glisseo

(gli-SAY-oh)

Spell which transforms a staircase into a smooth slide (DH32). This is likely the spell which is triggered when boys try to climb the staircase to the girls' dormitory in Gryffindor tower (OP17).

from 'glisser' = Fr. 'slip, slide'

Gnome, garden

(Gernumbli gardensi)

Common garden pest resembling a potato with legs. Gnomes live in gnome-holes underground, where they dig up plant roots and generally cause a mess; their presence is a dead giveaway that a home belongs to a witch or wizard (Sch1). Crookshanks loved chasing gnomes around the Weasleys' garden and the gnomes seemed just as much to love being chased (GF5). Xeno Lovegood studied gnome magic. He called them 'gernumblies' and 'wise little gnomes', and raved about their special magic abilities (DH8).

goats

Aberforth Dumbledore has a strange fascination with goats; he was prosecuted for 'practicing inappropriate charms on a goat' (GF24), and his bar, the Hog's Head, smells like goats (OP16). What's more, as a child, when he was angry at someone he'd show it by throwing goat dung at them (DH18). Today his Patronus is a goat as well (DH28). On an unrelated note, the bezoar is a stone-like object found in the stomach of a goat (PS8).

Gobbledegook

The language of Goblins (GF7), described as 'a rough and unmelodious tongue, a string of rattling, guttural noises' (DH15).

Goblet of Fire

A large, wooden magical cup, which was kept in a very old jewelled chest. The Goblet of Fire is a very powerful enchanted artefact. In order to make the selection of Triwizard champions completely fair, the decision was left up to the Goblet, which filled with blue flames for the occasion. Students who wanted to compete placed their names in the Goblet, which then 'spit out' the names of the one who would be Triwizard Champions. Once the names had been chosen, the Goblet's flames went out, waiting for the next Tournament (GF16).

goblin

One of the primary magical races in the Wizarding world: short and dark-skinned, with long fingers and feet, pointed ears, and dark, slanted eyes (PS5, GF24, HPM). Goblins speak Gobbledegook (GF7, DH15). Although goblins are considered inferior by wizards (GF24), they have established themselves as a vital part of Wizarding society, running the wizarding bank Gringotts (PS5) and thereby controlling the economy. (*See also* OP5, c.f DH15).

Goblin Liaison Office

Ministry office for dealing with the goblin population. Dirk Cresswell was head of this office at one point (HBP4, DH15). Cuthbert Mockridge also worked in this office (GF7).

Goblin metalwork
Apart from their cleverness with money and finances, goblins are also very capable metalsmiths. Their silverwork is well known and prized (OP6, 21). Goblins actually mint the Galleons, Sickles, and Knuts used in the Wizarding world; each coin is stamped with a serial number identifying the goblin who cast it (OP19).

goblin rebellions
Uprisings where goblins have fought for the right to use wands and be treated as equal members of society. Described as 'bloody and vicious', these were most prevalent in the 1600s (PA5) and 1700s (GF15, OP31). One rebellion, in 1612, took place in the vicinity of Hogsmeade; the Inn there was used as headquarters for the rebellion (PA5, JKR). Subversive goblin groups still work in secret against the Ministry, according to the *Daily Prophet* (OP15). In the 1990s, some goblin groups met with representatives of the Ministry of Magic, hoping to create a Bill of Goblin Rights (DP3). Oswald Beamish was a pioneer of goblin rights (FW).

Gobstones
A game similar to marbles, played with stones which spit disgusting liquid at the opposing player when they lose a point. Many of the kids at Hogwarts have a set of Gobstones and it is played fairly regularly (CS10, PA16, GF20). There are Gobstone clubs at Hogwarts (OP17) and also an International Gobstones League (DP1). The offices of the Official Gobstones Club are in the Department of Games and Sports on level seven of the Ministry of Magic (OP7).
'gob' = Br. slang 'saliva or phlegm, particularly when spit out'

Gobstones Tournament
Recently the Welsh National Gobstones Team defeated the Hungarian national side to win this tournament (DP1).

Godelot
Wizard who was killed by his son Hereward to steal the Elder Wand (DH21).

'God Rest Ye, Merry Hippogriffs'
A Wizarding Christmas carol, possibly just made up on the spot by Sirius (OP23).
This is an obvious take on a Muggle Christmas carol, 'God Rest Ye Merry

Gentlemen'. It would be interesting to hear what the rest of the song's lyrics might be.

Godric's Hollow

Though a Muggle village, for over a thousand years it has been home to notable wizards and witches, and has been most famous as the birthplace of Hogwarts founder Godric Gryffindor. Over the centuries, Godric's Hollow has had a number of magical residents; 'the graveyard is full of names of ancient magical families' (DH16). Ignotus Peverell, one of the three brothers of Deathly Hallows lore, is buried here (DH35). Bowman Wright also lived here when he invented the Golden Snitch in the 1300s (DH16). Among those who have lived there more recently are the Dumbledore family, Bathilda Bagshot, and the Potter family (DH16, 17).

golden flames

A powerful but very mysterious spell, inexplicably cast by Harry's wand during the Battle of the Seven Potters (DH4, 36).

Golden Snitch

See SNITCH.

Goldstein, Anthony

(b. 1980; Ravenclaw, 1991; Prefect, 1995; Dumbledore's Army)

A student in Harry's year (OP10) who became a member of the D.A. (OP16, DH29).

Golgomath

A huge, violent giant who favoured the Death Eaters (OP20).

Goliath

Mercenary giant used by the Philistines in their war with the Israelites around 1000 BC; for more information, see the Famous Wizard cards (FW).

The story of Goliath and his defeat by the shepherd boy David is found in the Bible, in I Samuel 17.

Golpalott's Third Law

Golpalott's Third Law, a lesson Slughorn teaches in Potions, says that 'the antidote for a blended poison will be equal to more than the sum of the antidotes for each of the separate components' (HBP18).

This magical 'law', along with Gamp's Law of Elemental Transfiguration, suggests that in the Wizarding world, magic is researched and studied in the same way that scientific principles are studied in the Muggle world.

Gordon

(b. circa 1980)

A Muggle boy living in Little Whinging, one of Dudley's gang (PS3, OP1).

Gorgovitch, Dragomir

Chaser transferred to the Chudley Cannons for a record fee in 1995. He didn't do so well, however; he ended up breaking the record for the most Quaffle drops (DH7).

Gornuk

A Goblin on the run from the Ministry because he refused to be treated like a house-elf (DH22).

Goshawk, Miranda

Author of *The Standard Book of Spells* series of books (*Grade One, Grade Two,* etc.) which are required textbooks for students at Hogwarts (PS5, PA4, GF10, OP9, HBP9).

'miranda' = L. 'worthy of wonder'; a 'goshawk' is a bird of prey

Gouging Spell

See DEFODIO.

Goyle, Gregory

(b. 1980; Slytherin 1991; Inquisitorial Squad; Quidditch Beater 1995-?)

One of Draco Malfoy's thuggish cronies (PS6). Goyle has short, bristly hair that extends down onto his forehead. His eyes are small, dull, and deep set, and he speaks with a low, raspy voice. He's a bully who enjoys bossing people around, whether as a member of the Inquisitorial Squad in his fifth year (OP28) or using the Cruciatus Curse on other students in his seventh (DH29). Not surprisingly, he doesn't like writing (OP10).

Goyle, Mr

A large, somewhat oafish Death Eater (GF33). He is the father of Gregory Goyle (OP26).

Grades for exams

There are three passing and three failing grades given for O.W.L.s (OP15, JKR). The possible grades are:
Passing:
- Outstanding (O)
- Exceeds Expectations (E)
- Acceptable (A)
Failing:
- Poor (P)
- Dreadful (D)
- Troll (T)

Grand Tour

Around the year 1900, it was a tradition for young wizards after leaving Hogwarts to take a 'Grand Tour', a trip around the world to visit famous

Wizarding locales and foreign wizards (DH2,18).

In the 17th through 19th centuries, it became fashionable for young British aristocrats to take a 'Grand Tour', a year or two of travel on the Continent as a way of finishing off their education. They would visit the cities of Paris and Rome, immerse themselves in the art and antiquities, and learn about the culture and politics of Europe. In some ways, this form of travel — to satisfy personal curiosity and learn about other places — was the precursor to modern tourism.

Granger, Hermione Jean

(b. September 19, 1979; Gryffindor 1991; Dumbledore's Army; Prefect 1995; Slug Club)

Resourceful, principled and brilliant, Hermione is probably the brightest witch of her generation. Along with Ron Weasley she is one of Harry Potter's closest friends (PS10 ff.). Muggle-born, (her parents were dentists) (PS12), Hermione is a living, breathing example of the fallacy of pure-blood wizard supremacy. Hermione reads voraciously and prefers concrete, knowable subjects like Runes and Arithmancy (PA12) to the more inexact subjects like Divination (PA15). Viktor Krum, an international Quidditch star, pursued her in her fourth year (GF23 etc.), but all along she harboured a secret fondness for someone else (DH31, /e). Hermione developed a social conscience very early, sticking up for Neville and supporting house-elf rights (GF15). In her third year at Hogwarts, she bought Crookshanks from a magical creatures store because no one had wanted him (PA4), and spent hours preparing a defence for Buckbeak, a falsely-accused hippogriff (PA11 ff.). Harry and Ron owe many of their successes to Hermione's planning and research (DH9). (*See also* BLC).

'Hermione' is a reference to a character in Shakespeare's play A Winter's Tale, *chosen because it sounded clever and a bit pretentious. Viktor Krum and Grawp had a very hard time pronouncing it properly, as do many fans. In fact, J.K. Rowling included the pronunciation in book four for the benefit of fans who were uncertain about how to say the name. J.K. Rowling said she chose that name because*

> *. . . it just seemed the sort of name that a pair of professional dentists, who liked to prove how clever they were...[would give] their daughter a nice, unusual name that no-one could pronounce! (NPC)*

'Jean' is one of the middle names of J.K. Rowling's daughter Mackenzie.

Granger, Mr and Mrs

Hermione's parents. They are Muggle dentists (PS12, GF3) who are very proud of their brilliant daughter. While accepting the Wizarding world and their daughter's place in it (EBF, CS4), they don't approve of using magic for quick fixes, for example insisting that Hermione's somewhat oversized front teeth be dealt with using braces (GF23). During the Second War, Hermione took desperate precautions to protect her parents (DH6, BLC). *J.K. Rowling has stated that she kept Hermione's family in the background, not even giving the first names of her parents. She did this intentionally, in part to contrast with Ron's family, who we get to know very well (EBF).*

Graphorn

A large, two-horned creature which lives in the mountains of Europe (JKR).

Graphorn (Rune)

According to *Ancient Runes Made Easy*, the rune symbol for the number 2 because of its two long, sharp horns (JKR).

Graves, Merton

(b. 1978)

Member of the popular wizarding band The Weird Sisters; for more information, see the Famous Wizard cards (FW).

Grawp

Hagrid's half-brother, a giant whose mother was Fridwulfa. Grawp is small for his age and was abused by the other giants in their mountain stronghold. When Hagrid found him, he insisted on bringing Grawp back to live in the forest near Hogwarts, despite Grawp's initial resistance to the plan. Though Grawp struggled to acclimatise to civilization, Hagrid told Harry that he was 'loads better' towards the end of the school year (June 1997) (OP30, also c.f. DH31). He's particularly fond of Hermione, calling her 'Hermy' (OP30).

Great Fire of London

In 1666 this fire destroyed much of London. According to Wizarding legend it was not, as Muggles believe, started in a bakery, but rather by a young Welsh Green Dragon that was being housed next door (JKR).

Great Hall

The main hall at Hogwarts used for meals, feasts, and other celebrations and events. Running the length of the room are four long tables, one for each house, and at the top of the room is a high table for the teachers. The ceiling is enchanted to show the sky outside and is frequently filled with floating candles for illumination. Students gather here for meals three times a day (esp. GF21). The Hall has also functioned as a place for exams (OP31), for fancy balls (GF23), and on one memorable occasion, a slumber party (PA9).

The arrangement of the Hall is somewhat ambiguous. While it seems logical that the doors to the hall open in the centre of the wall opposite the High Table (which is the way it is portrayed in the film), this does not fit this description in the fourth book:

> *Harry, Ron, and Hermione walked past the Slytherins, the Ravenclaws, and the Hufflepuffs, and sat down with the rest of the Gryffindors at the far side of the Hall . . . (GF12)*

In order to walk past all four house tables, Harry must have entered the Hall from the side, not the back. However, J.K. Rowling has stated in an interview that the Great Hall in the film looked just like she had imagined it:

> *'There are, for sure, going to be people out there that will say that this is not my Great Hall but, I can promise them, it is my Great Hall. So, from my point of view, it's obviously wonderful.' (Alderson, Andrew.) 'They really do look as I'd imagined they*

would inside my head.' Telegraph. co.uk November 11, 2001.)
Therefore the passage from GH12 might be just a minor continuity error.

Great Hangleton

Great Hangleton, neighbouring village to Little Hangleton, is found about two hundred miles from Little Whinging (which places it somewhere in Yorkshire, most likely). Great Hangleton is approximately six miles (HBP10) from Little Hangleton and contains a small police station that serves both towns (GF1).

Great Humberto, The

A character on a television show that Dudley, at age eleven, liked to watch on Monday nights (PS3).

Great Wizarding Events of the Twentieth Century

Not surprisingly, Harry is mentioned in this book (PS6).

Great Wizards of the Twentieth Century

Not surprisingly, Nicolas Flamel is *not* mentioned in this book (PS12).

Greece

The country of Greece, comprising a peninsula and numerous islands in the

Mediterranean Sea, is steeped in history and mythology. References to Greek mythology abound in the lore of the Wizarding world. Quite a few famous ancient witches and wizards came from Greece, including the first Dark Wizard, Herpo the Foul (FW), who created the first Horcrux (PC-JKR1).

Greengrass, Asteria

(b. circa 1982; Slytherin? 1993)

Younger sister of Daphne (PC-JKR2). *While not stated, it is likely that Asteria was a Slytherin considering who she married.*

Greengrass, Daphne

(b. 1980; Slytherin 1991)

Hogwarts student in Harry's year (OP31).

According to an early list of Harry's classmates that J.K. Rowling displayed during an interview (HPM), Daphne's name may originally have been Queenie Greengrass. If so (and this document can't really be considered canon), she is a Slytherin student from a pure-blood family (HPM).

greenhouses

At Hogwarts, these greenhouses are where Herbology classes are held; there are at least three, with plants of varying levels of danger (CS6).

Gregorovitch

(d. 2 September 1997)

European wand maker, a heavy-set man with white beard and hair (DH14). He made Krum's wand (GF18). At one time he owed the Elder Wand and bragged about it, but Grindelwald stole it from him in the early 1940s. Gregorovitch retired in the late 1980s (DH8).

Gregory the Smarmy

A medieval wizard who invented Gregory's Unctuous Unction (FW). There is a secret passage at Hogwarts located behind a statue of Gregory the Smarmy (PS9).

'smarmy' = Eng. 'smug, ingratiating, or false earnestness'

Gregory's Unctuous Unction

Potion which persuades the drinker that the giver is his or her very best friend. Invented by Gregory the Smarmy (FW).

The name of this potion is clever:

'unction' = Eng. 'an ointment', derived from a Latin term meaning 'to anoint with oil'

'unctuous' is derived figuratively from 'unction' and refers to being flattering and friendly in an oily, slimy sort of way

Grenouille

Character in the play 'Alas, I've Transfigured My Feet' by Malecrit.

'grenouille' = Fr. 'frog'

Greyback, Fenrir

Werewolf, low-level Death Eater. He killed for fun and especially enjoyed infecting children. Greyback was a follower of Voldemort since at least the 1970s, though he was in it for the access to victims, not for ideological reasons (HBP16, 27, DH23, 32, 36).

Fenrir comes from 'Fenriswolf,' ('Fenrisulv,' 'Fenrisulf'), the gigantic wolf of the God Loki in Scandinavian mythology.

Grey Lady, the

A tall, beautiful, but somewhat haughty-looking ghost, the ghost of Ravenclaw tower. Her real name was Helena Ravenclaw and she was the daughter of one of the Founders of Hogwarts. (PS12, DH31).

The name 'Grey Lady' is a term often used to refer to female ghosts. One such apparition, the Grey Lady of Rufford Old Hall, is the ghost of a young woman in a wedding dress who is said to be waiting in vain for the return of her betrothed who died in battle.

griffin

Strange creature with the front body of an eagle and hindquarters of a lion. There is a statue of a griffin in a corridor in Hogwarts, near a girls' bathroom (PS10). Godric Gryffindor, the founder of Gryffindor house, may be named for this beast. The griffin-shaped knocker on the door of Dumbledore's office (CS11) may be a reference to Gryffindor's name, assuming that Dumbledore was a Gryffindor.

Creatures resembling the griffin appear in various mythologies from around the world.

'gryphus' = L. 'hooked', probably a reference to its curved beak

Griffiths, Wilda

Outstanding Chaser who switched from the Harpies to Puddlemere United, much to the chagrin of Gwenog Jones, the amazingly talented but dangerous Captain of the Harpies (DP1, 2, 3).

Grim

The Grim is a ghostly image of a large dog-like beast; seeing one portends death. It is also one of the tea-leaf symbols which mean 'death' (PA6).

The Grim is based closely on the 'Church Grim' of British folklore. This spectral black dog would haunt churchyards to protect the church and the souls of those buried there from the devil.

Grimmauld Place

Muggle street in London on which Twelve Grimmauld Place is found (OP3). The dingy square is within about a mile of King's Cross Station (OP10) and a few Underground stops away from the Ministry of Magic and St. Mungo's Hospital (OP23). The Muggles living there have become used to the fact that apparently Number 11 and Number 13 are adjacent, with no Number 12 (OP3, 4).

The name 'Grimmauld Place' is a homophone for 'grim old place', especially since 'auld' is a Scottish word for 'old'. There is an additional play on words since it is the home of Sirius Black, who was mistaken for a Grim by Harry when they first encountered each other in Little Whinging (PA3).

Grindelwald, Gellert

(c.1883–1998)

A powerful Dark wizard. After expulsion from Durmstrang as a teenager, Grindelwald visited Britain, searching for the Deathly Hallows. There, Grindelwald and Dumbledore became friends, but the friendship ended abruptly (DH18). Grindelwald believed in Wizard supremacy 'For the Greater Good' of the world and tried to impose his rule on wizards and Muggles alike. He was finally defeated by Dumbledore in a spectacular duel in 1945 (PS6) and imprisoned in Nurmengard (DH18). In 1998, Grindelwald lied to Voldemort about ever having the Elder Wand, hoping to throw Voldemort off the trail (DH23). Perhaps in this small way, he showed remorse for the terrible things he had done (DH35).

'Grindelwald' is a small village in the Alps of Switzerland; the name could also refer to Grendel, the troll-like monster of the Anglo-Saxon epic Beowulf. *J.K. Rowling pronounces Grindelwald's name 'GRIN dell vald' (TLC).*

Grindylow

A pale green creature that lives in the weed beds on the bottom of lakes in Britain. It is also known as a water demon. Grindylows have long, brittle fingers which they use to grip their prey, sharp little horns, and green teeth. Lupin taught his third year students about them (PA8). Some grindylows appear to have been domesticated by merpeople (GF26).

The grindylow is a water creature from the folklore of Yorkshire. It's a type of bogeyman, a tale told to children to frighten them into not going near deep water.

Gringott

The goblin founder of Gringotts Wizarding Bank (FW).

Although the bank is named after the founder, it is not written with an apostrophe (as Gringott's), but without.

Gringotts Wizarding Bank

An imposing snow-white marble building in Diagon Alley, near its intersection with Knockturn Alley (CS4), Gringotts is the place where British witches and wizards store their money and other valuables in heavily-guarded vaults miles below ground. The centuries-old bank is run by goblins, and they alone know the secrets of the twisting underground passages and the enchantments and creatures in place to defend against intruders (PS5). (*See also* DH26).

J.K. Rowling said she created the name Gringotts by combining 'ingot', which is a bar of precious metal, with an aggressive sounding 'grrrr' (ITV).

Griphook

Goblin who operated the underground tram at Gringotts which takes wizards to their vaults (PS5). Several years later, having seen Harry's genuine care for house-elves and goblins even though they aren't wizards, Griphook agreed to help Harry, although his allegiance was always in some doubt (DH25, 26).

grooming charms

Minor spells for personal grooming. Examples include Parvati curling her eyelashes around her wand (OP27) and Molly Weasley's 'a proper haircuts', for which she uses her wand (GF5, DH7). Magic isn't the best choice for some grooming tasks, however. Eloise Midgen tried to curse her pimples off, but it didn't work out the way she intended. Madam Pomfrey did manage to reattach her nose, however (GF13).

Growth Charm

Spell to make things grow in size (OP31).

Grow-Your-Own-Warts kit

Harry once got a package of these in his Christmas crackers (PS12).

Grubbly-Plank, Wilhelmina

Substitute teacher who covered for Hagrid when he was indisposed after Christmas break (January 1995) and again when he was off negotiating with the giants (OP11); Grubbly-Plank knew a lot about unicorns and to Lavender Brown and others of Harry's year seemed to be a particularly good teacher compared to Hagrid, who devoted most their class time looking after Skrewts (GF24). She nursed Hedwig back to health at one point after the owl was injured delivering mail. Grubbly-Plank is an elderly witch with short-cropped hair who smokes a pipe (OP17).

Grunnings

A Muggle firm which makes drills. Vernon Dursley is a director of the company (PS2). As such he drives company cars (PA1) and entertains prospective clients in his home (CS2). His office is on the ninth floor and he sits with his back to the window and yells at people on the phone a lot (PA2).

Grunnion, Alberic

(1803-1882)

A wizard inventor, creator of the Dungbomb (FW, PS6).

Gryffindor, Godric

(c.900s)

One of the four Founders of Hogwarts over a thousand years ago. Gryffindor believed that anyone who showed magical ability should be allowed to attend Hogwarts. Gryffindor was from what is now the village of Godric's Hollow, which was named after him. He was the most accomplished dueller of his time and the magnificent Sword of Gryffindor was his, as was the Sorting Hat (DH15, 19, 25, 26).

Gryffindor House

One of the four houses of Hogwarts, valuing above all else loyalty, bravery, and chivalry (PS7, DH19). The head of Gryffindor is Professor McGonagall (PS8), and the house ghost is Nearly Headless Nick (PS7). Its shield is red and gold, and features a rearing lion (GF15). Gryffindor Quidditch teams are usually in the running for the Cup. Gryffindor has always produced strong leaders from its ranks, including Albus Dumbledore, the Weasley family, Hermione Granger, Harry Potter, and Neville Longbottom.

Gryffindor House common room

Located at the base of Gryffindor Tower, with the entrance on the seventh floor behind a large painting of a Fat Lady in a pink silk dress. The room is comfortable, with squashy armchairs, a fireplace, and tables (esp. PS7).

Gryffindor Tower

Harry's dormitory room is at the top (PS7, GF12) of this tower, which extends skyward from the House common room on the seventh floor.

Grymm, Malodora

A hag who used a sleeping potion to get what she wanted; for more details, see the Famous Wizard cards (FW).

The story of Malodora Grymm is a nod to the fairy tale 'Snow White', which was part of the collection of the Brothers Grimm, hence the last name 'Grymm'.

Gubraithian fire

Spell to make the target object burn forever (OP20).

The name comes from the Scottish phrase 'gu braith', meaning 'forever'.

Gudgeon, Davy

(Hogwarts student c. 1970s)

Foolhardy student who once tried to get past the Whomping Willow, nearly losing an eye (PA10).

'gudgeon' = Eng. 'a small freshwater fish used as bait; a gullible person'

Gudgeon, Galvin

The ineffectual Seeker for the Chudley Cannons (DP1).

Gudgeon, Gladys

Writes weekly fan-mail to Lockhart, even now, although he has no idea why she does (CS7, OP23).

Guffy, Elladora

Next-door neighbour to Ethelbart Mordaunt. Madam Guffy is fond of practical jokes and has been known on occasion to enchant Mordaunt's garden furniture (DP1).

Guide to Advanced Transfiguration

Cedric Diggory carried this in his book bag during his sixth year (GF20), which means both that Cedric was working toward a N.E.W.T. qualification in Transfiguration, and that this is the required textbook for sixth-year Transfiguration students.

Guide to Medieval Sorcery, A

One of the books that Harry, Ron, and Hermione examined while preparing for the second Triwizard task (GF26).

Guidelines on House-Elf Welfare

A wizard law that exists, but isn't enforced (JKR).

Guidelines for the Treatment of Non-Wizard Part-Humans

A Ministry policy which annoyed Percy (GF10).

Gulch, Zamira

Author of *Practical Household Magic*, who also writes for the *Daily Prophet* advice column (DP3).

The name comes from Elmira Gulch, the name of the Kansas alter ego of the Wicked Witch of the West in the film version of The Wizard of Oz.

Gulping Plimpies

Plimpies are a kind of magical fish.

Luna uses Gurdyroot to ward off the Gulping variety (HBP20).

Gumboil, Alastor
Employee in the Department of Magical Law Enforcement, to whom applicants for Hit Wizard positions need to apply. He works in Room 919 (DP2).

Gunhilda of Gorsemoor
Described on her Famous Wizard card as a 'one-eyed, hump-backed witch', Gunhilda was a healer known for developing a cure for Dragon Pox (FW). A statue of Gunhilda stands in the corridors of Hogwarts (PA10).

Gurdyroot
A green onion-like plant. Luna uses these to ward off Gulping Plimpies (HBP20). Her father makes a deep purple and unpleasant beverage from Gurdyroots to serve guests (DH20).

Gurg
The title for the leader of a Giant colony. The toughest, strongest Giant typically holds this title for life, but that might not be particularly long (OP20).

Gytrash
A huge, spectral hound that lives in forests (CS/g).
The Gytrash, in the form of a huge dog, horse, or mule, haunts solitary places and attempts to waylay travellers; it is found in the folklore of Northern England.

Hagrid, Rubeus

(b. 6 December 1928; Gryffindor 1940, expelled June 1943; Order of the Phoenix) A half-giant with shaggy hair and a 'wild, tangled beard' (PS1) who serves as the Keeper of Keys and Grounds, Gamekeeper, and Care of Magical Creatures professor at Hogwarts (PS4, PA6). He is excessively fond of 'interesting creatures' that anyone else would call fearsome monsters. Hagrid's appearance is very intimidating, but his disposition is kind (PA11). He lives in a hut on the Hogwarts grounds with his pet boarhound, Fang (PS8). The son of a wizard and a giantess (GF23), Hagrid tends to stick out (PS6) and has been subjected to much prejudice (GF24, OP15). Hagrid was fiercely loyal to Dumbledore, who has been heard to say that he 'would trust Hagrid with my life' (PS1). From the moment he was sent to retrieve Harry for his first year at Hogwarts, Hagrid and Harry Potter have been firm friends. Harry, Ron, and Hermione visit Hagrid's hut regularly while in school (PS8, etc.).

J.K. Rowling chose Hagrid's name because of an old English dialect word, 'meaning you'd had a bad night. Hagrid's a big drinker. He has a lot of bad nights' (Con).

'rubeus' = L. 'red'

'hagrid' = Eng. 'haggered, run-down', from the phrase 'hag-ridden' which referred to the superstition that nightmares were caused by a hag sitting on one's chest during the night.

Hagrid Sr.

(d. 1941 or 1942) The father of Rubeus Hagrid. He must have been an unusual man, since he married a giantess, Fridwulfa, and fathered a son by her. Fridwulfa left the family c. 1931 and Hagrid Sr. raised his son alone. He died during Rubeus's second year at Hogwarts (GF24).

hag

Magical being which appears to be an old woman. However, hags are less adept than witches at disguising themselves from Muggles (PA4, GF19). Hags are what one might refer to as 'fairy-tale witches'. They are wild in appearance and they have a reputation for eating children (DP1, FW), although this may not be true (JKR). Hags have only four toes on each foot (JKR).

hair-care products
Gilderoy Lockhart's secret ambition, according to his books, is 'to rid the world of evil and market his own line of hair care products' (CS6).

Hair-Loss Curse
A curse which features prominently in the book *Curses and Countercurses* (PS5).

Hair-Raising Potion
Ingredients include rat tails
Second-year potions students are assigned homework about this potion (CS13).

Hair-thickening Charm
A spell that affects hair, sometimes used as a grooming charm by witches (OP19).

'half-blood'
A witch or wizard with one wizarding parent but at least one Muggle parent or grandparent. Though the term can be somewhat disparaging, it includes most of the population of the Wizarding world (CS7, c.f. OP35).

Half-Blood Prince, The
A nickname used by some mysterious person who wrote notes in a Potions textbook many years ago. (HBP28).

Hall of Prophecy
A vast hall in the Department of Mysteries at the Ministry of Magic where records of prophecies are stored in glass balls on row upon row of towering shelves (OP34). Nobody may remove a prophecy from the shelf except one of the people who are the subjects of the prophecy (OP34). The Unspeakables — those witches and wizards who work in the Department of Mysteries — do not admit the existence of the room (HBP3).

Hallowe'en
An important holiday for wizards, as it is the one day they can 'let their hair down', so to speak (DP4). At Hogwarts it is celebrated with a feast, for which the Great Hall is elaborately decorated with bats, candles, and pumpkins (PA8). Hallowe'en has also been an eventful day in Harry's life (DH17, PS10, CS8, PA8, GF16).
The name is written 'Halloween' in the US editions of the books. The holiday probably originated in Britain with the

Celtic festival of autumn known as Samhain. On the evening of October 31, the barrier between the living and the dead was thought to disappear and celebrations were held to ward off or placate ghosts and evil spirits. The name comes from 'All-hallow-even', the name for the night in the Christian calendar before November 1, which was All Hallows' Day. Nowadays, Hallowe'en has become a holiday devoted to wearing costumes, often of witches, monsters, or ghosts, and of celebrating the darker, more macabre side of things. Part of the pleasure of reading J.K. Rowling's stories is the tongue-in-cheek assertion that many of the things which we find mysterious and a bit scary are actually real and even a bit mundane. Members of the Wizarding world enjoy Hallowe'en because it is the one day that they don't have to hide, when the barrier between the Muggle and Wizarding worlds disappears. Interestingly, the holiday is celebrated in the first four books but is completely ignored in the last three. This is one example of the huge shift between books one through four and books five through seven. Humongous pumpkins and ghostly 'formation flying' fit the whimsical overtones of the earlier novels a lot better than they do the darker plot which dominates the rest of the series.

Hampshire

A county in southern England. Location of the hamlet of Little Dropping — or at least it was until Archibald Alderton was there (FW).

Handbook of Do-It-Yourself Broom Care

Part of Hermione's present to Harry for his thirteenth birthday (PA1, 2).

Handbook of Hippogriff Psychology

Ron studied this book while preparing for an appeal for the Committee for the Disposal of Dangerous Creatures (PA15).

Hand of Glory

A withered hand which, when a candle is inserted into it, gives light only to the holder (CS4, HBP27).

J.K. Rowling didn't invent the Hand of Glory, although she modified it from its historical description. The object is first mentioned in tales from the 1400s, although the name 'Hand of Glory' isn't used for it until 1707. A Hand of Glory is a mummified hand of a hanged criminal turned into a candle by a complicated procedure. The Hand was a thieves' amulet, a tool which when lit would render the inhabitants of a house unconscious so that robbing them would be easy.

Hanged Man, The

The village pub in Little Hangleton, where villagers gathered to gossip about the Riddle family (GF1).

The Hanged Man is the name of a card found in a Tarot fortune-telling deck. It signifies that a questioner is trapped or stuck in a position, perhaps between opposites. In this case, since nothing can be proven one way or another, Frank Bryce is the one trapped, always suspected of murders he didn't commit.

Harkiss, Ciceron

Gave Ambrosius Flume (owner of Honeydukes) his first job. Favourite student of Horace Slughorn, and probably a member of the Slug Club (HBP4).

Harper

(Slytherin, mid-1990s; Quidditch Chaser 1996 —1997)

Substitute Chaser for the Slytherin Quidditch team after Vaisey was injured during a practice session (HBP14).

Harris, Warty

A wizard whose toads were stolen by someone named Will, and then again by Mundungus Fletcher, who sold them back to Warty (OP5).

The name is no doubt a connection to the commonly held (but false) belief that handling toads causes warts.

hat, cursed

Hat that makes the wearer's ears shrivel. Bill Weasley once had a pen-friend from Brazil who was so offended when Bill couldn't travel all the way to South America for a visit that he sent Bill one of these hats (GF7).

Hate Potion

Potion which reveals to the person drinking it the worst aspects of another person. This potion is recommended by the *Daily Prophet*'s advice columnists to help witches and wizards get over emotional attachments to people who don't love them back (DP3).

Hawkshead Attacking Formation

A Quidditch formation with three Chasers together, one in the centre and slightly ahead of the other two (GF8).

hawthorn

A wand wood. Draco Malfoy's wand is made of hawthorn (DH24).

Draco's birthday, 5 June, falls within Huath, the month in the Celtic lunar calendar which is represented by the hawthorn tree. The lore associated with hawthorn is contradictory: it represented hope and marriage to the ancient Greeks and Romans, but to the Celts it represented witchcraft and bad luck. The hawthorn, after all, has both beautiful flowers and very sharp thorns. In folklore, the hawthorn tree is closely associated with fairies. In fact, a solitary hawthorn is said to be a marker pointing to the fairy realms, while a grove which includes hawthorns, oak, and ash trees are thought to be where fairies will be visible to normal humans. According to tradition, wand wood must be taken from a hawthorn only on Beltane, a holiday celebrated in mid-May.

Head Boy and Girl

Seventh-year Hogwarts students selected each year to hold a position of authority in the school, helping with discipline and maintaining order. Those who have held the position include Albus Dumbledore (DH18), Tom Riddle (HBP20), James and Lily Potter (PS4), Bill Weasley (PS12, OP9), and Percy Weasley (PA1).

The Head Boy and Girl are typically chosen from the Prefects. How James Potter became Head Boy is a mystery, then, since he was never a Prefect. However, a possible solution to this turned up in Half-Blood Prince. James was the Captain of Quidditch, and when Harry is given that post in his sixth year, Hermione exclaims that he is then on equal status with the Prefects.

Head Juggling and Head Polo

Two sporting activities engaged in by members of the Headless Hunt, using their severed heads as balls (CS8).

Headless Hunt

A group of ghosts who died by decapitation, and who now carry their heads under their arms as they ride ghostly horses. Nearly Headless Nick longed to be part of the Hunt, but the leader, Sir Patrick Delaney-Podmore, wouldn't allow it because Nick's head wasn't completely severed (CS8, also DH31).

Tales of a ghostly hunting party riding through the sky or along deserted moors abound in the folklore of Northern Europe. Frequently, these hunts are associated with thunderstorms and death. One tale from Devon tells of a drunken farmer who encountered the Hunt while on his way home in a thunderstorm, only to discover that they had been riding off with the body of his son who had died during the storm.

Headmaster/Headmistress

The chief administrator of Hogwarts School of Witchcraft and Wizardry carries the title of Headmaster or Headmistress. This person carries a lot of status in the Wizarding community in that he or she influences most young witches and wizards from ages eleven through seventeen. Recent Heads of Hogwarts include Albus Dumbledore (c. 1956–1997), Dolores Umbridge (1996), and Severus Snape (1997-1998) (PS4, OP28, DH12).

Headmaster's office and residence
A large circular room where the Headmaster or Headmistress lives. The entrance on the seventh floor is guarded by a statue of a gargoyle which demands a password. From there a spiral stone staircase moves upward like an escalator to a polished oak door (CS11). The walls are covered with portraits of previous Headmasters and Headmistresses which offer advice to the current Head (GF30, DH15). In the centre of the room is a large claw-footed desk (CS12). During Dumbledore's tenure, the room contained the Pensieve, the Sorting Hat, the Sword of Gryffindor, and Fawkes the Phoenix as well as a collection of strange magical devices (e.g., OP22).

Healers
The title for witches and wizards who work at St. Mungo's hospital, similar to Muggle doctors and nurses (OP22).

Healer's Helpmate, The
Book of first aid, home remedies, and cures. Includes a chapter on 'Bruises,

Cuts, and Abrasions' which Mrs Weasley consulted while trying to heal a black eye Hermione had received from a rather unusual telescope (HBP5).

Hebridean Black
A dragon species native to the Hebrides Islands on the coast of Scotland (PS14).

Hedwig
d. 27 July 1997
A large female snowy owl with amber eyes, purchased by Hagrid at Eeylops Owl Emporium as a present for Harry's eleventh birthday (PS5). Harry found the name in his book *A History of Magic* (PS6) and came to regard her as a companion and friend (DH5). Hedwig was unusually intelligent even for a post owl, and often communicated her feelings toward Harry with affectionate nips of her beak or reproachful looks (e.g. GF3).

Heir of Slytherin
According to legend, Slytherin created a chamber under the school which contained a monster only his direct heir could control. Years later, everyone wondered who the Heir of Slytherin might really be. Harry was suspected for a while (CS17).

Heliopath

One of Luna Lovegood's imaginary creatures, a large flaming creature that runs across the ground and burns everything in its path. Luna believed during Harry's fifth year that then-Minister for Magic Cornelius Fudge had an army of Heliopaths at his command (OP17). 'helios' = Gr. 'the sun' + '-path' = Gr. 'feeling'

Hengist of Upper Barnton

Giant killed by the famous giant-slayer Gifford Ollerton in the 15th century (FW).

Hengist of Woodcroft

The founder of Hogsmeade village; for more information, see the Famous Wizard cards (FW).

heptomology

A branch of Divination on which Umbridge quizzed Trelawney during her evaluation (OP25). *This word was invented by J.K. Rowling, unlike some of the other Divination forms which are mentioned in the books (e.g. ornithomancy). The word is derived from 'hept-', a Greek prefix meaning the number seven. In the Potter universe, the number seven 'the most powerfully magical number' (HBP23), which is why Tom Riddle wanted to split his soul into* seven pieces. *Bridget Wenlock achieved fame as an Arithmancer for discovering the magical properties of the number seven (FW), so perhaps she could be said to have practiced heptomology. In an interesting side note, while there are runes for all the other numerals, there is none for the number seven because it hasn't been discovered yet (JKR).*

Herbology

The study of plants, both magical and common. Some plants are studied because they are essentially magical creatures, others because they are used for potion-making (PS8). During Harry's time, Hogwarts Herbology classes are taught in the greenhouses by Pomona Sprout (PS8, CS6, etc.).

Hereward

Son of Godelot who took the Elder Wand from him (DH21).

Hermes

Owl belonging to Percy Weasley, which he received for becoming a Gryffindor prefect (PS6). Percy used him for sending personal correspondence, such as letters to Penelope Clearwater (CS3), and letters to his youngest brother Ron (GF, OP14). *Hermes is a figure from Greek mythology. He is the god of travellers, thieves, athletics (particularly* running), and literature. He served as the messenger to the gods, wearing a pair of winged sandals to move between the realms of the gods and mortals on earth.

Herpo the Foul

The first great Dark wizard; he lived in ancient Greece. Herpo was the first known creator of a basilisk (FW) and the inventor of the Horcrux (PC-JKR1).

'herp-' from 'herpeton' = Gr. lizard, serpent, so J.K. Rowling is connecting the serpent symbol with the Dark Side already back in the ancient history of the Wizarding world.

'He-Who-Must-Not-Be-Named'

After Voldemort came to power in the 1970s, wizards were so terrified of him and his Death Eaters that they refused to say his name, referring to him instead as 'He-Who-Must-Not-be-Named' or 'You-Know-Who' (PS4 etc.). This later took on added significance when a Taboo was placed on Voldemort's name (DH20).

In some traditions, a person's true name is considered something personal, almost sacred, and it is never shared for fear that it could be used in a magical attack. J.K. Rowling discussed this in an interview (TLC) where she also mentioned the infamous Kray brothers, gangsters who held sway over London's East End during the 1950s and 1960s. They instilled such fear in people that no one dared to speak their name for fear of violent reprisals.

hex-deflection

Hex-deflection was included in Harry's fourth-year Defence Against the Dark Arts classes (GF28).

Hiccough Sweet

A kind of sweet sold at Zonko's Joke Shop (PA14).

US spelling: 'Hiccup'

Hiccoughing Solution

Malfoy made this in sixth-year Potions for an assignment to make 'something amusing', but Slughorn pronounced it as merely passable (HBP22).

US spelling: 'Hiccupping'

Higgs, Bertie

Hunting mate of Cormack McLaggen's uncle Tiberius, along with Rufus Scrimgeour (so Higgs is probably someone of some importance) (HBP7).

Higgs, Terence

(Slytherin 1985; Quidditch Seeker c. 1991–1992)

The Slytherin Quidditch Seeker during the 1991-92 school year (PS11); he was replaced by Draco Malfoy the following school year (CS7).

High Street

The main street of a village where most of the shops are located. Hogsmeade has a High Street, but also a number of side streets where smaller or less reputable shops are to be found (the Hog's Head, for example) (PA14).

High Table

A long table standing on a raised platform at the top of the Great Hall. This is where the teachers sit, visible to the rest of the school (PS7 etc.).

hinkypunk

A little one-legged creature with the appearance of being made of smoke; the hinkypunk carries a light with which it lures travellers into bogs (PA10).

'Hinky punk' is a Somerset and Devon name for the will-o'-the-wisp, ghostly lights sometimes seen over bogs at night. Since this creature is studied in Defence Against the Dark Arts class, we can assume that it is not simply a magical creature but one which actively seeks to harm.

hippogriff

A flying creature with the head, wings, and forelegs of a giant eagle and the body (including hind legs and tail) of a horse. The eyes are orange, but individual hippogriff colours vary as those of mundane horses do. An adult hippogriff's wingspan is approximately twenty-four feet (PA6). To approach a hippogriff, one should bow first; if the animal bows in return, it can be touched and even ridden. Hogwarts third-years learned about them in Care of Magical Creatures class, with the dozen or so hippogriffs which live in the Forbidden Forest (PA6).

The hippogriff is a legendary creature born of the union of a horse and a gryphon. Since horses are the natural prey of gryphons, the fact that they would mate makes the hippogriff a symbol of love and impossibility.

Hipworth, Glover

(1742–1805)

Wizard inventor who created Pepperup Potion, which cures common colds (FW).

Glover's last name suggests 'rose hips', an herbal remedy high in vitamin C, a vitamin commonly thought to help prevent the common cold.

'His Eyes Are as Green As A Fresh Pickled Toad'

Valentine's Day poem written to Harry Potter by Ginny Weasley in 1993 (CS13).

History of Magic

Class at Hogwarts taught by Professor Binns, a ghost. Binns gives extremely boring lectures on various aspects of magical history. However, the boredom is due to Binns' teaching style, not the material itself, which tends to emphasize vicious goblin riots and giant wars (PS8). Harry barely even opened the class textbook (DH16). At one point during the 1992-1993 school year, Hermione managed to get Binns talking about the Chamber of Secrets, but he soon lapsed back into his usual boring style after reminding her that he deals in 'facts . . . not myths and legends' (CS9).

It's too bad, really, since a surprising number of those myths and legends turned out to be true.

History of Magic, A
by Bathilda Bagshot

This is a required textbook for first-years (PS5), and appears to be used by second- and third-years as well in History of Magic (PA1). It does not cover anything later than the end of the 19th century (DH16). Harry didn't read this book very attentively (DH16), but he did discover the name 'Hedwig' there (PS6).

Hitchens, Bob

A Muggle who married Isla Black; she was consequently blasted off the Black Family Tree (BFT).

Hit Wizards

The Department of Magical Law Enforcement maintains squads of trained Hit Wizards whose job it is to capture dangerous wizarding criminals. A group of these Hit Wizards captured Sirius Black after he supposedly killed Peter Pettigrew (PA10). The job requires five O.W.L.s, including Defence Against the Dark Arts, and pays 700 Galleons a month — though it also comes with a private bed at St. Mungo's Hospital (DP2).

Hobday family

A birth announcement for Egmont Elvert Hobday was posted in the *Daily Prophet*, saying he'd been born November 30 to Hilliard and Violetta Hobday (DP2).

Hobday, Oakden

This name appears (along with Mylor Sylvanus) on an early planning chart for Order of the Phoenix *in a list as the fifth of the Defence against the Dark Arts Professors. Moody is not mentioned (JKR).*

Hobgoblins, the

A rock band, now disbanded, which included musician Stubby Boardman. The band broke up in 1980 after Boardman was hit in the ear by a turnip at a concert in Little Norton Church Hall (OP10).

Hobgoblins in folktales are typically friendly versions of goblins, sometimes suggesting a superficial or imagined fear.

Hodrod the Horny-Handed

Notorious goblin activist who shrank three wizards and attempted to squish them (DP3).

Hog's Head, the

A pub on a side street in Hogsmeade, known for its cheapness and 'interesting' clientele (OP37). Aberforth Dumbledore has been the bartender for over twenty years (OP17, DH28). The bar is small and filthy, and smells strongly of goats (OP16).

Hogsmeade

The only entirely Wizarding village in Britain. It's a picturesque village of little thatched cottages and shops with a long, storied history (PA5). According to tradition, Hogsmeade was founded by Hengist of Woodcroft, who was fleeing persecution by Muggles (FW). One of the Goblin Rebellions took place in the area in 1612 (PA5). The citizens of Hogsmeade took part in another battle in May 1998 when they rallied to the defence of Hogwarts castle (DH36). Students of third year and above may visit Hogsmeade on selected weekends if they have a signed permission form (PA1). During the holiday season, enchanted candles hang in the trees (PA10).

The name: 'hog' from the same source as Hogwarts, most likely, which according to legend is from a dream in which Rowena Ravenclaw saw a warty hog leading her to the cliff by the lake where the castle was eventually built (JKR) + 'meade' = Brit. 'meadow'.

Hogsmeade Station

A station with a fairly small platform where the Hogwarts Express ends its journey north from King's Cross. It is located near the lake and a small boat landing. A road extends from the train station around the lake to Hogwarts Castle (PS6, PA5, GF11). The station is actually quite a distance from the town itself, being on the opposite side of the Hogwarts grounds (PA/dvd).

Hogwarts castle

A huge magical castle set on a cliff overlooking a lake (PS6) in the highlands of Scotland (BN2). The main structure is eight stories tall, with towers rising above that. The castle contains classrooms, a huge Entrance Hall with a majestic marble staircase, a Great Hall, a library, a hospital wing, and many other rooms and corridors. Beneath the castle are vast dungeons, in which are located the cold, dark Potions classroom and the Slytherin common room. Secret passageways, hidden corridors, strange staircases and doors, and unexpected rooms make navigating the castle a challenge (esp. PS8). However, clever students soon learn their own shortcuts. Secret passages also lead out of the castle, if one is lucky enough to locate an entrance (esp. PA10). However, no one knows all the secrets of the ancient building (GF23). The grounds of the castle include a large lake, a forest, a Quidditch pitch, a curious old animated tree called a Whomping Willow (CS5), and greenhouses in which Herbology classes take place (PS8, etc.). Hogwarts castle is hidden from Muggle eyes by a number of enchantments. Muggles, should they wander near, will see only an old ruin with signs warning them to keep out (SN). Other spells protect the castle from magical intrusion; for example, it is impossible to Apparate anywhere on the Hogwarts grounds (HBP4).

According to J.K. Rowling, she borrowed the name for the school from a variety of flower she saw in Kew Gardens (SMH). She then decided, by way of explanation within the story, that Rowena Ravenclaw dreamed of a warty hog leading her to the place near the lake where Hogwarts was eventually founded (JKR).

Hogwarts: A History

A famous book about Hogwarts school, over a thousand pages long. Discusses the manner in which Hogwarts is hidden from Muggles (GF11) and describes the enchanted ceiling of the Great Hall (PS7), but surprisingly never mentions the Hogwarts house-elves (GF15, OP17, 23). Like *A History of Magic*, it is a book which Ron and Harry never got around to reading. *The name of this book was slightly different in earlier editions of the books, when the colon was written as a comma, thus:* Hogwarts, A History.

Hogwarts Express

A passenger train which makes a run on 1 September between King's Cross Station, London, and Hogsmeade Station, leaving at 11am from Platform Nine and Three Quarters, King's Cross, and arriving at Hogsmeade Station in the early evening (PS6); it makes similar runs for Christmas, Easter, and the summer holidays (PS17, CS12). There is no dining service, but a witch pushes a trolley through the train midway through the trip, selling various sweets and iced pumpkin juice (PS6). There are usually no adults aboard the Hogwarts Express except the driver and the witch with the trolley (PA5).

Hogwarts High Inquisitor
In response to concerns about what was going on at Hogwarts, and more specifically to monitor Albus Dumbledore, Cornelius Fudge on 8 September 1995 passed Educational Decree 23 making Dolores Umbridge the first ever 'Hogwarts High Inquisitor'. She was given the power to oversee, inspect, and if she chose, dismiss other teachers (OP15, 26, 31).

Hogwarts schedule
The Hogwarts school year begins on 1 September with the Welcoming Feast and finishes towards the end of June with the Leaving Feast, at which the House Cup is awarded to the house which has accumulated the most House Points. The first term ends in December with two weeks off for Christmas and the second with a two-week Easter holiday around the first of April. The summer term takes up the rest of the school year. Exams are held at the be-

ginning of June (e.g., PS5, 7, 12, 17, PA16, HBP29).

Hogwarts School of Witchcraft and Wizardry
Hogwarts School, located in Hogwarts Castle (q.v.), was begun over a thousand years ago by the four Founders, Rowena Ravenclaw, Helga Hufflepuff, Salazar Slytherin, and Godric Gryffindor, great witches and wizards of that age who wanted a place where they could train young people to use their magic wisely (CS9). The students at Hogwarts are Sorted into one of four houses. These houses vie for house points and compete on the Quidditch field (esp. PS7). Students attend Hogwarts for seven years, beginning when they are eleven and leaving when they are seventeen and of age, at which point they are considered to be fully trained.

Hogwarts school song
When in a particularly festive mood Dumbledore directs the school song at the end of the start-of-term feast (JKR). The rest of the staff does not appear to share Dumbledore's delight in this little ritual, but he conducts the singing with gusto and even gets a bit misty at the end of it (PS7). Dumbledore only called for the song to be sung when things seemed to be going well (JKR).

Hokey

A tiny, ancient female house-elf who was bound to serve Hepzibah Smith. Tom Riddle framed Hokey for the death of her mistress by modifying her memory so she believed she accidentally poisoned Hepzibah's cocoa (HBP20).

'Hold your hippogriffs!'

A saying akin to the Muggle phrase 'hold your horses!' (OP20).

Holidays With Hags

by Gilderoy Lockhart

One of the many required textbooks for Defence Against the Dark Arts in Harry's second year (CS4), filled with lies about wonderful things Lockhart had done (CS16).

holly

A wand wood, used to make Harry's wand (PS5).

Holly was originally associated with the winter holidays such as Saturnalia and Christmas because it symbolised renewal and resurrection in the darkest months of the year. J.K. Rowling had decided on a holly wand for Harry before realising that in the Celtic tree calendar, holly was assigned to July 8 — August 4, which includes his birthday (JKR). In Celtic, lore, holly is a symbol of good fortune.

The wood of holly is white in colour and has a heavy, solid feel.

Holyhead Harpies

The only all-witch Quidditch team in the British and Irish Quidditch League, famously captained by the fiery Gwenog Jones (HBP4, DP). Ginny Weasley played for the Harpies after leaving Hogwarts (BLC).

Home Life and Social Habits of British Muggles

by Wilhelm Wigworthy

A required textbook for third-year Muggle Studies (PA13).

Homenum revelio

(HOM-eh-num reh-VEL-ee-oh)

A spell that reveals human presence; for example, casting it on a house can tell the caster whether anyone is in that house (DH9). When this spell is cast, a person it touches feels something swooping low overhead (DH21).

'homoinis' = L. 'human being' + 'revelo' = L. 'to unveil, uncover'

Homorphus Charm

Lockhart supposedly used this charm to defeat the Wagga Wagga werewolf and demonstrated the feat in Defence Against the Dark Arts, using students to act it out (CS10).

'*homo*' = L. *man* + '*morph*' = *shortened from* '*metamorphose*' *Eng. to change shape. Given the etymology, we can assume that it's designed to be used against werewolves. It's uncertain what the effect of this spell is, however, since lycanthropy is not curable in the Potter universe.*

Honeydukes
Hogsmeade sweetshop, owned by Ambrosius Flume (HBP4) and his wife, who live over the shop; an entrance to one of the secret tunnels from Hogwarts is in the cellar under a trapdoor (PA10). Honeydukes sells a wide variety of magical sweets as well as fudge and enormous blocks of chocolate made on the premises (PA8, GF28).

honking daffodils
Professor Sprout has some of these, which Lavender Brown mentions that she likes a lot less than normal daffodils (OP27).

Hooch, Rolanda
Teaches flying lessons (on broomsticks) to first-years at Hogwarts, and referees most inter-House Quidditch matches. She has short, grey hair and yellow eyes (PS9). She is an enthusiastic expert on racing brooms. Madam Hooch mentioned that she first learned to fly on a Silver Arrow (PA13).

Hookum, Daisy
(b. 1962)
Wrote bestseller *My Life as a Muggle*, after giving up magic for a year (JKR).

Hooper, Geoffrey
(b. 1983; Gryffindor, 1994)
Tried out for Gryffindor Keeper in autumn 1995 and flew better than Ron Weasley, but was rejected because Angelina said he was a 'real whiner' (OP13).

Hopkins, Wayne
(b. 1980; Hufflepuff, 1991)
Wayne's name appears in the draft of the class list of Harry's year that J.K. Rowling displayed during the 'Harry Potter and Me' TV interview (HPM). He is a half-blood. Wayne has never appeared in the canon, but his name is listed here because he existed in early plans for the books.

Hopkirk, Mafalda
A little grey-haired witch who works at the Ministry of Magic. She is responsible for sending warnings from the Improper Use of Magic Office when underage magic is detected (CS2, OP2, also DH12, 13).

Horcrux
An object within which a wizard hides a piece of his soul (esp. HBP23, JKR).

This is the Darkest of magic (PC-JKR1) and can only be performed after a wizard splits his soul by committing murder, an act of pure evil. A Horcrux protects the bit of soul encased within from anything that might happen to a wizard's body. Once a Horcrux has been created, the wizard who made it cannot be killed until the object is destroyed (HBP23). Herpo the Foul, an ancient Greek Dark wizard, created the first Horcrux (PC-JKR1). Only rare, very powerful magic can destroy Horcruxes, such as basilisk venom (DH6) or Fiendfyre (DH31).

Horcruxes, Voldemort's

Obsessed with avoiding death from a young age, Tom Marvolo Riddle learned to create Horcruxes and set out to make six, giving himself a seven-part soul. For each of his Horcruxes he chose an item of some significance (HBP23).

Interestingly, each of Voldemort's Horcruxes was destroyed by a different person.

horklump

A magical garden pest (JKR).

hornbeam

A wand wood, used by Gregorovitch to make Viktor Krum's wand (GF18).

The wood of the hornbeam is particularly hard. It is sometimes called 'ironwood'.

Hornby

Brother of Olive Hornby. Moaning Myrtle haunted his wedding back in the 1940s (GF25).

Hornby, Olive

(Hogwarts student, early 1940s)

Teased Myrtle about her glasses, but regretted it later (CS16).

horned toads

Horned toads are really lizards, and very fearsome-looking lizards at that. Neville once had to disembowel an entire barrel full of horned toads while in detention with Snape (GF14).

Poor Neville had quite an evening, one would guess. One can't help but wonder why anyone would need hundreds of dead lizards, or indeed where Snape would have even found an entire barrel full of them, since they're native to North American deserts and their population is in decline (and are considered endangered in Texas). The callous way the Wizarding world deals with animals can be very disturbing.

Horn Tongue

A spell listed in *Basic Hexes for the Busy and Vexed*. Harry came across it while searching for a spell to use on his dragon, but decided it would just give the dragon one more weapon (GF20).

horses, flying

Twelve gigantic flying horses pull the Beauxbatons carriage as it flies through the sky. These magnificent animals are very powerful and require 'forceful handling'. Hagrid was up to the task (GF15). (*See also* THESTRAL; *c.f.* HIPPOGRIFF.)

Pegasus was the winged horse of Greek mythology. He was the son of Poseidon. The hero Bellerophon captured Pegasus with a golden bridle and rode him into battle against the Chimera and the Amazons. Pegasus married Euippe and their offspring were the ancestors of all other flying horses.

hospital wing

Hogwarts castle includes a hospital wing where injured or ill students are cared for by Madame Pomfrey, the school matron (nurse). The hospital wing includes a ward with a number of beds and an office for Pomfrey (PS17 etc.). If a patient requires a higher level of care than can be provided in the hospital wing, they are moved to St. Mungo's hospital (HBP13, OP32).

hot air charm

Hermione used this charm, which involves a complicated wand motion, to melt snow and dry her snow-covered robes (OP21).

hourglasses

Four giant hourglasses, one for each house, stand opposite the main doors in Hogwarts' Entrance Hall (PS15). Each uses gemstones of the house colour to track house points (OP28). Gryffindor's is filled with rubies, Ravenclaw's with sapphires (OP38), and Slytherin's with emeralds (DH32).

The gems used for Hufflepuff are not identified in the books.

Houses (Hogwarts)

Students at Hogwarts are grouped into four houses: Gryffindor, Ravenclaw, Hufflepuff, and Slytherin, each named for one of the founders of the school. Each student attends classes and spends free time with other students in his or her house. The houses compete each year for the House Cup and the Quidditch Cup (e.g., PS7). Each house also has its own common room and dormitories. In addition to the headmaster of Hogwarts, each house has a head of house, a resident ghost, and an animal mascot.

See entries for the individual houses for more information.

House Cup

Awarded to the house that wins the House Championship, determined by which has accumulated the most

House Points through the year (PS7). The Cup is presented at the Leaving Feast (PS17, CS18, PA22).

house-elves

Small humanoid creatures with large floppy or pointed ears and enormous eyes. House-elves are 'bound' to a wealthy Wizarding house and family, serving as slaves until they die. House-elves are happy with this arrangement and consider it a matter of pride that they serve faithfully and do not betray their families. House-elves wear no clothing (and they would consider it dishonourable to do so); instead, they cover themselves in towels, tea cosies, or pillowcases. If their owner gives them clothing, they break the 'enslavement' and the house-elf is free. For most house-elves, this would be the ultimate insult and they would be shamed forever (esp. CS3).

house-elves, Hogwarts

There are over a hundred house-elves at Hogwarts, the largest number in any dwelling in Britain (GF12). They lay the fires, do the laundry, light the lamps, and perform countless other such tasks. The house-elves are also the chefs of the castle and they create wonderful meals in the huge kitchens (GF12, 21). Helga Hufflepuff origi-

nally made these arrangements because she knew that house-elves who worked at Hogwarts would be treated well and not abused (PC-JKR1).

house points

Points used to reward or punish the behaviour of students. Points are accumulated over the course of the school year, at the end of which a House Cup is awarded to the house with the most. Giant hourglasses in the entrance hall record the points for all to see; as a teacher speaks the words awarding or deducting points, the appropriate hourglasses are automatically updated (PS15, OP28, 38). The number of points for various infractions is random and subject to the capriciousness of the teacher, making the contest almost meaningless. Points scored on the Quidditch pitch also count toward the house points (PA22).

Hover Charm

Makes an object float in the air (CS2, DH17).

Howler

A nasty letter sent to tell someone off. It arrives in a red envelope, smoking slightly, and if it is not opened immediately it explodes. Upon opening, the Howler screams at the recipient in a voice magically magnified for maximum effect (CS6).

Hubbard, Old Mother

Old Mother Hubbard was a medieval hag who lured stray animals into her home and starved them to death (FW).

This character is based on the nursery rhyme of the same name: 'Old Mother Hubbard went to the cupboard/To get her poor dog a bone/But when she got there the cupboard was bare/And so the poor dog had none.'

Hufflepuff, Helga

(c. 900s)

One of the four founders of Hogwarts, from 'valley broad' (GF12). Hufflepuff was known for bringing together a wide variety of people in the founding of Hogwarts (FW), and valued hard work and fair play (PS7). Hufflepuff was especially adept at cooking and various food-related charms, originating many recipes still served at Hogwarts feasts today (JKR). Hufflepuff arranged for the house-elves of Hogwarts to be treated kindly and not abused. This was enlightened behaviour for that time (PC-JKR1).

Although by no means conclusive, the reference from the Sorting Hat's song might indicate that Hufflepuff was Welsh. The

term 'The Valleys' commonly refers to a populous region of South Wales.

Hufflepuff House

One of the four houses of Hogwarts, valuing above all else loyalty and hard work (PS7, GF16). The head of Hufflepuff is Professor Pomona Sprout (GF36), and the house ghost is the Fat Friar (CS8). Its shield is yellow and black, and features a badger (GF15). According to Hagrid, 'everyone says Hufflepuffs are a lot o' duffers' (PS5); however, Hufflepuff has produced many brave, heroic witches and wizards, including Cedric Diggory (GF37) and Nymphadora Tonks (JKR).

Hufflepuff House common room

A 'cosy and welcoming place', the Hufflepuff common room is located near the kitchens. It is accessed through a still-life painting, and features underground tunnels leading to the dormitories. The doors are round (BLC).

The round doors and burrow-like architecture, not to mention the sense of comfort and hospitality, are suggestive of Hobbit houses in The Lord of the Rings *and* The Hobbit *by J.R.R. Tolkien.*

Hufflepuff's Cup

An ancient relic once owned by Helga Hufflepuff, a small golden cup with two handles and with a badger engraved on it. It had been in Hepzebah Smith's family for generations (HBP20, DH26).

humpbacked witch statue

This statue on the third floor of Hogwarts masks a secret passageway out of the school, labelled on the Marauder's Map (PA10). This statue is probably of Gunhilda of Gorsemoor (FW).

Hungarian Horntail

A particularly nasty species of dragon, native to Hungary and sporting a distinctive spiked tail (GF20).

Hungary

Country in Eastern Europe. In addition to being home to the Hungarian Horntail dragon, Hungary has a national Gobstones team which was beaten by Wales. The *Daily Prophet* didn't cover the match (DP1).

Hurling Hex

A nasty kind of hex that can be placed on a broom (PA12).

Hurtz, Grizel

The 'agony aunt' of the *Daily Prophet* (DP3).

The term 'agony aunt' refers to a person who writes an advice column about relationships. In this case, the last name of the 'agony aunt' is particularly appropriate.

hut, Hagrid's

A wooden hut near the Forbidden Forest. The hut is a single room with a table, fireplace, bed, chest, and a basket for Fang, Hagrid's pet boarhound (CS7, OP20). A variety of objects, from cured hams (GF16) to unicorn tail hairs (HBP22) can be found hanging from the rafters. It was a place that Harry, Ron, and Hermione visited frequently while at Hogwarts, where they often kept Hagrid company and ate very sticky treacle fudge (CS8). (*See also* HBP28).

Hut-on-the-Rock

A tiny, broken-down shack on a rock in the sea, some distance from but within sight of shore. The shack smelled strongly of seaweed, and had gaps in the walls (PS3, 4).

Hydra

An ancient rune symbolising the number nine, represented by the nine heads of the Hydra. A picture can be found in *Ancient Runes Made Easy* (JKR).

ζ

Ice Mice

A sweet sold at Honeydukes (PA10).

Ilfracombe Incident

Incident in the seaside town of Ilfracombe in 1932, in which a Welsh Green dragon descended on a beach full of Muggle holidaymakers. Tilly Toke and her family happened to be there, and cast the largest Mass Memory Charm of this century (FW).

Ilkley Moor

A moorland located northwest of Leeds in Yorkshire, the location of a twelfth-century Quidditch pitch. This stadium also recently hosted a match between Puddlemere United and the Holyhead Harpies. With bad feelings between the two teams threatening to result in violence, the Ministry of Magic took fans' wands at the gate (DP3); in spite of precautions, the match ended in riots (DP3).

Imago, Inigo

Author of *The Dream Oracle*, a text that Trelawney uses in her fifth year Divination classes (OP12, 13).

'inigo' = uncertain origin (but immediately makes us think of Inigo Montoya from The Princess Bride) + 'imago' = L. 'image'

Impedimenta

(im-ped-ih-MEN-tah)

'Impediment Curse', 'Impediment Jinx', 'Blocking Jinx'

This very useful and much-used spell stops an object or slows it down (e.g., OP21).

'impedimentum' = L. 'hindrance'

Impediment Jinx/Curse

See IMPEDIMENTA.

Imperio

(im-PAIR-ee-oh)

'Imperius Curse'

One of the Unforgivable Curses, causes the victim to be completely under the command of the caster, who can make the victim do anything the caster wishes (GF14, etc.). A person who has had an Imperius Charm placed on them is said to have been Imperiused

(DH5). The spell can be resisted, but doing so is very difficult (GF15).

'impero' = L. 'order, govern, command'

'Imperius Curse'

See IMPERIO.

Imperturbable Charm

A spell which creates a magical barrier. When placed on a door, for example, the charm makes it impossible to listen through it to what's being said on the other side (OP4).

'imperturbable' = Eng. 'not easily disturbed', from 'im-' = prefix from L. meaning 'not' + 'perturbo' = L. 'disturb'

Impervius

(im-PER-vee-us)

Hermione used this spell to make Harry's glasses repel water during a rainy Quidditch match (PA9).

'im-' = prefix from L. meaning 'not' + 'pervius' = L. 'letting things through'

Important Modern Magical Discoveries

Nicolas Flamel isn't mentioned in this book (PS12).

Improper Use of Magic Office

An office located on the second level of the Ministry of Magic (OP7) that, among other things, enforces the De-

cree for the Restriction of Underage Wizardry (CS2) and registers Animagi (GF26). Cornelius Fudge's irresponsible nephew, Rufus Fudge, worked for this office but got caught in a scandal when he made a Muggle tube train vanish to see how long it would take the Muggles to notice (DP2).

Inanimatus Conjurus

(in-ahn-i-MAH-tus kon-JU-ris)

Fifth-year Transfiguration students had to do an essay on this spell for homework (OP14). The meaning suggests that it involves conjuring up non-living objects.

'in' = L. 'against' + 'anima' = L. 'breath, living' + 'conjure' Eng. 'to call up'

Incarcerous

(in-CAR-ser-us)

A spell which binds a victim with rope. Umbridge used this spell on the centaur Magorian, not a particularly bright thing to do (OP33).

'in' = L. 'into, toward' + 'carcer' = L. 'prison'

Incendio

(in-SEN-dee-o)

Spell Arthur Weasley used that started a fire in the Dursleys' fireplace (GF4, also HBP28).

'incendo' = L. 'to set fire to'

Inferius
(plural: Inferi)
Animated corpses who do the bidding of the Dark wizard who created them (HBP4, 26, DH10).
'inferi' = L. 'the dead'
Legends and tales of reanimated corpses are found in many traditions, notably in the Voodoo religion. The term 'zombie' is frequently used for a reanimated corpse, which is interesting because zombies are mentioned in the Daily Prophet *newsletters and may be the same thing as Inferi. Zombies are portrayed in folklore and popular culture as having no mind of their own and shuffling along with their arms out, hoping to catch live humans to devour.*

Inquisitorial Squad
Group of students hand-picked by Umbridge for their support of the Ministry (and specifically who were willing to support Umbridge). The members wore a small silver letter 'I' on their robes, and seemed all to be Slytherins. Among other things, members inspected incoming mail, reported people to Umbridge, and docked lots of points from other students (OP28).

insect jinx
An unnamed jinx Harry was tempted

to use on Dudley, which would have made him sprout feelers and force him to crawl home (OP1).

instant scalping
This spell appears in *Basic Hexes for the Busy and Vexed*, which Harry consulted to find a spell to work against dragons (GF20).

Institute of Muggle Studies
Conducts studies of familial relations between wizards and Muggles (JKR).

Intermediate Transfiguration
The required textbook for third-year (and probably fourth-year) Transfiguration students at Hogwarts (PA4).
In his sixth year, Cedric Diggory was using a textbook called Guide to Advanced Transfiguration, *which presumably is the N.E.W.T.-level textbook (GF20).*

International Alchemical Conference
Albus Dumbledore won a gold medal award in his youth for 'Ground-Breaking Contribution' to this conference, held in Cairo (DH18).

International Association of Quidditch
The body overseeing international Quidditch teams, rules, and tournaments. Its chairwizard at the time of

the Quidditch World Cup in 1994 was Hassan Mostafa (GF8).

International Ban on Duelling

According to Percy, the Department of International Magical Cooperation was trying to get the Transylvanians to sign this in 1994 (GF23).

International Confederation of Warlocks

Another name for the International Confederation of Wizards (CS2, PA3).

International Confederation of Wizards

An organisation that, among other things, oversees the International Statute of Secrecy, which was passed in 1689 (DH16), and the control of magical creatures by member countries (FB). It was chaired by Albus Dumbledore (OP5).

International Magical Cooperation, Department of

A Ministry department that employs Percy Weasley (GF3) and, for a time, was overseen by Barty Crouch, Sr. (GF7, 16). Among other things, it organised the Quidditch World Cup (GF5) and the Triwizard Tournament (GF12). Among their more mundane projects is standardizing cauldron bottom thickness (GF5).

International Magical Office of Law
International Magical Trading Standards Body

These two groups have offices on level five of the Ministry of Magic, along with the Department of International Magical Cooperation (OP7).

International Statute of Wizarding Secrecy

A law enacted by the International Confederation of Wizards in 1689 that changed wizarding life for good (DH16). The Statute made it illegal to reveal any form of magic to Muggles, although magic can still be used in self-defence (OP6). Though it has presented some challenges, such as concealing magical creatures (e.g.DP1), the Statute has held for over three hundred years. As Hagrid says, wizards are 'best left alone' (PS5).

There is a discrepancy between sources as to the date of this important Statute. According to Fantastic Beasts and Where to Find Them, *the Statute was passed in 1692. The date is given as 1689 in* Deathly Hallows, *however.*

International Warlock Convention of 1289

Professor Binns gave an excruciatingly boring lecture on this event to second-year History of Magic students (CS9).

Invigoration Draught

Potion assigned to the fifth-year Potions class. Harry found this rather easy to do because for once Snape wasn't harassing him (OP29).

Invisibility Charm/Spell

One of these spells was placed on a Quidditch stadium in Exmoor in an attempt to hide it from Muggles; however, it failed spectacularly when none of the spectators could find the game (DP1).

Invisibility Cloak

See CLOAK OF INVISIBILITY.

Invisible Book of Invisibility, The

Flourish and Blotts bookstore once lost a lot of money on this book, since they never found the copies they ordered (PA4).

Invisible Ink

Hermione suggests that Riddle's diary might appear blank because it's written in invisible ink; however *Aparecium* revealed nothing (CS13). Snape also wondered whether the Marauder's Map might be a letter written using this ink (PA14).

Ireland

Wizarding Ireland is closely intertwined with wizarding Britain; children from Ireland, Seamus Finnigan for example, attend Hogwarts (GF6), and cities in Ireland are part of the British and Irish Quidditch League (DP1, 2, 3, 4). Notable wizards from Ireland include Cliodna, Queen Maeve, and Morholt (FW).

Ivanova

Bulgarian Chaser (GF8).

J

Jarvey

A ferret-like magical creature (JKR).
In Ireland, a 'jarvey' is a coachman. Perhaps this refers to the idea that a coachman might be prone to rude language and rough talk, as Fantastic Beasts and Where to Find Them *notes that Jarveys are verbally abusive.*

Jelly-Brain Jinx

During the riot that took place during a recent Puddlemere/Holyhead game, many Harpy fans used this jinx (DP4).

Jelly-Fingers curse

Spell which makes the target's fingers like jelly, so that they cannot grasp anything properly.
After a recent match between Pride of Portree and the Appleby Arrows, the losing Seeker accused his opposite number of putting this curse on him (DP3).

Jelly-Legs Jinx

Spell which makes it difficult for a person to walk (GF31, JKR).

Jelly Slugs

A sweet sold at Honeydukes; on weekends when Hogwarts students visit Hogsmeade, the shop goes through these rather quickly (PA10).

Jenkins, Joey

Beater for the Chudley Cannons. His photograph, hitting a Bludger toward a Ballycastle Bats Chaser, is a moving picture in the book *Flying with the Cannons* (GF2).

Jigger, Arsenius

Author of *Magical Drafts and Potions* (PS5).
'jigger' = Eng. 'a small liquid measure of an ounce and a half'; 'arsenic' = 'a chemical element, also a common poison'

jinx

A spell cast to cause damage or other negative effect. It is similar to a curse, but typically not as powerful or cast with such negative intention (OP12).

Jinxes for the Jinxed

The Room of Requirement contained

a copy of this book during the D.A.'s first meeting there (OP18).

Johnson, Angelina

(b. October 1977; Gryffindor, 1989; Quidditch Chaser 1990-1996, Captain 1995–6; Dumbledore's Army)

A tall black girl (GF16) and an excellent Quidditch player (PS11). She put her name in for the Triwizard Tournament but wasn't chosen (GF16). She is in Fred and George's year and seems to be friends with the two of them, as well as Lee Jordan (GF22, 23). Angelina became Quidditch captain in 1995 (OP12), which stressed her out and gave her something of a mean streak (OP13).

joke cauldron

A customer came into Weasleys' Wizard Wheezes looking for one of these (HBP6).

Jones, Gwenog

(b. 1968; Hogwarts 1979-1986)

Captain and Beater of the only all-female professional Quidditch team, the Holyhead Harpies (FW). She herself believes that the Harpies 'are easily the most exciting team playing' (DP1). Gwenog was a favourite of Horace Slughorn's while at Hogwarts; she still sends Slughorn free tickets to see the

Harpies play whenever he wants them (HBP4). Gwenog visited one of Slughorn's Slug Club parties at Hogwarts. Hermione met her but thought she was 'a bit full of herself' (HBP14).

Jones, Hestia

A member of the Order of the Phoenix assigned to escort the Dursleys to safety before Harry's departure (DH3).

Jones, Megan

(Hufflepuff 1991)

Megan's name appears in the draft of the class list of Harry's year that J.K. Rowling displayed during the 'Harry Potter and Me' TV interview (HPM). She is a half-blood. Megan has never appeared in the canon, but her name is listed here because she apparently existed in early plans for the books.

Jordan, Lee

(b. 1978; Gryffindor 1989; Dumbledore's Army)

A compatriot of Fred and George Weasley who commentated Quidditch matches while at Hogwarts; he occasionally let himself drift off topic (PS11). He is a black boy with dreadlocks (OP10). (*See also* DH22).

Jorkins family

Primrose and Albert Jorkins, already

the parents of Grimwold and Granville, had a third baby, Griselda Harmonia, whose birth was announced in the *Daily Prophet* (DP2).

Jorkins, Bertha

(1958?–1994; Hogwarts c.1969)
Two years ahead of Sirius, James, and their friends at Hogwarts, Bertha Jorkins was gossipy and not especially bright (GF27, 30). After leaving Hogwarts, Bertha went to work for the Ministry of Magic, where she earned a reputation for being scatterbrained; when she went missing on a vacation to Albania in 1994, most people simply assumed she'd lost track of time and would come wandering back eventually (GF7, c.f. GF33).

The tale of Bertha Jorkins is undoubtedly one of the weakest links in J.K. Rowling's plot. That Jorkins would have happened to learn of Barty Crouch's existence at his father's home is at least plausible. However, that she of all people would have just happened to visit Albania, and then out of that entire country just happened to meet Pettigrew and therefore reveal this information to Voldemort is a bit difficult to believe. J.K. Rowling has said that she discovered a major plot hole while writing book four and had to scramble to fix it. Perhaps Bertha's improbable fate was the result of J.K. Rowling's frantic plot fixing as she tried to meet her deadline.

Jorkins, Stamford

Ministry spokesperson, interviewed by the *Daily Prophet* for the story about new Ministry regulations on Hallowe'en celebrations (DP4).

Jugson

Death Eater who fought in the Battle of the Department of Mysteries (OP35).

junk shop

A shop in Diagon Alley (CS4).

Kappa

A water-dweller resembling a scaly monkey with webbed hands, a kappa will grab and strangle waders in its pond (PA8). According to Snape, the kappa is commonly found in Mongolia (PA9), though the Care of Magical Creatures textbook states that the kappa is a Japanese creature (FB).

Kappas are water sprites from Japanese folklore. They are said to have bowl-like depressions on the tops of their heads and they keep these filled with water. This is the source of their strength. To overcome a kappa, according to folklore, one must bow to it, enticing it to bow in return and spill the water from its head.

Karkaroff, Igor

(d. 1996)

Headmaster of Durmstrang and a former Death Eater. Karkaroff was a coward and a bully; he treated his students unfairly and didn't even take the trouble to pilot the school ship (GF15 ff.). (*See also* HBP6).

Karkus

(d. 1995)

The Gurg of the giants in Europe, first contacted by Hagrid and Maxime in the summer of 1995 (OP20).

Keeper

Quidditch player who guards the goal hoops. Oliver Wood (PS10) and later Ron Weasley (OP13) played this position for the Gryffindor team.

Keeper of the Keys and Grounds

Hagrid's title at Hogwarts, along with Gamekeeper (PS4).

Kegg, Roland

(b. 1903)

President of English Gobstones team (FW).

kelpie

A carnivorous, shape-shifting water creature (CS7). The world's biggest and most famous kelpie is the Loch Ness Monster, which is known to give wizarding authorities some trouble because it tends to be a bit of a show-off (DP1).

In Celtic folklore, the kelpie is a shape-shifting horse which haunts the lochs and rivers. A kelpie looks like a lost pony with a perpetually dripping mane. According to some legends, the kelpie will lure humans into the water to kill and eat them.

Kenmare Kestrels

An Irish Quidditch team. (DP1–4).

Kent

A southeastern English county, the home of Dedalus Diggle (PS1). The Wailing Widow (CS8) ghost also hails from Kent.

Ketteridge, Elladora

(1656–1729)

Discovered Gillyweed. For more information, see the Famous Wizard cards (FW).

Kettleburn, Professor

Care of Magical Creatures professor at Hogwarts until September 1993, when he retired to spend time with 'his remaining limbs', as Dumbledore put it. Hagrid took over his position (PA6).

Kevin

Two-year-old wizard boy, hanging around his parents' tent early in the morning at the Quidditch World Cup campground. He played with his father's wand and managed to enlarge a slug, much to his mother's dismay (GF7).

keys

One of the chambers which had to be crossed to reach the hiding place of the Philosopher's Stone was filled with hundreds of brightly-coloured flying keys (PS16). Keys are also bewitched by wizards as a form of 'Muggle-baiting' — they shrink the keys so the Muggle owners can't find them (CS3).

Kiely, Aidan

Kenmare Kestrels Seeker (DP2).

This player gets his name from Aine Kiely, a friend of J.K. Rowling's when she lived in Portugal. J.K. Rowling dedicated the third book to Aine and another friend, Jill Prewett.

Killing Curse

See AVADA KEDAVRA.

King's Cross Station

A railway station in London. Between Platform Nine and Platform Ten in this station is a metal barrier and a ticket box, but witches and wizards can push right through these onto magical Platform Nine and Three Quarters. There, under a wrought-iron archway with the name of the platform on it, they find the Hogwarts Express leaving on September 1 for Hogwarts and the start of term (PS6, etc.). (*See also* DH35).

J.K. Rowling wrote King's Cross into the stories because it was the place her parents met; however, she admitted she was accidentally picturing the layout of Euston Station in her head while writing it (HPM). In the films the platform scenes are shot on King's Cross platform four, while Marylebone Station is used for the Hogwarts Express departure scenes. Trains bound for Scotland do in fact leave King's Cross every day.

Kirke, Andrew

(Gryffindor, mid 1990s; Quidditch Beater, 1996)

Kirke was at least a second year during the 1995-1996 school year, and became a Beater on the Quidditch team after Fred and George were banned (OP21). Unfortunately he wasn't very good; the most memorable moment of his season was when he fell backwards off his broom in fright during a match against Hufflepuff (OP26).

This minor character's name may be a nod to the character of Professor Diggory Kirke in C.S. Lewis's Narnia tales.

kitchens, Hogwarts

Located one floor below the Great Hall, reached through the door to the right of the main staircase in the entrance hall, continuing on to a painting of a bowl of fruit, and tickling the pear until it giggles and becomes a door handle. The kitchens are staffed by more than a hundred house-elves. Food preparation tables are located directly below the four house tables in the Hall above; when the time comes for the food to be served, it is magically transported up through the ceiling of the kitchen and onto the plates (GF21).

Knarl

Very similar to a hedgehog, except that knarls have very suspicious natures (OP31). Fred and George use the quills in their products (OP9).

The name probably comes from 'gnarl', which means 'growl or snarl'.

kneazle

(NEE-zul)

This very intelligent cat-like creature can detect unsavoury or suspicious persons very well and will react badly to them. However, if a kneazle takes a liking to a witch or wizard, it makes an excellent pet. The kneazle has spotted fur, large ears, and a lion-like tail.

Crookshanks is part kneazle (Nr, JKR). Mrs Figg raises Kneazles (JKR).

Knight Bus, The

A magical purple bus that provides 'emergency transport for the stranded witch or wizard' (PA3). It is also possible to book a seat on the Knight Bus for trips around Britain (PA14). The ride is rather uncomfortable (e.g., OP24). The bus travels anywhere you want to go, 'as long as it's on land', according to the conductor, Stan Shunpike (PA3). The driver is Ernie Prang, an elderly wizard in thick glasses (PA3). During the day, the bus is filled with armchairs for passengers (OP24), though at night the seats are replaced by half a dozen brass bedsteads on each level (PA3).

The name of the bus is a play on words. Buses which run all night in London and other British cities are called Night Buses. Using the word 'knight', however, suggests a heroic rescuer. Since the Knight Bus can be called from anywhere in Britain with just a wave of the wand, it certainly can rescue witches and wizards from tight spots.

Knightley, Montague

(1506–1588)

Wizard Chess Champion; for more information, see the Famous Wizard cards (FW).

Knights of Walpurgis

Original name for the Death Eaters (HPM).

The name comes from Walpurgis Night, a celebration in central and northern Europe. Walpurgis Night, which is celebrated on the night of April 30/May 1, was believed to be one of the days when the barriers between the realms of the dead and the living break down. The other such day, Hallowe'en, is exactly six months opposite from Walpurgis Night on the calendar. In Germany, 'Walpurgisnacht' is also called 'Hexennach' ('witches night'), and is said to be the night when witches gather and celebrate the arrival of spring.

knitting charm

Spell which bewitches knitting needles to knit elf hats (OP17).

Knockturn Alley

A dingy alleyway connecting to Diagon Alley near Gringotts which is full of disreputable shops devoted to the Dark Arts, including stores selling shrunken heads, live gigantic black spiders, and poisonous candles. Street vendors include an old witch with a tray full of whole human fingernails (CS4). Prominent in the Alley is Borgin and Burkes, a Dark items shop where Tom Marvolo Riddle once worked and which is now frequented by the Malfoy family (CS4, HBP6, 20).

The name is a play on words, just like the name of Diagon Alley. Knockturn Alley is a homophone of 'nocturnally'. This kind of word play is actually called an 'oronym'. A classic example of this is the 'Four Candles' sketch of 'The Two Ronnies' television show in Britain, in which a man asks the clerk in a shop for 'fork handles' and is given four candles.

knotgrass

An ingredient in Polyjuice Potion (CS10) that is kept in the student store-cupboard in the Potions classroom. It also grows in the Forbidden Forest (OP30).

Culpeper's Complete Herbal, a famous book of herbal lore from the 1600s which J.K. Rowling has mentioned as one of her sources, lists many uses for knotgrass, including the relief of gallstones and inflammation. There's no mention of transforming a person into someone else, though.

Knut

(kuh-NUT or kah-NOOT)

A small bronze coin, the smallest unit of wizarding currency; there are twenty-nine Knuts to a silver Sickle (PS5). One bronze Knut is worth about £0.01 (about 2 US cents) (CR).

Knut (or Canute) is a Scandinavian first name. Several kings of Denmark were named Knut, two of whom ruled over parts of Britain as well during medieval times.

Kreacher

An aged house-elf whose family has served the Black family for generations. He was devoted to Sirius Black's mother and father, as well as their younger son Regulus (OP6). Kreacher's allegiances were always to the House of Black, but his mistreatment at the hands of the last of the Blacks, induced the elf to betray his master (OP37). (*See also* DH10, 11, 36).

Krum (grandfather)

Grandfather of Viktor Krum, a victim of the dark times in Europe in the 1940s (DH8).

Krum, Mr and Mrs

Viktor Krum's parents; his father has a hooked nose like his son, and his mother is dark-haired. Mr and Mrs Krum travelled from Bulgaria to Hogwarts for the third and final task of the Triwizard Tournament (GF31).

Krum, Viktor

(b. 1977; Bulgarian National Quidditch Team Seeker 1994; Durmstrang Triwizard Champion 1994–1995)

A famous international Quidditch player while still in school (GF8), Viktor Krum attended Hogwarts for the 1994-1995 school year, and represented Durmstrang as their Triwizard champion (GF16). (*See also* GF27, DH8).

Kwikspell

'A Correspondence Course in Beginners' Magic', which arrives in a purple envelope with silver lettering. The Kwikspell course is aimed at those whose magical abilities are unusually low, but not completely absent (or at least those who would like to believe that that is the case). Filch, the caretaker at Hogwarts, is a Squib. He sent for and received the Kwikspell course in October of 1992 (CS8), though it never worked for him (JKR).

Laburnum Gardens

A street located in Clapham, London, which at number two is the home of Sturgis Podmore (OP14).

Lachlan the Lanky

A statue of this wizard stands on the seventh floor of Hogwarts Castle, just to the right of the top of the stairs leading down to the floor below, between the stairs and the Fat Lady's portrait (OP13).

LaFolle, Fifi

(1888 - 1971)

Author of the 'Enchanted Encounters' series (JKR).

J.K. Rowling's Wizard of the Month for October 2005. This was the first new character to appear on the Wizard of the Month; previously they had all previously appeared on a Famous Wizard card. LaFolle's image on J.K. Rowling's website bears a striking resemblance to romance writer Barbara Cartland.

Lake, the

Before the castle lies a large lake which is home to the giant squid, merpeople, and grindylows. First-years approach the castle for the first time across this lake in magically self-propelled boats (PS6).

Although never referred to as such in the books, any lake in Scotland would more properly be called a loch.

Lancelot

Cousin of Aunty Muriel who worked at St. Mungo's around 1900. He told Muriel that the Dumbledores never brought Ariana into the hospital, which naturally made Muriel suspect the worst. After all, *not* going to the hospital certainly suggests that someone is sick, doesn't it (DH8).

While the name Lancelot is well known from the stories of King Arthur and his knights, in this case the name was more likely chosen because it is related to the term 'lancet', which is a surgical instrument. 'The Lancet' is the name of one of the leading British medical journals.

Langlock

(LANG-lok)

A jinx that glues the target's tongue to the roof of his or her mouth (HBP19).

'langue' = Fr. *'tongue'* + *'lock'* = Eng. *'to fasten'*

Languages
Giant — speak their own language; some do not speak English, and possibly do not speak any human language (OP20).
Gobbledegook — Goblin language (GF24, DH15).
Mermish — Merfolk language (GF7); it sounds like horrible screeching if heard in air (GF21).
Parseltongue — The language of snakes which sounds like extended hissing (HBP10).
Troll — The Trolls' crude form of language consists of grunts (from the viewpoint of a human listener, at any rate), although some can be trained to speak a few words of English (PS10, GF7).
Unlike Tolkien, J.K. Rowling makes no effort to create the actual languages of her world. The only word given in the books from one of these languages is 'bladvak', which we are told means 'pick-axe' in Gobbledegook. Instead, the noises and sounds of the languages of magical creatures and races are described from the point of view of Harry, who doesn't speak those languages himself.

Lawson, Artemius
Outspoken campaigner for the suppression of trolls. He has strong objections to letting them wander free, referring to trolls as 'creatures weighing over a ton, with brains the size of a bogey'. He has a pretty good point (DP2).

Leach, Nobby
Minister of Magic from 1962–1968 (JKR).
'nobby' = Br. slang *'a rich man, an aristocrat'*

Leaky Cauldron, The
A small, shabby-looking inn on Charing Cross Road, London, sandwiched between a big book shop and a record store. The Leaky Cauldron is not in Diagon Alley itself; rather, it serves as a 'bridge' between the two worlds. The pub was built by Daisy Dodderidge around 1500 'to serve as a gateway between the non-wizarding world and Diagon Alley' (FW). The Leaky Cauldron has rooms to let upstairs and a bar and dining room on the ground floor (PA3, 4, 5). The innkeeper in the 1990s was named Tom (PS5, HBP6, 13). The current innkeeper is Hannah Abbott (OBT/CH).

Leanne
(Hogwarts student, 1990s)
Friend of Katie Bell's (HBP12).

leaping toadstools

The second-year Herbology students worked with these (CS14).

leech

A small slug-like creature that lives in water. Leeches attach themselves to other creatures and suck their blood. Leeches are used as potion ingredients (CS10, 11), both sliced and in the form of leech juice (PA7).

leek jinx

Results in leeks growing out of the target's ears (PA15).

Legilimency

(le-JIL-i-men-see)

The magical ability to extract emotions and memories from another person's mind. Someone who practices Legilimency is known as a Legilimens. Legilimency is easier when the spell-caster is physically near the target, and when the target is off-guard, relaxed, or otherwise vulnerable. Eye contact is often essential, so it is useful for a Legilimens to verbally manipulate his or her target into meeting the Legilimens' eyes, with the fringe benefit that the target's emotional state may bring relevant associated memories to the surface (OP24, 26).

Legilimens

(le-JIL-i-menz)

Incantation for performing Legilimency (OP24). This term is also used for a wizard who has learned the art of Legilimency, sensing the thoughts of another person (OP37, HBP2).

'legens' = L. 'reader' + 'mens' = L. 'mind'

Leg-Locker Curse

See LOCOMOTOR MORTIS.

lemon drop

A sour hard sweet shaped like a tiny lemon (PS1). A password to Dumbledore's office (CS11).

This term appears only in the US editions of the books. In the UK editions, it's given as 'sherbet lemon'.

leprechaun

A tiny fairy-like creature native to Ireland. They are able to produce a gold-like substance that vanishes after an hour or two (GF8, 28) which they think is funny (but Ron Weasley doesn't). Leprechauns are the Irish National Quidditch Team's mascots (GF8). For more information, see the book *Fantastic Beasts and Where to Find Them.*

Leprechauns are fairies from Irish mythology and folklore. They are typically described much as J.K. Rowling describes them in the books, as little old men. Ac-

cording to the tales, leprechauns are very clever and fabulously wealthy, but it is very difficult to convince or trick them into revealing the location of their gold.

Lestoat, Amarillo
(1776-1977)
An American vampire author (FW).
'Lestoat' is a reference to the name 'Lestat,' a main character of Anne Rice's vampire novel Interview with a Vampire *and that novel's sequels. The first book was published in 1976, exactly two hundred years after this character was born, which suggests an intentional reference by J.K. Rowling to Rice's novel.*

Lestrange
(b. late 1920s, Slytherin late 1930s)
One of the earliest (c. 1955) members of the Death Eaters (HBP20); attended Hogwarts with Tom Riddle (HBP17). Probably related to Rabastan and Rodolphus Lestrange, who attended Hogwarts with Severus Snape.
Bellatrix married into an ancient and aristocratic family. The family line originated in the Norman Conquest, with Roland Le Strange ('the stranger', since he was French). The Lestrange family coat of arms has the family motto: 'mihi parta tueri' ('I will fight for what is mine'). Seems a fitting motto for Death Eaters and Slytherins.

Lestrange, Bellatrix (Black)
(1951-1998; Slytherin c. 1962)
Fanatical member of Voldemort's inner circle of Death Eaters, a member of the pure-blood Black family (DH33). Bella, as she is called, went to Azkaban for her crimes as a Death Eater in the 1970s (GF27, 33). Bella was tall with black hair and heavily-lidded eyes; she enjoys causing pain using the Cruciatus Curse (e.g. OP35). Once beautiful, she was forever marked by the horror of Azkaban (GF30, OP25). (*See also* DH36)
'Bellatrix' = L. 'female warrior'; also the name of a brilliant star in the constellation Orion that is sometimes called the 'Amazon star'.
In a way, Bellatrix is the 'anti-Molly'. Where Molly is devoted to her husband and children, Bellatrix forsakes her husband and loves only Voldemort. Far from being nurturing and compassionate, as Molly is, Bella delights in harming others, including children. How fitting that these two women faced off in such a memorable duel.

Lestrange, Rabastan
(Slytherin, early 1970s)
A Death Eater; brother of Rodolphus Lestrange (GF30, OP6). Rabastan and his brother Rodolphus were given a life sentence in Azkaban (GF27, 33);

however, they escaped in January 1996 (OP25).

Lestrange, Rodolphus
(Slytherin, early 1970s)
A Death Eater, brother of Rabastan, husband of Bellatrix (GF27, 30, OP6).

Lethifold
Flavius Belby was attacked by this very dangerous magical creature in the 1700s and managed to survive, the only person known to do so (FW).
'lethe' = Gr. 'forgetfulness, concealment', or perhaps more directly from 'lethal' Eng. 'deadly' + 'fold' Eng. 'a crease or doubling-over of cloth'

Levicorpus
(leh-vi-COR-pus)
Dangles the target person upside-down by the ankle in mid-air. The counter-jinx is *Liberacorpus* (HBP12, DH26).
'levo' = L. 'to lift up, raise' + 'corpus' = L. 'body'

Levitation Charm
A basic charm (OP31) that allows the target to float up to five feet above the ground.
Possibly the same as 'Wingardium Leviosa' (q.v.).

Levski
Bulgarian National Team Chaser for the 1994 World Cup (GF8).

Li, Su
(Ravenclaw 1991–1998)
Su's name appears in the draft of the classlist of Harry's year that J.K. Rowling displayed during the 'Harry Potter and Me' TV interview (HPM). According to the class list she is half-blood. Su has never appeared in canon, but her name is listed here because she apparently existed in early plans for the books.

Liberacorpus
(lee-ber-ah-COR-pus)
Counter-jinx to *Levicorpus*. When cast on someone hanging by their ankle from the *Levicorpus* spell, the person crashes to the ground (HBP12, DH26).
'liber' = L. 'free' + 'corpus'= L. 'body'

library, the
The Hogwarts library, on the fourth floor, contains tens of thousands of books on thousands of shelves (PS12). Included in its many sections are an Invisibility Section (CS11), a section with information about dragons (PS14), and a Restricted Section (PS12, CS9, 10, GF26, HBP18). The library closes at 8 pm (GF20). Madam Pince is the librarian.

Licorice Wands

Sweets sold from the snack trolley on the Hogwarts Express (PS6). This was among the list of sweets' names Harry said when trying to guess the password into Dumbledore's office (GF29).

Liechtenstein

A tiny, mountainous country located between Austria and Switzerland, Liechtenstein is home to only about 33,000 people. Though it has not played a central role in Muggle history, it did have a place in wizarding history: the warlocks of Liechtenstein refused to join the International Confederation of Wizards at its first forming. Harry's History of Magic O.W.L. asked why this was the case, though he never did come up with the answer (OP31).

Life and Lies of Albus Dumbledore, The

by Rita Skeeter

A 900-page biography of Dumbledore. Chapters 9 to 12 discuss his mother and sister. Chapter 16 discusses the uses of dragon's blood and argues that Dumbledore might not have been the first to find some of them after all. An entire chapter is devoted to his relationship with Harry Potter (DH2). The book also has a chapter entitled 'The Greater Good' discussing Albus

Dumbledore's friendship with Gellert Grindelwald.

The chapter entitled 'The Greater Good' is quoted in its entirety in DH18.

lion

The animal symbol of Gryffindor house (PS3, GF15).

Little Dropping

A hamlet in Hampshire which was blown up by Archibald Alderton when he tried to mix a birthday cake (FW).

The name was no doubt chosen to fit the fact that it was 'blown up', after which it may be assumed that bits of the town were dropping all over the countryside. There is no actual town called Dropping in Britain, although there is one called Dropping Well in South Yorkshire.

Little Hangleton

A town of massive importance to recent Wizarding history and yet unknown to most modern wizards. Little Hangleton is found about six miles from its neighbour, Great Hangleton, (HBP10) and is the location of the Riddle House (GF1, 32, HBP10). Nearby, in a copse on the hillside, was the Gaunt House, wherein lived the Gaunt family, the last remaining descendants of Salazar Slytherin (HBP10).

Little Norton

At a 1980 Hobgoblins concert in Little Norton church hall, lead singer Stubby Boardman was hit in the ear by a turnip, prompting him to retire (OP10).

Little People, Big Plans

by Ragnok the Pigeon-toed

Book written by an activist for Goblin rights (DP3).

Little Whinging

A quiet, perfectly normal suburb of London, where the houses are large and square (OP1), and where you'll find the perfectly normal residence of number four, Privet Drive, home of the perfectly normal Dursley family (PS1).

'whinging' = Br. 'whining, complaining'

Liverpool

A famous port town on the western coast of England and the site of a Celestina Warbeck concert some years back. As late ticket-holders raced to the event, there was a three-broom crash over the Mersey River, which runs through Liverpool (DP2).

Livius

One of two wizards who, according to history, might have taken the Elder Wand from Loxias (DH21).

Llewellyn, 'Dangerous' Dai

Famous Quidditch player for the Caerphilly Catapults. He was known for his reckless and foolhardy style of play. The St. Mungo's ward for treating magical bites is named for him (OP22).

This foolhardy character bears the name of two famous Welshmen. The more famous is of the two is a baronet who is a socialite and self-proclaimed playboy. The other, however, is a Wales international rugby union player, which fits better for a Quidditch player.

Loch Lomond

Perhaps the most famous loch in Scotland, Loch Lomond is home to merpeople. Mirabella Plunkett fell in love with a merman from Loch Lomond (FW).

Loch Ness

A large, deep lake in the Highlands of Scotland. It is home of the Loch Ness Monster, a large kelpie that prefers to take the form of a sea serpent. The monster is notorious for showing off for Muggles. In fact, the Ministry has been looking to move the monster (DP1).

locked room

A mysterious room, connected to the circular entrance chamber in the Department of Mysteries, which stayed locked despite everyone's best efforts. Even Harry's magical penknife from Sirius couldn't open it (OP34, 37).

Locket of Regulus Black

A plain non-magical locket which Regulus Black left as a decoy. Years later, Harry gave Regulus's locket to Kreacher as a gift, earning the house-elf's deep respect and gratitude (DH10).

Locket of Slytherin

A heavy gold locket carrying Salazar Slytherin's mark (an ornate serpentine S) and originally owned by Marvolo Gaunt. The locket had a strange, tragic history, passing from one person to another and leaving misery in its wake (OP6, HBP20, DH13, 19).

Lockhart, Gilderoy

(DADA professor, 1992–1993)
Defence Against The Dark Arts professor, a pompous buffoon. Lockhart is obsessed with himself and his image (esp. CS7). In his many books, he tells of his exploits fighting various types of magical creatures, but the truth is that he simply interviewed the people who really dealt with the creatures, then performed Memory Charms on them and took the credit (CS16).

Locomotion Charms

A series of spells which use the word *'locomotor'* for moving objects around. Usually the objects name is part of the incantation. Parvati and Lavender practice these as they get ready for their O.W.L.s (OP31).

Locomotor

(lo-co-MO-tor)
Moves an object. Typically, the spell word *'Locomotor'* is followed by a target word, which is the object to be moved (e.g. *'Locomotor* trunk!') (OP3, 26, DH30).
'loco' = L. *'from a place'* + *'motionem'* = L. *'motion'*

Locomotor Mortis

(lo-co-MO-tor MOR-tis)
'Leg-Locker Curse'
Locks together the legs of the victim, making him or her unable to walk (PS13).
'loco' = L. *'from a place'* + *'motionem'* = L. *'motion'* + *'mortis'* = L. *'death'*

London

Located in southeastern England, one of the largest and most famous cities in the world. For Wizards as well as Muggles it is the centre of commerce and government. London is the location of the Ministry of Magic (esp. OP7, 34, DH12, 13) and St. Mungo's Hospital (esp. OP22, 23). It is also the location of Grimmauld Place, near King's Cross Station (OP10) and The Leaky Cauldron, on Charing Cross Road (PS5 etc.).

Longbottom, Alice
(Order of the Phoenix)
A respected Auror during the first Wizarding war, wife of Frank Longbottom. Alice is a round-faced woman; her son Neville looks a lot like her. Along with her husband, she was a member of the original Order of the Phoenix (OP9, c.f. OP23).

Longbottom, Augusta 'Gran'
Neville's paternal grandmother who is raising him in the absence of his parents. She is a forceful, strong woman. Neville loves her, but he's a bit scared of her as well (PA7). In the spring of 1998, when Neville was causing problems for the Death Eaters, Dawlish was sent to try to take her into custody to put pressure on the boy. It didn't go so well for Dawlish (DH31).

Longbottom, Frank
(Order of the Phoenix)
Auror, popular in the Wizarding world, who fought against Voldemort and his supporters during the 1970s. He was a member of the Order of the Phoenix and Neville's father (OP9, c.f. OP23).

Longbottom, Grandfather
Under interrogation, Neville tells Umbridge that he can see Thestrals because he saw his Grandad die (OP21).

Longbottom, Harfang
On the Black Family Tree, Harfang Longbottom married Callidora Black, daughter of Arcturus Black. No dates are given for Harfang, but Callidora was born in 1915 and appears to still be alive (BFT).

In the Chronicles of Narnia, the House of Harfang was the large (even by giant standards) castle of a clan of Northern Giants.

Longbottom, Neville
(b. July 30, 1980; Gryffindor 1991; Dumbledore's Army; Herbology professor, early 21st C.)
A staunch friend of Harry Potter's and a true Gryffindor. Neville is described as 'round-faced'; he looks like his mother (OP23). His bravery is a different sort than Harry's. It is the bravery of children who keep trying even though they have repeatedly failed in the past, of the unpopular child who never succumbs to peer pressure, even from friends. At Hogwarts, he was rather forgetful and often had trouble performing magic; it didn't help that Professor Snape relent-

lessly singled Neville out for ridicule (e.g., PA7). While broom-flying (PS9) and Potions (GF14) were problems, Neville excelled at Herbology (GF14). When he joined Dumbledore's Army, he gained confidence and skill through sheer hard work (OP19, etc.). (*See also* OP35, HBP28, DH29, 36, /e, BLC).

Loser's Lurgy
Luna suggests that Zacharias Smith is suffering from this ailment during her commentary on the Quidditch match (HBP19).

The 'dreaded lurgy' was a humorous disease invented for an episode of the Goon Show on BBC Radio in the 1950s (and spelled 'lurgi', incidentally). The term is popularly used to refer to a vague, non-specific illness one gets occasionally, sometimes as an excuse not to do something. It also has become a British playground slang term for the sort of vague 'different-ness' children use to exclude another child from their games ('You can't play, you've got the dreaded lurgy!'). In other words, Luna is saying that Smith has cooties. It's pronounced with a hard g, rhyming with 'Fergie'.

Love Potion
Potion which causes the drinker to develop a powerful infatuation or obsession with someone (HBP9). The du-

ration of the effects of a love potion vary depending on such factors as the weight of the person drinking the potion and the attractiveness of the person with whom the potion is supposed to make the drinker obsessed (HBP6). The effects wear off naturally over time but can be renewed by administering further doses (HBP10). After taking an antidote to a love potion, the drinker does not forget what he or she did while under its influence, which can be terribly embarrassing (HBP18).

Lovegood House
Located in the hills near Ottery St. Catchpole, the Lovegood house looks something like a castle tower, tall and black. The cluttered rooms inside are circular and have been painted with colourful designs of flowers and insects. A wrought-iron staircase runs up the centre of the tower, connecting the rooms. The ground floor is the kitchen. The first floor is a combination living room and workplace, the next above that is Luna's bedroom (DH21).

Lovegood, Mrs
(d. circa 1990)
The mother of Luna, Mrs Lovegood was 'a quite extraordinary witch' who liked to experiment (OP38). Luna resembles her mother (DH21).

Lovegood, Luna

(b. 1981; Ravenclaw 1992; Dumble-dore's Army)

A witch in Ginny's year who simply wasn't like the other kids at all. She dressed unusually, she proclaimed her strange beliefs openly, and in some ways she seemed to be completely out of touch with what was going on around her (e.g., OP10). She tucked her wand behind her ear for safekeeping, wore odd items as jewellery such as a necklace of butterbeer corks and Dirigible Plums for earrings, which she believes 'enhance the ability to accept the extraordinary' (DH20). Luna was often the butt of jokes. She was called Loony Lovegood behind her back. Through it all, Luna was surprisingly patient and accepting. She didn't fight back or even seem to notice, although she was certainly aware of much of the teasing (OP38). Luna proved to be a faithful friend to Harry and his friends (e.g. OP13) and a valiant member of the Order of the Phoenix (e.g. OP35, DH32). *(See also BLC).*

See SCAMANDER, ROLF.

Lovegood, Xenophilius

Editor of *The Quibbler*, father of Luna Lovegood and a rather odd fellow. Unusually open-minded, he agreed to publish Rita Skeeter's exclusive interview giving Harry Potter's side of things, which helped turn public opinion (OP25). *(See also DH20, 21).*

'Xenophilius' comes from 'xenophile' = Eng. 'one who loves unusual things, other cultures, and appreciates differences'

Loxias

Described as a 'dreadful' fellow, Loxias once owned the Elder Wand (DH21).

Luckless, Sir

A Muggle knight in the story 'The Fountain of Fair Fortune' from *The Tales of Beedle the Bard*. Sir Luckless, along with three witches, Amata, Asha and Altheda, was a competitor for a drink of the curative water from the Fountain (TBB).

Sir Luckless is probably a reference to 'Sir Luckless Woo-All' a knight addressed in some of Ben Jonson's Epigrams (1616): 'Sir LUCKLESS, troth, for luck's sake pass by one; He that wooes every widow, will get none.'

Ludicrous Patents Office

This office is part of the Department of Magical Games and Sports and is located on Level Seven of the Ministry of Magic (OP7).

Lufkin, Artemisia

(1754–1825)

First witch to become Minister for Magic, serving from 1798–1811 (FW).

Lumos

(LOO-mos)

Causes a small beam of light to shine from the end of the caster's wand (CS15).

'lumen' = L. *'light'*

lunascope

Some kind of astronomical model or instrument which shows the phases of the moon. Dumbledore kept a lunascope in his office (OP37). It was invented by Perpetua Fancourt (FW).

Lupin, Remus John

(1960–1998; Gryffindor, 1971; Prefect, 1975; Order of the Phoenix; DADA professor, 1993-1994)

Friend of James Potter and Sirius Black and for a year, Harry Potter's Defence Against the Dark Arts teacher. He was a very capable wizard and an excellent teacher (e.g. PA7), although his personal problems relegated him more often than not to the fringes of Wizarding society (PA17, HBP16). At Hogwarts, Lupin was one of the Marauders (PA17) and after leaving school he joined the Order of the Phoenix (esp.

OP34-35, HBP28, DH4, 31, 35). (*See also* DH25).

Both Lupin's first and last names have wolf connections. The mythological founders of Rome were Romulus and Remus, who as babies were suckled by a she-wolf. 'Lupin' comes from 'lupus' = L. 'wolf'. J.K. Rowling revealed his middle name in an interview (WBD).

Lupin, Teddy

(b. 1998; Hogwarts, 2009)

Son of Remus Lupin (DH11). Apparently from the photos, he's a metamorphmagus since as a baby his hair kept changing colours (DH25). (*See also* DH/e, BLC).

Luxembourg

A tiny European country sandwiched between France, Germany, and Belgium, Luxembourg had a Quidditch team that slaughtered Scotland's team in the World Cup playoffs of 1994, according to Charlie Weasley (GF5).

Lynch, Aidan

Irish National Quidditch Team Seeker for the 1994 World Cup (GF8).

ℳ

MacDonald, Mary

(Hogwarts, 1970s)

Student at Hogwarts at the same time as Lily Evans and Severus Snape (DH33).

MacDougal, Morag

(Hogwarts, 1991)

A young witch who was Sorted as a member of Harry's class (PS7).

According to an early list of Harry's classmates that J.K. Rowling displayed during an interview, Morag's name may originally have been Isabel MacDougal. If so (and this document can't really be considered canon), she is a Ravenclaw student from a pure-blood family (HPM).

Macmillan, Ernie

(b. 1980; Hufflepuff, 1991; Prefect 1995; Dumbledore's Army)

Though sort of a pompous fellow, Ernie's heart and loyalties are in the right place (CS15, OP13, 16, DH31, 32). Ernie became a prefect in his fifth year, together with his close friend Hannah Abbott (OP10).

MacMillan, Melania

(1901-1991)

Wife of Arcturus Black, and Sirius Black's paternal grandmother (BFT).

Macnair, Walden

A Death Eater (OP20, 38, DH36) who sports a black moustache. Macnair worked as an executioner of dangerous creatures for the Ministry of Magic (PA16, 21, GF33).

According to a (non-canon) planning chart for Order of the Phoenix, Macnair was the one visiting Bode at St. Mungo's on Christmas Eve (JKR). It seems likely, then, that Macnair was the 'friend' who brought Bode the Devil's Snare (OP25).

Madam Malkin's Robes for All Occasions

A Diagon Alley shop next door to Flourish and Blotts, and the primary seller of Hogwarts school robes (PS5, HBP6). During one summer sale, the store offered a wide range of magical robes and included a 'free frog-skin belt with every purchase' (DP1).

Madam Primpernelle's

Located at 275 Diagon Alley, this company brews Beautifying Potions. They recently advertised in the *Daily Prophet* classifieds, looking for a Junior Potion Mixer (DP2).

Madame Puddifoot's Tea Shop

A small, cramped tea shop with decor on the tacky side of frilly (which included floating golden cherubs throwing pink confetti), located just off the High Street in Hogsmeade. The only Hogwarts students who seem to patronise the place are trysting couples (OP25).

Madcap Magic for Wacky Warlocks

One of the books that Harry, Ron, and Hermione examined while preparing for the Second Task of the Triwizard Tournament (GF26).

Maddock, Alasdair

Chaser for the Montrose Magpies who was a bit over-interested in Muggle sports (DP1, 2, 3).

Madley, Laura

(Hufflepuff, 1994)

A girl sorted during Harry's fourth year (GF12).

Maeve, Queen

Medieval witch from Ireland who trained young witches and wizards there (FW).

According to Irish mythology, Maeve was a warrior queen who lived in the 1st Century BC. She is perhaps most famous for the war she fought to claim the brown bull of Ulster, which she desired because it would make her wealthier than her husband.

Mafalda

A character who never appeared in the books, though J.K. Rowling originally wrote her to be in Goblet of Fire*. Mafalda was a Weasley cousin, a Slytherin, who came to stay with the Weasleys for a summer. She was quite annoying, though an intellectual match for Hermione (JKR).*

magic

Magic is the heart and soul of the Wizarding culture in the same way that science and technology are for Muggle culture. Where a Muggle would pound a stake into the ground using a sledge hammer (a simple machine), a wizard would use a wand (GF18). Both the Muggle and the wizard view their choice of tool as completely and utterly logical and ordinary, although each would find the other's tools fascinating and even mysterious. In the Wizarding world, magic is just 'the way you do things' and is studied systematically just like science is for Muggles (e.g. HBP18, DH15).

Magical Accidents and Catastrophes, Department of

A Ministry department, located on level three of the Ministry of Magic, that includes the Accidental Magic Reversal Squad, Obliviators, and generally anyone who deals with breaches of the Statute of Secrecy (DH23).

Magical Drafts and Potions

by Arsenius Jigger

A potions textbook on the booklist for Hogwarts first-years in 1991 (PS5).

Magical Equipment Control

A Ministry department that once issued a warning about sub-standard wands, which were being sold by a street peddler named 'Honest Willy' Wagstaff (DP1).

Magical Games and Sports, Department of

Formed in the wake of the Statute of Secrecy in 1689 to enforce Quidditch regulations and ensure that the sport did not attract Muggle attention (esp. OP7). The department was recently

was led by Ludo Bagman (GF7) until he resigned in 1995. It helped organise the Quidditch World Cup and the Triwizard Tournament, along with the Department of International Magical Cooperation (GF7, 12). Other sports are overseen by this Department, including Gobstones, but let's face it, what's Gobstones compared to Quidditch?

Magical Hieroglyphs and Logograms

Book that Hermione sits reading in the common room during her fifth year, most likely for Ancient Runes class (OP26).

A logogram is a symbol used in writing to indicate an entire word. The alphabet used in most languages today employs letter symbols by themselves or in combination to represent sounds. We use the letter 'B', for example, to represent the sound at the beginning of the word 'baby'. A logogram, on the other hand, represents the whole word in one go, not tied to pronunciation at all. In modern written language, for example, the numeral 3 represents the word 'three' in English, while in Spanish that same symbol represents the word 'tres'. The numeral is a logogram. The term 'hieroglyph' refers to any symbol used in a writing system which includes logograms. The most familiar to many people is the hieroglyphs of Ancient

Egypt. Hermione is studying Ancient Runes using this textbook, which suggests that magical runes are often logograms. In fact, the rune symbols we do know of — a three-headed Runespoor to symbolise the number three, for example — are logograms.

Magical Law Enforcement, Department of

The largest department in the Ministry of Magic, headed once by Barty Crouch, Sr. (GF27) and more recently by Amelia Bones (OP8), Pius Thicknesse (DH1), and Yaxley (DH12). Its six primary branches are Auror Headquarters, the Wizengamot, the Magical Law Enforcement Squad, the Improper Use of Magic Office, Magical Equipment Control, and Misuse of Muggle Artefacts (esp. OP7). Other offices set up at one time or another include the Office for the Detection and Confiscation of Counterfeit Defensive Spells and Protective Objects (HBP5) and the Muggle-Born Registration Commission, headed by Dolores Umbridge (DH13).

Magical Law Enforcement Squad

Headed at one time by Bob Ogden (HBP10), this squad is within the Department of Magical Law Enforce-

ment and serves as a basic police force for the Wizarding world. Among other things, it employs Hit Wizards to handle dangerous criminals (PA11).

Magical Maintenance

An office that oversees the basic functions of the Ministry of Magic headquarters, including its magical windows (OP7, DH12). The department's employees include Reg Cattermole (DH12).

One can't help but wonder if the rainstorms in various people's offices during the takeover of the Ministry by Death Eaters weren't caused by Magical Maintenance as a subtle way of fighting back.

Magical Me

by Gilderoy Lockhart

Lockhart's autobiography, which apparently had just come out in the summer of 1992, since he was doing book signings for it at the time (CS4).

Magical Menagerie

Diagon Alley pet shop where Hermione bought Crookshanks. The walls are covered with cages and the place is noisy with the sounds of all the animals. The proprietor is a witch who wears heavy black spectacles. She offers advice and sells things like rat tonic (PA4).

Magical Theory
by Adalbert Waffling
Required textbook for first-years, possibly for Charms (PS5).

Magical Transportation, Department of
Located on level six of the Ministry of Magic, this office regulates Portkeys, brooms (OP7), the Floo Network (OP27), and Apparition (GF6), among other things.

Magical Water Plants of the Mediterranean
Barty Crouch Jr., disguised as Mad-Eye Moody, gave Neville a copy of this book after the first Defence Against the Dark Arts lesson of Neville's fourth year (GF14); it discusses gillyweed, a plant which can come in very handy sometimes (GF35).

magic, disciplines of
There are five fundamental branches of magic taught at Hogwarts: Charms, Herbology, Potions, Transfiguration, and the Dark Arts (taught at Hogwarts as 'Defense Against the Dark Arts'). Other magical disciplines in the Wizarding world include Arithmancy, Divination, Herbology, wandlore, Legilimency, medical magic, Magizoology, and Occlumency (PS8, OP31).

All the classes at Hogwarts are not separate disciplines. Astronomy and History of Magic, for example, seem to be informational classes teaching necessary background knowledge rather than separate magical disciplines of their own.

'Magic is Might'
Slogan adopted by the Ministry of Magic in 1997 to justify the oppression of Muggles and Muggle-borns. A huge black stone statue in the Ministry Atrium paid homage to this idea, depicting a witch and wizard sitting on a throne made from suffering, naked Muggles in their 'rightful place' (DH12).

Magick Most Evile
A library book in the restricted section that refers to Horcruxes in its introduction, but only to call them 'the wickedest of magical inventions' and to say that the book will not speak of the subject further (HBP18).

Magi-Me-More
A pill that is advertised as making a wizard feel younger and more powerful. However, the side effects from this drug sound dire indeed, including 'tusks'. It pays to read the fine print sometimes (JKR).

Magizoology

The study of magical creatures from all over the world (FB); at Hogwarts it's taught in the form of Care of Magical Creatures classes (PA5).
'magic' + *'zoology'* = *'the study of animals'*

Magnolia Crescent

'Several streets away' from Privet Drive (PA3), Magnolia Crescent is a street on which several of Dudley's friends probably live, as he bade them goodbye 'at the entrance to Magnolia Crescent' when they were all walking home (OP1).

Magnolia Road

Also found in Little Whinging, Magnolia Road is on the opposite side of Magnolia Crescent from Privet Drive (OP1).

Magorian

Acts as the leader of the centaurs of the forest. He is not as rash as Bane, but he does not trust humans (OP30, DH36).

mahogany

A wand wood that Mr Ollivander used to make James Potter's first wand, which was 'excellent for Transfiguration' (PS5).

Maidenhead

A town on the River Thames in Berkshire, to the west of London. In a *Daily Prophet* story about out-of-control Hallowe'en celebrations, a Maidenhead barbecue is mentioned as an example of a Wizarding party gone awry (DP4).

Majorca

A Mediterranean vacation spot where the Dursleys wanted to buy a vacation home (CS1) and where Petunia's friend Yvonne once vacationed (PS2).

Malcolm

Malcolm is one of Dudley Dursley's gang, which certainly tells you something about Malcolm (PS3, OP1).

Malfoy, Abraxas

Draco's grandfather who died of dragon pox (HBP9).

Malfoy, Draco

(b. 5 June, 1980; Slytherin 1991; Quidditch Seeker 1992–?; Prefect, 1995; Inquisitorial Squad)
The archrival of Harry Potter, son and only child of Lucius and Narcissa Malfoy. Draco worships his stern father and is doted on by his mother. The rivalry between Harry and Draco began on the Hogwarts Express at the start

of their first year (PS6) and continued in classes, in the corridors, and on the Quidditch pitch for the next six years (e.g., PS9, CS10, 11, etc.). Draco is a good student, although he wishes that Hogwarts actually taught how to perform Dark Magic, not just defend against it (GF11). Draco was seldom seen without his two friends, Crabbe and Goyle, who were much larger than he and function as bodyguards (e.g.PS6). (*See also* DH/e, PC-JKR2). Draco has white-blond hair and a pale, pointed face (PS5).

'draco' = L. 'dragon'; 'malfoy' = Fr. 'bad faith'

Malfoy, Lucius

(b. circa 1954; Slytherin 1965; Prefect, 1969)

Rich, haughty wizard, father of Draco Malfoy. Lucius was a Death Eater during the Voldemort's first rise to power, but after Voldemort fell Lucius 'came back saying he'd never meant any of it' (CS3). He used his position in the Wizarding world to wield considerable power in the Ministry of Magic; impressing people with the 'purity' of his wizarding blood and amount of Galleons he donated (CS14, OP9). (*See also* OP34, DH1).

'lucius' from 'lux' = L. 'light', probably a reference to 'Lucifer', a name for the Devil meaning 'light-bearer'

Malfoy Manor

A fine old manor house with extensive grounds (DH1) located in southwestern England in Wiltshire (OP15). Draco Malfoy grew up here with his parents, Lucius and Narcissa. (*See also* DH1, 23, 26).

Malfoy, Narcissa Black

(b. 1955; Slytherin, c. 1966; Death)

Lucius' wife and Draco's mother; blonde, blue eyes, with a haughty expression (GF8). Narcissa doted on her son (e.g. GF11, 13) and would do anything to protect her family (HBP2). When events threatened to tear the family apart, she became the strong one, holding things together and taking what steps were necessary to ensure that her son and husband were safe (DH1, 35).

'Narcissa' is the feminine form of the name Narcissus of Greek mythology. Narcissus fell in love with his own reflection and died gazing at himself.

Malfoy, Scorpius Hyperion

(b. 2006; Hogwarts, 2017)

Son of Draco Malfoy, and similar to him in appearance (DH/e).

'scorpius' = L. 'scorpion'

'Hyperion' = a Titan (the original gods) in Greek mythology (ITV-YIL)

Malkin, Madam

Proprietor of a robe shop in Diagon Alley called 'Madam Malkin's Robes for All Occasions'. She is a squat witch who is generally very friendly (PS5), though she becomes alarmed when wands are drawn in her shop (HBP6).

'malkin' = Brit. 'an untidy woman'

mallowsweet

A plant which, along with sage, is burned as part of the centaur divination ritual. They observe the fumes and flames to refine the results of their stargazing (OP27).

There are a number of plants which are called 'mallow', including the marsh mallow, the roots of which were originally used to make marshmallows.

manager of Flourish and Blotts

A much-put-upon wizard who has to deal with bizarre and dangerous books assigned by Hogwarts teachers. He complained that the store's copies of the *Invisible Book of Invisibility* 'cost a fortune, and we never found them' and dealt with the fact that his copies of the *Monster Book of Monsters* attacked him and each other (PA4).

Mandrake

Also known as the Mandragora, this plant is used to make Mandrake Re-storative Draught, a powerful potion which can cure the effects of Petrification (CS9). Mandrake seedlings are tufty little plants, purplish-green in colour, with what look like tiny babies growing where the roots would be (CS6). The cry of the Mandrake is fatal to humans — even as a baby, the howls can knock a person out for a couple of hours — so special care must be taken when handling them (CS6, DH31).

J.K. Rowling's version of the mandrake plant comes directly from folklore, although embellished with her typical humour. The root of a mandrake was thought by ancient sorcerers to resemble the human form and therefore was considered to be powerfully magical. When pulled from the ground, the root was said to emit a scream that would kill any who hear it, which necessitated some rather drastic measures for obtaining it. One account suggests tying a dog to the partially-exposed root, then walking away quickly. The dog would try to follow and pull out the root. The dog would then be killed by the scream (reflecting the same cavalier attitude toward animal life that we see in the Wizarding world). Mandrakes were thought by some alchemists to be the original human form, as created by God from the ground, and as such were cultivated with a variety of strange rituals and procedures in the hope of cre-

ating a 'homunculus', a tiny animal-like humanoid which would serve the alchemist who created it.

manticore

A sentient creature, capable of intelligent speech but classified as a beast due to violent tendencies. A manticore has a human-like head, a lion's body, and the venomous tail of a scorpion (GF24). In 1296, a manticore seriously wounded someone but was let off because no one dared go near it (PA11).

The manticore comes originally from Persian mythology. The name comes from the Persian word 'martikhoras', meaning 'man-eater'. Like a sphinx, the manticore was said to pose a riddle to its victims before eating them.

maple

A wand wood used on occasion by Ollivander (PS5).

The maple wand might have been a pretty good fit for Harry, actually. In tree lore it signifies an independent mind, with ambition and an eagerness to learn and experience new things, but also someone who can be reserved and complex. Sounds like Harry.

Marauders

Self-assigned nickname for James Potter, Sirius Black, Remus Lupin, and Peter Pettigrew, who created the Marauder's Map (PA17, HBP21).

Marauder's Map

Magical map of Hogwarts created by the Marauders that shows the castle and grounds and the location of people within the school (PA10). When not in use, the map looks like a blank parchment (PA14). (*See also* BLC).

Marchbanks, Madam Griselda
(b. mid-1800s)

Elderly witch, head of the Wizarding Examinations Authority (OP31) and at one point a member of the Wizengamot (OP15). She is at least a decade Dumbledore's senior, since when he was about seventeen, she was already working for the Wizarding Examinations Authority and personally administered his N.E.W.T.s (OP31).

Marius

Wizard bearing a Probity Probe in front of Gringotts (DH24).

Marjoribanks, Beaumont
(1742–1845)

Marjoribanks was a pioneer in the field of Herbology. Marjoribanks is also credited with discovering Gillyweed, although Elladora Ketteridge had discovered it about a century earlier (FW).

Mars Bars

Harry's idea of a real treat — that is, until he visited the trolley on the Hogwarts Express and discovered Wizarding sweets (PS6).

Marsh, Madam

An elderly witch who seems prone to motion sickness, but nevertheless braves the Knight Bus. (PA3, OP24).

Martha

A Muggle girl working at Tom Riddle's orphanage the time of Dumbledore's visit (HBP13).

Masking Fog

One of the methods used to hide Quidditch pitches from Muggles (DP2).

Mason, Mr and Mrs

Builder and his wife, who were dinner guests of the Dursleys' on Harry's twelfth birthday — an unfortunate night for all parties involved (CS1).

Their surname refers to someone who works in brick and stone, fitting for a builder.

Maxime, Madam Olympe

Headmistress of Beauxbatons Academy, respected both for her work at her job (GF29) and for her magical power (OP20). Though she's a half-giant with the height to prove it, she publicly denies her ancestry (GF23) and runs counter to all stereotypes of giants, as she dresses elegantly in silk and jewels, and is an excellent dancer (GF29). (*See also* GF19, GF23, GF28, HBP30).

Madam Maxime's names suggest her large size. The word 'maxime' in Latin means 'the very largest', while 'Olympus' is the name of a mountain in Greece where the gods were thought to live.

McBride, Dougal

Seeker for the Pride of Portree (DP3).

McDonald, Natalie

(Gryffindor, 1994)

Hogwarts student (GF12).

This character was named for a Canadian girl who wrote to J.K. Rowling in the late 1990s. Natalie at that time was terminally ill and J.K. Rowling wrote back and told her some of the secrets of the books to come. Sadly, Natalie had died by the time the letter arrived. Natalie's mother responded to the letter and she and J.K. Rowling have since become friends. J.K. Rowling sorted Natalie into Gryffindor as a tribute to the girl's courage (Mac).

McGonagall, Minerva

(b. circa 1925; Gryffindor c. 1937; Transfiguration professor, from Decem-

ber 1956; Head of Gryffindor House; Order of the Phoenix)

Hogwarts Transfiguration professor for over forty years, as well as its Deputy Headmistress. McGonagall is a powerful witch and Animagus (PS1, 4). McGonagall was known for teaching challenging classes (CS6). She did not break rules (PA8) or tolerate misbehaviour (CS5, PA14). Though generally respectful of her fellow teachers, McGonagall occasionally used her sharp wit to skewer those she considered frauds, most noticeably Lockhart (CS16) and Trelawney (PA11). However, when faced with Dolores Umbridge, she defended Trelawney (OP26) and Hagrid (OP31).

Minerva in Greek mythology was the goddess of wisdom. It's easy to see how that name fits the character. However, the last name, McGonagall, comes from a very unlikely source. William Topaz McGonagall was a self-styled poet in the late 1800s in Scotland. His clunky rhymes and faltering rhythms, along with his fondness for subject matter such as train disasters, have earned him the title of the worst poet of all time.

McGonagall's office

Located on the first floor of Hogwarts (PS15), with a window overlooking the Quidditch pitch (PA9). McGonagall's office has a fireplace with a mantelpiece (CS18) that can be connected to the Floo Network (HBP18). She keeps a tin of biscuits on her desk (OP12, OP19), tartan decorations, and more often than not these days, the huge silver Quidditch Cup (OP19).

McGuffin, Jim

Muggle weatherman on the evening news Vernon Dursley was watching on 1 November 1981 (PS1).

McKinnon, Marlene

(d. July 1981; Order of the Phoenix)

A member of the Order of the Phoenix in the 1970s (PS4, GF30, OP9, DH10).

McLaggen, Cormac

(Gryffindor, 1990; Slug Club; Substitute Quidditch Keeper, 1996)

A burly Gryffindor, arrogant and foolhardy. He was accepted into the 'Slug Club' because of his Uncle Tiberius who had been a favourite student of Horace Slughorn's (HBP7). During his seventh year Cormac tried out for Gryffindor Keeper, (HBP11). (*See also* HBP 19).

J.K. Rowling talked about the origin of McClaggen's name in an interview:

You have to be careful if you get friendly with me because you tend to turn up in my books, and if you offend me, you often turn up as a nasty character. I found the name McClaggen the other day, which I think is a great name. There is a McClaggen in book six because I thought that it is a surname that is too good to waste (EBF).

She never made it clear whether she took the name from someone who had actually offended her, but she certainly gave it to an unpleasant character. In the book, Cormack demonstrates what might be seen as the bad side of Gryffindor: courage and self-confidence turned into arrogance and boorishness.

McLeod, Cormack
Manager of the Montrose Magpies (DP2, 3).

McTavish, Tarquin
(b. 1955)
Wizard who got into trouble for magically inserting his Muggle neighbour into a teapot (JKR).

Meadowes, Dorcas
(died c. 1981; Order of the Phoenix)
Member of the Order of the Phoenix in the 1970s (OP9).

Medal for Magical Merit
Award given to Tom Riddle fifty years ago. Since Tom was one of the brightest wizards ever to attend Hogwarts, this award may be one for achievement in academic studies (CS13).

Medical magic
Healing magic performed by Healers (OP22), or occasionally mediwizards (GF8) or witch doctors (DP1). St. Mungo's Hospital for Magical Maladies and Injuries is the main centre for medical magic in Britain (OP22), in addition to a hospital wing at Hogwarts (PS8). Medical magic has healed and re-grown broken bones (PS9, CS10, DH25), fixed and replaced teeth (GF23, DH5), relieved the common cold (CS8) and repaired the scarring power of thoughts (OP38), and it's all done with treatments ranging from elaborate potions (OP38) and spells to chocolate (PA5).

Mediterranean Sea
Large sea which separates Europe from Africa. Somehow merpeople (including the Greek Sirens), the hippocampus and the sea serpent manage to live in this heavily trafficked sea undetected. The Mediterranean Sea is also the natural habitat of gillyweed, as described in *Magical Water-Plants of the Mediterranean* (GF35).

Mediwizard

Healers who were present to treat injuries at the Quidditch World Cup; they seem to differ from other Healers in the way that Muggle paramedics, or perhaps athletic trainers, differ from doctors (GF8).

Mega-Mutilation Part Three

Video game Dudley was fond of. It does sound like something he'd like (GF2).

megaphone, magical

Device used to give Quidditch play-by-play (PA15, HBP14, 19), to make announcements to the entire student body (CS14), and to address a rally (DP2).

Meliflua, Araminta

Cousin to Sirius Black's mother; she tried to have a Ministry bill passed that would make it legal to hunt Muggles (OP6).

Memory Charm

See OBLIVIATE.

Men Who Love Dragons Too Much

Harry and Hermione tried this book while searching for a simple spell for dealing with a dragon, but couldn't find anything (GF20).

Merlin

Considered to be the most famous wizard of all time, part of the court of King Arthur and a specialist in Charms magic (PS6). Merlin believed that wizards should help Muggles and therefore created the Order of Merlin to support laws protecting and benefiting Muggles (FW).

Merlin is probably the most famous wizard in folklore, figuring in a variety of tales from the history of Britain. He is most known as the advisor to King Arthur, although his role in the stories is not consistent and is sometimes portrayed as evil. Over the centuries of retelling, folklore paints Merlin most often as the wise magician who masterminded Arthur's birth and eventual ascent to the throne.

'Merlin's Beard!'

An exclamation of surprise, used frequently by Arthur Weasley (GF7). There are number of other variations on this as well (DH12).

Mermish

The language of merpeople, which some wizards can speak as well — Barty Crouch Sr (GF7) and Albus Dumbledore included. It sounds like screeching above water, but underwater it simply sounds like English spoken in a croaky voice (GF26).

Merpeople

Intelligent water-dwelling folk who have developed their own culture and social structures and have a great love of music (GF26). Merpeople are found all over the world, including Scotland in the Lake near Hogwarts (GF26) and Loch Lomond (FW). The merpeople of Hogwarts have greyish skin and long green hair (GF26). Merpeople live in underwater villages, which consist of crude stone dwellings (GF26).

Mermaids have appeared in legends and folklore from ancient times. Descriptions from all over the world are very similar: a creature which has the tail of a fish to the waist, with the torso, arms, and head of a human female. In some stories, mermaids kill humans accidentally because they forget that humans can't breathe water. In others, mermaids intentionally lure sailors to wreck their ships and drown them when they fall into the sea.

Merrythought, Galatea

Defence Against the Dark Arts professor from c.1895 to c.1945 (HBP20).

Considering the subject this professor taught, his name is interesting. Certainly a positive mental state would be helpful as a defence against any Dark magic. In some cases, for example the Patronus, 'merry thought' is absolutely required for spells to be effective. 'Galatea' was the name of a mythological sea-nymph.

Mersey River

A three-way broom crash occurred over this river involving wizards racing to get to a Celestina Warbeck concert in Liverpool (DP2).

Merwyn the Malicious

Medieval wizard known for creating many nasty jinxes and curses (FW).

metal-charmer

A wizarding occupation analogous to that of a Muggle metalsmith (FW).

Metamorphmagus

Witch or wizard born with the ability to change their appearance at will. Nymphadora Tonks is a Metamorphmagus (OP3), as is her son Teddy Lupin (BLC).

'meta' = Gr. 'changed, altered' + 'morphe' = Gr. 'form, shape' + 'magus' = Persian 'wise one, magician'

Metamorph Medal

A necklace marketed by a street vendor in Diagon Alley which was supposed to allow a person to change their appearance at will; in reality, it turned them orange and produced bizarre warts. While technically that is a change in appearance, it is not likely what the customer had in mind (HBP5).

Meteolojinx Recanto
(mee-tee-OH-lo-jinx ree-CAN-toh)
One of the spells used by Magical Maintenance to control the weather at the Ministry of Magic; in this case, it halts rain (DH13).
'meteorologia' = Gr. 'meteorology' + 'jinx' + 'recanto' = L. 'to recant; to charm back, charm away'

Midgen, Eloise
(Hogwarts, early 1990s)
Tried to curse off her acne and had to have her nose reattached by Madam Pomfrey (GF13). To this day, Harry, Ron, and Hermione speak of her as the standard against which bad acne must be measured. Eloise may be in Hufflepuff, since the Hufflepuffs chatted about her in a very familiar way in Herbology class (GF13).

Miggs, Martin
Fictional character in a wizarding comic book that Ron was reading, *The Adventures of Martin Miggs, the Mad Muggle* (CS3).

'Might as well be hanged for a dragon as an egg'
This is analogous to the Muggle expression about being 'hanged for a sheep as a lamb'. The sense of it is that if one is to be punished severely for a minor offence, one might as well go ahead and commit a more serious offence that won't be punished much more severely (OP2).

Millamant's Magic Marquees
Company that hires magical tents for special events (DH6).

Mimbulus mimbletonia
A very rare Assyrian plant that resembles a gray cactus, but with boils where the spines would have been. The boils spew Stinksap upon contact. This plant is a particular favourite of Neville Longbottom's, who received one as a present from his Great Uncle Algie for his fifteenth birthday. Like its owner, the plant grew a lot over that year (OP10, 11, 38). Password to get into Gryffindor Tower (OP11).
The name probably comes from the genus of plants called mimulus. *In the lore of flower remedies, as developed by British physician Dr Edward Bach in the 1920s, an essence made from the* mimulus *flower is said to counter anxiety and fear.*

Mimsy-Porpington, Sir Nicholas de
The full name of the Gryffindor house ghost, popularly known as Nearly Headless Nick (PS7, etc.).

Minister of Magic

The head of the Wizarding government. This is a position of great honour and prestige, as well as great re-
sponsibility. Unfortunately, the actions
of recent Ministers resulted in much
suffering and misery in the world.

Known Ministers of Magic:

- 1798-1811: Artemisia Lufkin, first
  witch to become Minister for Magic
  (FW)
- 1811–1819: Grogan Stump (FB,
  FW)
- 1819–1865: unknown
- 1865–1903: Faris 'Spout-Hole'
  Spavin (JKR)
- 1903–1962: unknown
- 1962–1968: Nobby Leach (JKR)
- 1968–1980: unknown
- 1980–1990: Millicent Bagnold
- 1990–1996: Cornelius Fudge
- 1996–1997: Rufus Scrimgeour
- 1997–1998: Pius Thicknesse
- 1998 ff.: Kingsley Shacklebolt

Ministry Cars

Cars that navigate traffic with magical
ease. The Ministry has loaned them for
the Weasleys to use on occasion (PA5,
HBP6).

Ministry of Magic

The governmental authority for the
Wizarding world in Britain. Its basic
mission is to keep the Muggles from
finding out about an entire culture of
magical folk (PS5). It's a huge, complicated, and inefficient bureaucracy, just
like most governmental organisations.
The Ministry consists of seven de-
partments, of which the Department
of Magical Law Enforcement is the
largest (OP7). The numerous Depart-
ments, Committees, Boards, and Offices make and enforce laws and regulations. Besides keeping the Wizarding
world secret, the Ministry also handles
commerce and international relations.

Ministry of Magic Decree of 1631

Legislation that forbade all 'Non-
Human Magical Beings' from carrying wands (JKR).

Ministry of Magic headquarters

Vast governmental office located in the
heart of London (OP7, DH12, 13).
The actual structure is underground,
although magical windows show whatever weather Magical Maintenance has
chosen for the day, from sunshine to
hurricanes.

Floor Guide:

- *Level One:* the offices of the Minister for Magic and administra-
  tive staff
- *Level Two:* Department of Magical Law Enforcement

- *Level Three:* Department of Magical Accidents and Catastrophes
- *Level Four:* Department for the Regulation and Control of Magical Creatures
- *Level Five:* Department of International Magical Cooperation
- *Level Six:* Department of Magical Transportation
- *Level Seven:* Department of Magical Games and Sports
- *Level Eight:* Atrium
- *Level Nine:* Department of Mysteries
- *Level Ten:* Courtrooms

Minsk

The capital city of Belarus, an Eastern European country which was at one time part of the Soviet Union. Hagrid and Madame Maxime passed through Minsk on their way to meet the giants in the mountains (OP20).

The fact that Hagrid and Madame Maxime passed through Minsk means that the mountains they were visiting were very likely in Russia, and that they travelled across the entire length of Europe.

Mirror of Erised

A large magical mirror with a gold frame and two clawed feet. The inscription carved around the top reads 'Erised stra ehru oyt ube cafru oyt on wohsi,' which is 'I show not your face but your heart's desire' written backwards (that is, in what is called 'mirror writing'). When a person looks into the Mirror, they see the 'deepest, most desperate desire of their heart' (PS12). Dumbledore used the power at one point to keep something safely hidden (PS17, HBP23).

Over the course of the books, J.K. Rowling introduces various magical artefacts and spells which reveal the innate qualities of her characters. The Mirror of Erised is one such artefact. According to J.K. Rowling, Voldemort would see 'himself, powerful and eternal' (TLC). Dumbledore would see 'his family alive, whole and happy — Ariana, Percival and Kendra all returned to him, and Aberforth reconciled to him' (BLC). Harry sees his family in the Mirror; Ron sees himself as Head Boy and Quidditch champion (PS12). When she was asked in an interview what Snape would see in the Mirror, J.K. Rowling wouldn't give an answer. That interview happened just before the last book came out, so it might be assumed that what she didn't want to reveal was that Snape would see himself and Lily, together.

mirrors, talking

Magical mirrors which give advice, whether you want them to or not.

Harry encountered one in the kitchen of the Burrow (CS3) and another one in room 11 of the Leaky Cauldron when he stayed there for a few weeks (PA4).

mirrors, two-way

Magical means of communicating, originally used by James and Sirius while they were in school. Sirius gave one to Harry, but he never even opened the package until it was too late (OP24, 38, DE23, 28, BLC).

Misericordia, Cordelia

(1298–1401)

Hag representative at fourteenth century summit of Wizard's Council (FW).

'misericordia' = L. 'tender-heartedness, pity, compassion, mercy'

mistletoe

The front yard of the Lovegood house has a sign advertising 'PICK YOUR OWN MISTLETOE' (DH20). Dobby decorated the Room of Requirement with mistletoe (OP21).

Mistletoe was one of the druids' most sacred plants. It signified, among other things, life-force and fertility, which in turn influenced the custom of kissing under the mistletoe.

Misuse of Magic Office

This appeared on the first W.O.M.B.A.T. exam as an answer choice, implying that it is a Ministry department (JKR). However this was likely a confusion between the Misuse of Muggle Artefacts Office and the Improper Use of Magic Office (which is what the test should probably read instead).

Misuse of Muggle Artefacts Office

A two-person office in the Department for Magical Law Enforcement at the Ministry of Magic, not even considered important enough to get its own window (OP7). Arthur Weasley worked in this office for years, along with an old warlock named Perkins. The office is charged with keeping enchanted items out of the hands of Muggles and with crafting legislation that determines legal — and illegal — uses for Muggle items (CS3).

Mnemosyne Clinic for Memory Modification

With the slogan, 'Helping witches and wizards find their marbles since 1426,' the Mnemosyne Clinic advertises in the *Daily Prophet* that they perform charms to help fix up faulty memories (DP4).

from 'mnemonikos' = Gk. 'of or pertaining to memory'

Moaning Myrtle

(d. 1943; Ravenclaw c. 1941)

A Ravenclaw (JKR) student at Hogwarts in 1943 (CS16, 17, GF25, HBP21, 24), now a ghost. After her death, Myrtle decided to haunt Olive Hornby to make her pay for teasing her, until the Ministry had to step in and stop her (GF25). She then returned to the site of her death, a toilet, which she has haunted ever since (CS8, 9).

The name 'Moaning Myrtle' is an interesting one. It is similar to the term 'Moaning Minnie' which was used in World War Two for a type of German mortar which made a shrieking sound when it was fired. The name came to be used as a slang term for someone who constantly moaned or complained about things.

Mobiliarbus

(MO-bi-lee-AR-bus)

Spell which moves a tree (PA10). The basic spell for moving something starts with the 'Mobili-' prefix. It is up to the caster to be able to tack on the correct Latinate word for the object to be moved, in this case a tree.

'mobilis' = L. 'movable' + 'arbor' = L. 'tree'

Mobilicorpus

(MO-bi-lee-COR-pus)

Spell which moves a body. Again the basic spell for moving something starts with the '*Mobili-*' prefix, and in this case, the Latin word for 'body' is tacked on the end (PA19, 20).

'mobilis' L. movable + 'corpus' L. body

Mockridge, Cuthbert

Head of the Goblin Liaison Office (GF7).

Modern Magical History

Harry is mentioned in this book, according to Hermione, who read it in preparation for her first year at Hogwarts (PS6).

Moke

A small magical lizard that can shrink at will (DH7).

Mokeskin pouch

Harry receives one of these from Hagrid for his seventeenth birthday, as Hagrid explains that only the owner can retrieve items from within this rare object (DH7, 10, 18).

MoM

Commonly used abbreviation in fandom and even by J.K. Rowling herself for Ministry of Magic.

money

There are three basic types of coins in the Wizarding world: the gold Galleon, the silver Sickle, and the bronze Knut. There are seventeen Sickles to a Galleon and twenty-nine Knuts to a Sickle, which seems like it would make for some rather confusing maths for anyone trying to make change, but Hagrid says it's 'simple' (PS5). Exchange rates (approximate):

  1 Galleon = £5.00 (US$7.65) (CR)
  1 Sickle = £0.29 (US$.45)
  1 Knut = £0.01 (US$.02)

Monster Book of Monsters, The
Required textbook for Care of Magical Creatures in Harry's third year. The book attempted to bite anyone who touched it, causing rather a lot of problems for the manager of Flourish and Blotts (PA4, 6).

Montague
(Slytherin, c. 1989; Quidditch Chaser c. 1992–1996, Captain 1995–1996; Inquisitorial Squad)
Member of Umbridge's Inquisitorial Squad who made the mistake of trying to take House Points from the Weasley twins without witnesses (OP19, 28, 30).

Montgomery sisters
(Hogwarts students, 1990s)
Twin sisters whose five-year-old brother was bitten by Fenrir Greyback in the spring of 1997 (HBP22).

Montmorency, Laverne de
(1823–1893)
Invented a number of love potions (FW)

Montrose Magpies
A Quidditch team in in the British and Irish league (DP1-4).

Moody, Alastor 'Mad Eye'
(d. 1997; Order of the Phoenix)
Retired Auror, considered one of the best Dark Wizard catchers the Ministry has ever had. Mad-Eye was noted for his paranoia, particularly in regard to food and drink, but also wand safety; this last may be related to his own missing leg (GF13, OP3), but that is mere speculation. Moody took command of any operation he was associated with. He was brusque and efficient (OP3, DH4, 5, also DH15). Moody's favourite expression was 'Constant vigilance!'
The name 'Alastor' was one sometimes given to the Greek god Zeus in mythology ('Zeus Alastor'). The name referred to the Zeus's role as an avenger of evil deeds.

Moon
(Hogwarts 1991)
A student in the same class as Harry, though sorted into a different house (PS7).

Mooncalf

A strange creature that dances by the light of the moon and whose dung is very valuable (JKR).

moon frog

Someone interviewed by *The Quibbler* claimed to have a bag of moon frogs, substantiating his claim that he had flown to the moon on a Cleansweep 6 (OP10).

Moonshine, Regulus

A professor who claimed to have developed a potion that would decrease a 'hag's natural desire to feast on human flesh'. He had several chunks of flesh missing from his face and neck, thanks to his test subjects (DP4).

'moonshine' = Eng. 'moonlight; illegally-distilled liquor; nonsense'

Moony

Remus Lupin gained this nickname as one of the Marauders because of his condition (PA17).

moor

Open land, usually raised higher than the surrounding terrain, where few trees grow. Moors tend to be sparsely inhabited. Most Quidditch pitches in Britain are located on deserted moors, far from Muggle eyes (GF6, DP1-4).

A moor is a broad tract of open land, often high but poorly drained, with patches of heath and peat bogs. Of the heather moorland in the United Kingdom, most of it lies in North Yorkshire, Wales, Cumbria and Dartmoor (with some moorlands in the far West Country in the county of Cornwall). Godric Gryffindor hailed from 'wild moor' according to the Sorting Hat, and could accordingly have been from the any of these regions (GF12).

Mopsus

Ancient Greek soothsayer; for more information, see the Fantastic Wizard cards (FW).

Mopsus was an ancient Greek seer who was a rival of Calchas, another seer. Both seers made predictions about an upcoming battle. When Mopsus' predictions proved to be true and Calchas' false, the latter died of grief.

Mopsy

A character initially included in GF, who was a batty dog-owner living on the outskirts of Hogsmeade, and adopted Sirius Black, thinking him a stray. Ms. Rowling cut the character because she 'added nothing to the plot' (JKR).

Moran

Witch who was an Irish Quidditch Team Chaser, one third of the famous trio of Chasers, 'Troy, Mullet, and Moran' (GF8).

Mordaunt, Ethelbard
Wizard whose next door neighbour, Elladora Guffy, was overly fond of practical joke spells. Ethelbard sent a letter complaining about Guffy to the *Daily Prophet* (DP1).

Morgan le Fey (Morgana)
A bird Animagus and King Arthur's half sister. She was a dark sorceress and an enemy of Merlin. For more information, see the Famous Wizard cards (FW). She appeared on one of the first Chocolate Frog trading cards Harry Potter ever saw (PS6).
The legendary figure of Morgan le Fey, also known as Morgana, takes a number of forms in various tales in which she appears. Originally, Morgana was a fairy ('le fey' = Fr. 'the fairy'). In later works, she was Arthur's half-sister who dallied with one of his knights and was subsequently estranged from the king. She was an enemy of Arthur and Guinevere for many years, but was finally reconciled and was one of the sorceresses who bore Arthur, gravely wounded, to Avalon to be healed.

Morgan, Valmai
Chaser who replaced Wilda Griffiths on the Holyhead Harpies team (DP3, 4).

Morholt
An ancient giant, brother of the King of Ireland. For more information, see the Famous Wizard cards (FW).
Morholt is not a giant but a mighty Irish warrior in the British folktales, including the Arthurian legends. In an early tale, Morholt comes to Britain to collect a debt owed to Ireland, whereupon Tristan battles him to erase the debt. He grievously wounds Morholt, leaving a piece of his sword in the wound, but the Irish warrior wounds Tristan in return with a poisoned spear. Morholt manages to return to Ireland to die. Tristan, poisoned and dying as well, travels to Ireland in disguise to be healed, but is found out when the piece missing from his blade is seen to match the piece taken from Morholt's wound. In the tales of King Arthur, Morholt is an Irish warrior who becomes a knight of the Round Table.

Morsmordre
(mors-MOR-druh)
'The Dark Mark'
Conjures an immense glowing skull in the sky, comprised of green sparks, with a snake coming out of the skull's mouth. This spell is known only to Death Eaters, who send it up in the sky when they kill. The Dark Mark

caused panic at the Quidditch World Cup in 1994 (GF9).

'mors' = L. 'death' + 'mordere' = L. 'to bite'

Mortlake

A Ministry raid on his house in August 1992 turned up some suspiciously unusual ferrets (CS3).

Mortlake is a district of Greater London, located on the south bank of the Thames. In Elizabethan times, the town of Mortlake was the location of one of the most impressive libraries in Britain, collected by Dr John Dee, a scholar and astrologist who was obsessed with the occult and who claimed to speak with angels and spirits. Sadly, his library was targeted by a mob in 1583 which feared him because he was a magician. The mob destroyed and looted much of the collection.

Mosag

An Acromantula, found by Hagrid to be a wife for Aragog (CS15). Together, Aragog and Mosag raised a family of scores of Acromantulas (HBP22).

'mosag' = urban slang: 'a very ugly girl'

Most Charming Smile Award

A somewhat silly award given out by *Witch Weekly* Magazine. It has been won five times by Gilderoy Lockhart, which is quite possibly his only genuine accomplishment (CS6).

Mostafa, Hassan

Chairwizard of the International Association of Quidditch in 1994, when he served as referee for the World Cup. Mostafa is small, skinny, and bald, with a huge moustache (GF8).

Most Extraordinary Society of Potioneers

Founded by Hector Dagworth-Granger (HBP9).

Moste Potente Potions

Illustrated book of very powerful and dangerous potions, kept in the Restricted Section of the Hogwarts library. It contains (among other things) the instructions for making Polyjuice Potion (CS9).

motorcycle, flying

An amazing magical flying machine once owned by Sirius Black. It's huge, big enough to carry Hagrid (or perhaps it magically expands as necessary to accommodate its rider (PS1, DH4).

Mould-on-the-Wold

A town where the Dumbledore's family lived when he was young, and where Ariana was attacked by Muggles (DH11).

The word 'wold' originally referred to a forested hill, but the meaning changed to refer to rolling hills. In any case, it only survives now as part of place names, such as 'Cotswolds'. Of the over two hundred place names in Britain which include the word 'wold', the town with the name closest is Stow-on-the-Wold, located in Gloucestershire.

Mountain Troll
The biggest and nastiest type of troll (PS10, OP31, DP2).

Mrs Scower's Magical Mess Remover
A magical cleaning product used extensively by Filch (CS9) and stored in various broom cupboards around Hogwarts (GF18).

'Mudblood'
A derogatory term used by 'pure-blood' wizards to describe someone of Muggle descent. Once considered absolutely foul and not to be used in polite company, the term unfortunately became more common during Voldemort's second war against the Wizarding world (CS7, etc.).

Muffliato
(muf-lee-AH-to)
A spell Harry learned from the Half-Blood Prince's notes in his potions book. It fills the ears of people nearby with a buzzing sound so they cannot overhear a conversation. Hermione disapproved of it (HBP12, c.f. DH7, DH14).

'muffle' = Eng. 'to wrap something up to deaden sound'

Muggle
Non-magical people (PS4). Muggles are completely oblivious to the existence of magic, going so far as to routinely create non-magical reasons for things that happen to them. Many wizards look upon Muggles with disdain, viewing them as lesser beings (DH12), while others, like Arthur Weasley, simply seem to think they're kind of cute (CS3). To most witches and wizards, Muggle society is essentially unknown. Hogwarts does offers a class in Muggle Studies (CS14). Despite this, wizards remain largely ignorant, and their attempts to act like Muggles can be humorous indeed (GF7).

Muggle-baiting
Considered a game by some wizards, but it's one Arthur Weasley despises. It consists intentionally confusing Muggles with magic, such as making keys shrink so they can't find them (CS3).

Muggle-borns
A term used for people of magical ability whose parents were Muggles,

like Hermione Granger or Lily Evans (HBP4, DH13).

Muggle-born Registration Commission

A Ministry of Magic program, headed by Dolores Umbridge, which was designed to persecute and imprison witches and wizards who had been born to Muggle parents (DH13). (*See also* BLC).

Muggle guard

Magical device that acts as an alarm when touched by a non-magical hand; one such device is a Muggle-deterring-gate (DP2, JKR).

Muggle Protection Act

A law written in part by Arthur Weasley. Lucius Malfoy saw this law as a threat to wizard superiority (CS4, 12, 18).

Muggle-Repelling Charm

See REPELLO MUGGLETUM.

Muggle Studies

A Hogwarts class taught recently by Quirinius Quirrell (BLC), Charity Burbage (DH1), and Alecto Carrow (DH12 ff.). Its textbook is *Home Life and Social Habits of British Muggles*, and class work includes creating charts showing Muggles using levers to lift heavy objects, understanding the importance of electricity to Muggle technology, and so on (esp. PA13).

Muggle-Worthy Excuse Committee

A branch of the Department of Magical Accidents and Catastrophes, which in the case of a magical accident or disaster is responsible for generating plausible explanations to be disseminated to the Muggle population (OP7).

Mulciber

The name of two Death Eaters. The first went to school with Voldemort (HBP20). The second was a school friend of Snape and Avery some twenty years later (DH33). One of the Mulcibers was an Imperius Curse specialist (GF30). (*See also* OP35).

The two Mulcibers, older and younger, are not differentiated in the stories.

'Mulciber' = alternative name for the god Vulcan in Roman mythology; Vulcan appears as a demon in Milton's Paradise Lost *with the name 'Mulciber'.*

Muldoon, Burdock

Chief of the Wizard's Council from 1448 to 1450 (FW).

The dates given on the chocolate frog cards are inconsistent with the reference in Fantastic Beasts *which places Muldoon 'in the fourteenth century'. J.K. Rowling may simply have made the common mistake of referring to events in the 1400s as being in the fourteenth century.*

mulled mead

A favourite drink of Hagrid's (PA10).

Mullet

Witch who was the Irish National Team Chaser, one third of the famous trio of Chasers known as 'Troy, Mullet, and Moran' (GF8).

mummy

A preserved human body, wrapped in clothes. Pavarti Patil is afraid of them (PA7). When the Weasleys toured the tombs of Ancient Egypt, they encountered mutant skeletons of Muggles who'd been cursed by spells put on the tombs by Egyptian wizards. Perhaps the mummies Parvati fears are similar to these (PA1).

Munch, Eric

A badly-shaven watchwizard at the Ministry of Magic, who during sits at the security desk in the Atrium where visitors are required to present their wands for registration (OP7, 14).

Murcus, Merchieftainess

The leader of the community of merfolk in the Hogwarts lake. She is on speaking terms with Dumbledore, which is saying something since she speaks Mermish (GF26).

Muriel, Auntie

(1890-present)

A great aunt of the Weasleys who is quite an eccentric and outspoken character. She doesn't seem to have any sense of tact; however, she is kind and generous in her own peculiar way (HBP29, DH5, 8, 24).

Murtlap

A magical water creature. Its tentacles can be made into a yellow liquid, Essence of Murtlap, which soothes and heals wounds (OP 15, 18, 26).

musical box

This mysterious object sat on the shelves in number twelve, Grimmauld Place, and when wound made everyone sleepy (OP6).

Myrtle's Bathroom

The gloomiest, most depressing bathroom Harry has ever entered, though its poor light and lack of proper maintenance probably have something to do with the fact that it is haunted by Moaning Myrtle (CS9, 16, DH31).

There is a continuity error in the second book's description of Moaning Myrtle's bathroom. Hermione tells Harry and Ron that it's on the first floor while chatting at the Deathday Party. However, a few chapters later the first Basilisk attack happens right outside of Moaning Myrtle's bathroom and the book clearly places that event on the second floor.

Mysteries, Department of

Section of the Ministry of Magic, deep in the lowest level, where wizards called Unspeakables research some of the deepest mysteries of existence, exploring and experimenting in various chambers which are clustered around a central, circular room lined with doors (OP24, OP34). Among the forces explored are time, death, thought, and love (OP35, OP37). Part of the time area consists of a vast Hall of Prophecies (OP34, 35). Because of the secret nature of the work done in the Department of Mysteries, strange rumours often arise about what goes on there (OP18).

𝔑

Nagini

(d. 1998)

Voldemort's massive snake. As a Parseltongue, Voldemort had unusual control over snakes; however, his attachment to and control over Nagini was particularly strong (esp. OP21, HBP23, DH17, 36).

'Nagini' = female snake deity, from 'naga' = Sanskrit 'snake'

In both Hinduism and Buddhism, the Naga are deities who take the form of large snakes. The feminine version of the Naga is called a Nagini. The Naga are generally evil in the stories and are in constant conflict with Garuda, a gigantic man-bird.

Nagnok

A Gringotts goblin several hundred years ago who was involved in a most unfortunate incident (JKR).

Nargle

A creature that Luna believes infests mistletoe (OP21).

Nastily Exhausting Wizarding Tests (N.E.W.T.s)

A standard exam taken by students at the end of their seventh year at Hogwarts. These tests are administered by the Wizarding Examinations Authority and are given at the same time as the O.W.L.s are given to fifth-year students. Passing scores on various N.E.W.T. exams are required for different professions in the Wizarding world (PA16).

The N.E.W.T.s are the equivalent of A-levels, standard exams given to British students prior to their entering university.

Nature's Nobility: A Wizarding Genealogy

Sirius' family kept a copy of this book (OP6, DH22).

Nearly Headless Nick

Nickname of the ghost of Sir Nicholas de Mimsy Porpington, a wizard who died in a botched execution on 31 October, 1492 (CS8). Nick wears a tunic with a ruff to hide the fact that his head is nearly severed (GF12, OP38).

He is the resident ghost of Gryffindor House and is always helpful to Gryffindor students (PS7). Nick occasionally entertains at Hogwarts banquets by re-enacting his own 'botched beheading' (PA8). On Hallowe'en of 1992, a five hundredth Deathday party was held in Nick's honour, attended by ghosts from all over the country as well as Harry, Ron, and Hermione (CS8).

Nettles, Madam Z.
An apparently happy customer of the Kwikspell course. Before Kwikspell, she writes that her feeble attempts at magic were laughed at (CS8).

newt
Mentioned as a potion ingredient during Harry's research for the Second Task of the Triwizard Tournament (GF26).

N.E.W.T.s
See NASTILY EXHAUSTING WIZARDING TESTS.

New Theory of Numerology
A book, Harry's Christmas present to Hermione during their fifth year (OP23).

Niffler
A '[f]luffy, black and long-snouted creature' which burrows in dirt. Although

Nifflers are gentle and even affectionate, they are strongly attracted to anything shiny, which can make them difficult to control (GF28). They can be very useful for finding treasure (OP31).
The name probably comes from the word 'sniff', since Nifflers use their noses to sniff out treasure.

Nigellus, Phineas
See BLACK, PHINEAS NIGELLUS.

Nimbus Racing Broom Company
Company that, beginning in 1967, was the leader in producing high-end sport brooms. The company was founded by Devlin Whitehorn (FW). Harry's first broom was a Nimbus 2000, given to him by Professor McGonagall (PS10, CS7).
'nimbus' = L. 'cloud'

'Noble and Most Ancient House of Black, the'
The self-appointed title of the Black Family, proud and protective of their pure-blood status (OP6, BFT).

Nogtail
Dark magical creatures which are sometimes hunted for sport (HBP7).

'non-human magical beings'
A broad category of creatures that are

forbidden from carrying wands, according to the Wand Ban of 1631. Included in the ban are goblins and house-Elves (JKR).

Norbert / Norberta

A dragon hatched from an egg and raised for two weeks by Rubeus Hagrid in his hut at Hogwarts. It didn't work out too well (PS14, 17, DH7).

Norris, Mrs

A cat owned by Argus Filch, who helps him patrol the corridors at Hogwarts. Mrs Norris is a scrawny gray cat who is always on the lookout for troublemakers (PS8). Filch dotes on her, talking to her constantly and calling her 'my sweet'. They have an inexplicable connection that brings Filch running whenever Mrs Norris spots a student out of line (CS8).

Filch's cat is named after a character in Jane Austen's novel Mansfield Park. *In that book, Mrs Norris was a meddlesome, shallow person who frequently interfered in the life of the main character, Fanny Price.*

North Sea

Sea which lies to the north and east of Britain. Azkaban fortress is located on an island in the middle of the North Sea (HBP1).

North Tower

One of the towers of Hogwarts castle, where Trelawney's residence and the Divination classroom are located (PA16); access to the classroom at the top of this tower is by way of a silver ladder through a trap door (PA6).

Norwegian Ridgeback

Dragon species, native to Norway, which has black scales and characteristic black ridges along its back. Hagrid once obtained a black Ridgeback egg and hatched it, naming the baby Norbert (PS14).

Nose-Biting Teacup

A product sold at Zonko's Joke Shop (PA14).

Nosebleed Nougat

The most popular of Fred and George's Skiving Snackboxes, which gives a nosebleed designed to get students out of class (HBP6). One end, the Blood Blisterpod, causes the bleeding, and swallowing the other end stops it immediately (OP14).

Notable Magical Names of Our Time

A book in the Hogwarts library in which Harry, Ron, and Hermione unsuccessfully searched for Nicholas Flamel (PS12).

Nott

A longtime Death Eater (OP35, HBP20). His son is Theodore Nott, a Slytherin in Harry's year (JKR).

Nott, Theodore

(b. 1980; Slytherin, 1991)

Son of the Death Eater Nott, Theodore is a scrawny boy (OP26) who is something of a loner, not feeling the need to join anyone's clique (JKR).

Nottingham

A large city in the East Midlands region of Britain. A goblin family was murdered near Nottingham during the first war against Voldemort (OP5).

Nox

(noks)

Spell which extinguishes the wandlight cast by *Lumos* (PA17).

'nox' = L. 'night'

number four, Privet Drive

The home of Vernon and Petunia Dursley, their son Dudley, and for sixteen years their nephew Harry Potter. Located in Little Whinging, Surrey, the house is large, square, and it's kept immaculately clean (PS1, OP3). This house played a crucial role in protecting Harry throughout his childhood.

'privet' = a type of shrub commonly used for hedges

number twelve, Grimmauld Place

An Unplottable London row house on a shabby Muggle street, protected by many magic spells and protections. Grimmauld Place has been handed down through the generations of the Black family (OP6). The house itself is quite large, and rather scary-looking, with rows of house-elf heads mounted on the wall and creepy décor (OP4).

Numerology and Gramatica

An Arithmancy textbook. Hermione has a copy (PA16).

It seems strange that the title of an Arithmancy book would include the word 'Gramatica'. However, that word can be used to indicate the basic elements and understandings of any art or science, so in this case it suggests that the book covers the basic 'grammar', or structure, of Arithmancy, as well as the theories of Numerology, which might be the more esoteric philosophies of the subject.

Nurmengard

A prison built by Gellert Grindelwald, with his slogan — 'For the Greater Good' — over the door. Though it was designed to hold his enemies, he ended up incarcerated there himself after being defeated by Albus Dumbledore (DH18, 23).

The name of this prison comes from the Nuremberg Palace of Justice in the city of Nuremburg, Germany, where the famous Nazi trials after World War II were held. A prison is part of the palace complex. Nuremberg had been the site of Nazi rallies for many years before and during the war, which made the trials and prison a symbol of the defeat of the Nazis and justice being served.

Nutcombe, Honoria
(1665–1743)
Founder of the Society for the Reformation of Hags (FW).

oak

A wand wood which Ollivander used to make Hagrid's wand (PS5).

J.K. Rowling assigned an oak wand to Hagrid because the oak tree is considered 'King of the Forest' and it symbolises strength (JKR).

Oakby, Idris

(1872-1985)

Founder of the S.S.S. — the Society for the Support of Squibs (JKR).

Oblansk, Mr

The Bulgarian Minister for Magic, who watched the Quidditch World Cup along with Cornelius Fudge in the top box (GF8).

This is most likely not the Minister's name. Fudge tried to introduce him to the Malfoys but stumbled over the name ('Mr Oblansk - Obalonsk - Mr - well, he's the Bulgarian Minister of Magic'). Fudge passed it off with an undiplomatic 'he can't understand a word I'm saying anyway, so never mind' (GF8). As it turned out, the Minister could speak English just fine, but was leading Fudge

along. One wonders what other blunders Fudge made, assuming that his foolish words weren't being understood.

Obliteration Charm

Spell which can wipe out footprints in the snow (OP20).

Obliviate

(oh-BLI-vee-ate)

'Memory Charm', 'Memory Modifying Charm'

This charm modifies or erases portions of a person's memory. The Ministry of Magic has a team of Obliviators who erase the memories of Muggles who have seen evidence of magic (PS14). Memory Charms can be reversed (DH6), though in some cases not without permanent brain damage (CS16, GF33).

According to J.K. Rowling, there are two kinds of Memory Charms. One changes memories while the other totally erases them (BLC). This explains why Hermione says she's never cast a Memory Charm before (DH9) when she'd modified the memories of her parents just a few weeks

before. She was saying that she'd never cast the kind of charm that erases memories completely.
'oblivisci' = L. 'forget'

Obliviator

Title given to Ministry employees who cast Memory Charms on Muggles, helping keep the Statute of Secrecy intact (GF7). Their headquarters is on Level Three of the Ministry of Magic (OP7).

Obscuro

(ob-SCOO-roh)

Hermione used this spell to place a blindfold on Phineas Nigellus Black. Since Phineas Nigellus was a painting, the blindfold magically appeared, painted in place (OP15).
'obscuro' = L. 'to cover, darken, obscure'

Occlumency

Occlumency is the art of magically defending the mind against attempts to read or influence it, the defensive counter to Legilimency. A practitioner of Occlumency is referred to as an Occlumens. Elementary Occlumency involves clearing the mind of thought and emotion, so that the Legilimens can find no emotional ties to memories that the target wishes to conceal. In its more advanced form, Occlumency al-

lows the user to suppress only feelings and memories that contradict what the user wishes a Legilimens to believe, thus allowing the Occlumens to lie without self-betrayal (OP24).
'occulto' = L. 'to hide, conceal, cover' +
'mens' = L. 'mind'

Oddpick, Winkus

Wrote an editorial for the *Daily Prophet* titled 'Why can't goblins be more like elves?' after the Chipping Clodbury riot (DP3).

'oddsbodikins'

One of Sir Cadogan's strange passwords to get into Gryffindor Tower (PA12).
'oddsbodikins' = an archaic interjection, from 'Gadsbodikins' = 'God's body', a mild oath

'Odo the Hero'

A Wizarding drinking song (DH8).

Office for the Detection and Confiscation of Counterfeit Defensive Spells and Protective Objects

A Ministry office created in the wake of Voldemort's return, and headed by Arthur Weasley (HBP5).
The Ministry meets the threat of Voldemort's return by, what else, creating new bureaucracy.

Official Gobstones Club

This club has an office on Level Seven of the Ministry of Magic (OP7).

O'Flaherty

The name Professor Binns uses to refer to Seamus Finnigan; he doesn't seem to know his students particularly well (CS9).

Ogden, Bob

(c. 1920s)

Head of the Department of Magical Law Enforcement in the 1920s. Ogden was a short, pudgy man who wore thick glasses (HBP10).

Ogden, Tiberius

Wizengamot elder who resigned in protest when Fudge appointed Dolores Umbridge as the first Hogwarts High Inquisitor (OP15); friend of Professor Tofty of the Wizarding Examinations Authority (OP31).

Ogden's Old Firewhisky

See FIREWHISKY.

Ogg

Gamekeeper at Hogwarts during Molly Weasley's era, probably the man who held the job before Hagrid. Molly seemed to be rather fond of him (GF31).

Oglethorpe, Dunbar

(b. 1968) Head of Q.U.A.B.B.L.E., the Quidditch Union for the Administration and Betterment of the British League and its Endeavors (FW).

ogre

A monstrous magical creature, but one which can be around witches and wizards relatively safely, since Ron and Hermione thought they saw an ogre at the Three Broomsticks (PA8).

Ogres in folklore are horrible, grotesque, man-eating creatures, which doesn't seem to describe the creature Ron and Hermione saw. No ogre of the folklore variety would be found hanging about a pub. Considering the context, it's certainly possible that Ron and Hermione didn't see an ogre at all. The word ogre has the same roots as the word 'orc', which was used by Tolkien for the grotesque creatures who were servants of the Dark Lord.

Olde and Forgotten Bewitchments and Charmes A spellbook that Harry, Ron, and Hermione examined while preparing Harry for the Second Task of the Triwizard Tournament (GF26).

Oldridge, Chauncey

(1342–1379)

The first known victim of Dragon Pox (FW).

However, Gunhilda Kneen suffered a bout of Dragon Pox 250 years before that, according to Fantastic Beasts and Where to Find Them. Perhaps Oldridge is the first to actually die from the disease.

Oliphant, Gondoline
(1720–1799)
A famous Troll expert; for more information, see the Famous Wizard cards (FW).

Ollerton, Gifford
(1390—1441)
Famous giant slayer; killed the famous giant Hengist of Upper Barnton (FW).

Ollivander, Mr
An old wandmaker who owns a shop in Diagon Alley (PS5, HBP6). Ollivander has eerie, moon-like eyes and makes Harry a bit uncomfortable, as he seems just as fascinated by the power of wands used for evil as those used for good. Ollivander remembers every wand he has ever sold, and greets people by rattling off the specifications of their wands (PS5, DH24). (*See also* HBP6, DH5, 23.)

Ollivander's
('Makers of Fine Wands since 382 BC')
A narrow little shop in Diagon Alley where everyone goes to buy wands (PS5). (*See also* HBP6, DH5).

Omnioculars
Magical devices which look like a pair of brass binoculars, except that they are covered with knobs and dials (GF7). *'omni'* = L. *'all'* + *'-oculars'* from *'binoculars'*, which is from *'oculus'* = L. *'eye'*,

One Minute Feasts — It's Magic!
Wizarding cookery book. The Weasleys keep a copy of this book in their kitchen (CS3).

One Thousand Magical Herbs and Fungi
by Phyllida Spore
A textbook required by Snape for Potions classes at all levels (PS5, HBP25).

opal necklace
A Dark Item with a heavy curse (CS4) and a 1500-Galleon price tag, on sale at Borgin and Burkes (*See also* HBP6, 12, 27).

'open' or 'open up'
This password is all it takes to open the Chamber of Secrets, spoken to one particular copper tap in Moaning Myrtle's bathroom. Of course, you must say the words in Parseltongue . . . (CS16, DH31).

Oppugno

(oh-PUG-noh)

A spell which causes something to attack (HBP14).

'oppugno' = L. 'to attack, assault'

Orchideous

(or-KID-ee-us)

Spell which makes a bouquet of flowers come out of the wand's end (GF18).

'Orchideae' = L. 'name for the orchid plant family'

Order of Merlin

An award given to witches and wizards who have done great deeds (PS4, CS6, 13, PA10, 21, OP6, 19, HBP7, DH10, FW).

Although we now think of the Order of Merlin as an award, the text of the Famous Wizard card for Merlin suggests that it was originally conceived by Merlin himself as an organisation which made rules against using magic on Muggles. With the exception of Tilly Toke, the recipients of the Order of Merlin we know about from the books don't seem to have done things which specifically protect Muggles.

Order of the Phoenix

A resistance organisation originally formed by Dumbledore in the 1970s to fight Voldemort. It had limited suc-

cess during the First War when a large number of its members were killed (OP9). The Order was revived in 1995 (OP5). Its members communicated using the Patronus Charm (DH9).

Ordinary Wizarding Levels (O.W.L.s)

Tests given to Hogwarts students at the end of their fifth year for each of the classes he or she has taken. These are standardised tests administered by the Wizarding Examinations Authority, and scores can affect both the classes students may take in the future (HBP5) and their potential career choices (DP2). Each O.W.L. has a theory portion; for applicable classes a separate practical portion is given, so that many O.W.L.s are in two parts (OP31).

See GRADES ON EXAMS

Ornithomancy

A branch of Divination (OP25).

Ornithomancy, practiced by the ancient Greeks and Romans, is the foretelling of the future by watching the behaviour of birds.

'ornis' = Gr. 'bird'+ 'mancy' = 'divination by means of' from 'manteia' = Gr. 'oracle, divination'

orphanage

A London orphanage was where Tom Marvolo Riddle spent the first eleven years of his life. The orphanage was run by a Mrs Cole who kept the place clean and seemed to do her best with the children in her care (HBP13, DH15).

Ottery St. Catchpole

A small Muggle town along the River Otter in Devon, Ottery St. Catchpole is nevertheless home to a number of wizarding families (DH16). Included among these families are the Lovegoods, the Fawcetts, the Diggorys, and the Weasleys, who live in the Burrow on the outskirts of town (GF6).

Ottery St. Catchpole borrows its name from the town of Ottery St. Mary in Devon, near Exeter where J.K. Rowling went to university. She borrowed a few other names from that area as well, in each case changing the name somewhat (e.g., Budleigh Salterton, a town along the coast near Exeter, became Budleigh Babberton in book six). Of course, just because she borrowed the name of a town doesn't mean that the fictional town has to be in the same place, but in the case of Ottery St. Catchpole, it almost certainly is. The first part of the name, Ottery, refers to the fact that the town is on the River Otter. Since there are no other rivers with that name in Britain, it's safe to assume that Ottery St. Catchpole is somewhere along that river.

Ouagadougou

A small city in Burkina Faso, Ouagadougou is mentioned by Gilderoy Lockhart as the site of one of his fictitious exploits (CS9).

owl

A magical bird (JKR), very capable and intelligent. Owls understand instructions in English and are able to read names written on messages (OP14). They know who their deliveries are for and where the recipient will be (GF18). Owls' emotions can seem very human at times (e.g.,PS8, CS7, PA1, GF18, OP2).

The folklore about owls spans the globe, since these birds are found on every continent except Antarctica. Although some cultures saw the owl as a symbol of wisdom, many considered it to be a symbol of evil or of sorcery; the hoot of an owl was often considered to be a death omen. The ancient Romans considered it to be bad luck to see an owl in the daytime. Of course, seeing all the owls flying about after the first fall of Voldemort was actually very good luck, although the Muggles couldn't have known that. In some cultures, different species of owl have different connotations. A white owl is considered to be a friend and companion in India, for example, while at the same time, the Hindi word for owl, 'ulloo', is used as a slang term for a stupid person.

owl nuts

Treats that Harry and Ron keep on hand for their owls. Owl nuts are sold at Eeylops Owl Emporium (HBP6).
These can't be actual nuts, despite the name. Owls, after all, are carnivores.

owl post

The system whereby wizards send messages and parcels to one another tied to the legs of owls (GF3), or occasionally other large birds (PA1). The owls use magic to find their recipients (e.g. PA2, 22, OP17).

Owlery, the

The large chamber where Hogwarts school owls and owls belonging to students live, located on the top of West Tower. It is a circular stone room with open archways rather than windows, and perches holding hundreds of owls (GF15).

O.W.L.s

See ORDINARY WIZARDING LEVELS.

pack!

A spell that causes items to collect themselves into a trunk (OP3).

This isn't the actual spell word or name of the spell. Tonks just happens to wave her wand at the moment she says the word 'pack' in her sentence.

Paddington Station

One of the main railway stations in London, serving the western part of Britain. On Harry's eleventh birthday, after touring Diagon Alley for the first time, Hagrid took Harry here so he could catch a train back to the Dursleys. Before Harry's train departed, the two ate at a hamburger restaurant in the station (PS5).

Trains from Paddington don't run to Surrey, which makes it a bit odd that Hagrid would have taken Harry there for a trip to Little Whinging.

Padfoot

Nickname the Marauders gave Sirius Black, due to his Animagus form of a large dog (PA18).

Painswick

A small town in Gloucestershire, in the Cotswolds. A crowd of three hundred gathered there in 1836 to watch Xavier Rastrick tap-dance, a performance made famous when he vanished in the middle of it and was never seen or heard from again (FW).

Paisley

A good-sized Scottish town which was famous for textiles in the 1800s, lending its name to a very distinctive cloth design. A witch in Paisley wrote to Harry shortly after his interview with *The Quibbler* (OP26).

palmistry

A method of Divination taught to third-years where the lines on a person's hand are analysed for information about that person's life (PA12).

Palmistry, also called 'chiromancy', is an ages-old method of fortune-telling. It was practiced by ancient people in India, China, and Egypt, and it is still practiced today. Clues about the life and experiences of the person are thought to be 'written' in the lines on the palm of a person's hand. These lines are given names which correspond to area of the subject's life. Trelawney seems to be implying from her statement that Harry's short life line indicates that he won't live very long. However, the length of the life line — the curved line which encircles the base of the thumb — is not believed by practitioners of the art to indicate how long a person will live. Either Trelawney isn't the expert on palmistry that she thinks she is, or more likely, she's just trying to scare Harry with a bit of her usual mumbo-jumbo.

paper aeroplanes

Pale violet paper aeroplanes, used for interdepartmental memos in the Ministry of Magic, flying around the building by themselves. The Ministry switched to these from owls because of the mess the birds made while flying to and fro indoors (OP7).

paper shop

A Muggle shop in Ottery St. Catchpole that Fred and George enjoy visiting because there's a pretty Muggle girl who works there who enjoys Fred's card tricks (HBP16).

Paracelsus

(par-a-SELL-sus)

A 'secretive wizard' about whom little is known (FW). There is a bust of him in a Hogwarts corridor that Peeves has been known to drop on people's heads (OP14).

Paracelsus was born Phillip von Hohenheim in Austria in 1493. He was a physician and a astrologer who made important contributions to medicine. Unlike most scholars at that time, he didn't consider himself to be a magician at all. He was disdainful of many of his contemporaries — including Nicolas Flamel and Cornelius Agrippa — and rejected their teachings. He was rather arrogant and self-aggrandizing. He gave himself the title Paracelsus, meaning 'greater than Celsus', (Celsus being a famous Roman scholar).

parchment

Wizards write on scrolls of parchment, rather than on Muggle paper (OP3).

Actual parchment is very thick and heavy, made from the skin of sheep or goats. With the rate they go through parchment in the wizarding world, someone must be raising and skinning a lot of sheep.

Paris

The capital and largest city of France, and one of the world's great cities.

Gladrags Wizardwear has a location in Paris (along with London and Hogsmeade) (GF8).

Also, in an early, handwritten version of book one, J.K. Rowling mentioned that Flamel was spotted at the opera in Paris in 1762 — though this line never made it into the final book (JKR).

Parkinson, Pansy

(Slytherin, 1991; Prefect, 1995; Inquisitorial Squad)

An unpleasant Slytherin girl in Harry's year (PS8) who has been described as having a 'face like a pug' (PA6, GF27). She is the ringleader of a 'gang of Slytherin girls' who take pleasure in mocking other students, especially Hermione (OP25).

Pansy is one character J.K. Rowling really doesn't like. She said:

> *I loathe Pansy Parkinson... She's every girl who ever teased me at school. She's the Anti-Hermione (PC-JKR2).*

She said elsewhere (RAH) that, judging by the letters she's received, most girls know someone like Pansy.

Parselmouth

A wizard who can speak the language of snakes (CS11, HBP13).

According to J.K. Rowling, the term 'parselmouth' is an old word used for someone with deformed mouth, such as with a cleft palate (RAH).

Parseltongue

The language of snakes; to a human who cannot speak it, it sounds like hissing without taking a breath (GF1). There are only a few wizards who can speak Parseltongue, and it is something for which Salazar Slytherin was famous (CS11). (*See also* BLC).

Patented Daydream Charms

Sold at Weasleys' Wizard Wheezes, and according to Hermione, 'really extraordinary magic.' They give a realistic, undetectable, thirty-minute daydream (HBP6).

Patil, Padma

(Ravenclaw, 1991; Prefect, 1995; Dumbledore's Army)

Identical twin sister of Parvati, though they are in different houses (GF12). (*See also* GF24, OP16, DH29).

Patil, Parvati

(Gryffindor, 1991; Dumbledore's Army)

Identical twin sister of Padma (GF22) and best friends with Lavender Brown (PS10), who shares her fondness for Divination (PA6). Their favourite pastime is giggling, with a bit of gossiping thrown in for good measure (GF22, OP13, HBP13). Parvati was one of the first students to join Dumbledore's Army (OP16), and was able to produce quite a good Reductor Curse (OP19). She has long dark hair which she wears in a plait (GF15).

Patronus

The corporeal form created by a Patronus Charm, which takes an animal shape unique to each witch or wizard (DH28). The Patronus Charm was adapted by Dumbledore for the Order of the Phoenix to use as a messenger (JKR). When cast correctly, it appears talking with the voice of the wizard who cast the spell (DH7).

Known Patronuses:

- Harry — stag
- Hermione — otter
- Ron — terrier
- Aberforth — goat
- Snape — doe
- McGonagall — cat
- Umbridge — kitten
- Luna — hare
- Ernie MacMillan — boar
- Seamus — fox
- Cho — swan
- Tonks — wolf
- Kingsley — lynx
- Dumbledore — phoenix

Patronus Charm

See EXPECTO PATRONUM.

Pauncefoot, Randolph

Fan of the Magpies who didn't care so much if their Chaser wanted to give Muggle sport a try, although he pointed out that you have to be a bit crazy to play golf (DP3).

Paws, Mr

One of the pet cats, or perhaps Kneazles, of Mrs Figg (PS2).

Payne, Mr

A campground manager at the site where the 1994 Quidditch World Cup was held; the Diggorys stayed in his campground (GF7).

Peakes, Glanmore

(1677–1761)
Famous slayer of the Sea Serpent of Cromer (FW).

Peakes, Jimmy

(Gryffindor, 1994; Quidditch Beater 1996–?)
A short, solidly-built boy two years younger than Harry. He plays Quidditch 'ferociously' (HBP11).

Peasegood, Arnold

Obliviator for the Accidental Magic Reversal Squad (GF7) and trained Hit-Wizard (DP3).

Peeves

A poltergeist, not a ghost, but an 'indestructible spirit of chaos', who haunts the halls of Hogwarts (JKR). He is a little man dressed in loud, outlandish clothes, and is completely solid-looking, in contrast to the transparent ghosts (CS8, GF12). He swoops around the corridors and inside the classrooms of the castle causing mischief and trouble wherever he can. He answers to no one (except maybe the Bloody Baron) and particularly enjoys pestering Filch (e.g., PS7, 9). His jokes, which usually involve dropping things on people and using rude words, are fairly predictable; as Nearly Headless Nick says, 'Subtlety has never been Peeves's strong point' (OP14).
'peevish' = Eng. 'perverse, capricious, silly'

penfriend

A young wizard in Brazil who wrote back and forth with Bill Weasley years ago (GF7).

penknife, magical

A present given to Harry by Sirius for Christmas in 1994. This handy penknife had attachments to 'unlock any lock and undo any knot' (GF23, OP29, 32, 34).

Pennyfeather, Miss

Binns called Parvati Patil this when he couldn't remember her name (CS9).

Penrose, Professor Phoebus

Professor Penrose headed a committee that produced a report entitled 'A Study into Muggle Suspicions About Magic'. The report discusses crop circles (actually 'Contorting Cereals'), escaped Quaffles that Muggles have labeled UFOs, and the ongoing problem of hiding the kelpie in Loch Ness (DP1).

Pensieve

A shallow stone basin with odd runes and symbols carved around the edge which can be used to store thoughts and allow others to view them. When in use, a silvery light shines from the memories contained within. The Pensieve can be a useful tool to explore events of the past (GF30, OP24, 28, 37, HBP10, 13, 17, 20, 23, DH33).
'pensive' = Eng. 'pondering' from 'penser' = L. 'to think', combined with a double meaning of the word 'sieve', which is a gadget with a screen which is used in cooking to separate and 'un-clump' powdered ingredients, such as flour. In this case it conveys the idea of sifting through a number of options or thoughts.

pepper breath

Harry came across this charm while searching for a weapon against the dragon in the First Task of the Triwizard Tournament; he decided it would only increase the creature's firepower (GF20).

Pepper Imps

Small black candy that makes you '[b]reathe fire for your friends!' (PA5, 10).

Peppermint Toads

Peppermint creams shaped like toads (PA10).

Pepper, Octavius

Wizard who disappeared in the early spring of 1997, as reported by the *Daily Prophet*. It was implied that the disappearance was connected to an attack by Death Eaters (HBP21).

Pepperup Potion

A potion invented by Grover Hipworth that cures the common cold (FW). It leaves steam coming out of the drinker's ears (CS8).

Perkins

An elderly wizard who works with Arthur Weasley at the Ministry (OP7, GF7, DH14).

Perkins

The name by which Professor Binns mistakenly refers to Harry (OP17).
How out of touch must a professor be not to know Harry Potter's name?

Perks, Sally-Anne

(Hogwarts 1991)

A student in Harry's year (PS7).
Sally-Anne seems to have disappeared between Harry's first and fifth years. Although she was sorted just before him (PS7), when the alphabetical list of names was read off for O.W.L.s, the name 'Perks' was not called (OP31). It would seem that she left Hogwarts before fifth year.

Permanent Sticking Charm

A rather annoying charm, really, that sticks things to walls so tightly that they cannot be removed (OP6, DH10).

Peru

The most Quidditch-crazed country in South America. Peru's national team was flattened by that of Ireland in the World Cup semi-finals in 1994 (GF5). Instant Darkness Powder is imported from Peru (HBP6).

Peruvian Instant Darkness Powder

A powder imported by Weasleys' Wizard Wheezes for defensive use (HBP6);

when thrown, it casts the surrounding area into a blackness that even wand light cannot penetrate (HBP29).

Peskipiksi Pesternomi

(pes-kee PIK-see pes-ter-NO-mee)
Lockhart's version of a Freezing Charm (CS6).

These so-called spell words actually are a simplistic English phrase: 'pesky pixie pester no me'. Nice try, Gilderoy. It's kind of like someone pretending to speak a different language by affecting an exaggerated accent.

Pest Advisory Board

A Ministry office that keeps a list of known pests and suggests ways to get rid of them (JKR).

Petrification

Not a spell so much as a magical effect, caused by seeing the reflected eyes of a basilisk (looking at the eyes directly is deadly). It essentially turns a person into a statue until he or she is revived with a Mandrake Restorative Draught (CS9).

'petrificare' = L. *'to make into stone'*, *from 'petra'* = L. *'rock'*

Petrificus Totalus

(pe-TRI-fi-cus to-TAH-lus)
'Full Body Bind', 'Body-Bind Curse'

A spell that turns the victim's entire body rigid which Hermione reluctantly cast on Neville when he tried to stop them going after the Philosopher's Stone (PS16). It's also a favourite spell used by members of the D.A., though it's easily released by another witch or wizard (OP35).

'petrificare' = L. *'to make into stone'* + *'totalis'* = L. *'entire'*

Pettigrew, Peter 'Wormtail'

(1960–1998; Gryffindor, 1971; Order of the Phoenix)
One of the Marauders, a Gryffindor student who idolised his schoolmates James, Sirius, and Lupin (PA10). Pettigrew was weak-willed, following whomever had the most power (e.p PA19). Peter's life was one of tragedy, betrayal, and deceit. (*See also* GF33, HBP2, DH1, esp. DH23).

Peverell brothers: Antioch, Cadmus, and Ignotus

Though the extent to which the story is factually accurate is unknown, these are the three brothers in the wizarding fairly tale, 'The Tale of Three Brothers.' Legend (and, it seems, fact) holds that they were the original owners of the Deathly Hallows. Their story is not widely known among wizards, but among Hallows seekers, they are revered (DH21).

Philosopher's Stone

(U.S.: Sorcerer's Stone)

A fabulous magical item, the goal of alchemists for centuries. It transforms metal into gold, and can be used to create the Elixir of Life, thus, giving unlimited riches and immortality. Only one such stone was known to be in existence, created by Nicolas Flamel in the 1300s (PS14, 17).

The name of the stone was changed to 'Sorcerer's Stone' by the book's American publishers and J.K. Rowling, as this was thought to better appeal to a wide audience. Some of the richness of J.K. Rowling's created world is lost, however. The Philosopher's Stone was really a part of alchemical teaching and practice for centuries, symbolising purification and transformation of the soul. The Sorcerer's Stone, on the other hand, is purely an invented name, having no connection to legend or folklore whatsoever.

Philpott, Arkie

Wizard who ran afoul of a Probity Probe after the goblins tightened security at Gringotts (HBP6).

Phoenix

A magical bird the size of a swan, with crimson and gold plumage (CS17). Phoenixes can carry great weight (CS17) and have the ability to vanish and re-appear in another place, in a burst of flame (OP22). Phoenixes regenerate after they die; they are reborn from their own ashes following each death (CS12). Phoenix tail-feathers are used as wand cores (PS5, GF36). Phoenix tears are an immensely powerful healing solution, serving as an antidote even to basilisk venom (DH6).

The phoenix exists in the mythology and folklore from a number of cultures. Generally speaking, it was a large bird which, when it died, would transform — typically by fire — into a hatchling and begin its life over again. In the Classical tradition, the phoenix represented Christ, particularly his death and resurrection.

photograph potions

If photographs are developed in certain potions, the resulting images will move (CS6).

Piertotum Locomotor

(pee-air-TOE-tum lo-co-MOE-tor)

A variation on the *Locomotor* spell, used to animate armour and statues (DH30).

'pier' = ? + 'totum' = L. 'total, all' + 'loco' = L. 'from a place' + 'motionem' = L. 'motion'

What does 'pier' mean? Well, here's the best I can come up with:

'pier' = Eng. 'support of a span of a

bridge,' which according to etymological dictionaries is derived through Fr. from 'petra' = L. 'rock', and since this spell animates all the stone statues, it does make sense.

'pig snout'
Password to get into Gryffindor Tower (PS9).

Pigwidgeon
Ron's owl (PA22), a tiny bird, possibly a Scops owl. 'Pig,' as he is called, is very excitable. He annoys Ron (GF5) and irritates Hedwig, who apparently doesn't think Pig has the proper bearing and manners for a post owl (GF3).

Pilliwickle, Justus
(1862–1953)
Once the head of the Department of Magical Law Enforcement (FW).
The name 'Justus' is a homonym for 'justice', which is fitting for someone who heads the main law enforcement entity of the government.

Pillsworth, Bernie
A senior member of Magical Maintenance, at the Ministry of Magic (DH13).

Pimple Vanisher
A WonderWitch product sold at Weasleys' Wizarding Wheezes, guaranteed to work in ten seconds (HBP6). Apparently Marietta Edgecombe has yet to discover it (HBP7).

Pince, Irma
Librarian at Hogwarts, mean and nasty (CS10). She is highly suspicious of students, placing spells on books to make sure they're returned on time (QA/i) and getting irate when library rules are broken (OP29).
J.K. Rowling has apologised to librarians for writing Pince as stereotypically unhelpful, saying that she had to do so because of all the times she needed the trio to be forced to search for information. 'If they'd had a pleasant, helpful librarian, half my plots would be gone' (HCG).
'pincer' = Fr. 'pinch'; used in the term 'pince-nez' (literally 'pinch-nose') which are used for a pair of glasses with no bows which just perch on the bridge of the nose. Pince-nez are often used as reading glasses; they're the type of glasses one might imagine on a chain around the neck of someone like Madam Pince.

'pine fresh'
Password to get into the Prefects' Bathroom on the fifth floor of Hogwarts (GF23, 25).

Pinkstone, Carlotta

(b. 1922)

Famous for campaigning to lift the Statute of Secrecy; this has got her into trouble with the Ministry on more than one occasion (JKR).

Pips, Dagbert

Proprietor of Pumpkins R Us, who complained to a *Daily Prophet* reporter that a restriction on Hallowe'en celebrations would 'hit the pumpkin-growers particularly hard' (DP4).

Another word for a fruit seed is 'pip', so his is a fitting last name for someone who runs a pumpkin shop.

Pixie

Native to Cornwall, these mischievous creatures are a bright blue in colour (CS6).

In folklore, pixies, (or piksies, as they are also called), are typically found in Devon and Cornwall. They appear in various forms and are described as fond of music and dancing. Typically, they are helpful creatures who help with housework, and are even sometimes credited with creating clotted cream on Dartmoor for deserving housewives. On the other hand, pixies are just as likely to eat all the cream, since they're mischievous and fond of tricks. They will confuse travellers on the moors and have been accused of stealing chil-

dren. Pixies wear green clothing to better blend in with their surroundings. They have slanted eyes and pointed ears, but they definitely aren't blue-skinned. They resemble wildly-dressed humans, not the electric blue imps seen in the Harry Potter books or film.

Planet Room

Located in the Department of Mysteries, the dimly-lit Planet Room is described as an 'odd place' even by Luna Lovegood (OP35).

Models of the solar system and even of the whole galaxy are popular with wizards because these give the information needed for spell casting. From the fact that the solar system is studied in such detail in the Department of Mysteries, we can assume that the influence of the planets on magic is very great indeed — and not well understood.

Platform Nine and Three-Quarters

A hidden platform in Kings Cross Station in London, and the home platform of the Hogwarts Express. The platform is reached by running through the solid metal barrier between platforms nine and ten, which transforms into a wrought iron archway. Through the archway, the scene is like one from a hundred years ago: a beautiful scarlet steam train sits waiting, with hundreds of families crowding the steam-filled platform, loading trunks into the cars, and saying goodbye to their children for the start of the school year (PS6, DH/e).

Platform Nine and Three-Quarters is filled with romantic imagery, and intentionally so; J.K. Rowling's parents met at King's Cross Station, and it became part of her 'childhood folklore' that she wanted to include in Harry's life (HPM). This romanticism is reflected in many scenes, such as when the train pulls out of the station for the first time with Ginny Weasley running after it, waving (PS6), or when Harry sends his children off to school, and he finds himself still waving as the train rounds the corner and twists out of sight (DH/e).

Platt, Yardley
(1446 - 1557)
A famous serial goblin-killer (FW). Platt's murder spree was one of the factors which many believe led to the 1612 goblin rebellion (JKR).

PlayStation
Dudley owned a PlayStation, until he threw it out the window in a fit of rage. His favourite game was *Mega Mutilation Part Three* (GF2).

J.K. Rowling wrote the fourth book in 1999, when the term PlayStation was often used generically for 'video game console'. Trouble is, the events of the fourth book take place in 1994–1995, and the PlayStation wasn't released in the UK at that point. But no matter. It is doubtful that J.K. Rowling bothered to research the history of the PlayStation while writing book four. Instead she just used the name of the game console that was most popular at that time and didn't realise that she'd made an error in dates. Then again, who's to say when things happened in Harry Potter's universe? Perhaps the PlayStation was released before 1994 in that reality.

Plimpy
A magical fish. The stream near Bottom Bridge, behind the Lovegoods' house, contains Freshwater Plimpies that Xenophilius uses to make soup (DH20). Luna carries a Gurdyroot to ward off Gulping Plimpies (HBP20).

Plumpton, Roderick
(1889–1987)
Seeker for the England National Team and the Tutshill Tornados (FW).

Plunkett, Josiah
Quidditch referee for the match between the Pride of Portree and the Appleby Arrows during which one Seeker transfigured the other's head into a cabbage (DP3).

Plunkett, Mirabella
(b. 1839)
Famous for falling in love with a merman in Loch Lomond; for more information, see the Famous Wizard cards (FW).

Pocket Sneakoscope
See SNEAKOSCOPE.

pocket watch
It is a Wizarding world tradition for parents to give their son a pocket watch on his seventeenth birthday (DH7, *see also* DH/e).

Podmore, Sturgis
(Order of the Phoenix)
Square-jawed wizard with thick yellow-blonde hair. Member of the Order of the Phoenix and part of the Advance Guard (OP3, 14).

Point Me
'Four-Point Spell'
A simple spell, performed with the wand laying flat on the open palm of the caster. When the words are spoken, the wand rotates to point north (GF31).

Poke, Royden
One of the representatives of the Department for the Regulation and Control of Magical Creatures at a meeting with the Brotherhood of Goblins in Chipping Clodbury (DP3).

Pokeby, Gulliver
(1750–1839)
Author of *Why I Didn't Die When The Augurey Cried* and an expert on magical birds (FW).

Poliakoff
Male student from Durmstrang who was treated with disdain by Karkaroff despite the fact that he must have been a rather talented wizard to make the Durmstrang short list for the Triwizard Tournament (GF16).

Polkiss, Piers
(b. 1980)
A Muggle boy and Dudley's best friend, described as 'scrawny, with a face like a rat' (PS2). Piers attends Smeltings with Dudley (PS3).
The similarities between Piers and Peter Pettigrew are striking. He's a follower, hanging around the powerful kids and participating in their bullying. His first and last names start with P, just like Peter Pettigrew's, and Piers is actually a form of the name Peter. To top it all off, J.K. Rowling describes Piers as having 'a face like a rat' (PS2).

Polyjuice Potion

A muddy brown potion (HBP9) described as 'complicated' (CS10), The potion transforms the drinker to look exactly like someone else, requiring only that they have a bit of that person to add to the potion, usually hair (CS12, HBP21, DH4, 26,). However, the potion only lasts an hour each time it is drunk (GF35). For obvious reasons, Polyjuice Potion can cause major security headaches (HBP3).

Polyjuice Potion, like the Time Turner, is a complicated plot device to include in a story. J.K. Rowling included some limitations when she first introduced it in book two: it took a month to brew, the ingredients were hard to come by, it only lasts an hour, and so on. However, in book four, J.K. Rowling had Barty Crouch drinking a swig of it every hour, all day and every day, for nine months, in order to maintain his disguise as Mad-Eye Moody. No matter how you look at it, that's a lot of potion. How could his body stand up to that kind of abuse, and where would he have obtained all the ingredients for gallons and gallons of the stuff? Was he brewing it in his office? He would have to be making it constantly, since each batch takes a month. By the time we get to book seven, Polyjuice Potion is flowing like water. The one-hour time limit is all but ignored. Just consider the impact this kind of thing would have on a society, particularly on security. With all that Polyjuice Potion around, how could the Death Eaters have been fooled by Harry, Ron, and Hermione as they infiltrated the Ministry and Gringotts just because they happened to look like someone else? They would have been on the lookout for such things. On the plus side, Polyjuice Potion has given us some delightful moments, such as Crabbe and Goyle as little girls or Hermione trying to be as nasty as Bellatrix when she took that appearance.

'poly' = Gr. *'many'* + *'juice'*

Pomfrey, Poppy

The Hogwarts school matron (U.S.: 'nurse'), who is very adept with curing spells, potions, herbs, and other remedies (PS17). Among other things we've seen her re-grow bones (CS10), cure a poisonous dragon bite (PS14), fix Eloise Midgen's nose after she cursed it off (GF13), remove beards (GF16), and shrink overgrown teeth (GF23). Madam Pomfrey works hard to protect her patients' peace and quiet, not hesitating even to throw out Dumbledore when necessary (PS17, PA21). She has been the matron at Hogwarts for a long time, as she was there when the Marauders were in school (PA18).

'poppy' = *flower from which a number*

of medicines are derived, including morphine and codeine

'pomfrey' = may be a reference to 'comfrey', an herb used in medieval times as a remedy for internal bleeding

Pontner, Roddy

Wizard who bet on the World Cup with Ludo Bagman (GF7).

Porlock

A magical creature studied in Care of Magical Creatures (OP15, 20).

Porlock is a small coastal village in Somerset, near Exmoor.

Porskoff Ploy

Complicated Quidditch manoeuvre involving several Chasers (GF8).

Portable Swamp

Created magically by Fred and George in a corridor at Hogwarts, to annoy Umbridge (OP29, 30, 38).

Portkey

An enchanted object, typically a piece of seemingly worthless junk, which when touched will transport a person to a pre-programmed location (GF6). Any object can be transformed into a Portkey by the Portus spell (OP36). The Portkey Office, part of the Department of Magical Transportation at the Ministry of Magic, authorises the creation of Portkeys (OP7).

portraits

Painting of a person's face. Wizarding portraits are very life-like, as the wizards depicted within them are able to talk and hold conversations. However, the wizards are not as fully realised as ghosts are, only able to 'repeat catchphrases' from the wizard's life. The most lifelike portraits exist in the head's office at Hogwarts, as the previous heads of the school leave their 'aura' in that room (EBF). We see evidence of this in the portraits of Phineas Nigellus (DH15) and Dumbledore (DH33), which seem to repeat much more than the usual catchphrases so evident in the portrait of, say, Walburga Black (OP6).

Portree

See PRIDE OF PORTREE.

Portuguese Long Snout Dragon

A breed of dragon not listed in *Fantastic Beasts and Where to Find Them* which appears in *Dragon Breeding for Pleasure and Profit*. The Long Snout has scales of light green and black eyes, and is found in the north of Portugal, around Geres, an area of rocky summits and valleys (JKR).

Portus

(*POR-tus*)

A spell that turns an object into a Portkey (OP22).

'*portus*' = L. '*door*'

possession

A very powerful and mysterious magical ability. A soul or soul fragment that has no body can possess other living things (PS17, OP36). Horcruxes can also possess people who get too emotionally close to one (CS17, DH7).

post office (Muggle)

The Weaselys have used the Muggle post office in Ottery St. Catchpole on occasion, but Molly notes that the postman probably doesn't know where the Burrow is located (GF3, 11).

Very likely a Wizarding house like the Burrow has Muggle-Repelling enchantments on it to gently divert Muggle attention away. In this case, we might guess that the Muggle postman just conveniently doesn't notice that there's a house down that particular lane.

post office (Wizarding)

Located in Hogsmeade, an office filled with owls waiting to take messages (PA8). It is also referred to as an 'Owl Office' (PA22).

potion-making kit

Hogwarts students use these (GF10), although curiously they aren't listed on the supply list sent to first-years (PS5).

potions

Magical liquids created by mixing various ingredients in a cauldron according to very specific rules; they can only be brewed by someone of magical ability (HCG). These mixtures must usually be drunk to give their magical effect. The ingredients in potions range from the mundane (caterpillars, pomegranate juice) to the bizarre and fantastic (Ashwinder eggs, unicorn horns) (PA7, OP17, FB, PS15), and the procedures for creating some potions can be complicated and time-consuming; Felix Felicis, for example, has to brew for six months (HBP24).

Potions class

Potions class is one of the seven fundamental classes at Hogwarts, taught starting first year (PS8).

Severus Snape was the Potions Master at Hogwarts from c. 1980 to the fall of 1996. Horace Slughorn, an earlier Potions Master, came out of retirement for the following two school years (OP15, HBP4, 8, DH30).

Potions class is a good example of how the various fields of study at Hogwarts fit together. In order to obtain the necessary ingredients for a potion, a wizard needs to have quite a wide understanding of the magical world. Herbology, for example, gives wizards the knowledge of plants such as Mandrakes, which are grown for the purpose of creating certain potions. Other ingredients come from magical creatures, which are studied in Care of Magical Creatures. The power of some ingredients comes from when they're picked, such as when the moon is full, and other potions obtain full strength if brewed under specific astronomical conditions; this is why students study Astronomy at Hogwarts. The world of Harry Potter was very carefully created by J.K. Rowling to be believable and consistent, and this is particularly clear in the way magical training is portrayed.

Potions classroom

A 'creepy' room in the Hogwarts dungeons where Potions classes are held (PS8). In the corner stands a gargoyle with water pouring from its mouth into a basin, for washing hands (PA7). The walls hold a variety of dead animals in jars, probably to be used in potions making. The room can get cold enough in the winter so that students can see their breath (PS12).

Potter, Albus Severus

(b. 2006; Hogwarts, 2017)

Middle child of Harry and Ginny Potter, named for Albus Dumbledore and Severus Snape (DH/e).

Potter, Charlus

(20th century)

Husband of Dorea (Black) Potter and father of one son (BFT).

Potter cottage

On the outskirts of Godric's Hollow, the house where James and Lily Potter lived with their son Harry. It was protected by a Fidelius Charm, but despite this they were attacked by Voldemort (DH16, 17, c.f. PA19).

Potter, Dorea (Black)

(1920–1977)

Daughter of Cygnus and Violetta (Bulstrode) Black, sister to Cassiopeia, and wife of Charlus Potter; they had one son (BFT).

It is doubtful that Dorea is Harry's grandmother because J.K. Rowling has stated that James's parents 'were old in wizarding terms' when they died, (TLC), but Dorea died at age 57 (BFT).

Potter, Harry James

(b. 1980; Gryffindor, 1991; Quidditch Seeker, 1991-1997, Captain, 1996-

1997; Dumbledore's Army; Slug Club)
Born under a prophecy (OP37) to parents who were desperately fighting Voldemort and the Death Eaters, Harry Potter was destined to become a hero. After the strange events in Godric's Hollow which resulted in the deaths of Harry's parents and a lightning-shaped scar on his forehead, not to mention the complete disappearance of Voldemort (DH17), he was sent off at age one to live with his Muggle relatives, the Dursleys (PS1), where he stayed, downtrodden and abused, for ten years. At age eleven, his true heritage was revealed to him (PS4) and he travelled for the first time to Hogwarts. He was sorted into Gryffindor (PS7) and became the Seeker for the house Quidditch team. He made excellent friends in Hermione Granger (PS10) and Ron Weasley (PS6), and with their support over the years, Harry faced a reborn Voldemort and his Death Eaters on several occasions as the Dark Lord gained power (esp. CS17, GF32, OP37). During those years, the strange connection between Harry and Voldemort became more and more obvious, leading Harry, with Dumbledore's guidance, to discover secrets behind the existence of the Dark Lord, secrets which allowed Harry to weaken his enemy, bit by bit.

Eventually, Harry faced Voldemort one final time, and the prophecy was fulfilled (DH35).

Potter, James
(b. circa 2005; Gryffindor, 2016?)
The oldest son of Harry and Ginny Potter, named for Harry's father. He seems to have inherited a bit of Weasley — interrupting his cousins while snogging (DH/e) — as well as a bit of his namesake, stealing the Marauder's Map from his father's desk (BLC).

Potter, James 'Prongs'
(27 March, 1960–31 October, 1981; Gryffindor, 1971; Quidditch Chaser; Head Boy 1977; Order of the Phoenix)
Father of Harry Potter. At Hogwarts, James was very popular; he was a Quidditch Chaser (Sch2) and liked to show off (OP28). He was one of the Marauders, boys who became Animagi and created the Marauder's Map (PA22). James had a particular disdain for Snape (PA19). He 'deflated his head a bit' his seventh year, was named Head Boy, and started dating Lily Evans, whom he later married (PS4, OP9, 30). James joined the Order of the Phoenix (OP9, 30), but was betrayed and killed along with Lily on October 31, 1981, in their cottage at Godric's Hollow (DH17).

Potter, Lily

(b. 2008; Hogwarts, 2019)
Youngest child and only daughter of Harry and Ginny Potter, named for Harry's mother, Lily. Like her mother twenty-eight years earlier, Lily was jealous as she stood on Platform Nine and Three-Quarters, watching her older brothers go off to Hogwarts (DH/e).

Potter, Lily Evans

(30 January, 1960 –31 October, 1981; Gryffindor 1971; Head Girl 1977; Slug Club; Order of the Phoenix)
Mother of Harry Potter, from whom he inherited his green eyes (OP28). Lily was a gifted witch (HBP4) born to a Muggle family, and had a sister named Petunia. Lily discovered she was a witch when she befriended a young wizard at the playground (DH33). After Hogwarts, Lily joined the Order of the Phoenix to fight Voldemort (OP9, 30) and married James Potter (OP30); their only child, Harry, was born on July 31, 1980. (*See also* OP37, DH33, 36).

Potter, Mr and Mrs

James's parents, a wealthy and elderly couple when he, their only son, was born; they considered him a 'gift' and pampered him throughout his childhood (TLC, AOL). They were kind enough to let James's best friend Sirius Black come live with the family after he ran away from home (OP6).

Potterwatch

A radio show hosted by Lee Jordan (code name: 'River') during the second war against Voldemort. Hidden behind a different password each week on the Wizard Wireless, the show discussed news that was being ignored by the *Daily Prophet* and other mainstream media. They also reported on the resistance being put up by the Order of the Phoenix (DH22).

Powers You Never Knew You Had and What To Do With Them Now You've Wised Up

One of the books that Harry, Ron, and Hermione examined while preparing for the Second Task of the Triwizard Tournament (GF26).

Practical Defensive Magic and Its Use Against the Dark Arts

Harry's Christmas present from Sirius and Lupin in his fifth year (OP23).

Practical Household Magic

by Zamira Gulch
A book of solutions to everyday magical problems (DP3).

Practical Potioneer, The

One of the scholarly journals of the Wizarding world; Albus Dumbledore had at least one paper published in it when he was still quite young (DH2).

Prang, Ernie

Elderly, bespectacled driver of the Knight Bus (PA3).

Ernie is named after J.K. Rowling's grandfather. His last name, 'prang', is a British slang term for an automobile accident, as in 'I missed a turn and pranged the Rolls Royce . . .'

Predicting the Unpredictable: Insulate Yourself Against Shocks

A book in the Divination section of Flourish and Blotts (PA4).

prefect

Starting fifth year, one boy and one girl in each Hogwarts house are named prefects, giving them duties supervising younger children and assisting the teachers in maintaining discipline (OP9, c.f. OP37).

prefects' bathroom

Located behind the 'fourth door to the left of the statue of Boris the Bewildered on the fifth floor' (GF23). Inside there is an enormous white marble bathtub, the size and depth of a swimming pool, with a diving board. The tub is also lined with over a hundred taps, releasing various types of perfumed bubble bath (GF25),

Prefects Who Gained Power

A book that, not surprisingly, interested Percy (CS4).

Prentice, Mr

A Muggle neighbour of the Dursleys (OP2).

Prewett, Fabian and Gideon

Brothers of Molly Weasley (JKR, OP9). Among the 'best witches and wizards of the age' (PS4). When Harry turned seventeen, the Weasleys gave him the traditional gift, a watch. The one they gave him had belonged to Fabian (DH7).

The Prewett family name is borrowed from one of J.K. Rowling's best friends when she lived in Portugal, Jill Prewett. The third book is dedicated to Jill, along with another good friend, Aine Kiely.

Prewett, Ignatius

Husband of Lucretia Black and a paternal uncle of Sirius Black (BFT).

J.K. Rowling intentionally included familiar names on the Black Family Tree to show the way the various pure-blood families were related. Prewett is Molly Weasley's maiden name, and Percy Wea-

sley's middle name is Ignatius, likely after this relative.

Pride of Portree
A Quidditch team in the British-Irish League (DP1-4).

Prime Minister
The Prime Minister is one of the only Muggles to whom wizards intentionally reveal their existence. It is frustrating for him, particularly when events in the Wizarding world negatively affect his constituency and he is powerless to do anything about it. A small portrait hanging in the Prime Minister's office serves to announce the impending arrival of the Minister for Magic for meetings (HBP1).

Primpernelle, Madam
Witch who produces a line of Beautifying Potions in Diagon Alley (DP2).
'primp' = Eng. 'to dress with care, to make oneself pretty', blended with 'pimpernel', a red-coloured flower commonly referred to as a 'scarlet pimpernel'.

Prince, Eileen
Severus Snape's mother, a witch (HBP13). Described as skinny, sullen woman (HBP25). Eileen was the captain of the Hogwarts Gobstones Team during her years there (HBP25). Her husband was Tobias Snape, a Muggle who treated her badly (HBP30).

Pringle, Apollyon
Caretaker at Hogwarts when Arthur and Molly Weasley attended (1960s), preceding Argus Filch (GF31).
'Apollyon' = Gr. 'Destroyer', a name used for one of the terrible Beasts in the book of Revelation in the Bible.

printing press, magical
Xenophilius Lovegood runs a magical printing press in his home to churn out copies of the *Quibbler* (DH20).

Priori Incantatem
(pry-OR-ee in-can-TAH-tem)
'Reverse Spell Effect'
The strange magical effect which happens when two wands are forced to duel that have core material from the same single creature. The effect is a ghostly display, in sequence, of the last spells one of the wands cast (GF36). Which wand will show the spell effect depends on the willpower of the two wizards involved (GF34, c.f. DH5).
'prior' = L. 'former, earlier, preceding' + 'incantatare' = L. 'to bewitch or enchant'

Prior Incantato
(pry-OR in-can-TAH-toe)
A spell that, when cast on a wand,

forces it to emit a ghost image of the last spell it cast. The images can be dispelled using *Deletrius* (GF9).

Pritchard, Graham
(Slytherin, 1994)
A student sorted into Slytherin at the start of Harry's fourth year (GF12).

private hospital
London hospital where the Dursleys took Dudley to have his tail removed on 1 September 1991 (PS6).

Privet Drive
A street in Little Whinging, Surrey. Privet Drive is an ordinary Muggle street with boring, boxy houses. It is also, at number four, home to the Dursley family (PS2).

Probity Probes
Magical security devices used to scan wizards for Dark items upon entering Gringotts (HBP6, DH26).
'probity' = Eng. 'honesty'

Prod, D. J.
Warlock living in Didsbury who was excited about the Kwikspell course and wrote a glowing testimonial (CS8). Possibly the same person as the late Demetrius J. Prod.

Prod, Demetrius J.
Died, according to the *Daily Prophet*, 'very noisily' after an argument with his wife Elsie (DP2).

Prod, Elsie
Widow of Demetrius J. Prod, according to the *Daily Prophet* (DP2).

Prongs
James Potter's nickname among his closest friends (PA18).

Prophecy
A prophecy is an uncommon magical effect where someone with the gift of Seeing gives information about the future. The prophecy is often in a cryptic form which then itself requires some interpretation. Prophecies are recorded and stored in glass spheres in the Hall of Prophecies in the Department of Mysteries (OP34).
J.K. Rowling wrote about the nature of prophecy on her website. She said:
> *As for the prophecy itself, it remains ambiguous, not only to readers, but to my characters. Prophecies (think of Nostradamus!) are usually open to many different interpretations. That is both their strength and their weakness (JKR).*
> *Much of the plot of the books revolves around the prophecy made about Voldemort and Harry. Specifically, it is*

Voldemort's lack of appreciation for the ambiguity of prophecy — his own hubris in thinking that he understood what it meant — that drove him to set events in motion which caused the very result he was trying to avoid.

Protean Charm

(PRO-tee-an)

A complex charm that Hermione cast on fake Galleons which were used by the D.A. to communicate meeting times. When Harry changed the numbers on his coin, they automatically changed on the others. It is a very advanced N.E.W.T.-level spell (OP19).

'protean' = Eng. 'able to readily assume a different form', from Proteus, a sea god from Greek mythology who could change his shape rapidly

Protego

(pro-TAY-go)

'Shield Charm'

Spell that creates an invisible magical barrier to deflect spells (GF31, OP25, 26, 35, 36, HBP6, 9, DH9, 15, 19, 26, 36).

'protego'= L. 'to defend'

Protego Horribilis

(pro-TAY-go ho-RIB-i-lis)

An advanced Shield Charm, cast by Flitwick to help defend Hogwarts from oncoming Death Eaters (DH30).

'protego'= L. 'to defend' + 'horribilis' = L. 'horrible, frightful'

Protego Totalum

(pro-TAY-go to-TAL-um)

A semi-permanent version of the Shield Charm, cast routinely by Hermione to protect the trio's campsites (DH14).

'protego' = L. 'to defend' + 'totalum' = L. 'total, entire'

Proudfoot

Auror stationed at Hogwarts during Harry's sixth year, along with Tonks, Dawlish, and Savage (HBP8).

Ptolemy

Famous wizard who appears on a Chocolate Frog trading card (PS6, FW).

Ptolemy, whose full name was Claudius Ptolemaeus, lived from 83–161 AD in Egypt. He was a scholar who wrote books on astronomy, mathematics, and astrology. Several of these books were a great influence on scientific thought in Islamic and Western culture.

Pucey, Adrian

(Slytherin, 1989 or 1990; Quidditch Chaser c.1991–1996)

Slytherin student who played in matches against Harry's Gryffindor team (PS11, OP19).

Since he was on the Slytherin team during Harry's first year, he was at least a year ahead of Harry; since he was still there during Harry's fifth year, he's no more than two years ahead of Harry, assuming he's up to scratch academically.

Puddifoot, Madam

The owner of a small tea shop in Hogsmeade, blessed with the kind of taste in decorating that involves a lot of frilly doilies (OP25).

Pudding Lane

The street where the Great London Fire of 1666 started; however, there is some debate as to whether it began in a Muggle bakery (as Muggles believe) or in the basement of the house next door, where a young Welsh Green dragon was being kept (JKR).

Puddlemere United

A Quidditch team in the British and Irish League, managed by Philbert Deverill. The team recently changed the colour of its robes from mud brown to the bright blue (DP2). Oliver Wood joined this team as a reserve Keeper after leaving Hogwarts in 1994 (GF7).

Puffapod

Plant with fat pink pods with seeds that burst into flower if dropped (PA8).

Puffskein

A magical creature which looks like a little furball. These pleasant creatures are often kept as pets, particularly by wizarding children. Weasleys' Wizard Wheezes breeds and sells miniature Puffskeins called Pygmy Puffs (HBP6).

Puking Pastilles

Perhaps the most dramatic of the sweets in the Skiving Snackboxes sold by Weasleys' Wizard Wheezes. Eating the orange end makes a person vomit continuously until they eat the purple end, which makes the vomiting instantly stop (OP6).

Pumpkin Fizz

Some type of treat, possibly a beverage, which Fred and George brought back from Hogsmeade (PA13).

Pumpkin juice

A beverage, usually served iced, which is available on the Hogwarts Express and at Hogwarts (CS5, PA6). It seems to be the drink of choice for wizarding children, giving way to butterbeer (PA8) and even firewhisky (DH5) as they get older.

Pumpkin Pasty

Treat sold on the Hogwarts Express (PS6).

Pumpkins R Us

For a *Daily Prophet* article on Ministry laws cracking down on Hallowe'en celebrations, the proprietor of Pumpkins R Us was interviewed, clearly upset at restrictions he feared might hurt his business (DP4).

pure-blood

According to some wizards, being a 'pure-blood' — that is, not having any Muggle ancestors — is an elite status symbol. It's a form of racism, really, but families like the Malfoys (CS7), the Blacks (OP6), and the Gaunts (HBP10) have clung to it for generations and refuse to marry anyone of Muggle descent. Used as a password to enter the Slytherin common room (CS12).

Purge and Dowse, Ltd.

An old abandoned department store in Muggle London, Purge and Dowse, Ltd. is actually a false front that prevents Muggles from seeing St. Mungo's Hospital for Magical Maladies and Injuries. Wizards enter by talking to the dilapidated mannequin in the window, then walking straight on through the glass (OP22).

The names of this abandoned department store both have interesting meanings. To 'purge' means to cleanse or purify by removing whatever is undesirable. It's used in a medical sense to refer to cleansing out the intestinal tract. A medication which causes this to happen is called a 'purgative'. 'Dowse' doesn't have a medical meaning, although in some ways it connects to the word 'purge'. 'Dowse', or 'douse', means to drench something with water. 'Dowse' can also refer to a pseudoscientific procedure where a person holds 'divining rods', often two wires or sticks, and walks around trying to detect underground water by the movements of the rods. The method, while not supported by science, is still practiced today.*

Purkiss, Doris

In the summer of 1995, *The Quibbler* printed an interview with Doris Purkiss, who claimed that Sirius Black was really Stubby Boardman, and that Stubby had been enjoying a romantic dinner with her the day of the murder of the Potters and therefore had an alibi (OP10).

Put-Outer

See DELUMINATOR.

Pye, Augustus

Trainee Healer on the Dai Llewellyn Ward of St. Mungo's who tried to heal Arthur Weasley's snakebite in December 1995. He was very interested in 'complementary medicine' (using Muggle techniques along with the magical approaches) (OP23).

Pygmy Puff

Miniature Puffskeins, bred and sold in Weasleys' Wizard Wheezes. They sell so quickly that Fred and George 'can't breed them fast enough' (HBP6). Ginny convinced her mother to buy one for her, and she named it Arnold. Arnold is frequently seen riding around on Ginny's shoulder in the Gryffindor common room, often with a curious Crookshanks trailing behind (HBP14).

pyramids

Huge stone tombs, arguably the most recognisable ancient structures in the world. Some of the most famous pyramids are located in Egypt. Wizards have discovered that they were protected by curses cast by ancient wizards. The Weasley family toured some of them when they visited the country in the summer of 1994, where they saw, among other things, mutant skeletons of Muggles who had broken in and 'grown extra heads and stuff,' according to Ron (PA1). Fred and George tried to shut Percy in a pyramid, but unfortunately were spotted by Mrs Weasley (PA4).

Pyrites, Arthur

A character J.K. Rowling included in early drafts of PS1, but discarded eventually. His name means 'fool's gold'. J.K. Rowling described him as a servant of Voldemort, 'a dandy' who wore white gloves (JKR).

Q.U.A.B.B.L.E.

Acronym for the 'Quidditch Union for the Administration and Betterment of the British League and its Endeavours' (FW).

Quaffle

A seamless red leather ball, twelve inches in diameter, which is used in playing the game of Quidditch. The Quaffle is the ball with which Chasers score goals, and due to the nature of the game must be caught and thrown one-handed, since the player must at the same time control his or her broomstick (PS10).

Quaffle Drops

A statistic kept in Quidditch. Dropping the Quaffle is not something one would wish to be known for. The record for the most dropped Quaffles not surprisingly belongs to a member of the Chudley Cannons, Dragomir Gorgovitch. He broke the record shortly after transferring to the team c. 1995 (DH7).

Quality Quidditch Supplies

Harry Potter's favourite shop in Diagon Alley. He visited it often when he stayed for three weeks at the Leaky Cauldron in 1993, since that summer the new Firebolt racing broom had been introduced and the shop had one on display (PA4). Quality Quidditch Supplies also displayed a full set of Chudley Cannons robes in the front window (CS4).

Quibbler, The

The tabloid newspaper of the Wizarding world, edited by Luna Lovegood's father, Xenophilius (DH8). It publishes an edition every month (OP26), usually filled with wild, silly, and bizarre stories about famous people, particularly involving conspiracy theories (OP10).

'quibble' = Eng. 'to evade the truth in an discussion with petty objections or meaningless arguments'

Quick-Quotes Quill

A quill that is enchanted to be set up on a sheet of paper without human support, which when activated will write an exaggerated account of whatever is said in its presence. Rita Skeeter famously carries an acid-green Quick-Quotes Quill in her crocodile skin handbag (GF18).

'quid agis'

Password to get into Gryffindor Tower (HBP24).

'quid agis' = L. 'how do you do?'

Quidditch

Quidditch is the premier sport of the Wizarding world. It is a fast, dangerous, exciting game in which two teams flying on broomsticks compete for points scored by throwing a ball through hoops on either end of a large grassy pitch (PS10). Quidditch is played by kids on broomsticks in the back apple orchard (HBP6), by teams of students at Hogwarts (PA15), and by professional athletes whose exploits are followed avidly all over the world. The World Cup matches attract hundreds of thousands of fans (GF8).

After a fight with her boyfriend, J.K. Rowling checked into a hotel and spent some time working on the rules of the sport she was inventing for her books. She knew she wanted the name of the sport to start with a Q, so she scribbled a lot of names on a pad, looking

for one that 'worked'. When she wrote 'Quidditch', she knew she'd found it. Although the word was invented, it is possible that a real place name provided some inspiration. Near Exeter, where she went to university, is a small town named Quoditch. Perhaps she heard or saw that name at some point and it stuck in her mind. The colourful history of this thousand-year-old sport is detailed in the excellent book, Quidditch Through the Ages, written by J.K. Rowling using the penname Kennilworthy Whisp, and available in Muggle bookshops.

Quidditch Cup

Awarded each year to the top House Quidditch team at Hogwarts (esp. PA15, OP30, HBP24).

Quidditch stadiums

Teams in Britain do not have their own home fields for matches. Instead, Quidditch stadiums have been erected on a number of deserted moors, and players and fans come from all over Britain to attend these matches. Various charms and magical effects have been used, with varying degrees of success, to prevent Muggles from accidentally discovering these stadiums (DP1–4)

Quidditch Teams of Britain and Ireland

Hermione gave a copy of this book to Harry as a Christmas present during their fourth year (GF23); it was one of the books he tried reading as a distraction while cooped up in number four, Privet Drive before his fifth year (OP3).

Quidditch Through the Ages

by Kennilworthy Whisp

A general reference work about Quidditch, first lent to Harry during their first year by Hermione (PS11), who'd read it for tips before the Gryffindors' first flying lesson (PS9). It has since been produced for Muggles, and is highly recommended by Albus Dumbledore, among others (QA/i).

The book Quidditch Through the Ages *is available in Muggle shops. Included in that book are lists of teams and fouls and other encyclopaedic information. We do not reproduce that information in here; instead, we encourage you to buy a copy of* Quidditch Through the Ages *for yourself and find out more.*

Quidditch Union for the Administration and Betterment of the British League and its Endeavors (Q.U.A.B.B.L.E.)

An organisation which supports professional Quidditch in Britain. The head of this organisation is Dunbar Oglethorpe (FW).

Quidditch World Cup

An enormously popular international sporting event. In 1994 it was held on a deserted moor in Britain, with Harry, Hermione, and the Weasleys in attendance for a spectacular match between Ireland and Bulgaria (GF8).

Quidditch World Cup stadium

The Ministry of Magic spent a year leading up to the event magically constructing a huge stadium for the Quidditch World Cup far out on a deserted moor, near a forest. With immense gold walls and seating for 100,000, it was an impressive place. The stadium was protected by Muggle-repelling charms and other spells (GF8).

Quietus

(KWY-uh-tus)

Reverses the effect of *Sonorus*, making the caster's voice normal in volume. Ludo Bagman used this in conjunction with *Sonorus* to allow himself to speak to large crowds at the World Cup and at the Triwizard Tournament (GF8).

'quietus' = L. 'quiet, peaceful'

Quigley

Beater for the Irish National Quidditch Team (GF8).

Like the other members of the Irish National Team, Quigley is named for one of J.K. Rowling's friends (JKR).

Quigley, Finbar

Captain of and Beater for the Ballycastle Bats, and possibly the same person as Quigley of the Irish National Quidditch Team (DP1, 2).

quill

Members of the wizarding community use quill pens and parchment for writing rather than modern Muggle pens and paper. Various birds' feathers may be used to create such quill pens, ranging from eagles (GF2) to pheasants (OP16), to phoenixes (OP37). Quills are sold in Diagon Alley at Scrivenshaft's Quill Shop (OP16).

quill, magical

A magical quill at Hogwarts detects the birth of every magical child and records the names down in a large parchment book. Professor McGonagall checks this book annually to know which children need to be sent owls as they approach their eleventh birthdays (Sch1). Other types of magical quills include Auto-Answer (OP31), Quick-Quotes (GF18), Self-Inking, Smart-Answer, and Spell-Checking (HBP6).

quill, Umbridge's

Umbridge had a quill that she used for detentions that wrote in blood and simultaneously etched the phrase being written into the back of the writer's hand (OP13).

Quince, Hambledon

(b. 1936)

Developed a bizarre theory about the origins of wizards and Muggles (JKR).

Quintaped

A dangerous, five-legged magical creature (JKR).

'quint' = L. 'five' + 'ped'= L. 'foot'

Quintaped (rune)

With an ancient symbol looking at a Quintaped head-on, this is the rune for the number five, thanks to the creature's five legs. The meaning appears in *Ancient Runes Made Easy* (JKR).

Quintessence: A Quest

Required reading in sixth-year Charms; the students were expected to have read it before Christmas (HBP15).

'quinta essentia' = L. 'fifth essence'

According to ancient science, the celestial

realm — the space in between the stars and other heavenly bodies — was composed of 'aether' (U.S. 'ether'), the fifth element. The other four elements comprised the terrestrial world: earth, water, air, and fire. Alternatively, the fifth element was thought by some ancient scholars to be 'idea', that which is not part of the physical world at all. Therefore they considered the fifth element to be thoughts, mathematical concepts, and the like. We have no way of knowing which of these definitions is being studied in Charms.

Quirke, Orla
(Ravenclaw, 1994)
Hogwarts student (GF12).

Quirrell, Quirinus
(d. June 1992; Muggle Studies professor, ?-1990; DADA Professor, 1991–1992)
A young wizard with a 'brilliant mind', Quirrell was a professor of Muggle Studies, and later of Defence Against the Dark Arts, at Hogwarts (PS5, BLC). At some point before he took the DADA job, he took a year off to gain experience dealing with Dark Arts (PS5). (*See also* PS17, GF33).

Quong Po
(1443–1539)
A Chinese Magical Creatures Specialist; for more information, see the Famous Wizard cards (FW).

rabbit

A long-eared, furry animal sometimes associated with Muggle stage magic ('pulling a rabbit out of a hat'). A fat white rabbit in the Magical Menagerie transformed itself into a top hat and back again; it was either a magical creature or simply one enchanted to perform this bit of Transfiguration (PA4).

Rackharrow, Urquhart
(1612–1697)

Inventor of the Entrail-Expelling Curse; a portrait of this nasty-looking wizard hung in the Dai Llewellyn Ward in St. Mungo's (OP22).
Urquhart is the name of a Scottish clan and also of a castle on the shores of Loch Ness.

Radford, Mnemone
(1562–1649)

The first Ministry of Magic Obliviator and the wizard who invented some useful memory charms (JKR).
from 'mnemonikos' = Gk. 'of or pertaining to memory'

Ragnok

A goblin of some influence. Bill, who works at Gringotts, knows Ragnok (OP5).

Ragnok the Pigeon-Toed

Author of *Little People, Big Plans*, and an activist for Goblin rights (DP3).

Ragnuk the First

A goblin king c.1000 A.D. who, according to goblin legend, was the true owner of the sword of Gryffindor, and the one from whom Godric Gryffindor stole it (DH25). The legend is untrue (BLC); however, it may have provoked a bloody goblin rebellion of the 17th or 18th centuries (JKR).

Railview Hotel

A gloomy-looking Muggle establishment in Cokeworth, to which Vernon Dursley took his family while attempting to avoid Harry's Hogwarts letters (PS3).
The name of this hotel suggests that it looks out on the railway line. Not a particularly upscale hotel, apparently.

'Rapier'

Fred (or perhaps George) Weasley's code name when he appears on *Potterwatch*, though Lee Jordan initially tried to call him 'Rodent' instead (DH22).

Rastrick, Xavier

(1750–1836)

A flamboyant wizarding tap-dancer; for more information, see the Famous Wizard cards (FW).

rats

In the Magical Menagerie was a cage full of black rats which were busy using their tails as skipping-ropes; the saleswitch implied that since they were magical, they would live longer than a common rat's three-year lifespan (PA4).

Ravenclaw, Helena

The daughter of Rowena Ravenclaw. She is now known as the Grey Lady, the House ghost of Ravenclaw (DH31).

Ravenclaw House

One of the four houses of Hogwarts, valuing above all else wit and learning (PS7, GF16). The head of Ravenclaw is Professor Filius Flitwick (HBP29), and the house ghost is the Grey Lady, Helena Ravenclaw (DH31). The house shield is blue and silver and features an eagle (GF15).

Ravenclaw House common room

Located in Ravenclaw Tower, this common room, like the other House common rooms, is decorated in House colours. The room is circular and very airy, with a domed ceiling painted with stars and arched windows. On a plinth stands a life-size statue of Rowena Ravenclaw wearing her diadem (DH29).

Ravenclaw, Rowena

(c.1000)

One of the four founders of Hogwarts, 'best remembered for her intelligence and creativity' (FW) and widely considered the most brilliant witch of her time (JKR). Ravenclaw was good friends with Helga Hufflepuff (OP11) and had a single daughter, Helena (DH31). Her motto was 'Wit beyond measure is man's greatest treasure,' and she selected students for Ravenclaw house accordingly (DH29). She also invented the ever-changing floor plan for Hogwarts (FW). Ravenclaw was famous for having a diadem that bestowed wisdom to anyone who wore it. It was stolen by her daughter, Helena, and lost for a thousand years; wizards have long coveted its powers (DH31).

Ravenclaw Tower

Located on the west side of the castle

(OP18), Ravenclaw Tower is one of the tallest towers in Hogwarts (HBP27, DH30). The entrance is a door at the top of a tightly winding spiral staircase that leads up from the fifth floor. The door has neither handle nor keyhole, but instead has a talking bronze doorknocker in the shape of an eagle. Rather than asking for a conventional password, the doorknocker will ask a question; if answered correctly, the knocker will compliment the person on the answer and the door will swing open (DH29).

razor, enchanted
Bill and Fleur gave Harry one of these for his seventeenth birthday (DH7).

Recent Developments in Wizardry
A Hogwarts library book in which Harry searched in vain for Nicholas Flamel (PS12).

Red Caps
Small, goblin-like creatures which love bloodshed, and will attempt to beat to death Muggles lost in dungeons or on battlefields on dark nights (PA8).
Red Caps in folklore are said to inhabit the castles on the border between Scotland and England, waiting to waylay travellers and kill them. Red Caps wear heavy iron boots and carry huge iron pikes, but

even so can run faster than a human. The only way to avoid being skewered is to stop and quote a Bible verse to the little monster.

Reducio
(re-DOO-see-oh)
Causes an Engorged object to return to its normal size; Barty Crouch Jr., disguised as Moody, used this after demonstrating the Unforgivable Curses on enlarged spiders (GF14).
'redusen' = Middle Eng. 'diminish', from 'reducere' = L. 'bring back'

Reducto
(re-DUC-toh)
'Reductor Curse'
A blasting spell that has at various times been used to create a hole in a hedge (GF31), smash shelves of prophecies (OP35), and reduce a table to dust (OP19).
'redusen' = Middle Eng. 'diminish', from 'reducere' = L. 'bring back'

'Reductor Curse'
See REDUCTO.

Refilling Charm
A rather difficult but handy N.E.W.T.-level Charm which fills empty glasses (HBP22).
Since J.K. Rowling has stated that food

cannot be created by magic, we might assume that the Refilling Charm is magically transporting the food (or drink, in this case) from somewhere else. *This is similar to the spell McGonagall cast on an empty plate to make it refill itself with sandwiches when Harry and Ron had been caught flying to Hogwarts in the Ford Anglia and weren't allowed to go to the feast for their dinner (CS5).*

Regerminating Potion

A green potion sold by Tilden Toots and marketed on his show, 'Toots, Shoots 'n' Roots'. It can be used along with a Rejuicing Potion to revive a dead Flitterbloom (JKR).

This potion, along with the Rejuicing Potion, was found on J.K. Rowling's website. Bottles of each sat next to a dead Flitterbloom plant in the Room of Requirement. If you listened to Tilden Toots' radio show on the site, you'd discover how to use the two potions to revive the Flitterbloom and gain a prize.

Registry of Proscribed Charmable Objects

This defines carpets as a Muggle item, at least in Britain; consequently it is illegal to bewitch one to fly (GF7).

Regulation and Control of Magical Creatures, Department of

A regulatory department at the Ministry of Magic, with a lot on its plate: this is the group responsible for overseeing all magical non-humans, from goblins and house-elves to ghosts. Responsibilities include hiding magical creatures like the Loch Ness Monster from Muggles, regulating the creation of new magical breeds (GF24), and dealing with creature-related crises (HBP1). The department takes up the entire Fourth Level of the Ministry of Magic (OP7), and its employees include Amos Diggory (GF6).

Rejuicing Potion

A red potion sold by Tilden Toots and marketed on his show, 'Toots, Shoots 'n' Roots'. It can apparently be used along with a Regerminating Potion to revive a dead Flitterbloom (JKR).

See the entry on Regerminating Potion for details of how to use this potion on J.K. Rowling's website.

Relashio

(re-LASH-ee-oh)

Spell that forces a person or object to release whatever it is holding, be it a wizard (HBP10), chains (DH13), or a Grindylow (GF26).

'rilascio' = It. 'to release, to relax, to issue'

Reluctant Reversers, A Charm To Cure

This spell is on page twelve of the *Handbook of Do-It-Yourself Broom Care* (PA2).

Remembrall

A glass ball the size of a large marble. In its default state (when nobody is touching it), a Remembrall is full of white smoke. When picked up and held in a person's hand, a Remembrall will glow scarlet if there's something the person has forgotten to do (PS9). Remembralls are banned from the examination hall at Hogwarts (OP31), which suggests that they are capable of telling a person whatever they're trying to remember.

remorse

Once a wizard has split his or her soul, only genuine remorse will allow that soul to be put back together. According to *Secrets of the Darkest Art*, 'you've got to really feel what you've done . . .' This is a horribly painful process, but it is the only way (DH6, esp. DH36).

What an interesting twist. No matter how numerous or terrible a person's crimes, then, true repentance is always possible and with that repentance will come restoration. This is a deeply religious theme, common to various faiths and belief systems. What would have happened if Voldemort had taken the opportunity to change his heart when Harry offered it to him? Perhaps we see a hint of this with Grindelwald, whose final actions in the tower of Nurmengard seemed to show a changed man. He sacrificed himself rather than tell Voldemort what he knew. Perhaps, somewhere on the other side of the Veil, Gellert Grindelwald and Albus Dumbledore will meet as friends once again.

Rennervate

(REN-er-vayt)

Spell used to revive a person who has been hit by a Stunner (GF9, 28, 35).

In early editions of GF, the spell was written 'Ennervate'. See the notes on that spell for details of the etymology and why this change was made.

're-' = L. 'back, return to the original place' + 'nerves' Eng. c.1603 'strength', from 'nervus' = L. 'nerve' (as in 'daring, courage')

Reparo

(re-PAR-oh)

A useful common spell that undoes damage to an object, fixing anything from wood (GF5) to ceramics (OP15) and glass (GF11). Didn't work so well for Hagrid trying to repair the sidecar to the flying motorcycle in mid-battle, though (DH4).

'reparare' = L. 'repair, restore'

Repello Muggletum

(re-PEL-oh MUG-ul-tum)

There are a number of different Muggle-Repelling Charms, including those which are placed on the Quidditch World Cup Stadium (GF8) or wizarding schools (GF11). This incantation is probably one of the most basic of such charms, though we don't know its exact effect on Muggles. Hermione casts this spell routinely when protecting the trio's campsite (DH14).

'repello' = L. 'to repel' + 'Muggletum' = a 'Latinised' form of the word Muggle

restoring spell

Forces an Animagus who has transformed into an animal to revert to his or her human form. The spell's effect is a bright blue-white flash of light (PA19).

Restricted Section

Section of the Hogwarts library, at the back, set off with a rope. A signed note from a teacher is required for younger students to peruse that section of the library; it contains books of Dark Magic only used by older students, such as those studying advanced Defence Against the Dark Arts (PS12, CS9, 10, GF26, HBP18).

Resurrection Stone

One of the Deathly Hallows, a stone which would bring back the dead. It was passed down from Cadmus Peverell through the generations, and made into a ring (HBP10). (*See also* HBP17, 23, DH34, 36).

Reusable Hangman

A product sold at Weasleys' Wizard Wheezes, this magical word game features a wooden man and an authentic reusable gallows (HBP6).

Revealer

Eraser-like object that makes invisible ink visible. Hermione owns one (CS13).

A Revealer appears on J.K. Rowling's website and can be used to show some secret writing (JKR).

Reverse Spell Effect

See PRIORI INCANTATEM.

Re-Visibility Spectacles

The Ministry of Magic handed these out to spectators for a Quidditch match between the Falmouth Falcons and the Pride of Portree, as an Invisibility Charm had been put on the stadium (DP1).

Revulsion Jinx

A spell which drives a person away from the caster; the spell produces a flash of purple light (DH13, 14).

Rictusempra

(ric-tu-SEM-pra)

'Tickling Charm'

Causes a person to laugh uncontrollably. Harry cast this spell on Draco at the Duelling Club (CS10).

'rictus' = L. 'gaping mouth, grin' + 'sempra' = L. 'always'

Riddikulus

(ri-di-KYOO-lus)

'Boggart Banishing Spell'

A simple charm requiring force of mind, this spell requires the caster to visualise his or her worst fear in an amusing form while reciting the incantation. When performed correctly, this forces the boggart to alter its form, which will be that of the person's worst fear, in such a way that it will inspire laughter. This forms an effective defence against the creature (PA7). It was tested for the Defence Against the Dark Arts O.W.L. (OP31).

'ridiculum' = L. 'joke', from 'ridere' = L. 'to laugh'

Riddle family

An unpleasant, snobbish Muggle family who lived in Little Hangleton fifty years ago, in a large manor house on a hill (GF1). The son, Tom, caught the eye of the witch Merope Gaunt, and she brewed a love potion and induced him to marry her. Together they had a son — Tom Marvolo Riddle (BLC).

Riddle House

Large manor house located on a hill overlooking Little Hangleton. The house was the home of Voldemort's paternal grandparents and his father, Tom Riddle. One summer day in 1943, the whole family died under mysterious circumstances. The house was briefly occupied, then fell into disrepair, watched over by the old caretaker, Frank Bryce (GF1, HBP17).

Riddle of the Potions

A challenge set by Snape to protect the Philosopher's Stone. He placed seven bottles of various sizes and shapes, with different potions in each, and left a riddle which, when solved, would reveal which potion needed to be drunk to pass safely into the next room (PS16).

Fans have made valiant attempts to solve the riddle. However, since description of the scene in the book does not give two key facts — the locations of the 'dwarf' and 'giant' vials — it is impossible to solve it completely. Fortunately, Hermione had all the clues she needed and worked it out. Even more fortunately, Quirrell had left a bit of potion in the bottle. If he had been smart, he would have emptied the whole thing to thwart anyone trying to follow him.

Riddle, Tom Marvolo

(b. 31 December 1926; Slytherin, 1938; Prefect, 1942; Slug Club?; Head Boy, 1944)

A boy born in an orphanage on 31 December, 1926, to Merope (Gaunt) Riddle, who named him after his grandfather and father and then died. He discovered that he could do magic, and when Dumbledore approached him at age eleven to come to Hogwarts, he was keen to go (HBP13). At Hogwarts he was outwardly a model student. After leaving school, he worked at Borgin and Burkes for a while and then vanished (HBP20).

See VOLDEMORT, LORD.

'Tom' was his Muggle father's first name 'Marvolo' was his maternal grandfather's name.

'Riddle' means 'a difficult problem, or to pierce with many holes'.

Ridgebit, Harvey

(1881–1973)

Dragonologist who established the Romanian dragon sanctuary (JKR).

Ring of Peverell

Set with the Resurrection Stone, this ring was passed down through the descendants of Cadmus Peverell, eventually ending up in the hands of Marvolo Gaunt (HBP10, 23, BLC).

See RESURRECTION STONE.

Ripper

One of Marjorie Dursley's twelve dogs, evil-tempered and mean. Ripper was Marjorie's favourite. She took him with her when she went visiting, because she said he pined for her when she wasn't there. Ripper enjoyed drinking from Marge's saucer and chasing Harry up trees (PA2).

Rise and Fall of the Dark Arts, The

Harry is mentioned in this book, which Hermione had read before meeting him for the first time on board the Hogwarts Express (PS6). It also discusses the Dark Mark (GF9).

'River'

The host of the wizarding radio programme *Potterwatch*. River is actually a code name for Lee Jordan (DH22).

Lee's code name comes from the River Jordan, one of the most famous rivers in the world, located on the border between the countries of Israel and Jordan and flowing into the Dead Sea.

Rivers

Hogwarts student in Harry's year.

This last name appears in the draft of the class list of Harry's year that J.K. Rowling displayed during the 'Harry Potter and Me' TV interview (HPM). This name cannot be considered canon, however, because the notes on this document conflict in too many places with the stories as they were actually published.

River Troll

River Trolls are fond of lurking beneath bridges. In the 1600s, a River Troll caused problems for travellers trying to cross the River Wye (FW).

Robards, Gawain

Head of the Auror Office in the Ministry of Magic, replacing Rufus Scrimgeour when he became Minister for Magic (HBP15).

Roberts family

A Muggle campground manager and his wife and two children who had a most peculiar couple of days in August 1994, though they've forgotten all about it (GF7, 9).

robes

See CLOTHING, WIZARD.

Robins, Demelza

(Gryffindor, 1990s; Quidditch Chaser 1996–?)

A Chaser for the Gryffindor team with a talent for dodging Bludgers, part of the team that won the House Cup in 1996-1997 (HBP11, 24).

rock cake

A kind of fruitcake. It's supposed to look something like a rock, and even to have a hard surface, but not to resemble a rock quite as closely as Hagrid's version seems to (PS8).

'Rodent'

While hosting *Potterwatch,* Lee Jordan initially used this code name to refer to Fred Weasley. A quick background conversation, though, revealed that Fred actually wanted to be called 'Rapier', so to keep the show moving, Lee relented (DH22).

Romania

An important country for dragon enthusiasts, located in Central Europe. The Carpathian Mountains dominate the central region of the country, and it is very likely in that region where can be found the famous Romanian Longhorn dragon reservation. Charlie Weasley works in Romania with the dragons there (PS14).

Romanian Longhorn dragon

A dragon species (JKR).

Romanian Longhorn Dragon Reservation

The largest dragon reservation in the world, founded in the mid-20th Century by Harvey Ridgebit (JKR). Charlie Weasley works at this reservation (PS6). A number of dragon species live on the reservation, not just Longhorns (GF19, DH7).

The reservation is almost certainly located in the Carpathian Mountains, one of the largest mountain ranges in Europe. These mountains dominate the central region of Romania.

'Romulus'

On *Potterwatch,* this was the code name for Remus Lupin (DH22).

For anyone with knowledge of Muggle history, this wouldn't have been a hard one to guess, as Romulus — the founder of Rome, according to legend — had a twin named Remus. Fortunately, most wizards know very little Muggle history.

Ronan

Red-haired Centaur who lives in the Forest near Hogwarts (PS15, OP30, DH36).

'ronan' = Celtic 'little seal; oath', but possibly from 'roan', which is a term for a type of grey coat found on some horses.

Rookwood, Augustus

Pockmarked, stooped Death Eater and Ministry wizard working in the Department of Mysteries; friend of Ludo Bagman's father (GF30, OP25, 35). He fought in the Battle of Hogwarts (DH32, 36).

In the first British editions of OP, Rookwood's name is erroneously given as Algernon.

Room of Hidden Things

A name for the Room of Requirement when it has configured itself into a vast storeroom filled with things hidden or thrown out by generations of students at Hogwarts (HBP24, DH31).

Room of Requirement

(Come and Go Room, The Room of Hidden Things)

Magical room at Hogwarts which can only be discovered by someone who is in need; located on the seventh floor. The Room magically adapts itself to whatever is needed by those who enter (OP18, HBP24, 27, DH29, 31).

room-sealing spell

Snape used a powerful magic spell to seal his office, a charm that only a powerful wizard could break (GF25).

Roper, S.

Hogwarts student in Harry's year.

This last name appears in the draft of the class list of Harry's year that J.K. Rowling displayed during the 'Harry Potter and Me' TV interview (HPM). This name cannot be considered canon, however, because the notes on this document conflict in too many places with the stories as they were actually published.

ropes, magical

Ropes are sometimes conjured from thin air to bind a person; Quirrell did this to Harry, for example, in front of the Mirror of Erised (PS17), and Dumbledore did it to bind Barty Crouch Jr. after 'outing' him (GF36). Wormtail also memorably conjured these to bind Harry in the graveyard (GF32). (*See also* BINDING/FASTENING MAGIC.)

rosewood

A wand wood that was used to make Fleur Delacour's wand (GF18).

Rosewood is a beautiful, richly-coloured wood often used for fine woodworking, such as musical instruments or furniture. The wood has a sweet smell which lingers for many years, hence the name. When cut, rosewood changes hues almost before one's eyes, through yellow and orange to a deep reddish colour. The wood is highly prized, and as a result some species are endangered. In folklore, rosewood is associated with the highest goddesses: Aphrodite, Venus, Hera, and so on.

Rosier

One of the earliest members of the Death Eaters (as early as 1955), along with Nott, Mulciber, and Dolohov (HBP20). Possibly related to Evan Rosier, a Death Eater friend of Snape's.

According to tradition, Rosier is a fallen angel, the patron demon of seduction.

Rosier, Druella

Druella was the wife of Cygnus Black and had three daughters: Bellatrix Lestrange, Andromeda Tonks, and Narcissa Malfoy (BFT).

This is another example of how J.K. Rowling uses the Black Family Tree to show the complex connections between the pure-blood families. Druella would be a relative of the Rosiers who became Death Eaters.

Rosier, Evan

(born late 1950s or early 1960s, died c.1980; Slytherin)

Attended Hogwarts with Severus Snape (GF27), so he was probably a child of the elder Rosier who was a contemporary of Tom Riddle at school (c.1980) (GF27, 30).

Rosmerta, Madam

The proprietor of the Three Broomsticks in Hogsmeade since at least the 1970s, though she is quite young-looking. She is well known by witches and wizards from all over, including the teachers from Hogwarts, rowdy groups of warlocks and goblins, and even the Minister for Magic himself (PA10). She has been described as 'a curvy sort of woman' (PA10) and 'pretty' (GF19). Ron gets a bit red in the face when he gets near her (PA10), a fact which Hermione is only too happy to point out (HBP12). (*See also* HBP27).

Rosmerta is a late-Roman goddess of fertility and abundance, her symbol being the cornucopia. She was not part of the classical Roman pantheon. She appeared in the Gallo-Roman religion which came from the combination of Roman traditions with the religions of Gaul (western areas of Europe, particularly what is now France).

Rotfang Conspiracy

A crackpot theory which suggests that the Aurors are secretly working to destroy the Ministry of Magic via the use of Dark Magic and gum disease (hence the name: 'rot fang') (HBP15).

rowboat spell

Propels a rowboat along without oars (PS5). Possibly it is this spell which propels the fleet of small boats from the dock near Hogsmeade station to Hogwarts castle (PS6).

Rowle, Thorfinn

A large blond Death Eater who was involved in an altercation with Harry, Ron, and Hermione (DH9) and fought against the Order of the Phoenix (HBP28).

'Royal'

On *Potterwatch,* this was the code name for Kingsley Shacklebolt (DH22).

'Royal' is a reference to his first name, Kingsley. Very likely his distinctive bass voice would give him away, regardless of his code name.

Rufford, Grugwyn

Disgruntled member of the National Welsh Gobstones Team, who complained to the *Daily Prophet* because they didn't cover the Welsh victory over Hungary. The editor responded that this was because people thought Gobstones was 'deeply boring' (DP1).

Runcorn

Hogwarts student in Harry's year (HPM).

This last name appears in the draft of the class list of Harry's year that J.K. Rowling displayed during the 'Harry Potter and

Me' TV interview (HPM). This name cannot be considered canon, however, because the notes on this document conflict in too many places with the stories as they were actually published.

Runcorn, Albert

A tall, bearded wizard who works for the Ministry of Magic, an imposing fellow who bullies some of the other Ministry employees (DH12, 13).
There is no evidence that Runcorn was a Death Eater. More likely he, like Umbridge, was happy to follow the lead of the Death Eaters when they took over and to use that excuse to bully other people. In some ways he is similar to Peter Pettigrew and Piers Polkiss, although he is much more physically imposing than either of those characters.

rune dictionary

An untitled book that Hermione carries around during her fourth year (GF20), possibly her copy of *Ancient Runes Made Easy.*

runes

See ANCIENT RUNES.

Runespoor

A magical three-headed snake (JKR).

Runespoor (Rune)

According to *Ancient Runes Made Easy,* the rune symbol for the number three is an icon of a Runespoor, a three-headed snake (JKR).

rune stones

A method of Divination using stones with various runes carved or inscribed on them (OP25).

Ryan, Barry

Keeper for the Irish National Quidditch Team (GF8). In 1995 he made a spectacular save against Poland's top Chaser, Ladislaw Zamojski (OP19).

sage

Centaurs burn this herb, observing the fumes and flames to refine the results of their stargazing (OP27).

In North American Indian lore, sage is burned as part of many rituals to drive away bad influences or feelings.

Sahara Desert

Vast desert in Africa, covering a large portion of the northern half of the continent. A place where Quidditch referees have been known to turn up after disgruntled fans Transform their brooms into Portkeys (PS11).

St. Brutus's Secure Centre for Incurably Criminal Boys

A Muggle boarding school Vernon Dursley publicly claims that Harry attends, so neighbours and relatives don't wonder about his strange behaviour or absences (PA2).

From what we can tell, St. Brutus's was entirely invented by Uncle Vernon, which is pretty amazing when you recall that he 'didn't approve of imagination' (PS1).

St. Mungo's Hospital for Magical Maladies and Injuries

Founded in around 1600 by Mungo Bonham (FW), St. Mungo's Hospital is located in London disguised as an abandoned department store called Purge and Dowse, Ltd. To gain entry, a wizard speaks to the dummy in the window and walks into the glass when it nods. Once inside, patients suffering from strange (and often humorous) problems wait in a reception area or hurry along for treatment. The Healers (the Muggle equivalent of doctors and nurses) wear lime green robes bearing an emblem of a crossed wand and bone. St. Mungo's has six floors, each dedicated to different types of afflictions (OP22, 23).

The real St. Mungo was a Scottish saint who, among other things, founded the city of Glasgow. He lends his name to a real-life institution in London called St. Mungo's which assists homeless and other vulnerable people. St. Mungo's headquarters on Hammersmith Road is located in a large, red-brick building. Far from being derelict, however, it's a very new and smart-looking office block.

salamander

A small white lizard which lives in fire and which is studied at Hogwarts (CS8).

The salamander is a legendary creature rumoured to eat fire. It is said that it can poison a tree's fruit simply by wrapping itself around the trunk.

salamander (rune)

An icon of a salamander forms the rune symbol for the number six — as salamanders can survive for only six hours outside a fire. A picture can be found in *Ancient Runes Made Easy* (JKR).

Salem Witches' Institute

A group of American witches from the Salem Witches' Institute came to the Quidditch World Cup in 1994; Harry noticed them while walking by their tent (GF7).

Salem, in Massachusetts, is infamous in the history of the United States as the place where over 150 people were tried on suspicion of being witches in 1692. Of those, twenty-nine were convicted and nineteen were executed. Public outcry against the proceedings began very soon after the events. Thomas Maule, a noted Quaker, wrote that 'it were better than one hundred Witches should live, than that one person be put to death for a witch, which is not a Witch'. In 1697,
just a few years after the events, a day of fasting was declared and an apology read to the congregation of the church in Salem, referring to the trials as being the work of Satan.

Salvio Hexia

(SAL-vee-oh HEX-ee-ah)

One of the many defensive and protective spells that Hermione, and sometimes Harry, routinely cast around their tent (DH14, 22).

'salvia' = L. 'without breaking' + 'hexia' = L. 'hexes'

Sanguina, Lady Carmilla

(1561–1757)

A female vampire who used her victims' blood for bathing; for more information, see the Famous Wizard cards (FW).

'sanguineus' = L. 'of blood, also bloody, bloodthirsty'

Sanguini

Vampire who attended Slughorn's Christmas party with his friend Eldred Worple (HBP15).

'sanguineus' = L. 'of blood, also bloody, bloodthirsty'

Sardinia

A large island in the Mediterranean Sea, near Italy. Professor Binns had begun a lecture about a subcommittee of Sardinian sorcerers when Hermione interrupted him to ask about the Chamber of Secrets (CS9).

The term 'sorcerer' is seldom used in the books, and usually refers to evil, Dark wizards. In this case, J.K. Rowling was probably word-playing with alliteration more than anything else ('In September of that year, a subcommittee of Sardinian sorcerers . . .'). Try saying that five times fast.

Saucy Tricks for Tricky Sorts

One of the books that Harry, Ron, and Hermione examined while preparing for the second Triwizard task (GF26).

Savage

An Auror stationed at Hogwarts during Harry's sixth year, along with Tonks, Dawlish and Proudfoot (HBP8).

Sawbridge, Almerick

(1602-1699)

Battled a River Troll who was making life difficult along the River Wye (FW).

This wizard's name relates to the fact that River Trolls like to lurk under bridges, waiting for unwary travellers.

Scabbers

A most unusual pet rat belonging to Ron Weasley, inherited from his older brother Percy. Ron often complained of Scabbers's uselessness (PS6), although when Hermione's new cat, Crookshanks, took an interest in chasing Scabbers, Ron was quite upset (PA4). (*See also* PA19, GF33).

See PETTIGREW, PETER.

Scabior

A Snatcher working with Fenrir Greyback (DH23).

Scalerot

According to Dragon Breeding for Pleasure and Profit, Scalerot is an affliction that can affect dragons, where their scales seem flaky and fall off. It can be treated by rubbing the area with sea salt, tar, and white spirit (JKR).

Scamander, Newton 'Newt' Artemis Fido

(1897–present)

Author of *Fantastic Beasts and Where To Find Them* (PS5) and a number of other books. His illustrious career with the Department for the Regulation and Control of Magical Creatures included the establishment of the Werewolf Registry and the Ban on Experimental Breeding. A full biography of this amazing wizard can be found in the introduction to the book *Fan-*

tastic Beasts and Where to Find Them, available at your local book shop (FB). Scamander currently divides his time between his Dorset home and field expeditions to observe new magical species (FW).

All of Scamander's names have some connection to animals and nature. 'Scamander' suggests 'salamander'. 'Newt' is the name of a small lizard. 'Artemis' was the Greek goddess of forests and hills, as well as of hunting, and was the twin sister of the god Apollo. 'Fido' is a name commonly given to dogs which comes from the Latin word 'fidelis', which means 'faithful'.

Scamander, Rolf

The grandson of Newt Scamander, a naturalist and husband to Luna Lovegood (BLC). They have two children, Lorcan and Lysander (ITV-YIL).

Scarpin's Revelaspell

See SPECIALIS REVELIO.

Scintillation Solution

A witch who found the Kwikspell course helpful wrote that people were now begging for her recipe for Scintillation Solution (CS8).

'scintillatus' = a form of of 'scintillare' = L. 'to sparkle', from 'scintilla' = L. 'spark'

Scotland

The country which comprises the northern portion of the British mainland. Hogwarts School is located in the Highlands of Scotland (BN, etc.).

Scourgify

(SKUR-ji-fy)

A cleaning spell (OP3, 28).

from 'excurare' = L. 'clean off'

Scouring Charm

Another cleaning spell (GF14). Possibly the same thing as *Scourgify*.

screaming yo-yo

Added to Filch's list of 437 objects forbidden inside Hogwarts castle at the start of the 1994-1995 school year (GF12).

Screechsnap

A semi-sentient plant that wriggles and squeaks uncomfortably when given too much dragon manure. The fifth years worked with seedlings of this plant in Herbology (OP25).

Scrimgeour, Rufus

(d. 1 August 1997; Minister of Magic, July 1996–August 1997)

Head of the Auror Office who was tapped to replace Fudge as Minister of Magic. Scrimgeour took over at a dangerous time, but he was a warrior and took the threat of the Dark Lord very seriously. His approach, however, was not all that different from that of his successor (esp. HBP3). (*See also* DH11).

'rufus' = *L. 'red'; for the meaning of Scrimgeour, see above.*

Scrivenshaft's Quill Shop
A shop in Hogsmeade (OP16).
'scrivener' = *archaic Eng. 'professional penman, copyist'* + *'shaft', which in English can mean the barrel or handle of a pen.*

scrofungulus
Magical disease listed on the directory in the lobby of St. Mungo's Hospital (OP22).
The details of this disease are not given in the books, but the name certainly sounds like something unpleasant, the second part suggesting the word 'fungus', which in humans can cause a number of ailments such as athlete's foot.

'scurvy cur'
A password to get into Gryffindor Tower thought up by Sir Cadogan (PA11).
'scurvy' = *Eng. 'contemptible; cowardly'* + *'cur'* = *Eng. 'mongrel dog; detestable person'*

sealing spell
Seals a roll of parchment with a touch of the wand. A parchment sealed this way is also opened with a wand touch (OP12).

sea serpent
A gigantic water snake (FW).

'second'
In a proper wizard's duel, each wizard has a 'second' — a person who takes over for them if they die (PS9).

second-hand robe shop
Mrs Weasley took Ginny here to buy her robes for Hogwarts; the shop is located in Diagon Alley (CS4).

Second Wizarding War
(1995–1998)
Voldemort's second rise to power, beginning with his re-emergence after the Triwizard Tournament in 1995 and ending with a climactic battle in the spring of 1998 (esp. GF2, 33, OP35-6, 38, HBP27, DH4, 31-36).

Secrecy Sensor
Magicial device which resembles a collection of old-fashioned television aerials. These pick up vibrations of evil approaching (GF20, HBP12).

Secrets of the Darkest Art

A book in the Hogwarts library that Dumbledore later banned and kept in his private office instead. It gives instructions for making — and destroying — a Horcrux (DH6).

Sectumsempra

(sek-tum-SEM-pra)

Spell invented by The Half-Blood Prince 'for enemies' (HBP21) which produces slashing cuts (HBP24). It is Dark Magic; anything severed from a target's body by this spell cannot be grown back by magic, according to Molly Weasley (DH5).

'sectus' = L. past participle of *'seco'* = *'to cut'*, + *'sempra'* = L. *'always'*

security Troll

Trolls are often used as guards in the Wizarding world, since they don't have brains for much else. Training security Trolls was one of the careers suggested in pamphlets offered to fifth years when they were deciding which N.E.W.T.-level classes they would take (OP29, DP1, PA14).

Seeker

Quidditch player whose objective is to spot and catch the Golden Snitch, earning 150 points for his or her team and ending the game. Harry plays this position on the Gryffindor Quidditch team (PS10, etc.).

Seer

A wizard who possesses the Inner Eye, or the ability to prophesy. Trelawney is the great-great-granddaughter of a very famous and very talented Seer, Cassandra Trelawney (OP15). Judging by the thousands upon thousands of prophecies recorded in the Hall of Prophecy, there have been quite a number of Seers throughout history (OP34).

self-correcting ink

One of many items banned for use during exams at Hogwarts (OP31).

Self-Defensive Spellwork

The Room of Requirement contained a copy of this spell book during the D.A.'s first meeting there (OP18).

self-fertilising shrubs

Magical plants. Harry and other fifth-years had to write an essay on self-fertilising shrubs for Professor Sprout (OP14).

self-stirring cauldrons

A cauldron which stirs itself, which would be very handy for potion-making. Many cauldrons seem to be at least partially magical; for example self-stirring, collapsible, and other cauldrons are for sale in a shop on Diagon Alley (PS5).

Selwyn

A Death Eater whose day job is working for the Ministry (DH4, 21). Selwyn is a very old, pure-blood family name (DH13).

Serpensortia

(ser-pen-SOR-sha)

Spell which causes a large serpent to burst from the end of a wand (CS10). *'serpens' = L. 'serpent' + 'ortus' = L. past participle of 'ortir', 'to come into existence'*

seven

See HEPTOMOLOGY.

Severing Charm

Spell to cut something (GF23).

shack

Igor Karkaroff's body was found in a shack that the *Daily Prophet* described as 'up north'. The Dark Mark was hovering in the sky above (HBP6).

Shacklebolt, Kingsley

(Order of the Phoenix)

Tall, bald black wizard with a deep voice who wears a single gold hooped earring. Kingsley is an Auror for the Ministry of Magic and a valued member of the Order of the Phoenix (OP3, 4–9, 35, HBP1). (*See also* DH36, BLC).

Name meaning: Shacklebolt = 'bolt which passes through the eyes of a shackle' (OED) in heraldry, the shacklebolt symbolises 'victory; one who has taken prisoners or rescued prisoners of war'.

Shell Cottage

The quaint seaside home of Bill and Fleur Weasley. Located on the outskirts of Tinworth in Cornwall (DH23, 24, 25), the cottage sits on a clifftop with views of the sea, an airy garden, and the sound of the waves pulsating through the house. The house is not large — the upstairs has just three small bedrooms and downstairs a modest kitchen and a sitting room with a fireplace. At the end of the garden, a small mound of red earth covers a grave for one of the bravest heroes of the Wizarding world (DH25).

sherbet lemon

(US: lemon drop)

Muggle sweet that Dumbledore is fond of (PS1). One of the passwords to the Headmaster's office (CS11, GF28).

Lemon drops and sherbet lemons are very different from each other. Lemon drops are hard sour lemon candies with a dusting of powdered sugar. Sherbet lemons are also a hard, lemon-flavoured sweet, but they are filled with sherbet powder which fizzes inside the mouth. The sherbet lemon is completely unknown in the U.S., however, so the editors chose a sweet which would be familiar and have the same sense of being a simple, Muggle treat.

Shield Charm
See PROTEGO.

Shield Cloaks, Shield Gloves, and Shield Hats
Though Fred and George initially developed Shield Hats as a joke item, the Ministry of Magic unexpectedly bought five hundred of them, intending them to be used as protection for its staff. As a result, the twins decided to expand into this more serious line of defence merchandise. Though not much help against serious curses, they do repel 'minor to moderate hexes or jinxes' (HBP6).

Shimpling, Derwent
(b. 1912)
Comedian known for his boldness and his purple skin; for more details, see the Fantastic Wizard cards (FW).

Shingleton, Gaspard
(b. 1959)
Wizard inventor; for more information, see the Famous Wizard cards (FW).

Shock Spells
Spell used at St. Mungo's to treat mental illnesses. One reader of *The Quibbler* wrote to Harry after his interview was published and suggested that he needed a course of Shock Spells at St. Mungo's, since he was obviously a nutter (OP26).
This is a reference to electric shock therapy, a technique used in the treatment of mental illness in the Muggle world. Some see it as barbaric, but it does produce results in certain cases.

Shooting Star
Ron had an old Shooting Star broom that Harry noted was often 'outstripped by passing butterflies' (CS4). The Hogwarts school brooms include Shooting Stars (PA10).

Shrake
A magical fish (JKR).

Shrieking Shack
Falsely rumoured to be 'the most haunted building in Britain' (PA5), the Shrieking Shack is a favourite stop on any Hogsmeade visit (PA8). However,

the wails that were once heard emanating from this creepy building were not caused by ghosts at all (PA14, 17, 18).

Shrinking Solution / Shrinking Potion

A potion studied in Potions class (PA7). Harry had to write a particularly nasty essay on Shrinking Potions as one of his holiday assignments for Potions the summer before his third year (PA1).

shrunken heads

There were shrunken heads in a window display in Knockturn Alley when Harry accidentally got lost there (CS4); Crabbe also had a shrunken head confiscated when he arrived for his sixth year at Hogwarts (DH11).

Shunpike, Stan

Conductor of the Knight Bus, a young wizard with prominent ears, quite a few pimples, and a Cockney accent. He wears a purple uniform (PA3). Stan has been known to tell a few tales now and then to try to impress people (GF9, HBP11) which has landed him in quite a bit of trouble (DH4, 23).

'shunpike' = slang 'a side road used to avoid the toll on or the speed and traffic of a superhighway'. Stan = named after one of JKR's grandfathers, Stan Volant.

Sickle

A unit of Wizarding currency. There are seventeen Sickles to a Galleon, and one silver Sickle is worth twenty-nine Knuts, or roughly £0.29 (US: about 50 cents).

'sickle' = Eng. 'a farm tool consisting of a handle with a curved blade'

Side-Along Apparition

A form of Apparition in which the person Apparating touches someone else, such as a child too young to Apparate themselves or a wizard without a wand, and Apparates with that person as a passenger. Side-along Apparition is mentioned in a Ministry leaflet as something to practice with children as a safety precaution (HBP3).

Silencio

(si-LEN-see-oh)
'Silencing Charm'
A charm taught to fifth-years (OP18, DH36)

'silens' = past participle of 'silere' = L. 'to be quiet'

Silver Arrow

A type of racing broom. Madam Hooch once had one and remembers it fondly (PA13).

Sinistra, Aurora

Professor of Astronomy at Hogwarts (CS11).

'Aurora' is given in an early planning draft for Prisoner of Azkaban available on JKR's website. However, we cannot consider this canon because other information on this page changed by the time the book was actually published (JKR). Aurora was the Ancient Roman goddess of the dawn ('Eos' in Greek). 'Sinistra' = the name of a magnitude 3.5 star in the constellation Ophiuchus, the Serpent Handler.

Sites of Historical Sorcery

Book that mentioned some notable buildings in Hogsmeade (PA5).

Skeeter, Rita

(b. circa 1951)

Reporter for the *Daily Prophet*, known for her brutal and sensational writing. She wears jewelled spectacles and carries a Quick-Quotes Quill, which she uses to write flowery prose filled with innuendoes and veiled accusations (GF18, 27, OP25, DH2, 18).

'skeeter' = slang term for a mosquito, a blood-sucking pest . . . how fitting.

Skele-Gro

Potion used by Healers to re-grow bones. The effect takes about eight hours and can be quite painful (CS10, DH24).

skeletons, dancing

According to the rumour mill at Hogwarts, Dumbledore booked a group of dancing skeletons as entertainment for the Halloween feast during Harry's second year. Harry never confirmed the rumour, as he didn't attend the feast that year (CS8).

skinning

A Quidditch foul, defined as intentionally colliding with another player while flying (GF8).

Skively, Harold

In a letter to the *Daily Prophet*, the appropriately-named Skively suggested that the Wizarding community celebrate a day to honour Merlin, since, as he put it, he 'could do with an extra day's holiday around August' (DP1)

'skive' = Br. Slang 'to avoid doing one's task or duty; to skip, as in skipping classes at school'

Skiving Snackboxes

One of the most popular products of Weasleys' Wizard Wheezes, Skiving Snackboxes contain a variety of sweets that make the wizard who eats them intentionally ill. Each sweet also comes with an antidote, allowing the wizard to fake illness for as long as necessary, and then, hidden safely away, cure themselves instantly. As the advertisement states, you can then 'pursue the leisure activity of your own choice during an hour that would otherwise have been devoted to unprofitable boredom' (OP6). Skiving Snackboxes include Fainting Fancies, Fever Fudge, Nosebleed Nougat and Puking Pastilles (OP6, 18).

Skull, the

One of the signs that can be read from a cup of tea leaves in Divination. It means 'danger in your path' (PA6).
The skull doesn't seem to appear in lists of real tasseography symbols. J.K. Rowling is probably making the obvious connection here, but tea leaf reading is not always so simple. The symbol 'The Gallows', for example, actually means 'good luck' according to some guides.

Sleekeazy's Hair Potion

Hermione used this to style her hair for the Yule Ball, though she considers it too much of a bother to do every day (GF24).

Sleeping Draught / Potion

Potion to put someone into a magical sleep (CS12, GF19, 36).

Slinkhard, Wilbert

Author of *Defensive Magical Theory*, an utterly worthless book assigned for Defence Against the Dark Arts classes by Umbridge. The theme of the book was that using spells, even in self defence, was bad (OP9 ff.).
This author's name suggests slinking away in cowardice. J.K. Rowling mentioned that she patterned Fudge's attitude about the return of Voldemort to that of Neville Chamberlain before World War Two, who ignored the warning signs of the burgeoning power of Hitler and the Nazis and was willing to give into any demands simply to avoid a war. This book is a clear example of that kind of thinking: reasonable on the surface (since fighting really should be a last resort) but ultimately nothing but cowardice and capitulation.

Sloper, Jack

(Gryffindor, 1990s; Quidditch Beater, 1996)
A Gryffindor student in the mid-1990s and a replacement Beater on the Quidditch team after Fred and George were banned for life (OP26).

Sloth Grip Roll

Quidditch manoeuvre where a player rolls upside down to avoid a Bludger (OP17).

Slug Club

During both periods he taught Potions at Hogwarts, Horace Slughorn hand-picked favourite students — those who have influential parents, or who he believes will be important one day — and invited them to social networking events (HBP4, 7). Through this group, casually called 'The Slug Club', Slughorn ensured that he had friends in high places and received his share of lavish gifts (HBP4).

Slughorn, Horace E. F.

(Slytherin; Potions Master until 1981, then again from 1996; Head of Slytherin House)

Potions master and head of Slytherin House twenty years ago. During that time, he founded the 'Slug Club', a group of his favourite students in whom he saw potential or whose connections might be useful to him (HBP7, etc). He retired after the 1980-81 school year (HBP22). As a favour to Dumbledore, he returned to teach at Hogwarts again in 1996 (HBP4, 8). Slughorn is a short, very portly man with a moustache. He wears lavish clothes: waistcoats with gold buttons and luxurious velvet smoking jackets (HBP4, 7).

slug-vomiting charm

Causes the victim to belch up slugs (CS7, OP19).

There are no spell words given for this charm (which seems more like a jinx or curse, really). Interestingly, the four days before, on the first day of classes, Ron had told Draco off with the phrase 'Eat slugs, Malfoy!' (CS6). Perhaps this was in Ron's mind when he tried to cast the slug-vomiting charm on Malfoy the following Saturday (CS7).

Slytherin House

One of the four houses of Hogwarts, valuing above all else cunning and use of any means to achieve one's ends (PS7). The Head of Slytherin was Professor Snape (GF36) until spring 1997 (HBP29) and thereafter Slughorn became Head of Slytherin (DH30). The house ghost is the Bloody Baron (CS8). Its shield is green and silver, and features a snake (GF15). Slytherin House has the unseemly reputation for producing wizards prone to the Dark Arts (PS5) and supporting pure-blood supremacy ideals (OP7). Famous Slytherins include Tom Riddle, Lucius and Draco Malfoy, Phineas Nigellus, Regulus Black, and Bellatrix Black Lestrange.

Slytherin House common room

Located in the dungeons and under the lake (TLC), accessed through a sliding stone door concealed in the wall. The password is 'pure-blood' (or was in December of 1992) (CS12, DH23).

Slytherin, Salazar

(c. 900s)

One of the four founders of Hogwarts. Slytherin had many unique skills. He was a Parselmouth and an accomplished Legilimens. According to the Sorting Hat's song, Slytherin came from the fens, which are located in the eastern portion of England, East Anglia and in particular Norfolk. He believed that only pure-blood witches and wizards should be allowed to attend Hogwarts; he clashed with Godric Gryffindor over this and eventually left the school. There was a legend that Slytherin built a secret chamber somewhere in Hogwarts that only his true heir would be able to open. This chamber, called the Chamber of Secrets, contained a monster that would finish his 'noble purpose' of killing all the Muggle-born students at Hogwarts.

Even in the twentieth century, the conflict between Gryffindor and Slytherin is played out in the rise of Voldemort, Slytherin's heir, and his defeat by Harry Potter, a 'true Gryffindor'.

'Slytherin' is basically the word 'slithering' without the 'g', which is certainly a nice snake-ish word. There is nothing particularly snake-ish about the name Salazar. Antonio Salazar was dictator of Portugal from 1932 to 1968. Since J.K. Rowling lived in Portugal for a time, she would have certainly heard that name. But why Salazar specifically? Probably because she wanted a somewhat unusual name that started with 'S', since all of the founders (and many of the current teachers) have alliterative names.

'Smallest Bedroom'

One of the four bedrooms in number four, Privet Drive, which the Dursleys gave to Harry after his first Hogwarts letter came addressed to him at the 'Cupboard Under the Stairs' (PS3).

Smeek, Enid

A witch who lived in Godric's Hollow at the same time as the Dumbledore family. She was quoted in *The Life and Lies of Albus Dumbledore* as saying that Aberforth Dumbledore used to throw goat dung at her, and that Bathilda Bagshot is 'nutty as squirrel poo' (DH18).

Smeltings School

Exclusive Muggle school, Vernon Dursley's *alma mater* and now Dudley's school. The Smeltings uniform includes a maroon tailcoat, orange knickerbockers, a straw boater hat, and a knobbly stick with which to hit things (and people) (PS3).

Smethley, Veronica
One of many witches who wrote fan mail to Gilderoy Lockhart (CS7).

Smethwyck, Hippocrates
Healer-in-Charge on the Dai Llewellyn ward at St. Mungo's Hospital when Arthur Weasley was there recovering from a snake bite (OP22).
Hippocrates is known as the 'father of medicine'. He lived in ancient Greece, where he championed the idea that diseases are not caused by divine punishment but by environmental factors.

Smethwyck, Leopoldina
(1829–1910)
First British witch to referee a Quidditch match (FW).

Smith, Hepzibah
(d. late 1940s)
A very rich, very fat old witch who collected magical antiques. She befriended Tom Marvolo Riddle while he was working for Borgin and Burkes, or rather, he befriended her in order to wheedle her out of her treasures. She

lived in a grand house, filled with so many possessions that it was difficult to walk through the rooms (HBP20).

Smith, Mr
The father of Hogwarts student Zacharias Smith; described as 'haughty-looking' (HBP30).

Smith, Zacharias
(Hufflepuff, 1990s; Quidditch Chaser c. 1996–1997; Dumbledore's Army)
A real winner of a guy who seems to annoy Ginny quite often (HBP7, 14). Joined Dumbledore's Army and scoffed at learning the simple *Expelliarmus* spell until Harry pointed out that it had saved his life while duelling with Voldemort (OP18).

Smythe, Georgina
Witch who wrote in to Tilden Toots's herbology radio show 'Toots, Shoots 'n' Roots' to ask about a sick Flitterbloom plant (JKR).
The name is only heard, not seen in print, so it may be spelled 'Smithe'.

snails
Poisonous orange snails were for sale in the Magical Menagerie (PA4).

snake

The animal symbol of Slytherin house (PS3, GF15).

See BOA CONSTRICTOR; NAGINI; SERPENSORTIA.

Snape house

See SPINNER'S END.

Snape, Severus

(January 9, 1960–May 1998; Slytherin 1971; Order of the Phoenix; Potions Master 1981-1996; Head of Slytherin House; DADA Professor, 1996-1997; Headmaster 1997-1998)

The only child of Tobias Snape, a Muggle, and Eileen Prince Snape, a witch (HBP30). An unhappy, neglected child, he befriended another girl from the same town, Lily Evans, and they went to Hogwarts together. Snape tried to maintain his friendship with Lily even though they were sorted into different houses and he knew she deplored his interest in the Dark Arts. Snape made an enemy of James Potter (PS17, OP28, 29). After leaving school, Snape applied for a position at Hogwarts. For the next sixteen years Severus Snape was the Potions Master at the school and became head of Slytherin House. His teaching style was based on intimidation and bullying (e.g., PA7). It was a fateful moment atop the Astronomy Tower which seemed to seal his allegiance to the Dark Side forever (HBP27). (*See also* DH32).

So much more could be written about this fascinating character than will fit here. In many ways, the story of Harry Potter is just as much the story of Severus Snape. His hidden motivations and secret agenda drive the entire saga. Take this short synopsis of his complicated and tragic life as a tiny taste of all that this character — and J.K. Rowling's amazing story about him — have to offer. Go read the series through again, watching and appreciating the character of Severus Snape.

'Severus' has obvious connotations of severity and strictness. There are also several saints with the name 'Severus'.

'Snape' is a village in North Yorkshire near Hadrian's (also known as 'Severus's') Wall where there is a 'Snape Castle'.

'snape' — archaic Eng. 'to be hard upon, rebuke, snub' from 'sneypa' = Old Norse 'to outrage, dishonour, disgrace'

'sneap' = Eng. 'to nip; pinch; put down; repress; snub'

Snape's office and private stores

A dimly lit room in the dungeons (CS5), its walls lined with glass jars filled with different coloured potions and slimy bits of plants and animals (CS11, GF27, OP26, 30).

Snape, Tobias
The Muggle father of Severus Snape, husband of Eileen Prince (OP26, HBP30).

Snargaluff
A plant which looks like a gnarled stump most of the time but which has prickly branches that attack when the plant is touched. Inside are a number of small pods that, when poked with something sharp, emit dozens of small squirming tubers (HBP14, c.f. DH30). One of these plants sits in the garden of the Lovegoods' house (DH20).

Snatchers
Bands of renegade wizards who hunted fugitives for the Ministry. Snatchers tried to capture those on the run, collecting the reward money of five Galleons per capture (DH19, 23).

Sneakoscope
A device which looks something like a gyroscope and which gives off a whistling sound when someone untrustworthy is around (PA1, DH7).

Snell, Barnaby
A fan of the Chudley Cannons who was quoted in the *Daily Prophet* expressing his disbelief after the team defeated the Wigtown Wanderers,

ending a seventeen-game losing streak (DP3).

Snitch
A 'walnut-sized golden ball' with 'silver wings' invented by Bowman Wright in the 1300s to be used in Quidditch. A Snitch is bewitched to avoid capture for as long as possible while remaining within the boundaries of the pitch. The capture of the Golden Snitch ends the game and gives the team whose Seeker caught it 150 points, which usually determines which team wins the game (PS10). Snitches also have a unique flesh memory charm cast on them, so that in the event of a close call, referees can tell which Seeker first caught the ball (DH7).

snitch jinx
A delayed-action jinx which writes the word 'sneak' across someone's face in pimples if they break an agreement they sign (OP16, HBP7).

snowball, bewitched
Snowballs enchanted to fly around and hit things (PS12).

snow, enchanted
A magical imitation snow, which unlike real snow is warm and dry. It is sometimes made to fall from the en-

chanted ceiling of the Great Hall as a Christmas decoration (CS12).

Snowy

One of Mrs Figg's cats (or perhaps Kneazles), of whom she forced Harry to look at pictures when he stayed at her house on Dudley's birthdays (PS2).

snuffbox

There was a silver snuffbox filled with Wartcap powder in the drawing room of number twelve Grimmauld Place that bit Sirius as he was trying to clean out the house (OP6).

Snuffles

Sirius asked Harry, Ron, and Hermione to refer to him as this when talking among themselves about him, so that if they were overheard, no one would know who they were talking about (GF27).

Society for Distressed Witches

Founded in the 1800s by Dorcas Wellbeloved (FW).

Society for the Promotion of Elfish Welfare (S.P.E.W.)

Founded in 1994 by Hermione Granger in response to what she saw as gross injustice in the treatment of house-elves. The Society didn't exactly catch on among Hogwarts students, but she persevered (GF15, OP14, 18).

Society for the Reformation of Hags

Founded by Honoria Nutcombe around 1700 (FW).

Society for the Support of Squibs (S.S.S.)

This society was founded by Idris Oakby, most likely sometime in the early-to mid-twentieth century (JKR).

Society for the Tolerance of Vampires (S.T.V.)

This society has a candle-lit office in London. They advertised for someone to run the office, and indicated that a preference would be given to applicants with a garlic allergy (DP2).

Somerset

A county in the West Country. It borders on Wiltshire, where Malfoy Manor is located. A lot of damage was caused in the summer of 1996 by what appeared to be a freak hurricane in Somerset (HBP1).

Somnolens, Leticia

This spiteful medieval hag was jealous of the king's daughter and caused her to prick her finger on a poisoned spindle. For more information, see the Famous Wizard cards (FW).

'somnolentia' = L. 'sleepiness'. This story is a nod to the fairy tale 'Sleeping Beauty'.

Sonnets of a Sorcerer

Anyone who read this cursed book spoke in limericks for the rest of their lives (CS13).

Sonorus

(so-NO-rus)

reverse: Quietus

Spell which makes the caster's voice carry over long distances (GF31).

'sonorus' = L. 'resounding'

Sopophorous bean

A 'shrivelled bean' that is one of the ingredients in the Draught of Living Death. It exudes a juice which is used for the potion, and will give up more liquid when crushed with the flat side of a silver knife rather than cut up (HBP9).

'sopor' = L. 'deep sleep'

Sorcerer's Saucepot

Company sponsoring Celestina Warbeck's upcoming concert in Exmoor, according to an advertisement.

In the Rumours section of J.K. Rowling's website, an advertisement for tickets to see Celestina Warbeck proclaims that the Sorcerer's Saucepot 'is offering three additional tour dates on the 11th, 12th, and 13th of this month' (JKR).

Sorcerer's Stone

Name given to the Philosopher's Stone by U.S. publishers.

See PHILOSOPHER'S STONE.

Sorting Hat

Originally the hat of Godric Gryffindor, the Sorting Hat was bewitched by the Founders of Hogwarts with brains and some amount of personality (GF12) in order to determine which of the four houses each new student will enter. It does so at the beginning of the start-of-term feast; first it sings a song of introduction, explaining the basic criteria for each house. First-year students then place the Hat on their heads and their House is announced (PS7 etc.). (*See also* OP11, CS17, DH7, 36).

Spattergroit

A nasty, very contagious wizarding skin disease (OP23). A wizard who has been afflicted becomes covered in purple blisters, to the point of being nearly unrecognisable. Once the disease spreads to his uvula, he also loses his ability to talk (DH6, 25).

Spavin, Faris 'Spout Hole'
Minister of Magic from 1895-1903. *Spavin was mentioned in the third W.O.M.B.A.T. test posted on J.K. Rowling's website (JKR).*
'spavin' = Eng. 'a swelling of a horse's hock joint that results in lameness'
'faris' = Arabic 'horseman' or 'knight'
'spout hole' = Eng. 'blowhole of a whale or other sea mammal' (How Spavin earned this odd nickname must be an interesting story)

Specialis Revelio
This spell — probably the incantation for Scarpin's Revelaspell — reveals the enchantments of an object or potion (HBP9, 18).
'specialis' = L. 'particular, individual, marked by something unique' + 'revelo' = L. 'to expose, reveal'

Spectrespecs
A pair of 'psychedelic spectacles', given away free with an issue of *The Quibbler* during Harry's sixth year (OP10).
'spectre' = Eng. 'ghost, phantom' + 'specs' = Eng. slang 'spectacles, glasses'

Spellman's Syllabary
One of the many books Hermione consulted as she worked on her Ancient Runes homework in the common room (OP26).

A syllabary is a set of symbols where each one represents a specific syllable. The title of this book suggests that the words used to cast spells are sometimes represented by sets of symbols other than our usual alphabet. However, since English and Latin are not well suited at all for a syllabary, this book might actually be designed for use with another language or perhaps a separate spell-casting language composed of morphemes which have discrete magical meanings. See HEIROGLYPHS AND GRAMATICA *and* MAGICAL HIEROGLYPHS AND LOGOGRAMS *for more information.*

Spellotape
Repairs magic items (CS6, PA6, GF10, OP23, DH13, JKR).
'Spellotape' is a play on words: 'Sellotape' is the British term for 'cellophane tape'.

Sphinx
Native to Egypt, this human-headed creature has a lion-like body, the capacity for human speech, and an innate love of puzzles and riddles (GF31, DP1).
The ancient Egyptians carved sphinxes with various combinations of animal bodies and heads as temple and tomb guardians. To the Greeks, there was only one sphinx, a terrifying death demon. She also functioned as a guardian, and

as in the Potter books, she asked a riddle of anyone wanting to pass. If the person couldn't answer the riddle, she strangled and ate them. According to one tale, when the hero Oedipus answered her riddle correctly, she threw herself from the rock on which she'd been perched and died.

Spinks

Both 'Spinks' and 'Spungen' were names J.K. Rowling considered for Draco Malfoy's last name. They appear together in the draft of the class list of Harry's year that she displayed during the 'Harry Potter and Me' TV interview (HPM). These names have never been used in the books.

Spinner's End

Spinner's End is a street in an unnamed industrial Muggle town, most likely somewhere in northern England. Severus Snape grew up in a house on this street (HBP2, DH33).

Spinnet, Alicia

(b. 1978; Gryffindor, 1989; Quidditch Chaser, 1991-1996; Dumbledore's Army)

Part of the Gryffindor Quidditch team during Harry's first five years at Hogwarts, Alicia was a strong Chaser whose talent was discovered by Oliver Wood (PS7, PA8).

Spleen, Professor Helbert

A Healer at St. Mungo's Hospital, Professor Spleen also writes for a *Daily Prophet* advice column. In one such issue, he gives advice to a wizard with Dragon Pox (DP3).

'spleen' = an organ in the body which helps to fight infection and filter the blood

Splinching

Incomplete Apparition where part of the body is left behind. It occurs when the mind is not concentrating fully on the desired destination (HBP18). Though in some cases it can be almost comical (HBP22), more extreme cases can be very serious, even life-threatening (GF6, DH14).

Splinter and Kreek's

Second-hand broom shop which advertised in the *Daily Prophet* (DP4).

The name suggests old, broken-down wood, 'splintering' and 'creaking' with age.

Sponge-Knees Curse

During the recent riot that took place during the Puddlemere/Holyhead Quidditch match, a group of Puddlemere supporters were using this curse (DP4).

Spore, Phyllida

Author of *One Thousand Magical Herbs and Fungi* (PS5).

'spore' = reproductive cell of some kinds of plants, eg. fungi.

Sprout, Pomona

(b. May 15, year unknown; Hufflepuff, Head of House)

A squat little witch with grey hair who teaches Herbology at Hogwarts. In the greenhouses, Sprout must deal with a variety of magical plants, some of which are strange and even dangerous. She handles them with aplomb, even the Venomous Tentacula. Her robes and fingernails are often earthy (CS6), and her hat is patched (HBP14). Professor Sprout is Head of Hufflepuff House (GF36), and in true Hufflepuff spirit is kind and nurturing to the students.

'sprout' = Eng. 'to germinate, for example, a seed; also a young plant'
'Pomona' = Roman goddess of fruit trees and orchards

Spungen

See SPINKS.

Squabbs Syndrome

According to *Dragon Breeding for Pleasure and Profit*, one of the symptoms of this dragons' disease is that they lose their fire. Squabbs Syndrome can be treated with hot baths, chilli powder and pepper, and four crates of rum daily (JKR).

squeaking sugar mice

Wizarding sweets (OP26).

Squib

A non-magical person born of wizarding parents. Squibs are a much rarer phenomenon than a Muggle-born witch or wizard. Squibs cannot attend Hogwarts or even live a full life within the Wizarding world (JKR). Having a Squib son or daughter has long been considered an embarrassment, although people have become a bit more enlightened in recent years (DH8, 11, FW). Today some Squibs are able to find niches within wizarding society; Filch works at Hogwarts, for example, and Mrs Figg breeds and trades cats and Kneazles (JKR).

'squib' = a dud firework that won't ignite properly

Squib Rights

Witches and wizards favouring rights for squibs once held a march that sparked major pure-blood riots (JKR).

staff room

Guarded by stone gargoyles (OP17, DH31), this room, located off the Entrance Hall in Hogwarts (PS16), is a fairly reliable place to find teachers when you need them during the day (PS8, CS16).

Stainwright, Erica

(1950s)

Witch who made a fortune selling 'cleaning' potions, but got into trouble when it was revealed that they really made things dirtier (JKR).

'wright' = Eng. 'craftsman, artisan', so the name means 'one who works with stains'.

Stalk, Blenheim

(b. 1920)

Stalk is a well-known expert on Muggles who has written many books on the subject (FW).

Standard Book of Spells, The

by Miranda Goshawk

Series of books for magical training, with a different edition for each year at Hogwarts; one of these can be found on the booklist every year (PS5, PA4, GF10, OP9, HBP9).

Starkey, Hesper

(1881–1973)

Famous witch who studied moon phases and their relation to potions (FW).

statues

Stone figures of famous wizards, animals, gargoyles, and so on. Many statues are found in the halls of Hogwarts (GF23, OP17). Other statues include the Fountain of Magical Brethren which once stood in the atrium of the Ministry of Magic (OP7, 36, c.f. DH12) and a statue of James, Lily, and Harry Potter that sits in the town square of Godric's Hollow, visible only to wizards (DH16).

Stealth Sensoring Spells

Spells to detect anyone sneaking past them which can be placed on physical objects such as doors (OP32).

Stebbins

(Hufflepuff, 1990s)

Snape took ten points from Stebbins' house after catching him in the roses with a Ravenclaw girl during the Yule Ball (GF23).

Stebbins

A Hogwarts student in the same year as James Potter and his friends (OP28).

Stimpson, Patricia

(Hogwarts, 1989)

A Hogwarts student in Fred and George's year. George mentioned that she had a minor breakdown as their O.W.L.s approached (OP12).

Stinging Hex

A hex that causes a stinging pain in the victim (OP24).

Stink Pellet

Joke item that releases a nasty smell when dropped. Evidently a Zonko's product sold in Hogsmeade, and definitely one of the many, many items Filch does not like having in the castle (PA8).

Stinksap

A smelly liquid. When the *Mimbulus mimbletonia* is prodded, its defence mechanism kicks in, spraying Stinksap all over its surroundings (OP10).

stoat sandwiches

A small mammal similar to a weasel which is found in Britain and Ireland. It is not usually eaten by humans, in sandwiches or any other form. Nevertheless, Hagrid makes stoat sandwiches and offers them to his guests (PS14).

Stoatshead Hill

Located outside Ottery St. Catchpole, this is a nondescript hill with a few pieces of rubbish littered around it (GF6).

Stonewall High

The public high school serving Little Whinging, Stonewall High is the school Harry would have been sent to had he never received his letter for Hogwarts. The uniforms for Stonewall High are a drab grey, which Aunt Petunia attempted to create for Harry by dyeing some of Dudley's old clothes (PS3).

Strengthening Solution

Potion to give strength. Apparently this potion takes a few days to make, since the fifth-year Potions students making it had to allow their mixtures to mature over a weekend (OP17).

Stretching Jinx

Spell to make something or someone taller. Mrs Weasley said before their sixth year that Harry and Ron had grown so much that they looked as though they'd had this jinx put on them (HBP5).

Stroulger, Edgar

(1703-1798)

Invented the Sneakoscope (FW).

Strout, Miriam

Motherly, cheerful Healer in charge of the Janus Thickey ward (a closed, long-term ward for patients with permanent spell damage) at St. Mungo's Hospital at the time of Broderick Bode's assassination (OP23, 25).

Stubbs, Billy

A Muggle orphan at Tom Riddle's orphanage who had chicken pox (HBP13).

'Study into Muggle Suspicions About Magic, A'

This study, undertaken by the Ministry of Magic and spearheaded by Professor Phoebus Penrose, determined that Muggles are less stupid than is generally assumed by wizards. The findings were published in the *Daily Prophet* (DP1).

Study of Recent Developments in Wizardry, A

Not surprisingly, Nicolas Flamel isn't mentioned in this book (PS12).

Stump, Grogan

(1770–1884)
Very popular Minister for Magic from 1811 until 1819 (FW).

Stunning Spell (Stunner)

See STUPEFY.

Stupefy

(STOO-puh-fye)
'Stunner', 'Stunning Spell', Stupefying Charm'
reverse: 'Rennervate'
A commonly used spell that shoots a red bolt of light and renders someone unconscious (GF9, 29, OP21, etc.).
'stupefacere' = L. 'to make senseless', from 'stupeo' = L. 'stunned'

Substantive Charm

Seamus Finnigan, the day before Harry's year's first O.W.L., was reciting the definition of this charm aloud (OP31).

sugar quills

Treat sold at Honeydukes that is particularly easy to sneak into class because they look like normal quills (PA5). Sometime around 1996, deluxe sugar quills were also released, which Hermione said 'would last hours' (HBP12).

Summerbee, Felix

(1447–1508)
Invented Cheering Charms (JKR).
'felix' = L. 'happiness'

Summerby (wizard)

(Hufflepuff, 1990s; Quidditch Seeker, 1995–?)
The year after Cedric Diggory's death, Summerby took over as the Hufflepuff Seeker (OP26).

Summers (wizard)

(Hufflepuff, 1990s)
Like Fred and George Weasley, he tried taking an Ageing Potion in order to put his name in the Goblet of Fire, and was sent to the hospital wing with a beard (GF16).

Summoning Charm

See ACCIO.

Sun, the

One of the symbols that can be read from a cup of tea leaves, according to *Unfogging the Future*. It means 'great happiness' (PA6).

In actual tasseography, tea leaves in the shape of the Sun represent 'a new beginning'.

Supersensory Charm

A spell allows the caster to sense things out of his or her line of sight. Ron says that he can use this spell instead of looking in the wing mirrors when driving a car (DH/e).

superstitions

Ron says that his mother is 'full of' wizarding superstitions, including 'May-born witches will marry Muggles', 'Jinx by twilight, undone by midnight', and 'Wand of elder, never prosper' (DH21).

Supreme Mugwump

The head of the International Confederation of Wizards (PS4, OP15, 31, 38).

The term 'Mugwump' refers to a leader, derived from an Algonquian word meaning 'great chief' (Algonquian lan-guages are spoken by a number of Native American Indian tribes).

Surrey

A county in England just south and west of London. Surrey is the location of Little Whinging, and thus is the county in which Harry grew up (PS3).

Sweden

Scandinavian country located in the north of Europe. Luna Lovegood and her father took a trip to Sweden in the summer of 1996 to search for the Crumple-Horned Snorkack, but couldn't find it (OP38).

Swedish Short-Snout dragon

A silvery-blue species of dragon (GF19 ff.)

Sweeting, Havelock

(1634–1710)

Unicorn expert (FW).

Swelling Solution

The second-year students were making this when Harry threw a firecracker into Goyle's cauldron to create a diversion. Where the solution splashed, people's arms, noses, eyes, and other body parts were enlarged grotesquely. The antidote was a Deflating Draught (CS11).

Switch, Emeric

Author of *A Beginner's Guide to Trans-figuration* (PS5).

Switching Spells

A category of Transfiguration spells that swap one thing for another (GF15).

Sword of Gryffindor

Goblin-made magical sword, silver with large rubies in the hilt (CS17), once owned by Godric Gryffindor. Ragnuk the First, a Goblin king, accused Gryffindor of stealing it from him (DH25, JKR). (*See also* CS18, DH6, 19, 36).

Sylvanus, Mylor

Non-canon: this name appears (along with Oakden Hobday) on an early planning chart for Order of the Phoenix *in a list as the fifth of the Defence against the Dark Arts Professors.*

Taboo

Spell and law making it illegal to speak that name 'Voldemort' and allowing the Ministry to instantly track down anyone who does (DH20, 22, c.f. DH9).

The choice of name for this effect is clever, as is the magic it invokes; there was already a social taboo on saying the name before the spell was ever cast, so very few people would say it. The ones who would say it would be those who most strongly defy Voldemort, such as members of the Order of the Phoenix.

Tail-Twig Clippers

Broom accessory made of silver, one of the highlights of a Broomstick Servicing Kit that Hermione gave Harry for his thirteenth birthday (PA1).

'Tale of the Three Brothers, The'

Wizarding fairy tale from the *Tales of Beedle the Bard* revealing background of the Deathly Hallows. In it, three brothers escape Death, who grants each a wish, thereby creating the three Deathly Hallows. The first two brothers then have their death brought about by the objects they asked for, while the third uses the Cloak to escape death until he reaches old age (DH21, TBB).

Tales of Beedle the Bard, the

Bequeathed to Hermione Granger by Albus Dumbledore, this book contains a number of children's fairy tales written in ancient runes (DH7, 21, 35, TBB).

Like most fairy tales, the stories in this book are intended to teach a lesson. Because they are written for children of wizarding families, the lessons include the idea that magic isn't always the best solution for a person's problems ('The Fountain of Fair Fortune'). In 2007, J.K. Rowling created seven hand-written copies of The Tales of Beedle the Bard *and gave six of them to friends. The seventh was auctioned off for charity and purchased by Amazon.com.*

talisman

A small object, often with magical symbols on it, which is supposed to bring protection or good luck to the person possessing it. During Harry's second year, Hogwarts saw a 'roaring trade' in talismans that supposedly safeguarded students who purchased them (CS11).

The term 'talisman' (from 'telesema' = Gr. 'to initiate into the mysteries') is sometimes thought to refer to a good luck object which is carried, in a pocket for example, as opposed to being worn, like jewellery.

talon-clipping charm
A charm used for dragon care (GF20).

'tapeworm'
Password to get into Gryffindor Tower (HBP23).

Tarantallegra
(TAIR-an-tuh-LEG-ruh)
A spell that forces the victim's legs to do a crazy dance (CS10, OP35).

The tarantella is actually two very different dances. One is a short, romantic dance with very specific movements and cheerful music. The other is a frenzied, convulsive dance which can go on for hours. It is usually danced solo, supposedly to cure the dancer of the poison of a spider bite through perspiration. This type of tarantella is actually a form of folk magic.
'tarantella'= It. 'a dance, from Taranto, a city in Italy' + 'allegro'= It. 'fast'

tarantula
Lee Jordan had a tarantula on Platform Nine and Three Quarters at the start of Harry's first year (PS6). They're sold, among other places, in Knockturn Alley (CS4).

teakettle, biting
Arthur Weasley turned up a couple of these enchanted Muggle objects on one of his nighttime raids (CS3).

tea leaves
A method of Divination where a witch or wizard drinks the tea from a cup, then interprets the meaning of the leaves that remain in the bottom. Trelawney started Harry's first Divination class teaching this method. Among her favourite symbols are the club (a forthcoming attack), the skull (danger ahead), and — of course — the Grim. All of these symbols are listed in *Unfogging the Future*, on pages five and six (PA6).

The practice of reading fortunes using tea leaves is called 'tasseography'. The procedure is fairly standard and matches the description in PA fairly closely. However, the interpretation of the symbols seen in the tea leaves is a very personal thing, and the assumption is that what one person sees will not match what another person sees. A symbol for 'a friendly person', for example, might immediately bring a particular person to mind, thereby influencing the reading. Therefore, the best results by far will come when a person reads their own tea leaves. Although Trelawney may have seen 'the Grim' in Harry's cup, if he didn't see it that way it's just as likely to be a donkey, as Seamus suggests.

tea set, enchanted
When an old witch died and her enchanted tea set was sold to some Muggles, the teapot started going crazy and attacking the new owners. This kind of problem is sorted out by the Misuse of Muggle Artefacts Office (CS3).

Ted
Muggle Newsreader on the evening news, 1 November 1981, who had no idea that the odd events he was joking about were connected to the downfall of a terrible Dark wizard (PS1).

telescope, punching
Rather violent joke item created by Fred and George (HBP5).

Tenebrus
One of the thestrals who live in the Forbidden Forest. Tenebrus was the first to be born there and is Hagrid's favourite (OP21).
'tenebrosus' L. = 'dark, gloomy'

tent
The magic tents the Weasleys set up in the campground at the Quidditch World Cup looked normal from the outside, but inside were quite large, with a small kitchen and bunk beds. Other folks used tents which were more obvious in their magical nature, with, for example, chimneys (GF7, DH14).

Tergeo
(TAIR-zhee-oh)
A spell which is used to siphon off that which is unwanted, whether dried blood (HBP8), dust (DH17), or grease (DH6).
'tergeo' = L. 'to wipe off, to wipe dry; to scour, to clean'

Terrortours
Wizarding travel agents. Located at 59 Diagon Alley, Terrortours plans very adventurous (and dangerous) holidays to places like the Bermuda Triangle and Transylvania (DP3).

Thestrals
Huge winged horses with white shining eyes, reptilian faces and necks, and skeletal black bodies (OP11). They are invisible to anyone who has not seen death. Contrary to superstitions that they are unlucky, though (OP21),

thestrals are quite useful magical creatures. They have an amazing sense of direction and move magically fast through the air (OP34, DH4). Hogwarts has a herd of thestrals which pull the Hogwarts carriages (OP10).

When book five came out, fans immediately spotted an apparent inconsistency in Harry's suddenly being able to see the thestrals. He had seen the death of a fellow student at the end of the previous book, after all, and yet the 'horseless carriages' are specifically mentioned in that book, rolling up to the castle as the students prepare to leave (GF37). Since Harry has now seen death, shouldn't he have been able to see the thestrals already at that point? J.K. Rowling's response to this was that when he was leaving the castle at the end of book four, he hadn't come to terms with the death he had witnessed and therefore couldn't see the thestrals yet.

Thickey, Janus

A ward for patients with spell damage in St. Mungo's Hospital is now named for this hapless wizard who tried to trick his wife into thinking that he was dead. The use of his name suggests that he might have come out of this incident a little worse for the wear (OP23).

'Janus' was the two-faced deity after whom the month of January was named, *a fitting name for a man who essentially lived a double life.*

Thicknesse, Pius

Head of the Department of Magical Law Enforcement (DH1) until the death of Rufus Scrimgeour, when he became Minister for Magic (DH13). Pius had long black hair, a beard, and a prominent forehead (DH12, 31).

Thief's Downfall

A magical waterfall that can be released over the track at Gringotts which Griphook says 'washes away all enchantment, all magical concealment' (DH25).

third-floor corridor

A corridor in Hogwarts castle, a section of which is set off with a door. It was off-limits to all students during the 1991-1992 school year (PS7).

Thomas, Dean

(Gryffindor, 1991; Substitute Quidditch Chaser, 1996–1997; Dumbledore's Army) A classmate of Harry's and best friends with Seamus Finnigan (GF7). He is a black Londoner who grew up as a Muggle; he's a fan of the West Ham United football team (PS9). He dated Ginny Weasley during his sixth year (OP38, HBP24). (*See also* DH23, 29).

Thomas family

Dean Thomas grew up believing that he was a Muggle-born. However, his real father never told his family that he was a wizard as he feared for their safety. Sadly, his son doesn't know the real reason his father left, or even who he was (JKR, DH15).

Three Broomsticks, The

A well-known inn in Hogsmeade and a frequent haunt of Hogwarts students. It's warm and comfortable, packed every time Harry goes in, and is a great spot to drink butterbeer (PA10), although they also serve firewhisky (GF25), gillywater, mulled mead, red currant rum, and even cherry syrup and soda with ice and an umbrella (PA10). Tradition says that the inn was originally the home of Hengist of Woodcroft, the founder of the town (FW).

'Three D's'

Strategy for learning Apparition, at least as taught by Wilkie Twycross, wherein wizards need to focus on the desired Destination, be Determined, and move with Deliberation. As this was pretty much the extent of Wilkie's instruction, he earned a few unkind nicknames starting with D as well (HBP18).

Thruston, Orsino

(b. 1976)

Member of The Weird Sisters; for more information, see the Famous Wizard cards (FW).

Thurkell, Thaddeus

(1632 - 1692)

A wizard who had problems with his kids; for more information, see the Famous Wizard cards (FW).

tiara, goblin-made

Molly Weasley's Auntie Muriel owns this tiara, which bears a slight resemblance to the diadem of Ravenclaw (DH8, 25, 29).

Tibbles, Mr

One of Mrs Figg's cats, Kneazles, of whom Harry has seen quite a few pictures (PS2). He also kept an eye on Mundungus Fletcher, alerting Mrs Figg the moment he abandoned his post (OP1, 2).

Tiberius

Uncle of Cormac McLaggen. Tiberius was a favourite student of Horace Slughorn's. An avid hunter, his hunting buddies include Bertie Higgs and Rufus Scrimgeour. He holds high office in the Ministry of Magic (HBP7).

Tickling Charm
See RICTUSEMPRA.

Time Room
One of the more fascinating rooms in the Department of Mysteries, the Time Room has clocks everywhere and is filled with 'beautiful, dancing, diamond-sparkling light'. The light emanates from a very large crystal bell jar (OP34). The Time Room also contains a glass-fronted cabinet full of hourglasses (OP35), the Ministry's entire stock of Time-Turners (HBP11).

Time-Turner
The Time-Turner is a small silver hourglass worn on a chain around the neck. It's a very powerful and dangerous magical item which literally turns back time for the user, one hour per inversion of the glass. They are strictly controlled by the Ministry of Magic (PA21, OP35, HBP11).
The Time-Turner is a tricky magic item to work into a story because it creates a lot of plot problems. If characters can go back in time at will, they can change the past and avoid whatever dangers would otherwise come their way. Having all the Time-Turners destroyed during the battle at the end of book five solved those plot problems.

Timms, Agatha
Owner of an eel farm, who bet with Ludo Bagman over the Quidditch World Cup match (GF7).

Tinworth
A village in Cornwall that, though a Muggle village, is home to a large number of witches and wizards (DH16). Shell Cottage, where Bill and Fleur make their home, is on the outskirts of Tinworth (DH23).
There is no village or town in Britain called Tinworth. J.K. Rowling may have been making a veiled reference to Tintagel, on the western coast of Cornwall, which has connections to the legends of King Arthur. Tin mining has an important place in the history of Cornwall, which may also have suggested the name to J.K. Rowling.

'Tiptoe Through the Tulips'
A Muggle song that Vernon Dursley hummed while manically boarding up the cracks around the front and back doors of number four, Privet Drive, trying to keep Hogwarts letters from reaching Harry (PS3).

toads
Toads are allowed as pets for students at Hogwarts, but Hagrid says that they're 'out of fashion', so if you have one, you're

likely to be laughed at for it (PS5). It just figures, then, that Neville comes to Hogwarts with a pet a toad named Trevor, a gift from an older family member (PS6). Despite their unpopularity, judging from Mundungus' story on Harry's first night in Grimmauld Place, toads (at least in bulk) are valuable enough to go to quite a bit of trouble to steal (OP5).

toadstools, leaping

The second year Herbology students worked with these (CS14).

Toadstool Tales

by Beatrix Bloxam

A series of children's books now banned in the Wizarding world because they're so nice they're literally sickening (FW).

Judging by the name of the author, this would seem to be a reference to Beatrix Potter, whose best-known work is The Tale of Peter Rabbit. *Since children's books with scary or gross storylines are often challenged or even banned by adults trying to 'protect' children, perhaps J.K. Rowling is creating a contrasting series in the Potter universe which the adults want to ban because they're so sickeningly nice.*

Todd, Sidney

An 83-year-old fan of the Montrose Magpies who supported the decision to release Alasdair Maddock after he was caught dabbling in basketball, football, and golf (DP3).

toenail-growing hex

One of the spells invented by the Half-Blood Prince; causes rapid toenail growth (HBP12).

'toffee éclairs'

Password to get into Gryffindor Tower (HBP20).

Tofty

A very ancient wizard who is a member of the Wizarding Examinations Authority, a friend of Tiberius Ogden (OP31).

Toke, Tilly

(1903–1991)

Recipient of the Order of Merlin First Class as a result of the Ilfracombe Incident 1932 (FW). For more information, see the Famous Wizard cards.

Tom

Bald, toothless old innkeeper of the Leaky Cauldron (PS5, PA3, 4).

Tongue-Tying Curse

Mad-Eye Moody set up one of these in number twelve, Grimmauld Place to try to keep Snape from entering the house (DH6, 9, c.f. BLC).

Tonks, Andromeda Black

Sister of Bellatrix Lestrange and Narcissa Malfoy (and very similar in appearance to Bellatrix). Andromeda married a Muggle-born (BFT, DH5). They had one daughter, Nymphadora (OP6). (*See also* DH22, DH34). She single-handedly raised her grandson, Teddy Lupin, though she had plenty of help from family friends (BLC, DH/e).

Tonks, Nymphadora

(1973-1998; Hufflepuff, 1984; Order of the Phoenix)

A young Auror and a member of the Order of the Phoenix (OP3-9, 35). She is a metamorphmagus, able to change her appearance at will. She prefers to be called Tonks, but her father called her 'Dora.' She is the daughter of Sirius Black's favourite cousin, Andromeda, who married a Muggle-born wizard, Ted Tonks (OP6). While at Hogwarts, Tonks was not a Prefect because she had trouble behaving (OP9). However, she must have been a very capable student, since becoming an Auror requires high marks in many subjects (HBP27, DH4, 31, 35).

Nymphs are spirits of nature in Greek mythology. They are minor female deities who appear as young, pretty girls, and are the protectors of springs, mountains,

and rivers (EM). A nymph is also a stage of metamorphosis in the insect world.

Tonks, Ted

(d. 1997)

Muggle-born wizard, father of Nymphadora and husband of Andromeda (OP6). He was described by his daughter as a 'right old slob,' in contrast to the Dursleys, whose house seemed unnaturally clean to Nymphadora (OP3). Ted Tonks had fair hair and a large-ish belly (DH5). (*See also* DH15, 22).

Ton-Tongue Toffees

Imbued with an Engorgement Charm, these sweets make a person's tongue swell up to ten times its normal size (GF4, 5).

Toothflossing Stringmints

A sweet sold at Honeydukes that Hermione says her parents would love — presumably because they're dentists (PA10).

Toothill, Alberta

(1391–1483)

Witch talented with a Blasting Curse; for more information see the Famous Wizard cards (FW).

'Toots, Shoots, 'n' Roots'

An award-winning radio program, hosted by Tilden Toots (JKR).

The tail end of one episode can be heard on J.K. Rowling's website, where Tilden gives a tip on rejuvenating a Flitterbloom before signing off for the day. This is actually a clue for one of the 'Easter eggs' on the site (JKR).

Topsham

A small village in Devon, the home of Madam Z. Nettles, a witch who used Kwikspell to improve her magical abilities. Her statement is part of the Kwikspell literature that Harry once read in Filch's office (CS8).

Tottenham Court Road

Shopping street in central London, very near Charing Cross Road. Hermione, Harry, and Ron fled to Tottenham Court Road during a crisis, then decided to Apparate to the relatively safer Grimmauld Place instead (DH9).

It's interesting that this was the place that 'popped into' Hermione's head. The Tottenham Court Road underground station is adjacent to Charing Cross Road, home of the Leaky Cauldron. It's possible that this was the station she and her parents would have used to reach Diagon Alley (CS4).

'Toujours Pur'

The motto on the Black family crest,

meaning 'always pure' in French — a reference to the family's blood status (OP6).

Towler, Kenneth

(Hogwarts, 1989)

A student who took his O.W.L.s at the same time as Fred and George, who developed boils as the test approached (OP12).

toy broomsticks

Two small girls at the Quidditch World Cup were playing with toy broomsticks that barely lifted them high enough for their toes to be clear of the grass (GF7). Harry had a toy broomstick as a child (DH10).

Trace, the

A charm, placed on all underage wizards that detects magic performed in their vicinity (CS2). The Trace is automatically removed when a wizard turns seventeen (DH4, 7, 11).

Transfiguration

The complex magic of changing one object into another (PS7), conjuring or Vanishing objects (OP13), or changing the fundamental nature of an object. Transfiguration has been part of magic since ancient times, when Circe famously turned lost Greek sailors into pigs (FW). Transfiguration is subject to rules; for example, Gamp's Law of Elemental Transfiguration has five exceptions, one of which is that food cannot be conjured from thin air (DH15). Transfiguration is one of the seven primary subjects at Hogwarts that all first- through fifth-year students are required to take, most recently taught by Minerva McGonagall (OP15, DH30).

Transfiguration classroom

Hogwarts classroom where McGonagall teaches her lessons. Little description is given since her lessons tend to be very work-focused, so Harry doesn't seem to notice his surroundings much, aside from McGonagall's desk that she transforms into a pig on his first day of class (PS8). The classroom is quite far away from Umbridge's office, though (OP32).

Transfiguration Today

A magazine that published an article written by Dumbledore when he was a young man (DH18). Nearly one hundred years later, he still read it (DH33).

Transforming Spells

These have to be adapted for Cross-Species Switches, at least according to a homework assignment fourth-years had to do for Transfiguration (GF21).

Transmogrifian Torture

When Mrs Norris was stunned, Gilderoy Lockhart pronounced with certainty that she was dead, killed by the Transmogrifian Torture (CS9).

'transmogrify' Eng. from L. 'to change or alter greatly and often with grotesque or humorous effect'

Transylvania

A region in the country of Romania. Its national team defeated England in a match leading up to the Quidditch World Cup in 1994 (GF5). As of Christmas of that year, Transylvania was to sign an International Ban on Dueling (GF23).

This is another example of the Wizarding world being a bit out of synch with the geography and politics of the Muggle world. Transylvania is not an independent country and has seldom been so during its long history. Yet not only does it have a Quidditch team, it also signs international treaties. Of course, since Transylvania is known as the fictional home of Dracula, using that name for a 'country' in Harry Potter stories evokes mystery and danger, lending credence to the tale of the Transylvania Quidditch team in 1473 being particularly vicious and underhanded. Incidentally, the mid-1400s was the era of Vlad the Impaler, a ruler in Transylvania thought by some to be the inspiration for the Dracula character.

Travels With Trolls
by Gilderoy Lockhart
One of the many not-so-worthwhile textbooks required for Defence Against the Dark Arts in Harry's second year (CS4).

Travers
Death Eater responsible for a number of murders during the 1970s (GF30). Travers joined the Ministry of Magic during the Second Wizarding War (DH13). (*See also* DH26).

Trelawney, Cassandra
Great-great-grandmother of Sibyll Trelawney. Cassandra was a 'very famous, very gifted' Seer in her day (OP37).
Cassandra in mythology was a Trojan seer gifted with true prophecy, but cursed (by Apollo) so that no one would ever believe her. The people of Troy ignored her warnings not to allow the Trojan Horse within the city's walls, a mistake that allowed the Greeks to capture Troy. Trelawney suffers the same fate repeatedly. For example, she wanders the hallways of Hogwarts, producing cards that tell of upcoming danger and trouble, but no one pays any attention at all.

Trelawney, Sybill Patricia
The Divination professor at Hogwarts

and the great-great-granddaughter of Cassandra Trelawney, a very gifted, famous Seer (OP37). Hermione considers her to be nothing but 'an old fraud' (GF13), a view shared by many at Hogwarts. Trelawney typically shuns the company of the rest of the school, spending her time in her tower apartments (esp. PA11). Her version of Divination is fortune-telling: reading palms and tea leaves, interpreting astrological charts, and reading crystal balls, for example (PA6).
In ancient times a Sibyl was a prophetess who, in a state of ecstasy and under influence of Apollo, prophesied without being consulted. Trelawney's first name is spelled differently in the British version than it is in the U.S. version. The British version has 'Sybill' while the U.S. version has 'Sibyll'.

Tremlett, Donaghan
(b. 1972)
The member of the Weird Sisters, and a big Kenmare Kestrels supporter (FW, JKR). According to the *Daily Prophet* he was married in the fall of 1995 (OP14). For more information, see the Famous Wizard cards.

Trevor
Neville Longbottom's pet toad. Trevor was constantly getting lost (PS6). On

at least one occasion, Neville brought Trevor to Potions class, which didn't turn out so well (PA7).

Trimble, Quentin

Author of *The Dark Forces: A Guide to Self Protection* (PS5).

Trip Jinx

A jinx which catches the target's legs and makes them stumble (OP27).

Triwizard Cup

Awarded to the winner of the Triwizard Tournament and held as an honour by the victorious school until the next tournament. In the 1994-1995 Tournament, the cup was placed in the centre of a dangerous and difficult maze (GF32).

Triwizard Tournament

A famous contest between the schools of Hogwarts, Durmstrang, and Beauxbatons, originating some 700 years ago as a friendly competition between the three schools. Each school took turns hosting the Tournament, which took place every five years, until it was discontinued due to a high number of deaths. It consisted of a series of tasks given to a single champion from each school, designed to test their magical and mental capabilities. Modern wiz-

ards grew up hearing stories of these great magical contests of years gone by (GF16) and were thrilled to learn that the Tournament was to be held again. *Dumbledore works hard to reinstate this ancient contest between the three schools in order to bring people together. His impassioned speech at the end of the book, saying that 'we are only as strong as we are united' and begging students from all three schools to consider themselves friends, gives a clear indication of why he would insist on holding a contest this elaborate and complicated when the world is in turmoil and with rumours of Voldemort returning. He is hoping to forge a bond of friendship and respect in the face of Voldemort's attempts to break down trust between wizards (GF37). The name of the contest was originally 'The Doomspell Tournament', which was also part of the working title of the fourth book:* Harry Potter and the Doomspell Tournament.

Troll

Tall, stupid creatures, violent in nature and very smelly (PS10). Some of the more intelligent species of Trolls participate in wizarding society to some extent, mostly as security guards (PA14, OP30). However, due to their low intelligence, they are not recognised as magical beings. This has caused some recent conflicts between the Troll Rights Movement and wizards favouring the creatures' continued suppression (DP2).

Trolls come from Norse mythology. They are giant, ugly, man-eating creatures who only come out at night. If exposed to sunlight, they will turn to stone. Tolkien included a memorable scene in The Hobbit *in which Bilbo managed to keep three Trolls distracted until the sun came up and petrified them. J.K. Rowling doesn't include this aspect of Troll lore in her books.*

Troll (language)

Apparently this is actually a language, since Percy Weasley names it as one of the two hundred or so languages that Mr Crouch can speak. As Fred points out though, it's hard to imagine it's all that difficult to learn, considering the low level of Troll intelligence (GF7).

Troll Rights Movement

An organised movement, spearheaded by Miss Heliotrope Willis, that campaigns for the rights of Trolls. They often use Trolls to forcefully break up meetings of wizards that oppose their views. The movement's members themselves also get clubbed on occasion, though, Trolls being what they are (DP2).

trophy room

Hogwarts has a trophy room on the third floor where all the old awards, trophies, statues, cups, plates, shields, and medals are kept in crystal display cases. There is also a list of all the head boys and girls (PS9, CS7, CS13). Peeves likes to bounce around the trophy room (PA10, GF25).

In the first film, we visit the trophy room and Harry sees a plaque showing names of famous Gryffindor Quidditch players. His father's name is on that plaque, listing him as a Seeker in 1972. This works well as a way to move the story along in the film, but the details don't match the facts given elsewhere. James Potter entered Hogwarts in 1971. This means that he would have received this award at the end of his first year, when he wasn't even on the team, or the beginning of his second year, when he could have played at most two games. Also, according to J.K. Rowling, James was a Chaser (Sch2).

Troy

Irish Chaser, one third of the famous 'Troy, Mullet, and Moran' (GF8).

trunk

The luggage of choice in the Wizarding world, at least among Hogwarts students and teachers. Trunks are quite large — Harry can barely lift his when he's younger (PS6) and it's long enough to fit a broomstick (PA15). Some have far more space in them than is obvious; Moody's trunk, for example, has six trunk-sized compartments and a seventh that's as deep as a pit (GF35). However those carried by young students don't seem to have these types of abilities, as Hermione mentions in her second year that she couldn't fit all the books she wanted to bring in hers (CS9).

Truth Potion/Serum

Truth Potion (GF27), Truth Serum (FB), and Veritaserum (GF27) are all names for potions which force the drinker to tell the truth.

tuba, exploding

This interesting musical instrument featured prominently in The Wizard Suite, composed by Musidora Barkwith (FW).

Tufty

One of Mrs Figg's cats and/or Kneazles, of which Harry isn't particularly fond (PS2).

Tugwood, Sacharissa

(1874–1966)

Witch specializing in beauty products;

for more information see the Famous Wizard cards (FW).

'saccharine' = Eng. 'sickly sweet'

Turkey

A large country on the boundary between Asia and Europe, with a correspondingly diverse tradition and culture. Turkey's national Quidditch team was defeated by England in a match in the early 1980s, thanks in part to a performance by Ludo Bagman (GF30).

Turpin, Lisa

(Ravenclaw, 1991)

A girl who was sorted along with Harry's class, just before Ron (PS7).

Tutshill Tornados

Quidditch team which hails from the small town of Tutshill in the Forest of Dean, on the border between Wales and England. Cho Chang has supported the Tornados since she was six years old, though according to Ron, the team has recently attracted a number of fair-weather fans (OP12). The team has recently been captained by Brevis Birch and included Keeper Merwyn Finwick, and according the the *Daily Prophet* they have a 900-year history (DP2).

J.K. Rowling lived in Tutshill for a few years as she was growing up.

Twelve Fail-Safe Ways to Charm Witches

A book which, according to Ron, 'explains everything you need to know about girls'. He received a copy from Fred and George, and gave Harry a copy for his seventeenth birthday (DH7). Judging by his behaviour, it includes advice on giving compliments and acting concerned for the girl's feelings.

Twiddle, Mallory

Wrote a letter to the *Daily Prophet* complaining that Gringotts was using Sphinxes to guard its high security vaults (DP1).

Twilfit and Tattings

A competitor to Madam Malkin's, probably located in Diagon Alley or Knockturn Alley (HBP6).

The name 'Twilfit' is a contraction of 'it will fit', suggesting that the clothing sold there is of good quality; 'tat', on the other hand, is a British term meaning something which is shabby and cheap.

Twitchy Ears Hex

Harry was hit with this hex as fourth-years practiced Hex-Deflection in Defence Against the Dark Arts (GF28).

Twonk, Norvel

(1888–1957)

Wizard hero; for more information, see the Famous Wizard cards (FW).

'twonk' = British slang 'idiot, fool'

Twycross, Wilkie

Apparition Instructor from the Ministry of Magic (HBP18).

𝔘

Ubbly's Oblivious Unction
A topical treatment for scars that are caused by thoughts, a type of damage that Madam Pomfrey describes as difficult to heal (OP38).
'oblivious' = Eng. 'unaware, forgetful'; 'unction' = Eng. 'salve or ointment'.

Ug the Unreliable
A very dishonest goblin; for more information, see the Famous Wizard cards (FW).

Uganda
African country located in East Africa. The Ugandan national team also defeated Wales in recent World Cup competition (GF5).

Umbridge, Dolores Jane
(DADA Professor, 1995–1996; Headmistress 1996)
Senior Undersecretary to the Minister of Magic (OP8). In fall of 1995, she was appointed by the Ministry to be the Hogwarts DADA teacher (OP12) and to weaken Dumbledore's authority at the school. Eventually Umbridge was made Hogwarts High Inquisitor, a position she used to terrorise the staff and students with class inspections, brutal detentions (OP13), and repressive Educational Decrees (e.g. OP17, 26), Umbridge continued to work for the Ministry of Magic over the next few years (DH13, *see also* BLC).

Umbridge and her role within the Ministry provide a chilling reflection of the tactics used by the Nazis to control the German people after Hitler was appointed Chancellor in 1933. The Nazis came to power by preying on people's fears and promising reform, then quickly and brutally silenced their critics and intimidated or co-opted the powerful. They made sure they controlled the news media and the ideas people might get from books, and made decrees aimed at stopping new resistance from forming. Umbridge didn't burn any books, but she seems to have learned Nazi tactics well.
'dolor' = L. 'pain, sadness, grief, resentment' 'Umbridge' = homonym for the English word 'umbrage' = 'to take offense', from 'umbra' = L. 'shade, shadow, ghost' Note: In an early planning chart for

Order of the Phoenix, *Umbridge's first name was given as 'Elvira' (JKR).*

Umbridge-itis

A fake (though fun) disease that swept through Hogwarts after Umbridge took over as Headmaster and Fred and George Weasley quit school. Umbridge never figured out what caused the illness and eventually resigned herself to letting students 'leave her classes in droves' (OP30).

Umbridge's office, Ministry of Magic

A fancy office on Level One of the Ministry of Magic. The office itself was eerily familiar to Harry, filled with lace, flowers, and sickeningly cute kittens. It also, notably, had the late Mad-Eye Moody's magical eye attached to the door so Umbridge could spy on her employees (DH13).

Umgubular Slashkilter

Something that Cornelius Fudge had in 1995 — according to Luna Lovegood, anyway. It's probably a creature of some kind, but who really knows . . . (OP18).

Unbreakable Charm

A spell which protects an object, a glass jar for instance, from breaking (GF37).

Unbreakable Vow

A magical contract, overseen by a caster, that if broken results in death (HBP16). As each clause of the oath being sworn is agreed to, 'a thin tongue of brilliant flame' shoots from the bonder's wand and winds itself around the joined hands of the participants (HBP2).

'uncontrollable giggling'

This condition is listed on the directory that stands in the lobby of St. Mungo's Hospital. Interestingly, it's listed as an example for 'Potion and Plant Poisoning', the department on the third floor of the hospital (OP22).

Undesirables

This term was used by the Ministry of Magic under the control of the Death Eaters to label the most wanted 'criminals', who were most likely all members of the Order of the Phoenix. (DH13).

The term 'undesirables' (Unerwünschten) was used by the Nazis for people such as Jews, homosexuals, gypsies, and communists who were to be eliminated from a 'perfect' German society.

Undetectable Extension Charm

A spell which allows one to carry a large number of useful items in a small pouch (DH9). It's unclear exactly how this charm works, but the pouch expands enough to squeeze a large painting through the opening (DH12), while still being small enough to hide the whole thing in one's sock (BLC).

Undetectable Poisons
One of the many things that third-years had to write an essay about for Snape's Potions class. The 'nasty' essay was due shortly after returning from the Christmas holiday (PA12).

Unfogging the Future
by Cassandra Vablatsky
Required textbook for Divination in Harry's third year (PA4). Ron and Harry were still using it as a reference book when working on Divination essays the following year (GF14).

Unforgivable Curses
Name given to three curses — the Cruciatus, the Imperius, and the Killing Curse — the use of which will result in a life term in Azkaban (GF14). They are all used extensively by Death Eaters, and occasionally by 'the good guys' (DH26, 29).
When a reader asked J.K. Rowling why she had Harry use Unforgivable Curses, she answered that he is 'flawed and mortal, just like Snape' and is subject to 'anger and occasional arrogance'. These flaws, combined with an extreme situation, led him to bad decisions (BLC). As

a story technique, however, Harry's use of Imperio *and* Crucio *leading up to the final battle is very important. When we see him use those curses, we realise that he could very well use the Killing Curse if he needed to. Part of the drama of that last confrontation came from wondering if Harry would in fact commit murder.*

unicorn
A white horse-like creature with a single horn on its head. Fourth-years study unicorns in Care of Magical Creatures (GF24, 26). Various parts of the unicorn — the horn and tail hair in particular — are used as potion ingredients (PS15) and as wand cores (PS5). Silver unicorn horns cost twenty-one Galleons each at the Apothecary in Diagon Alley (PS5) and the tail hairs are ten Galleons apiece (HBP22). The unicorn's blood can be drunk to extend life indefinitely, though according to Firenze the life will be forever cursed for killing something so pure (PS15). For more information, see the book *Fantastic Beasts and Where to Find Them.*
'unus' = L. 'one' + 'cornu' = L. 'horn'
The unicorn is first mentioned in ancient Greek texts, but not as part of any mythological tales. Rather, the unicorn was considered to be a real creature native to India, with a horn which was

thought to detect poisons. The only way to capture a unicorn was to have a young virgin accompany the hunters. The unicorn would immediately come to the girl and lie at her feet, subdued. J.K. Rowling borrows this idea when she describes her unicorns as preferring girls to boys. Unicorns have appeared in folktales and bestiaries through the centuries.

Unicorn (Rune)

According to *Ancient Runes Made Easy*, the Unicorn rune symbolises the number one, thanks to the animal's single long, straight horn (JKR).

U-No-Poo

A Weasleys' Wizard Wheezes product (of course) that causes constipation — and is the subject of a rather interesting display in the front window of the store (HBP6).

Unplottable

Spells can be cast on buildings, for example number 12 Grimmauld Place, that make them Unplottable — that is, they become impossible to include on maps (GF11). This simultaneously serves as an anti-Muggle charm and a precaution against wizards finding the place (OP6).

Unspeakables

Wizards, including Rookwood (GF30),

Broderick Bode (OP25), and Croaker (GF7), who work in the Department of Mysteries. They are forbidden to discuss what they do (OP24).

Upper Barnton

In the 1400s Upper Barnton was the home of a giant named Hengist (FW).

Upper Flagley

A Yorkshire village with a high concentration of wizards living among the Muggles (DH16, 22).

Urg the Unclean
(1700s)
Goblin activist (FW, JKR).

Uric the Oddball

A medieval wizard famous for his weird and seemingly insane behaviour (FW). Despite seemingly never doing anything of importance, he was discussed in the first-year's History of Magic classes (PS8).

Urquhart
(Slytherin, 1990s; Quidditch Chaser and Captain, 1996–?)
Captain of the Slytherin Quidditch team during Harry's sixth year (HBP14).
Urquhart is a Scottish clan name, and the name of a castle located along Loch Ness.

𝔳

Vablatsky, Cassandra

(1894–1997)

Celebrated Seer and author of *Unfogging the Future* (PA4).

'Cassandra' was the mythological daughter of Priam and Hecuba, given the power of prophecy by Apollo. When she spurned him, he added the curse that her prophecies should not be believed. 'Vablatsky' comes from Madam Helena Blavatsky, 1831–1891, who brought Eastern philosophical ideas to the West and founded the Theosophy movement.

Vaisey

(Slytherin, 1990s; Quidditch Chaser, 1996–?)

A Slytherin Quidditch player who Ron described as their best goal-scorer in 1996. He was hit by a Bludger just before the match with Gryffindor that year and couldn't play (HBP14).

valentine, singing

Lockhart's idea of a Valentine's Day treat was roving dwarfs dressed as cupids, delivering cards and singing love messages to various students (CS13).

Valentine's Day

Holiday observed on 14 February, celebrating romantic love. Several Valentine's Days were memorable occasions for Harry. The first was during Harry's second year, when Gilderoy Lockhart turned Valentine's Day into a 'morale-booster', decorating the Great Hall in disgusting pink tones and sending dwarfs carrying valentines around the school (CS13). Three years later, Harry had his first-ever date on Valentine's Day (OP25).

vampire

Though not wizards themselves, vampires are able to mix somewhat in the Wizarding world — they occasionally attend social events (HBP16) and products like blood-flavoured lollipops are marketed for them (PA10) — but a close watch has to be kept to ensure they don't attack innocent bystanders (HBP16, DP2, 3, 4). Generally speaking, though, they seem to be feared by wizards. Lockhart bragged about subduing a vampire in one of his books (CS10), for example, and they were covered in Lupin's Defence Against the Dark Arts classes (PA14).

Vance, Emmeline

(d. 1996; Order of the Phoenix)

Member of the Order of the Phoenix, both in the 1970s and in the 1990s. She was part of the Advance Guard that escorted Harry from number four, Privet Drive to number twelve, Grimmauld Place (OP3, 9). She is described as a 'stately-looking witch' who wore a green shawl. (*See also* HBP1, 2).

Vane, Romilda

(Gryffindor, 1993)

A Gryffindor with dark eyes and long, dark hair, Romilda was a bit boy-crazy and proved she would go to almost any lengths to try to catch the boy she fancied (HBP7, 11, 18).

Vanishing Cabinet

A magical device, very valuable and rare, paired in a set of two which allow someone to move magically between them (CS8, OP28, HBP27).

vanishing sickness

A wizarding malady listed on the directory in the lobby of St. Mungo's Hospital, under magical sicknesses, as something which would be treated on the second floor. Dragon pox and scrofungulus are listed here as well (OP22).

Vanishing Spell

See EVANESCO.

Vargot

(d. 1792)

A goblin rebel, though there is an unverified historical theory that when he died, Vargot was discovered to be a renegade house elf (JKR).

Varney, Sir Herbert

(1858–1889)

A Victorian vampire who attacked London women during the 1880s; for more information, see the Famous Wizard cards (FW).

This is probably supposed to imply that Jack the Ripper was actually a vampire who was taken care of by the Wizarding community, even though the Muggles never knew who it was. The Ripper murders took place in 1888.

vaults, Gringotts

Located deep underground in a labyrinth of caves and stone passages, Gringotts stores valuables for their patrons in vaults with varying degrees of security. The high security vaults are guarded by dragons and sphinxes, some with doors that only open when a Gringotts goblin touches them (PS5, PA22, DH26, DP1). The Lestrange family vault is one of the most heavily guarded. Even the treasure inside is jinxed with anti-theft spells (DH26).

Vauxhall Road

A street in South London, the location of a newsagent's where Tom Marvolo Riddle bought his diary (CS13).

Vauxhall is an area of South London which was neglected and run-down for many years. Much of the area was destroyed by air raids in World War II, which might account for the fact that the orphanage is no longer standing when Harry, Ron, and Hermione come to call (DH15). There is no road specifically called Vauxhall Road in London, but there is a Vauxhall Bridge in that area.

Vector, Septima

Arithmancy professor at Hogwarts (PA12, GF13, HBP24).

Professor Vector's first name appears on a list J.K. Rowling created while planning Prisoner of Azkaban*; however, her first name cannot be considered canon because other information on this page changed by the time the book was actually published (JKR scrapbook).*

veela

Female magical beings that have the ability to drive men uncontrollably wild, especially when they 'turn on' their charm or perform the sensual dance for which they're known (GF8, 22). However, when they get angry, they turn into bird-like creatures which throw fire. A group of veela served as the mascots for the Bulgarian National Quidditch Team at the Quidditch World Cup, though they were kicked out when they distracted the referee (GF8). Veela hairs can be used as wand cores (GF18).

The veela are based on Eastern European nature spirits of legend called 'Vily', Slovak fairies who can take the form of birds.

vegetable gardens (Hogwarts)

Located near the greenhouses (PA21), it was in these gardens where Harry found Professor Sprout and Professor Slughorn picking vegetables and chatting; fortuitously, they were exactly the people he needed to see (HBP22).

Venomous Tentacula

Spiky, dark red plant that when teething, reaches out vines toward people (CS6, OP9). 'venomous' = Eng. 'poisonous' + 'tentacle' = 'a long, flexible appendage used to grasp things'

Veritaserum

The most powerful Truth Serum available, this 'colourless, odourless potion' (which looks like plain water) forces the drinker to tell the truth (GF35, OP37, HBP9). Veritaserum is controlled by 'strict Ministry guidelines' (GF27)

veritas' = L. 'truth'

Verity

A 'young witch with short blonde hair' who worked as a shop assistant at Weasleys' Wizard Wheezes in Diagon Alley during the summer before Harry's sixth year (HBP6).

vine

The wood from which Hermione Granger's wand is made (JKR, c.f. DH36).

After assigning Harry a wand made of holly, J.K. Rowling discovered that she had unintentionally given him a wood that corresponded with his birth date according to Celtic lore. She decided to do the same for Ron and Hermione. The wood for September, the month Hermione was born, is vine (JKR). Vine wood in this case probably refers to grapevine, Vitis vinifera *(European wild grape).*

Violet ('Vi')

The Fat Lady's best friend, a wizened, pale old witch whose painting is located in the antechamber off the Great Hall (GF17).

Viridian, Vindictus

Author of the book *Curses and Counter-curses (Bewitch Your Friends and Befuddle Your Enemies with the Latest Revenges: Hair Loss, Jelly-Legs, Tongue-Tying, and Much, Much More)* (PS5).

To be 'vindictive' is to want revenge or to want to take things out on someone.

'viridis' = Latin 'green' (suggests the idea of being 'green with envy').

visitors' entrance (Ministry of Magic)

A run-down telephone box in a street surrounded by run-down offices and a pub. When a wizard dials 6-2-4-4-2 (spelling 'MAGIC') and states his name, he receives a visitors' badge and the telephone box lowers into the earth, dropping the visitor off in the beautiful Atrium of the Ministry of Magic (OP7, 34).

visitors' tearoom (St. Mungo's)

According to the sign in the St. Mungo's lobby, this room is located on the fifth floor of the hospital along with the hospital shop (OP22). Harry, Ron, Hermione, and Ginny decided to visit the tearoom during their visit to St. Mungo's over the Christmas holidays in 1995 (OP23).

Voldemort, Lord
(31 December, 1926–2 May, 1998)
The greatest Dark Wizard of the age. Voldemort took control of the Wizarding world by manipulating the festering prejudices in the Wizarding world. Voldemort delved deep into the darkest magic to find a way to make himself invincible and immortal. He stole the legendary Elder Wand to hold the ultimate weapon against his enemies (DH14, 23, 24) and created Horcruxes to protect himself from begin killed (esp. HBP23). In the end, however, it was his inability to understand love or feel remorse which led to his downfall (esp. DH36).
See RIDDLE, TOM MARVOLO; FIRST WIZARDING WAR; SECOND WIZARDING WAR.
'Voldemort' = Fr. 'flight from death', pronounced VOL-duh-more (the final 't' is silent, according to J.K. Rowling). Film pronunciation, however, is VOL-duh-mort.

Voldemort's potions
In order to return to his body, Voldemort had Wormtail make him two different potions. The first, consisting of unicorn blood and snake venom milked from Nagini, nursed him back to health (GF1, GF33); the second, which included bone from his father, Harry's blood, and Pettigrew's hand, restored him to his body (GF32).

Volkov
Bulgarian National Team, Beater at the World Cup of 1994 (GF8).

Voyages With Vampires
by Gilderoy Lockhart
One of the many, many required textbooks for Defence Against the Dark Arts in Harry's second year (CS4).

Vulchanov
Beater who played for the Bulgarian National Team during the 1994 Quidditch World Cup (GF8).

Wadcock, Joscelind

(b. 1911)

A famous Puddlemere United Chaser (FW).

Waddiwasi

(wah-di-WAH-see)

A useful spell that Lupin used to shoot gum out of a keyhole and up Peeves's nose (PA7).

Etymology uncertain; possibly 'vadd' = Swedish 'a soft mass' + 'vas y' = Fr. 'go there' Some magic theory here, because we're geeky enough to try to work this stuff out: The 'useful spell' that Lupin was showing them was probably the 'wasi' part, in this case with a target word attached, 'wad'. Again we see how important intention is to magic, since the wad was directed into Peeves' nose by intent with the 'go there' part of the spell. In another situation, the spell might be 'stolawasi' to send a robe into a student's trunk, but it would only work if the student focused his mind on where he wanted the robe to go.

Waffling, Adalbert

(1899–1981)

Adalbert was the author of *Magical Theory* (PS5, FW).

He would have enjoyed that little bit of theorising one entry back, I'll bet. The dates given for Waffling do not work when we learn in DH that Dumbledore corresponded with him while in school. Dumbledore had left Hogwarts by the time Waffling was born, according to the dates on the Famous Wizard card. His name is one of J.K. Rowling's sly jokes. This learned scholar of magical theory is 'addled' (confused) and tends to 'waffle' (blather on without coming to a conclusion).

Wagga Wagga Werewolf

The object of one of Gilderoy Lockhart's adventures, if you believe the Lockhart version of the story (CS10).

Wagga Wagga is a city in Australia. Funny how many of Lockhart's 'conquests' seem to have happened a long way from Britain.

Wagstaff, 'Honest Willy'

Street peddler who was accused by the Ministry of selling defective wands and loose-bottomed cauldrons in Diagon Alley. The wands caused burns to a number of people (DP1).

Wagtail, Myron

(b. 1970)

Member of the Weird Sisters rock group; for more information, see the Famous Wizard cards (FW).

Wailing Widow

A ghost from Kent that attended Nearly Headless Nick's five hundredth deathday party (CS8).

Wakanda

An 'elderly witch' with blonde hair that 'resembled an anthill,' who works at the Ministry of Magic (DH13).

Wales

A country, part of the United Kingdom, located in the western part of Britain. The Welsh National Quidditch team was defeated by Uganda in World Cup play in 1994 (GF5), though their Gobstones team did manage to defeat Hungary (DP1).

walnut

A wand wood that Ollivander used to create an 'unyielding' wand for Bellatrix Lestrange (DH24).

The lore about walnut wood fits with the kind of wand that Ollivander created. Walnut is said to be unrelenting, aggressive, and inflexible. It also signifies great ambition, jealousy, and passion. Sounds like it suits Bella just fine.

wand

A wand is the key to a wizard's power, a 'vessel' that channels the magical energy of its owner (HCG); though wizards can do some magic without one, it is far less controlled (CR). Wands are made of wood, with a core made from a powerful magical substance like unicorn tail hair or dragon heartstring (PS5). Though any wizard could use almost anything to channel their energy, it is a wand that has an affinity with its owner — that is, which has learned magic along with the owner, a 'mutual quest for experience' — that produces the best results (DH24).

Wand Ban of 1631

Currently it is illegal for any creatures other than witches and wizards to own a wand, pursuant to the Wand Ban of 1631 (JKR). Goblins in particular have been lobbying for changes to this law, but it remains enforced to this day (DP3, DH24).

wand effects

Unnamed category of minor spells. Wizards seem to be able to shoot things out of their wands at will, be it for celebration, decoration, or simply to get attention. Examples range from Dumbledore's purple firecrackers (PS10) to Ollivander's smoke rings and fountain of wine (GF18) and Hermione's streamers that decorated for Harry's birthday (DH7).

Wanderings With Werewolves
by Gilderoy Lockhart
One of the many, many required textbooks for Defence Against the Dark Arts in Harry's second year (CS4).

wand evaluator

Though this instrument is never named, the visitors' registration desk in the Ministry of Magic has one of these for checking in visitors' wands. Though the instrument is brass and looks like half a set of scales, it doesn't actually tell the wand's weight but its length, its core, and the length of time it's been in use. The Ministry then keeps the information, returning the wand to the wizard (OP17).
Chapter eighteen of Harry Potter and the Goblet of Fire *is named 'The Weighing of the Wands,' though Mr Ollivander's process of checking the wands*
of the Triwizard Champions doesn't seem to involve any sort of weighing device, or indeed measuring the weight at all (GF18).

wandlore

A particularly mysterious and complex ancient magic which governs the ownership and power of wands (esp. DH24). Wands have an affinity for specific wizards (PS5), and in some way even seem to have sentience all their own (e.g., DH4).

Wand of Destiny

Another name for the Elder Wand (DH21).

wand rights

Witches and wizards were given the 'right to carry wands at all times' by a law created in 1692 by the International Confederation of Wizards. This basic right was considered necessary because of the constant danger from Muggle persecution at that time. Wand rights do not extend to non-Wizard beings (JKR). In spite of this law, the Ministry took the extraordinary step of confiscating wands from spectators who attended a contentious Harpies-Puddlemere United match on Ilkley Moor (DP3), but trouble broke out anyway (DP4).

wand sparks

A basic spell that emits red or green sparks from the wand, used as a signal. This was a spell that first-years learned (PS15) that is used as a signal even by adult wizards (GF31, OP3).

wand writing

Emits an animated ribbon from the tip of the wand that spells words or forms numbers; Dumbledore used this effect to form the words of the Hogwarts School Song, so everyone could sing (PS7). The judges for the Triwizard Tournament used wand writing to show the marks they gave out of ten (GF21). (*See also* CS17).

War of the Roses

A popular historical theory holds that this war was actually started because of a wizarding conflict — neighbours fighting over a Fanged Geranium (JKR).

The War of the Roses was a series of conflicts between 1455 and 1487 fought between rival claimants to the throne of England.

Warbeck, Celestina

(b. 1917)

Known as the 'Singing Sorceress' (CS3), and one of the most well-known recording artists in the Wizarding world (FW). Her hits include 'A Cauldron Full of Hot, Strong Love' and 'You Charmed the Heart Right Out of Me' (HBP16). Concerts she has played include Liverpool (DP2) and Exmoor (JKR), and she is known to perform with a group of backup banshees (DP4). Miss Warbeck also sings Christmas Concerts on the WWN, which the Weasley family listens to enthusiastically (more or less) (HBP16).

A 'celesta' is a keyboard instrument which has a bell-like, ethereal sound, notably used for the melody of in Tchaikovsky's 'Dance of the Sugarplum Fairy' and John Williams' 'Hedwig's Theme' from the Potter films.

warlock

A word used more or less interchangeably with 'wizard', though it usually seems to refer to an older wizard. Dumbledore is Chief Warlock of the Wizengamot (OP5), a term that commands respect, and Ernie Macmillan proudly proclaims that he is descended from nine generations of warlocks (CS11).

Yet, while in the Leaky Cauldron, Harry contrasts 'venerable' wizards to a group of 'wild-looking' warlocks (PA4), and a book in the Hogwarts library is titled Madcap Magic for Wacky Warlocks *(GF26). Thus, the connotations of the word, aside from 'old,' are hard to tease out.*

Warlocks' Convention of 1709

This convention, a notable event in the Wizarding world, outlawed dragon breeding (PS14).

'Warlock's Hairy Heart'

One of the fairy tales in *The Tales of Beedle the Bard*. This dark, bloody story tells of a young warlock who goes to extreme measures to protect himself from love (TBB).

Warrington, (C. ?)

(b. 1977; Slytherin, 1988; Quidditch Chaser 1993–1996; Inquisitorial Squad)
Described by Dean Thomas as 'that big bloke from Slytherin who looks like a sloth' (GF16). While a member of the Inquisitorial Squad (and coincidentally just before a big match with Gryffindor), Warrington suffered an attack that left him with a horrible skin ailment (OP30).

Wars, Wizarding

See FIRST WIZARDING WAR *and* SECOND WIZARDING WAR.

Wartcap powder

When Sirius Black was bitten by a snuffbox that contained Wartcap powder in number twelve, Gimmauld Place, his hand instantly developed a strange skin condition. It didn't seem painful, though, and was quickly remedied by a swish of his wand. George snuck the box into his pocket after Sirius tried to discard it, so it's likely that the powder is now an ingredient in some Weasleys' Wizard Wheezes products (OP6).

Watkins, Fabius

(1940 - 1975)
Montrose Magpies captain and Chaser (JKR).

'wattlebird'

Password to get into Gryffindor Tower (CS5).
A wattlebird is a large honey-eating bird native to Australia.

Wazlib, Roonil

Inadvertent name for Ron. Eight months after buying a Spell-Check Quill from Fred and George, Ron discovered that the charm was wearing off. It misspelled 'belligerent' with a B-U-M, 'augury' with an O-R-G, and his own name as Roonil Wazlib (HBP21).

Weasley, Arthur

(b. February 6, c. 1950; Gryffindor; Order of the Phoenix)
An easy-going, middle-aged wizard with a passion for Muggles, Arthur is

a thin, balding man who wears glasses and long robes (CS3). Arthur met Molly Prewett at Hogwarts and fell in love; they eloped soon after graduation and eventually had seven children (HBP6). He raised his family to wear the 'blood traitor' label with pride (DH24). Arthur worked for years at the Ministry of Magic (GF11). He is particularly fascinated by Muggle technology (GF4). He also enjoys enchanting Muggle objects, such as a Ford Anglia he bewitched to fly (CS5). Arthur has been a very active member in the Order of the Phoenix (OP6), nearly dying in an attack in 1995 (OP23, 24) and fighting in the Battle of Hogwarts (DH35).

J.K. Rowling has said that she originally planned for Arthur to die when he was attacked by Nagini, but changed her mind (BLC).

'Weasley, Barny'

Though not a real person, Barny's name got thrown around a bit as a pseudonym Harry used during the war against Voldemort (DH8, 23).

Weasley, Bill

See WEASLEY, WILLIAM ARTHUR.

Weasley, Charlie

(b. December 12, 1978; Gryffindor 1984; Quidditch Seeker and Captain; Prefect, 1988; Order of the Phoenix)

An 'outdoor type', stocky and freckled (GF4), who has spent his whole adult life working with dragons in Romania (CS4, CS14). He is a member of the Order of the Phoenix despite living in Romania; he primarily helps by working to recruit foreign members (OP4). When he was at Hogwarts, Charlie was an excellent Seeker for the Gryffindor Quidditch team, and led his team to the Quidditch Cup; Oliver Wood claims 'he could have played for England' if he hadn't left to work with dragons instead (PS9).

Weasley, Fred and George

(b. April 1, 1978; Gryffindor, 1989; Quidditch Beaters, 1990-1996; Dumbledore's Army; Order of the Phoenix; Fred d. May, 1998)

Wizard twins known for, above all, having a sense of humour. By their fourth year at Hogwarts the twins had an entire file drawer in Filch's office devoted to their troublemaking (CS8). Both were short and stocky, with Weasley freckles and red hair (GF5). Fred and George always wanted to own a joke shop; from a young age explosions could be heard coming from their bedroom as they created and tested products (GF5). After leaving

Hogwarts (OP29), the twins set up shop in Diagon Alley (HBP6). Fred and George were eager to join the Order of the Phoenix and fought bravely against the Death Eaters (DH4, 31).

Weasley, Ginevra Molly 'Ginny'

(b. August 11, 1981; Gryffindor, 1992; Quidditch Seeker/Chaser, 1995–?; Dumbledore's Army; Slug Club)

The youngest child and only daughter of Arthur and Molly Weasley (CS3), and the first girl born to the family in several generations (JKR). Though consistently underestimated by her family, she is a powerful witch (OP6) and also quite popular (HBP24). From her first meeting with him, Ginny was quite taken with Harry (CS2), and according to her it was a romantic interest she never lost (HBP30). Ginny is all at once savvy, snarky, and very self-confident. She once told Harry that she believes almost anything possible, 'if you've got enough nerve' (OP29). (*See also* OP16, HBP6, 25, 30, DH/e, BLC).

Weasley, Hugo

(Hogwarts c. 2019)

The younger of Ron and Hermione's two children, Hugo seems to be good friends with Lily Potter (DH/e).

In the epilogue to Harry Potter and the Deathly Hallows, *Hugo was not yet old enough to attend Hogwarts, but instead hangs out laughing with Lily on Platform Nine and Three-Quarters while his older sister, Rose, prepares to head to her first year at Hogwarts. Though we don't know his exact age, Lily was nine at the time, and it's likely the two of them were within a year or so of each other's age. This would place Hugo's birth roughly between 2006 and 2009 (DH/e).*

Weasley, Molly Prewett

(b. October 30, c. 1950; Gryffindor; Order of the Phoenix)

A middle-aged witch, wife of Arthur and mother of seven, who puts her family first in everything she does. Molly is a very kind person, and gladly took on Harry as a sort of adopted son (OP5). When stressed out, though, she can be rather overbearing and tends to explode (CS3, OP24). This stems from her protectiveness; she lost both of her brothers to Death Eaters in the first war, and her greatest fear is the death of one of her own (OP9). Molly met Arthur (who in private calls her 'Mollywobbles') at Hogwarts, eloping shortly after leaving school (HBP5, 6). She home-schooled her children (WBD), along with doing the cooking and cleaning, while her husband worked at the Ministry (CS3). Molly is a capable witch in her own right, very faithful to Dumbledore and a valiant member of the Order of the Phoenix (DH36).

Weasley, Percy Ignatius
(b. August 22, 1976; Gryffindor, 1987; Prefect, 1991; Head Boy, 1993)
An ambitious and rather pompous young man, the third son of Arthur and Molly Weasley. Percy has always been devoted to rules and procedures (GF5). After Hogwarts, he got a job (GF3) at the Ministry of Magic. Despite his youth and inexperience, Percy was unexpectedly offered a position on Fudge's staff in 1995, and accepted it with pride. His parents voiced their concern that Fudge only wanted a spy in their family; this made Percy so upset that he broke ties with the Weasleys and moved to London (OP4). (*See also* DH30).

Weasley, Ronald Bilius 'Ron'
(b. March 1, 1980; Gryffindor, 1991; Prefect, 1995; Quidditch Keeper 1995-1997; Dumbledore's Army)
Harry Potter's best friend and the youngest son of Arthur and Molly Weasley. Ron was constantly being overshadowed by his family and friends, yet it was Ron's heart and humour that solidified his friendships and gave those around him the support they needed to carry through (BLC).

Ron is tall and gangly with bright red hair and freckles (PS6). He met Harry on the Hogwarts Express in 1991, and they quickly became friends. A funny sort of jealousy existed between them, with Harry in awe of Ron's family and knowledge of the Wizarding world and Ron of Harry's money and fame (PS6, 12). Ron was an avid Quidditch fan, particularly of the Chudley Cannons (CS3). Ron played a pivotal role in the struggle against Voldemort and the Death Eaters (DH36). (*See also* DH19, 31, /e, Today1, BLC).

Weasley, Rose
(b. 2006; Hogwarts 2017)
The older of Ron and Hermione's two children, and their only daughter. On 1 September 2017, Rose was preparing to take the Hogwarts Express to her first year at school, and was rather nervous about whether she'd be sorted into Gryffindor (DH/e).

Weasley, Septimus
The husband of Cedrella Black (born between 1912 and 1917). Cedrella's marriage to Septimus caused her to be 'blasted' from the Black Family Tree (BFT). Septimus was Arthur's father and could be the grandfather that gave Ron the Wizard Chess set (PS12).

Weasley, Victoire

(Hogwarts c. 2011)

Born most likely in either 1999 or 2000, Victoire is the daughter of Bill and Fleur, and therefore a cousin to the children of Harry, Ginny, Ron, and Hermione (DH/e).

Weasley, William Arthur 'Bill'

(b. November 29, 1970; Gryffindor, 1982; Prefect, 1986; Head Boy, 1988; Order of the Phoenix)

Oldest Weasley son. After leaving Hogwarts, Bill went to Egypt to work for Gringotts (CS4), then transferred to London to take an active role in the Order of the Phoenix and the struggle against Voldemort (OP4, HBP29, DH24, 25). (*See also* OP6, HBP5, 29, DH8, 23-25, /e, BLC).

Weasleys' Wildfire Whiz-Bangs

These magical fireworks were set off throughout Hogwarts on Umbridge's first day as headmistress. The Hogwarts professors refused to help get rid of them, and as neither Umbridge nor Filch had a clue how to do so, the fireworks disrupted classes all day and well into the evening. The fireworks included roaring dragons, rockets that left trails of stars, and sparklers that wrote vulgar words, like 'POO' (OP28). Compounding Umbridge's problem, the fireworks exploded when she attempted to Stun them, and multiplied by ten whenever she attempted to Vanish them (OP28).

Weasleys' Wizard Wheezes

Company formed by Fred and George Weasley while they were still in school to sell ingenious joke items of their own invention (GF4, 37). After leaving school, they set up shop at 93 Diagon Alley and did a booming business. Among their more popular items were Skiving Snackboxes, Extendable Ears, Weasleys' Wildfire Whiz-Bangs, Headless Hats, fake wands, and of course, U-No-Poo (GF22, OP24, OP28, HBP6). The creativeness and ingenuity of their products proved to be powerful and advanced magic. Not all of their products were jokes, some were very useful.

'Weatherby'

When Percy Weasley worked for Barty Crouch, Sr., he referred to Percy by this name, indicating that Percy perhaps hadn't made as much of an impression as he'd have liked (GF7).

Weatherby is a character in Jane Austen's Sense and Sensibility. *He is in love with Marianne, but forsakes her for a woman with money from a more influential family.*

Weather-Modifying Charms

The Committee for Experimental Charms conducted a survey about these, asking whether they should be 'regulated due to their effect upon the environment' (JKR).

Weighing of the Wands

Part of the official preparations for the Triwizard Tournament when the contestants' wands are examined by an expert to determine if they're in acceptable condition for the competition (GF18).

Weird Sisters

A musical group, very popular on the WWN. They are a group of eight musicians who sing and play drums, several guitars, a lute, a cello, and bagpipes (FW). They were quite hairy and wore artfully ripped black robes when Harry saw them at the Yule Ball (GF23).

'The weird sisters' is a term from Shakespeare's Macbeth, referring to the three witches who accost Macbeth and foretell the future when they hail him as 'king hereafter'. Also, in Norse mythology, there are three sister-goddesses of fate — the Norns — who are also referred to as the Wyrd Sisters. The archaic term 'wyrd' means 'fate' or 'destiny'.

Weird Wizarding Dilemmas and Their Solutions

One of the books that Harry, Ron, and Hermione examined while preparing for the Second Task of the Triwizard Tournament. The book discusses a spell for growing one's nose hair into ringlets, although it doesn't mention whether that was a dilemma or a solution (GF26).

Welcome Witch

This is the title used to refer to the receptionist at St. Mungo's Hospital for Magical Maladies and Injuries. Despite her title, she doesn't seem to be very welcoming (OP22).

Wellbeloved, Dorcas

(1812–1904)

Founded an aid society for witches; for more information, see the Famous Wizard cards (FW).

Wendelin the Weird

Medieval witch who so loved being burned at the stake that she allowed herself to be caught by witch hunters many times (PA1, FW).

Wenlock, Bridget

(1202–1285)

A famous Arithmancer; for more information, see the Famous Wizard cards (FW, JKR).

werewolf

A human who transforms into a very dangerous wolf-like creature at the full moon. A person becomes a werewolf when they are bitten by one (PA18); there is no cure (OP22). Recently, however, the Wolfsbane Potion was invented by Marcus Belby's uncle Damocles (HBP7), and though it does not prevent the transformation from happening altogether, it does control some of its worst effects (PA18). Werewolves are heavily regulated by the Ministry, for example by the 1637 Werewolf Code of Conduct (PS16) and by legislation drawn up by Dolores Umbridge which made it difficult for werewolves to find jobs (OP14).

See GREYBACK, FENRIR *and* LUPIN, REMUS.

Werewolf Code of Conduct (1637)

Hermione learned about this for her History of Magic final exam at the end of her first year at Hogwarts, but it didn't turn out to be on the exam (PS16).

West Country

A largely rural region of south-western England, that is home to many Wizarding families and the location of many important events (DH16, HBP1). Godric's Hollow is in the West Country, as is the Burrow and Malfoy Manor.

The West Country includes the counties of Devon, Cornwall, Somerset, Dorset, Wiltshire, and others all located to the west of London toward the sea.

West Ham football team

A Muggle football club, located in London. Dean Thomas, who grew up in a Muggle household, has long been a fan of this team (PS9).

West Tower

One of the towers of Hogwarts; it contains the Owlery (GF15).

Whalley, Eric

A Muggle orphan at Tom Riddle's orphanage who had chicken pox at the time of Dumbledore's first meeting with Riddle (HBP13).

Where There's a Wand, There's a Way

One of the books that Harry examined while preparing for the Second Task of the Triwizard Tournament; he fell asleep in the library over a copy on the night preceding the task (GF26).

Which Broomstick

A magazine that's particularly popular among the Quidditch-obsessed students at Hogwarts; Harry borrowed a copy from Oliver Wood when he needed to figure out what to buy to replace his broken Nimbus 2000 (PA10).

This magazine is styled after the magazine Which, *a monthly guide in Britain to products and best buys.*

Whisp, Kennilworthy

Wizard, living in Nottinghamshire, who is the author of a number of Quidditch-related books, notably *Quidditch Through the Ages* (QA).

Whitby, Kevin

(Hufflepuff, 1994)

A new Hogwarts student who was Sorted during Harry's fourth year (GF12).

Whitehorn, Devlin

(b. 1945)

Founded the Nimbus Racing Broom Company in 1967, revolutionising Quidditch (FW).

Whizzing Worm

An item sold in Hogsmeade, most likely by Zonko's joke shop, and apparently one of the many, many things that Filch does not like having in Hogwarts castle (PA8).

Whomping Willow

A very valuable, very violent tree that attacks anything within reach, from cars (CS5) to broomsticks (PA10) to people (PA17). One of these trees was planted at Hogwarts in 1971. The tree is too dangerous for students to go near, though prodding a particular knot on the tree with a branch freezes it (PA17).

Whopperwear

According to an ad for Madam Malkin's Robe Shop, Whopperwear is a range of robes for heavy-set witches and wizards (JKR).

Wiblin, Samson

(c. 1400s)

Duellist who was favoured to win the All-England Duelling Competition in 1430. He was defeated by Alberta Toothill instead, with a Blasting Charm (FW).

Widdershins, Willy

A ne'er-do-well fellow who set up a series of regurgitating toilets to confound the Muggles. Arthur Weasley spent some time tracking him down and hushing up the incidents in question, and Willy was finally caught in the explosion of one of the toilets and was captured (OP22). He was quite badly injured and spent some time heavily bandaged. Willy happened to be in the Hog's Head and overheard the first meeting of the D.A. (OP27).

'widdershins' = 'in a left-handed or contrary direction; counter-clockwise'

Wiggenweld Potion

A kiss from lips smeared with this potion revives people from the Draught of Living Death; a young wizard used this trick to marry a princess who had pricked her finger on a spindle coated with the Draught.

This is a reference to the Muggle fairy tale of Sleeping Beauty. Wiggenweld Potion first appeared in the video games from Electronic Arts and was subsequently mentioned on a Famous Wizard card, making it part of the canon.

Wiggleswade, Dempster

Writer for the *Daily Prophet*'s problem page (DP3).

Wight, Isle of

An island just a few miles off the south coast of England. Aunt Marge vacationed here and sent a postcard to the Dursleys, which arrived at the same time as Harry's first Hogwarts letter (PS3).

The Isle of Wight became a holiday destination during Victorian times. Queen Victoria and Prince Albert had a home

there, Osbourne House. *During World War Two, Hitler gave instructions that Osbourne House should not be bombed because he imagined that it would be one of his holiday retreats after he conquered Britain.*

Wigtown Wanderers

A Quidditch team in the British-Irish League (DP1–4).

Wildsmith, Ignatia
(1227–1320)

Invented Floo Powder (FW).

'Ignatia' (ig-NAY-sha) comes from 'ignis' = L. 'fire'

Wilfred the Wistful

A statue of this wizard stands in a corridor in Hogwarts (OP14).

Wilkes
(died c. 1980; Slytherin, c. 1971)

A Death Eater who was in a gang with Severus Snape at Hogwarts (GF27).

Wilkins, Wendell and Monica

Hermione modified her parents' memories, changing their names and convincing them to move to Australia. Their new names were Wendell and Monica Wilkins, who sadly had no idea that they had a daughter (DH6, BLC).

WILL — WINDOWS, ENCHANTED

Will

Wizard who stole a load of toads from Warty Harris, then was tricked out of the toads by Mundungus Fletcher (OP5).

Williams, Benjy

Seeker for Puddlemere United (DP4).

Williamson

Auror who wears scarlet robes; he has long hair in a ponytail (OP7, 36).

Willis, Heliotrope

The leader of the Troll Rights Movement. Some would say she's taken one too many knocks to the head from mis-aimed Troll clubs (DP2).

willow

A wand wood that Ollivander used to make Lily Potter's wand (PS5).

The willow has many properties, from healing to granting wishes, so many that the tree is sometimes called the Witch Tree. Willow offers magical protection; a willow tree planted near a home offers protection to that home and willow branches protect against evil sorcery. Willow wood is good for making wands (assuming that a person asks the tree for permission before taking a branch); the wood is particularly pliable (the word willow actually comes from the Anglo-Saxon word 'wellig' which means 'pliable').

Wiltshire

A county to the west of London, dominated by Salisbury Plain, where Stonehenge stands. Wiltshire is the location of Malfoy Manor (OP15, esp. DH1, 23).

Wimbledon

One of the sites of Willy Widdershins' exploding toilet pranks that Arthur Weasley investigated for the Ministry of Magic (OP7).

Wimbourne Wasps

A Quidditch team with black and yellow robes, for which Ludo Bagman was once a famous Beater. He still wears the robes now and then, although they're now a bit tight around the middle (DP1-4, GF7).

Wimple, Gilbert

Ministry wizard, Committee on Experimental Charms. Wimple had horns at the World Cup in 1994, and might still (GF7).

windows, enchanted

As the Ministry of Magic is located underground, their building can't have real windows. Instead the more important offices and some corridors have enchanted windows. The department responsible for the windows is

335

Magical Maintenance; they decide on the weather each day (OP7) and are in charge of fixing the windows when spells go awry, such as when Yaxley's office was raining (DH12). The last time Magical Maintenance wanted a pay raise, the Ministry had nothing but hurricanes for two months (OP7).

Wingardium Leviosa

(win-GAR-dee-um lev-ee-OH-sa)
'Levitation Charm'

A basic levitation spell, and one of the first spells learned by first-years in Charms (PS10).

In an excellent example of how intention affects magic, Ron was able to use this spell on a club, even though the 'wing' portion of the spell seems specific to feathers (PS10).

'wing' + 'arduus' = L.' high, steep' + 'levo' = L. 'to raise up, levitate'

Winged Catapult

These seem to be nothing more than catapults (U.S.: slingshots) that are able to fly. Harry notices them flapping around the Room of Requirement when it is transformed into a room for hiding his copy of *Advanced Potion-Making* (HBP24). He notices them again when he returns for Ravenclaw's diadem a year later as well (DH31).

Winky

A female house-elf who until 1994 worked for the Crouch family (GF8). For years, Winky cared for Barty Crouch Jr. until she was dismissed (GF35). Winky came to work at Hogwarts, but was considered a disgrace by the other house-elves. She took to sitting on a stool beside the kitchen fireplace and getting drunk on Butterbeer (GF21). Unfortunately it was an addiction from which she never completely recovered (WBD, BLC).

Wintringham, Herman

(b. 1974)

Lute player for The Weird Sisters (FW).

Wisteria Walk

A Muggle street in Little Whinging, intersecting Privet Drive. Mrs Figg lived on Wisteria Walk with her cats and kneazles (OP1).

witch-burnings

Though a tragic part of Muggle history, witch burnings don't have much of an effect on real witches and wizards, thanks to the Flame-Freezing Charm (PA1). However, it's probable that increasing numbers of witch-burnings, and of Muggles being burned by mistake, contributed to the enactment of the International Statute of Wizarding Secrecy in 1689 (JKR).

witch-doctor
Employed by Quidditch teams as trainers that oversee the health of Quidditch athletes (DP1).

Witching Hour
A popular program on the WWN (Wizarding Wireless Network), with Celestina Warbeck. Molly Weasley listens to it (CS3).

Witch Weekly
A well-known women's magazine that Mrs. Weasley subscribes to for its recipes (GF28) and that St. Mungo's Hospital keeps lying around its waiting room (OP22). The magazine gives an annual 'Most Charming Smile' award which Gilderoy Lockhart has won five times — a feat which he seems to consider his greatest accomplishment (CS6). *Witch Weekly* also published an article written by Rita Skeeter that defamed Hermione (GF27, 28).
This magazine is modelled on 'Women's Weekly', *a British magazine with tips and stories aimed at 'mature women'. The advertising blurb reads as follows:*
'Woman's Weekly *celebrates the home, family and lives of mature*

women, providing them with practical help, advice and inspiration.'

Withers, Lord Stoddard
(1642–1769)
Created a sport similar to Quidditch, but played on flying horses; for more information, see the Famous Wizard cards (FW).
'withers' = Eng. 'the highest point on the back of a horse, between the shoulders'

Wit-Sharpening Potion
Fourth-year Potions students make this (GF27).

'Wit without measure is man's greatest treasure'
The motto of Ravenclaw house, attributed to the Rowena Ravenclaw. This phrase was engraved on her famous Lost Diadem (DH29, 31).

'Wizard and the Hopping Pot, The'
One of the fairytales in the *Tales of Beedle the Bard*, a collection considered to be classics of Wizarding children's literature. The story tells of a foolish wizard whose magical cooking pot teaches him a lesson in using magic to help others. Since Harry and Hermione were Muggle-born, they did not read these stories until they were in their teens (DH7, TBB).

Wizard chess

A magical version of the game of chess in which the pieces are animated and fight for each square on the board under the command of the players. Individual pieces have distinct personalities. Some are more vicious than others. Many will bully and argue with an inexperienced player trying to order them around the board (PS12). Ron and Harry played quite a bit their first year; Hermione less so, because she tended to lose (PS13).

Wizarding Examinations Authority

A Ministry office, the Wizarding Examinations Authority is responsible for overseeing the development and administration of the O.W.L. and N.E.W.T. tests at Hogwarts each year. The panel, headed by Griselda Marchbanks, consists of 'a small group of ancient-looking witches and wizards', which also includes Professor Tofty (OP31). The Wizarding Examinations Authority title appears, along with Professor Marchbanks's name, atop the three W.O.M.B.A.T. exams administered for Muggles (JKR).

'Wizarding Suite, the'

An unfinished piece of music written by famous wizard composer Musidora Barkwith. The suite has only been performed once, in 1902, when its exploding tuba blew the roof off of Ackerly Town Hall. It has been banned from performance ever since (FW).

Wizarding Wars

See FIRST WIZARDING WAR *and* SECOND WIZARDING WAR.

Wizarding Wireless Network (WWN)

The Wizarding equivalent of a radio network, powered by magic instead of radio waves or electric energy (JKR). Among its programs are the Witching Hour, with Glenda Chittock and Celestina Warbeck (CS3, FW), music programs that play the Weird Sisters (GF22), and the Wizarding Wireless Network News (DH22), along with, most likely, 'Toots, Shoots, 'n' Roots' (JKR).

Wizarding Wireless Network News

A regular program on the WWN. The News, like the *Daily Prophet*, was heavily influenced by the Ministry of Magic (DH22).

Wizards' Ordinary Magic and Basic Aptitude Test (W.O.M.B.A.T.)

A range of tests of general knowledge of the Wizarding world that, like the O.W.L.s and N.E.W.T.s, are administered by the Wizarding Examinations

Authority. For a short time, three different stages of this test were available to Muggles as well (JKR).

wizard space

While not mentioned by name, this common effect allows magical objects to hold more space than they would otherwise seem to be able to (e.g. CS5, GF7). *See* UNDETECTABLE EXTENSION CHARM.

Wizard's Wireless

The equivalent of a Muggle radio; the Weasleys have one of these in their kitchen. The WWN (Wizarding Wireless Network) is listened to by many in the Wizarding world, and during the war against Voldemort, this device also allowed listeners to tune into *Potterwatch* if they had the correct password (DH22).

The Wizarding Wireless is an excellent example of the way in which Wizarding technology mimics that of the Muggle world. However, the actual functioning of the 'technology' is completely different, entirely a magical effect. Although it looks like a Muggle radio set, we see Ron operate the wireless set by tapping it with his wand and saying the correct spell words, not tuning the dial.

Wizengamot

The high court of Wizarding law in Britain, with about fifty members (OP8) who have an average age of 87 (JKR). When meeting, members of the Wizengamot wear purple robes with an elaborate silver 'W' on the left side (OP8). The head of the Wizengamot is the Chief Warlock (OP5). Other officials include Interrogators, who preside over the hearing; a Court Scribe, who records the proceedings (OP8); and Special advisors, who at one point included Elphias Doge (DH2)

The Wizengamot gets its name from the Witan, also known as the Witenagemot, from Anglo-Saxon England. The Witan was a gathering of influential people, including representatives from the clergy and high nobles, which advised the king on matters of national and social importance.

Wizengamot Administration Services

This support office for the Wizengamot office falls within the Department of Magical Law Enforcement at the Ministry of Magic. The office is located on level two of the Ministry of Magic, along with the Improper Use of Magic Office and Auror Headquarters (OP7).

Wizengamot Charter of Rights

One of the rights under this charter states that 'the accused has the right to present witnesses for his or her case' (OP8).

Wolfsbane Potion

While this potion doesn't cure lycanthropy, it does prevent the extremely dangerous dementia which would otherwise accompany the transformation from human into werewolf. It was invented (PA17) by Marcus Belby's uncle Damocles, who received the Order of Merlin for his work (HBP7). It's very difficult to brew and tastes awful (PA8).

WonderWitch

Sold at Weasleys' Wizarding Wheezes, WonderWitch is a line of products with pink packaging that caters to teenage girls. Products include a range of love potions, one of which, it seems, was later purchased by Romilda Vane (HBP18), and a ten-second pimple vanisher. The products apparently hit their target market, for when Harry and the Weasleys visit the store, a 'cluster of excited girls' is gathered around the display (HBP6).

woodlice

Tiny bugs which live in dark, damp places under rocks or logs. Bowtruckles feed on woodlice (OP13). People who annoy Gwenog Jones have a tendency to turn into them (DP1).

Wood, Mr and Mrs

Introduced to Harry by their son Oliver at the Quidditch World Cup (GF7).

wood nymph

Fleur told everyone at her table during dinner at the Yule Ball that the Christmas decorations at Beauxbatons included wood nymphs, who sing to the students as they eat (GF23).

Also known as dryads, wood nymphs of folklore and myth are shy creatures who live in trees to nurture and protect them.

Wood, Oliver

(Gryffindor, 1987–1994; Quidditch Keeper and Captain, c. 1990–1994)
Captain of the Gryffindor Quidditch team when Harry arrived at Hogwarts, and possibly the most passionate Quidditch fanatic in the school at that time (PS7). Oliver is known for giving particularly lengthy, impassioned locker room speeches (PS11, CS7, PA8), and gets quite depressed after losses (PA9). Fred Weasley once pointed out, fairly, that Wood might have 'bumped off' the entire Slytherin Quidditch team, except that he wouldn't have gotten away with it (HBP19).

'working like house-elves'

Ron (much to Hermione's chagrin) uses this phrase. Hermione takes offense at Ron's casual reference to what she sees as a gross injustice (GF14).

World Cup

See QUIDDITCH WORLD CUP.

'Wormtail'

Marauders' nickname for Peter Pettigrew (PA18). Pettigrew was called this by the Death Eaters, never by his given name.

See PETTIGREW, PETER.

Worple, Eldred

Author *of Blood Brothers: My Life Amongst the Vampires* and a guest at Slughorn's Christmas party with his friend Sanguini. Described as 'a small, stout, bespectacled man' (HBP15).

wound-cleaning potion

Medical magic; a purple liquid that Madam Pomfrey used to clean out injuries (GF20).

Wrackspurt

Invisible thing that Luna Lovegood believes floats in though a victim's ears and makes his or her brain go fuzzy (HBP7).

Wright, Bowman

(1492–1560)

A metal charmer from Godric's Hollow in the 1300s who invented the Golden Snitch, which replaced the Golden Snidget in games of Quidditch (FW).

A 'wright' is an English craftsman. There is some discrepancy as to when Bowman lived; according to his Famous Wizards card, it was from 1492–1560, but Quidditch Through the Ages *claims he invented the Golden Snitch in the 1300s. Clearly, one source is wrong.*

Wronski Defensive Feint

Seeker dives toward the ground as if he sees the Snitch, only to draw the opposing Seeker into a similar dive and drive him into the ground. This manoeuvre was used to great effect by Viktor Krum in the World Cup match of 1994 (GF8).

WWN

See WIZARDING WIRELESS NETWORK.

Wye, River

A Troll terrorised those hoping to cross this river, until it was killed by Almerick Sawbridge in the 1600s (FW).

The River Wye flows from Wales into the Severn Estuary near Chepstow, where J.K. Rowling lived as a child.

Yaxley

Death Eater who was one of the inner circle of Death Eaters who sat around the table at Voldemort's council before they took over the Ministry (DH1). He sat on the Muggle-Born Registration Commission with Umbridge (DH13).

Yaxley, Lysandra

(1884-1959)

Wife of Arcturus Black. They had three children: two daughters, Callidora and Charis, and one child who was disowned (BFT).

Year With The Yeti

by Gilderoy Lockhart

One of the many required textbooks for Defence Against the Dark Arts in Harry's second year (CS4).

Yeti

(Abominable Snowman, Bigfoot)

A Troll-like white furry creature native to Tibet. Yeti were discussed in Harry's second-year Defence Against the Dark Arts class (CS10), as one of Lockhart's books was *Year with the Yeti*.

The yeti is the name of a humanoid creature said to live in the mountains of Tibet. Although similar in some ways to the Bigfoot of North America, it is not considered to be the same creature. However, in the Harry Potter universe, the names are used interchangeably.

yew

A species of tree from which Tom Riddle's wand was made (PS5). Yew trees grow in the churchyard at Little Hangleton (GF32) and in the Forbidden Forest near Hogwarts (OP21).

Yew trees are symbolic of death and resurrection because the wood is particularly resistant to rotting. They are a traditional feature of graveyards in Britain. J.K. Rowling creates a nice contrast here with holly (Harry's wand wood). Both are evergreen and both have red berries, but the yew is very poisonous.

Yorkshire Moors

There is a professional Quidditch pitch on this moor. A notice in the *Daily Prophet* prior to a match between the Wigtown Wanderers and the Puddle-

mere United advised fans not to cheer too loudly, as Muggles had come looking for the source of the noise during the previous match (DP1).
See MOOR.

'You Charmed the Heart Right Out of Me'
A song performed by Celestina Warbeck (HBP16).

Youdle, Cyprian
(1312 - 1357)
Norfolk referee who was killed during a Quidditch match (FW).

You-Know-Who
A 'safe' way to refer to Voldemort.
See HE-WHO-MUST-NOT-BE-NAMED.

'Your Wheezy'
Dobby's nickname for Ron, when talking to Harry (GF26).

'You Went and Stole my Cauldron but You Can't have My Heart'
An album released by Celestina Warbeck; she planned to hold a concert promoting it on Hallowe'en (DP4).

Yo-Yo, Screaming
Added to Filch's list of objects forbidden inside Hogwarts castle at the start of the 1994–1995 school year (GF12).

Yule Ball
A 'traditional part of the Triwizard Tournament', the Yule Ball was hosted by Hogwarts School on Christmas Day 1994, to coincide with that year's tournament. The Ball was open to students fourth year and above, as well as to any younger students who they invited (GF22, 23).

Yvonne
A friend of Petunia Dursley who was on vacation in Majorca on Dudley's eleventh birthday, so she couldn't be imposed upon to look after Harry that day (PS2).

3

Zabini, Blaise

(b. 1980; Slytherin, 1991; Slug Club)
A tall, handsome, but somewhat haughty black boy in Harry's year. Blaise shares Draco's prejudice against Muggle-born witches and wizards; Ginny considers Blaise a 'poser' (HBP7).

Zabini, Mrs

Blaise Zabinin's mother, a witch well-known for her beauty and for the fact that each of her seven wealthy husbands died a mysterious death, leaving her a lot of gold (HBP7).

Zamojski, Ladislaw

Poland's top Chaser (OP19).

Zeller, Rose

(b. 1984; Hufflepuff 1995)
Hogwarts student (OP11).

Zograf

Bulgarian National Team Keeper at the World Cup in 1994 (GF8).

Zombie Trail

One of the main attractions of Terror-Tours, along with trips to Transylvania and the Bermuda Triangle. The Zombie Trail is advertised as allowing wizarding holidaymakers to see the 'living dead' first hand (DP3).

While not stated, it is possible that the zombies referred to are really Infiri. If so, this would be a dangerous holiday indeed.

Zonko's Joke Shop

A favourite place for Hogwarts students to shop in Hogsmeade. They carry such jokes and prank items as Dungbombs, Hiccup Sweets, Frog Spawn Soap, and Nose-Biting Teacups (PA14). During the dark time of 1996 and 1997, Zonko's closed and was boarded up. Fred and George visited Hogsmeade with an eye toward possibly buying the premises and turning it into a Weasleys' Wizard Wheezes (HBP18).

zoo

A local zoo to which the Dursleys took Dudley on his eleventh birthday, along with Piers Polkiss and, against their will, Harry. At the zoo, they bought ice cream treats, saw a gorilla, ate at the zoo restaurant, and visited the reptile house (which Dudley found boring because the animals weren't moving around much) (PS2).

The film version of the first book incorrectly shows Harry and the Dursleys at the London Zoo. This cannot be true, however, because when Harry travels to Diagon Alley for the first time, it is stated that he had never been to London before (PS5). Which zoo was it then? There is a zoo/adventure park in Surrey that fits the bill. It's called Chessington Worlds of Adventure, and it has both a reptile house and a family of gorillas. But it's mostly an amusement park, and it would seem very likely that Dudley would then ride the rides and forget about the animals.

zoological column

The *Daily Prophet* does a zoological column every Wednesday (GF21), which was Rita's excuse for interviewing Hagrid during his Care of Magical Creatures class to try to dig up dirt about him.

Sources

'A Highland Seer.' "Tea-Cup Reading and Fortune-Telling by Tea Leaves." Project Gutenberg. <http://www.gutenberg.org/files/18241/18241-h/18241-h.htm>.

Behind the Name — the Etymology and History of First Names. <http://www.behindthename.com/>.

Bunker, Lisa. Accio Quote!, the Largest Archive of J.K. Rowling quotes on the web. <http://www.accio-quote.org/>.

Conley, Craig. Magic Words: A Dictionary. <http://www.mysteryarts.com/magic/words/Ed.3/>.

Culpeper, Nicholas. Culpepers Color Herbal. New York: Sterling Publishing, 1987.

"Did you know the Great British map has some quirky, romantic, eccentric and funny place names?." Ordnance Survey, Britain's national mapping agency. <http://www.ordnancesurvey.co.uk/oswebsite/freefun/didyouknow/>.

Duckworth, Ted. Dictionary of English slang and colloquialisms of the UK. <http://www.peevish.co.uk/slang/>.

Ekwall, Eilert. The Oxford Dictionary of English Place Names. Oxford, Eng.: Clarendon Press, 1936.

Encyclopedia Mythica: mythology, folklore, and religion. <http://www.pantheon.org/>.

Evans, Ivor H. Brewer's Dictionary of Phrase and Fable. New York: Harper & Row, 1989.

Forthright. "Compendium of Lost Words." The Phrontistery: Obscure Words and Vocabulary Resources. <http://phrontistery.info/clw.html>.

Gay, Marcus. Occultopedia: The Occult and Unexplained Encyclopedia. <http://www.occultopedia.com/>.

Hall, James. Dictionary of Subjects and Symbols in Art. New York: HarperCollins, 1974.

Hill, Tara. "Sacred Woods and the Lore of Trees." Tara Hill Designs. <http://www.tarahill.com/treelore/trees.html>.

Hine, Phil. "The Magickal Use of the Sixteen Figures of Geomancy." Phil Hine: magic, sorcery, ritual, tantra. <http://www.philhine.org.uk/writings/rit_geomancy.html>.

"Learn about the family history of your surname" Ancestry.com. <http://www.ancestry.com/learn/facts/default.aspx>.

Leeflang, Tracy. Celtic Tree Lore. <http://www.dutchie.org/Tracy/tree.html>.

Mackillop, James. A Dictionary of Celtic Mythology. New York: Oxford University Press, 2004.

Martin, Gary. The Phrase Finder: The meanings and origins of sayings and phrases. <http://www.phrases.org.uk/ >.

Notre Dame University. "Latin Dictionary and Grammar Aid." Archives of the University of Notre Dame. <http://archives.nd.edu/latgramm.htm>.

Ogilvie, John, and Charles Annandale. The Imperial Dictionary of the English Language: A Complete Encyclopedic Lexicon, Literary, Scientific, and Technological. London [etc.]: Blackie & Son, 1883.

Online Etymology Dictionary. <http://www.etymonline.com/>.

Parkinson, Danny, and Ian Topham. Mysterious Britain, a guide to the legends, folklore, myths and mysterious places of Britain. <http://www.mysteriousbritain.co.uk/>.

Probert, Matt and Leela. Probert Encyclopaedia of Celtic Mythology. <http://www.probertencyclopaedia.com/ >.

Symbols.com. <http://www.symbols.com/>.

Tufts University. "Latin Lexicon." Perseus Digital Library. <www.perseus.tufts.edu/cgi-bin/resolveform?lang=Latin>.

Undiscovered Scotland. <http://www.undiscoveredscotland.co.uk/>.

Wikipedia, the free encyclopedia. <http://en.wikipedia.org/wiki/Main_Page>.

About the Author

Steve Vander Ark grew up in Grand Rapids, Michigan. He studied library science and media management at Grand Valley State University and worked as a school media specialist for many years. Vander Ark founded the Harry Potter Lexicon website in 2000. The internationally respected Lexicon site attracts an annual audience of over 25 million and is one of the most widely quoted and used sources of information on the Potter novels. The Lexicon has been named one of the top 15 websites for kids by the Association for Library Services for Children division of the American Library Association. Vander Ark has keynoted major academic conferences on the Harry Potter novels including Sectus in London, Patronus in Copenhagen, Lumos in Las Vegas, and Prophecy in Toronto. He has been interviewed on the novels by the BBC, the *Today Show,* the *New York Times, Time Magazine,* the Associated Press, the *New Yorker* and the *London Guardian.* His interview for an A&E television special on the series appears as part of the extra section on the DVD edition of *Harry Potter and the Order of the Phoenix.* Steve is the author of the book *In Search Of Harry Potter* (Methuen Publishing).